Religion as Empowerment

This volume shows how and why legal empowerment is important for those exercising their religious rights under various jurisdictions, in conditions of legal pluralism. At the same time, it also questions the thesis that as societies become more modern, they also become less religious. The authors look beyond the rule of law orthodoxy in their consideration of the freedom of religion as a human right and place this discussion in a more plurality-sensitive context. The book sheds more light on the informal and/or customary mechanisms that explain the limited impact of law on individuals and groups, especially in non-Western societies. The focus is on discussing how religion and the exercise of religious rights may or may not empower individuals and social groups and improve access to human rights in general. This book is important reading for academics and practitioners of law and religion, religious rights, religious diversity and cultural difference, as well as NGOs, policy makers, lawyers and advocates at multicultural jurisdictions. It offers a contemporary take on comparative legal studies, with a distinct focus on religion as an identity marker.

Kyriaki Topidi is a Senior Lecturer at the School of Law of the University of Lucerne, Switzerland. She is also associate director of the Centre of Comparative Constitutional Law and Religion at UNILU. She teaches and researches on comparative constitutional law with emphasis on religious rights, on which she has published widely.

Lauren Fielder is a Senior Lecturer at the School of Law at the University of Texas, USA. She teaches, writes and speaks about human rights issues in Africa.

ICLARS Series on Law and Religion
Series Editors:

Silvio Ferrari, University of Milan, Italy, Russell Sandberg, Cardiff University, UK, Pieter Coertzen, University of Stellenbosch, South Africa, W. Cole Durham, Jr., Brigham Young University, USA, and Tahir Mahmood, Amity International University, India

The *ICLARS Series on Law and Religion* is a new series designed to provide a forum for the rapidly expanding field of research in law and religion. The series is published in association with the International Consortium for Law and Religion Studies, an international network of scholars and experts of law and religion founded in 2007 with the aim of providing a place where information, data and opinions can easily be exchanged among members and made available to the broader scientific community. The series aims to become a primary source for students and scholars while presenting authors with a valuable means to reach a wide and growing readership.

Other titles in this series:

Religion and Equality
Edited by W. Cole Durham, Jr. and Donlu Thayer, Brigham Young University, USA

Church and State in Scotland
Francis Lyall, University of Aberdeen, UK

Religion as Empowerment
Edited by Kyriaki Topidi and Lauren Fielder, both at University of Lucerne, Switzerland

Religion as Empowerment

Global legal perspectives

Edited by Kyriaki Topidi and Lauren Fielder

Routledge
Taylor & Francis Group
LONDON AND NEW YORK

First published 2016
by Routledge
2 Park Square, Milton Park, Abingdon, Oxon OX14 4RN

and by Routledge
711 Third Avenue, New York, NY 10017

First issued in paperback 2018

Routledge is an imprint of the Taylor & Francis Group, an informa business

British Library Cataloguing in Publication Data
A catalogue record for this book is available from the British Library

Library of Congress Cataloging in Publication Data
A catalog record for this book has been requested

ISBN 13: 978-1-138-60660-9 (pbk)
ISBN 13: 978-1-4724-3759-4 (hbk)

Typeset in Times New Roman
by Swales & Willis Ltd, Exeter, Devon, UK

To Claire, Alexia and Eva-Maria for reminding me the real value of things in life and for asking the 'right' questions

K.T.

Contents

Illustrations

Figures

Tables

Contributors

Supriyanto Abdi is lecturer and researcher at the Faculty of Islamic Studies of Islamic University of Indonesia. He is also a PhD candidate at Asia Institute of the University of Melbourne writing a thesis on liberal Muslim discourse on religion-state relations and religious freedom in contemporary Indonesia. His recent publications include 'Islam, Religious Minorities and the Challenge of the Blasphemy Laws: A Close Look at the Current Liberal Muslim Discourse' in Bernhard Platzdach and Johan Saravanamuttu (eds), *Religious Diversity in Muslim-Majority States in Southeast Asia* (Singapore: Institute of Southeast Asian Studies, 2014) and 'Islam and (Political) Liberalism in Contemporary Indonesia: A Note on an Evolving Debate', *Journal of Indonesian Islam*, Vol. 3 No. 2, December 2009.

Waheeda Amien is an associate professor at the Faculty of Law, University of Cape Town (South Africa). Her teaching includes topics on International Protection of Human Rights (LLM), Legal Pluralism, Religion, Culture and Human Rights (LLB and LLM). Her research interests cover the areas of legal pluralism, religion, culture, women's rights, personal and family laws.

Lauren Fielder is a senior lecturer at University of Texas School of Law. She teaches international courses including African law, transnational litigation, US constitutional law, and international women and children's rights. She is also director of international and graduate programmes at UT.

Amos Israel-Vleeschhouwer is a research fellow at the Faculty of Law, Bar Ilan University (Israel), co-chair of the Jewish Law Association and deputy editor of the *Journal of Law Religion and State*. He holds an MA in social psychology and PhD in law, and teaches both psychology and law at various institutions. His main research interest is digital legal studies within digital humanities, as well as law and psychology and Jewish and religious law.

Kalindi Kokal is a PhD candidate at the Law and Anthropology Department of the Max Planck Institute for Social Anthropology. Her doctoral research focuses on understanding, in the Indian context, the influence of state law and its systems on dispute processing in the non-state arena. Her broader interests include legal ethnography, law and religion as well as non-state systems of dispute processing in South Asia, and more specifically in India.

Pietro Longo received his PhD in Middle-Eastern Studies at University of Naples l'Orientale. He has focused his doctoral degree on Islamic Law and on the so-called Islamic Constitutionalism, according to the Sunni and Shiite contemporary doctrines. After the 'Arab Spring', he started to study the processes of Constitution-making and the Constitutional politics adopted by the Islamists. For the academic year 2012, Pietro served as fellow, first, at the Faculty of Law at the University of Tunis and, then, at the Center for Comparative Constitutional Law & Religion of the University of Luzern. Currently, Pietro is a post-doctoral research fellow at University l'Orientale in Naples working for the EuSpring Project.

Adrian Loretan studied philosophy, theology, canon law and law in Lucerne, Tübingen, Rom, and Fribourg. He is Professor of Canon Law and Law and Religion at the University of Lucerne since 1996. He served as Dean of the Faculty of Theology at the University of Lucerne between 1999 and 2001. He has published 17 books and over 145 articles, translated in different languages. He has edited 18 books in his series 'ReligionsRecht im Dialog' since 2005. He is co-director of the Centre for Comparative Constitutional Law and Religion at the University of Lucerne.

Werner Menski, MA PhD, is Professor Emeritus of South Asian Laws at SOAS, University of London. He taught at SOAS since 1980 and was active in legal scholarship on South Asia, teaching numerous law courses at undergraduate and postgraduate level as well as supervising a large number of doctoral students. He was full Professor of South Asian Laws since 2004 until his retirement in 2014. He writes extensively on South Asian laws, Hindu law and Muslim law, comparative law and ethnic minority legal issues. Major books are *Comparative Law in a Global Context: The Legal Systems of Asia and Africa* (Cambridge University Press, second edition, 2006); *Hindu Law. Beyond Tradition and Modernity* (Oxford University Press, 2003); *Modern Indian Family Law* (Curzon Press, 2001); *Muslim Family Law* (with David Pearl, Sweet & Maxwell, 1998); *South Asians and the Dowry Problem* (Trentham Books, 1998). He remains editor of *South Asia Research* (New Delhi: SAGE) and acted as area editor for South and Southeast Asia, Africa, Oceania and Latin America for the *Oxford International Encyclopedia of Legal History* (6 volumes, New York: Oxford University Press, 2009).

Cosmina Paul has recently completed postdoctoral research in the History of Mentalities, focusing extensively on the study of the history of anti-Semitism and nationalism in Romania and employing oral history methodology. During her doctoral program, she benefited from a two-year fellowship at Yale University. Currently, she works as an expert collaborator with the Ministry of Education in the development of a food assistance volunteering programme.

Bogdan Mihai Radu is Senior Lecturer in the Department of Political Science at Babes-Bolyai University in Cluj-Napoca, Romania. His research revolves around conceptualizations of political culture in the context of post-communist democratic transformation and consolidation. Furthermore, he explores how political values and attitudes are formed and how attachment to democracy and the European Union is constructed in East Central Europe. He is also interested in the interaction between political culture and religious identity. More recently, he conducted research on public opinion and international development.

Federica Sona is a teaching fellow at the School of Law, SOAS University of London (UK), and a Visiting Research Fellow at the Law Department, University of Turin (Italy). She holds a PhD from SOAS/University of London. Her teaching and research interests encompass the comparison and interactions between Western legal systems (common law and civil law) and Islamic/ Muslim socio-legal cultures (including shari'ah-compliant legal systems and unofficial laws) with specific attention to family issues in migratory, international, transnational, multicultural and pluralistic scenarios.

Kyriaki Topidi is a senior lecturer at the School of Law of the University of Lucerne. She is also Assistant Director of the Centre of Comparative Constitutional Law and Religion of the University of Lucerne. She teaches and researches on comparative constitutional law and religious rights and has a background in human rights, minority protection and EU law. She has published widely in these areas.

Dennis Bonginkosi Xulu is a PhD candidate in KU Leuven Belgium. He obtained a Bachelor in Sacred Theology (BSC) through the Urbanian University (Rome) in 2002 and a Bachelor in Administration (Badmin) from the University of South Africa (UNISA) the same year. He obtained his Masters in Society, Law and Religion from KU Leuven in 2010. He holds a Licentiate in Canon Law (JCL) and a Masters in Canon Law, which he also obtained in KU Leuven in 2012.

Acknowledgements

This volume, like most edited volumes, represents a collective effort that extended over a lengthy period of time, largely exceeding our initial estimations. In many ways, it has been a difficult project to realize but a very rewarding and instructive one too. It was born out of the energetic emerging scholars doctoral programme that the School of Law at the University of Lucerne has run since 2010. In that sense, it reflects the cutting-edge work that takes place in the workshops that we organize and the exciting projects that young and more experienced scholars share with us on many levels.

Academically, this volume has benefited immensely from the advice, comments and suggestions that Professor Werner Menski has given us. He devoted a substantial amount of his time, and a chapter, to this project, to make sure that we are on the right track in our effort to 'fly our kites'.

The book is also, by definition and by nature, a collective work because it includes the precious contributions of all authors that, for the most, were involved in our doctoral workshops and that walked with us the path towards a meaningful academic exchange on the role of religion in modern legal systems.

Institutionally, the School of Law of the University of Lucerne and its Dean Prof. Dr Felix Bommer have been very supportive of our work, along with the Conference of Swiss Rectors that has endowed our efforts with generous financial support over the last few years. This support has been instrumental in building a solid network of knowledge in the broader area of Law and Society research that will hopefully develop further.

We are also very grateful to Alison Kirk and Alex Buckley of Routledge, who have been patient, understanding and welcoming with and to our ideas and their implementation. We appreciate their technical support and experience in transforming our ideas into a book. Linked to their work, we also acknowledge the useful advice of the anonymous reviewers of the volume who brought about improvements to the final work.

Similarly, and very importantly, we are thankful to Uta Dietrich for her continuous commitment to our work and her kind words at times when the project seemed to slow down.

1 Introduction

Religion as empowerment?

Werner Menski and Kyriaki Topidi

Law and religion

While law teaching remains in most law schools dominated by the demands and expectations of state-centric, doctrinal analytical approaches, the sociological study of law from a comparative perspective has long been a thriving legal industry. Relying on earlier stalwarts like Montesquieu, Maine and Weber, this direction of enquiry continues to generate exciting new studies[1] while largely still sidelining law and religion. Meanwhile, other prominent secular legal fields of fruitful exploration have developed, including transnational legal studies that combine state law and international law, again with the same blind spots. Closely related, development specialists, too, have joined the growing range of somewhat pluralist legal studies, in this case specifically in efforts to combine theory and development practice and to gain more insights into how law operates as a tool of empowerment 'on the ground'.[2]

Yet in all these increasingly plurality-conscious law-centric research efforts something is still missing in this post-secular age. That absent, more or less deliberately silenced element tends to be the inherently invisible force of 'religion', lurking in the background as another form of claimed legal authority.[3] Subtle and often not so subtle efforts to deny a voice to what earlier generations of lawyers will have studied and respected as various forms of natural law, which of course has religious as well as secular dimensions, can be observed.[4] In terms of empowerment, there is often outright fear that acknowledging religious claims will lead directly to theocracy, while often rather blind trust in what may be loosely described as 'rule of law' structures and arrangements remains common. Overall, one sees some progress in theorizing this complex scenario of law as a plurality of pluralities, as I call it now, but it is not yet brought out clearly that really no legal authority of any kind can be permanently and fully trusted. History, clearly, teaches that lesson, while all around

1 Cotterrell and del Mar (2015).

2 Tamanaha *et al.* (2012).

3 Habermas (2010).

4 Habermas (2008).

us, selective blaming of certain forces, specifically religion, involves political positioning rather than sustained legal analysis and sustainability testing of the various competing claims.

An instructive recent example of courageous navigation of these deeply contested conflicts is offered in the candid preface of Grillo, who lays his own secular cards on the table while trying to engage in a balanced debate of Muslim families and the law in Britain.[5] Knowing that all sides may be angered by such efforts to understand people's beliefs and practices, whatever his own personal feelings may be, this Emeritus Professor of Anthropology, who as he puts it, 'fell among lawyers',[6] dares to tackle a deeply contested field on which I have worked, too,[7] only to be treated as a pariah by many Eurocentric colleagues and their acolytes. Perhaps it is safer for retired professors to engage in such studies, as nobody can deny us promotion any longer for writing politically incorrect things. In 2015, we seem to be increasingly aware that law simply cannot be fully analysed by monist perspectives as it is indeed so intensely and deeply internally plural. Specialized legal industries, such as MILLI (an acronym for 'Muslims, Islam and the Law, a Legal Industry') claim now more focused attention in these troubled times of new 'religious' conflicts, which clearly not only concern Muslim issues and the religion of Islam. By reporting on the state of play in this complex field, new 'discursive ethnography' is, however, merely able to reflect on the confused and confusing effects of those largely silent shadow-boxing exercises that we have now observed for decades.[8]

While there is some progress here and there in pluralist navigation, it is becoming increasingly clear that simplistic banning of 'religion' as the legal 'other' is not only counterproductive but positively dangerous. A ban disempowers and cuts out a voice. But it also disables an ethical safety mechanism, if we are not careful. Banning 'religion' denies a place at law's debating table for those whose views and claims are inspired by whatever people mean by or take to be 'religion'. That 'religion' as commonly understood is largely a human construct is of course another matter, connected to empowerment. For, what do humans do when they invent gods or choose to bring themselves under a certain system, other than negotiating what many observers may treat as a form of insurance? If legal pluralism is one big unresolved issue, religious pluralism is a not altogether unconnected conundrum of a related kind. So while it is safer to discuss legal empowerment of poor and disadvantaged people and to avoid the hot potato of 'religion', more so in places like Bangladesh,[9] the present book explicitly tackles competitive claims relating to law and religion.

In one of the present authors' own work on the legal theorizing of Professor Masaji Chiba from Japan,[10] it was noted early on how Chiba as a 'Southern voice',

5 Grillo (2015).
6 Grillo (2015: ix).
7 Menski (2003); Pearl and Menski (1998).
8 Grillo (2015: x).
9 Khair (2008).
10 Menski (2006: 119–128).

facing severe criticism for attempting to add culture-specific 'basic values' to debates about legal normativity, perhaps also causing disquiet that this Eastern theorizing came too close to Kelsen's revered *Grundnorm*, coined the rather subtle term 'legal postulates'. This device was employed by Chiba as an empowering strategy to re-state a basic global truth, indicating that legal rules, whether in the form of official law or unofficial law, are always connected to values and ethics of some kind.[11] The same, as Hart and others have confirmed, applies of course also to law as process, but is often not mentioned. Evidently, by these 'legal postulates' Chiba meant not only 'traditional' cultural and religious values and ethics but also the then more prominently emerging ethical norms of international law and human rights theorizing. Law, this indicates and confirms without saying so explicitly, is composed of rules, values and processes. All of these are connected to power. Since all these intrinsically interconnected elements are also internally plural, law manifests as a highly dynamic hybrid superstructure that can evidently only be fully analysed by using interdisciplinary methodologies. As most legal scholars are not trained to be interdisciplinary scholars, however, legal studies today continue to struggle, as is also visible in this book, with the inputs and role of 'religion' as a law-related entity.

The factor of 'religion' thus becomes more than an irritant for many scholars. It is simply not trusted, is perceived as a terrorist threat, a force that kills and all too easily rides roughshod over basic rights entitlements, particularly of women and children. Whether something is really 'religious', for example polygamy, or rather more of a social normativity and a matter of practice, throws up precisely those thorny analytical challenges of interdisciplinary connectivity. Hence what is claimed to be 'religious' easily becomes a form of disempowerment, which therefore justifies, in the eyes of many, its relegation to the extra-legal sphere, even its ban from the legal arena. However, time and again, as also demonstrated in this book, particularly by Federica Sona, we realize that such monist action on the part of certain legal actors may change the formal or official law, but does not get rid of the underlying socio-legal issues. While one certainly cannot deny that grave abuses of law can and do occur in the name of religion (and culture), it also has to be acknowledged that equally gruesome rights abuses are perpetrated by secular legal systems and state-centric legal structures and mechanisms that simply fail to provide justice. Lack of accountability remains a burning issue. As the same damning criticism can at times also be directed against the international legal order and connected human rights ideologies, desperately confused post-liberal scholars and legal actors are left without useful clear-cut guidance, other than to guard against generating precariousness.[12]

The potentially nihilistic conclusion, that none of the elements of law-related claimants to power can be trusted to deliver what ideals of 'rule of law' seem to stipulate, however, needs to be turned into positive and empowering engagement

11 Chiba (1989).
12 Wacquant (2014).

in the never-ending search for 'justice' and 'the right law'. That, above all, justifies this book project, which arose from a series of intensive doctoral training seminars held in the past few years, led by the Law School at the University of Lucerne, with co-operation from London (SOAS), Naples, Lausanne, Halle and some other institutions engaged in doctoral research projects concerning legal pluralism. These intensive seminars confirmed that, whether we like it or not, pluralist theorizing in relation to law is part of a toolkit that is not just desirable, but essential for further studies about empowerment. It is clearly empowering in itself to be made to think about these pluralist tensions. Nihilism as an exit strategy still offers itself as an easy option for intellectually lazy observers. Pluralist theorizing, however, remains all too often still partial and segmentary, focusing only on some preferred elements and entities, often in adversarial constellations, while maintaining blind spots for others. I have come to characterize this as 'partial theorizing'. We see some examples in this book, too.

The present book project is a timely reaction to the very public re-emergence of religion as a major force to reckon with in today's world, and specifically in legal discussions. At the same time, there is intriguing new evidence of various methods of keeping religion deliberately hidden,[13] tucked away in the unofficial sphere behind more or less closed doors and in separate spaces, perpetuating what some may see as 'parallel lives', itself a deficient vision. Plurality management remains, everywhere, a hugely complex challenge, but we need to be aware that this is hardly a new challenge. Thousands of years ago, religious and legal pluralities were present, no doubt in different manifestations, but their existence and syncretizing effects cannot be denied.

Choosing to describe religion in the previous paragraph as 'a major force', and not 'the major force', reflects a pluralist mindset that informs revised use of legal language in this age of late modernity or maybe post-modern or post-liberal times. Clearly, 'religion' as a legal authority in the form of theocracy is not only perceived as a form of terror, all too visible presently in the Middle East and some parts of Africa, but it can also have the positive effects of empowering and inspiring others. Perhaps the key message of this book is that we urgently need to find sustainable balances between such competing claims and assessments. Portraying 'religion', despite risks of blatant abuse, as a relevant major force indicates not just respect for people's agency when it comes to belief and action inspired by such beliefs, but also knowledge and awareness that language matters for lawyers. It also highlights that no amount of secular legal engineering and state-centric domination has been able to completely silence the voices and authority claims of 'religion' in their many forms. Hence there is a need to tackle this conflict scenario, in a spirit of constructive criticism, seeking to identify the borders and limits of what is, at the end of the day, completely intolerable in some situations or scenarios.[14]

13 Degiorgis (2014).

14 Twining (2009: 218).

Menski has suggested the potential to theorize this predicament through models of law as a kite, with four competing, but inevitably connected, corners that all seem to need each other to pursue their own claims, otherwise the entire subtle and highly dynamic structure would crash.[15] This powerful and highly dynamic image of the kite confirms not only that law is culture-specific and situation-specific, it also illustrates the intrinsic connections and partial overlaps between these different types of law and thus their numerous inevitable interlinkages, as is also shown by Amos Israel-Vleeschhouwer in the present book. Any complete denial of a legitimate place and voice for any one of these four major, internally plural types of law rapidly leads, in this dynamic kite model, to a crash scenario, as it disables one of the crucial balancing elements. It is indeed like simply pressing the descent button of a plane that is then doomed. Since such legal kites can be perceived as four types, individual, social, state-centric and global, such a disaster scenario could indeed result in suicide or serious self-harm for an individual, turmoil and mayhem within any social group, revolt, uprisings and violent protests within a state, and it would generate various forms of terror at the international level.

The present book, then, seeks to argue that respect for religion may, in certain situations, and with certain safeguards, be an empowering experience. Such cautious wording is justified in view of the deep reservations that several contributors to this volume harbour about the power claims of 'religion'. Truly pluralist theorizing needs to extend this caution to all potential agents and players, as no legal actor can be fully trusted to avoid what Wacquant has so sharply identified as the risks of 'precariousness'.[16] At all levels, then, introspection and constructive conversations rather than simplistic juxtaposition and adversarial strategies could and should lead to a better future for all of us and should be an empowering experience. As noted earlier, this is what makes the concept of 'relative authority' so attractive and instructive.[17] Any monist claims would inevitably lead to some form of violence and disempowerment, which then quickly results in perceived or actual denial of justice in some respects. Conversely, simplistic claims that a particular law is a good law because it is conscious of other normative inputs and agents, whether such claims are made by state-centric speakers or agents of religion, or anyone else, simply seek to avoid fuller and deeper discourse about the various dimensions, constellations and manifestations of legal pluralism.

Taking a broad global perspective, we may realize that this globe, which we share and compete over with increasing intensity, is today not only marked by unifying effects of globalization but also by forces within such globalizing trends which have generated new awareness of continuing diversities and pluralities.[18] As noted, there is nothing new about this co-existence of difference and diversity. We quickly see, then, that any dreamy-eyed 'modern' monist assumptions that this world would

15 Menski (2014).

16 Wacquant (2014).

17 Cotterrell and del Mar (2015).

18 Robertson (2003).

ever become 'One Globe', or any city may become 'One', hides multiple pluralities below a thin veneer of claims to equally empowering recognition of differences. In other words, as we become of necessity more realistic and hence more plurality-conscious, because of globalization and its multiple pluralizing effects all around us today, it has become increasingly implausible to deny that difference remains – and will remain – a most basic fact of life. The main efforts of global scholarly *ijtihad* (for 'strenuous effort to get it right' is the basic meaning of that Islamic term) should thus be to find methods of empowered co-existence, rather than searching for methodologies that seek to reduce diversities. Muslims are frequently rather quick to claim their awareness of this, but fall at the hurdle of self-righteousness by not practising what they preach. Whether we talk about economics, politics or law here seems to make little difference in principle. Equality is everywhere a nice idea, but how that relates to justice – and what is meant by justice – are very different matters to debate. Monist, hegemonistic claims are being made by all cultures and religions and various kinds of law-related authorities that fail to account fully for the presence of others and the need to cultivate empowering balances, indeed what Cotterrell and del Mar's edited book theorizes as 'relative justice'.[19]

Focusing specifically on the role of religion in this wider context, sort-of-theocratic claims are of course still being made, sometimes openly, more often in hidden form or tongue-in-cheek. However, we have several recent examples to demonstrate that excessive claims by 'religious' authority to call the shots to the exclusion of other legal entities and concerns may badly backfire. I have written at length about the highly significant saga and wider impact of the much-misunderstood Shah Bano case in India.[20] Other examples can be given, for the Canadian brouhaha over Muslim Tribunals in 2006 only arose after some Muslims claimed that Islamic law was now the law of Canada, while more recent controversies over Islamic wills in the UK were blown out of all proportion by similar 'religious' claims that disturbed old, well-established balances as provided under England's Wills Act of 1837.

Educated lawyers should actually be more aware that religion was never the only force in the world and remains itself, like law, an internally plural entity, over whose definition there is no global agreement either. Religious pluralism as a fact should have – and has – made people think more deeply, since ancient times: if God of whatever name (if such an entity even exists) created and tolerates also religious difference, as also Muslims know so well, how then can any one form or manifestation of 'religion' make absolute claims to exclusivity? Some 'religions', which of course then face challenges about their status as a proper 'religion', opted for a route out of this cul-de-sac by claiming that the highest entity was neither this nor that, leaving adherents to decide for themselves what to believe and whom to follow. Hence Hindus can be atheists and still have so many gods. Everywhere, since 'religion' is not only about orthodoxy

19 Cotterrell and del Mar (2015).
20 Menski (2008).

but also about orthopraxis, it is evident that law and religion have to find empowering balances for constructive co-existence, as illustrated throughout this book.

So the constant question and challenge becomes how we respect and maybe tolerate what we hate and would love to be extinct or extinguished. While earlier duty-focused approaches had the effect of generating and managing live-and-let-live systems of equitable co-existence, we are tempted, encouraged and cajoled today by rights-based approaches to aim for systems of absolute equality. The standard remedy advised manifests as encouragement to excise the cancer of all kinds of rights abuses, to not just curtail, but ban perceived and actual abuses, to get rid of what we do not like and find intolerable.[21] Cheap monist rhetoric will never be good enough anymore to persuade anyone that a particular perspective can be maintained for all times and in all scenarios. Everything is in constant flux and highly dynamic, which is why I constantly advise using the image of kites flying in the air. What empowers those kites to fly, other than navigation skills? Indeed there appear to be some absolute truths serving as motivators, which even the cleverest scientists cannot finally uncover, but the majority of elements of truth and knowledge that we handle on a day-to-day basis is relative and malleable, and probably more secular than religious. This can all be managed, then, in navigational terms and in heuristic terms, too. For academia, this means that hiding behind 'rule of law' rhetoric becomes all too often academic gymnastics with toxic side-effects, hiding often brutal power claims. For what does 'rule of law' mean in terms of empowerment if Apartheid and Nazism were also quite manifestly rules of law? Similarly, simple demagogic ridiculing of 'the religious other' increasingly lacks credibility among lawyers, as all concerned parties, whether we look at individuals, social groups or societies, states, or also the international community, can at certain times and in certain scenarios be found guilty of violations of even the most basic rights of others. Such partial theorizing, a major academic preoccupation unduly privileged and exploited by those enjoying paid thinking time, has rightly come under intense challenge as yet another – and increasingly prominent – form of violence. If religion has now come back, not so much to rule the world in all kinds of theocratic horror scenarios, but as an increasingly articulate ethical voice in global re-thinking of development processes, it also has a rightful role in the re-thinking of what is meant by empowerment. Especially post-9/11, this has indeed been leading to many new debates, including a very significant revision of the earlier secular theorizing of Habermas.[22] In relation to public policy and state action, a realization that arose from the RELIGARE project,[23] states and their legal systems are certainly stuck with religion, but if handled carefully, respect for religion can be empowering. Moreover, because religions have moved across the globe, the need to address such deeply contested issues is increasing.[24] The case studies presented

21 Twining (2009: 218).
22 Borradori (2003).
23 See www.religareproject.eu.
24 Ventura (2014).

in this volume effectively problematize and illustrate the potential for abuses and empowerment of individuals, groups and state actors through using religion as an argument within a global framework of reference. There is a need for more of such studies. Indeed the series of workshops that led to the production of this particular book is continuing and will generate further fruitful debates.

The angle of the volume

Looking at the world today, one has the impression that religion is taking up more and more space both directly and indirectly. We are often 'trapped' in dilemmas that refer to religion as an element of non-modernity, as a perpetual violation of human rights, as an irrational force with tremendous power but little regard to human dignity.

Following recent developments in the legal discipline, this debate is acquiring new levels of intensity: can religion ever remain a strict element of one's private sphere? Do human rights have a problem with religion or is it the other way round?[25] Does the separation between the private and public sphere of religious rights exercise make any sense at all, or is this the outcome of a specific 'Western' perspective? The contributions in this volume problematize these issues from very different perspectives and geographical bases for their inquiries. Predictably, they do not all agree on possible answers but share one essential concern: they all aim to examine critically religion and religious rights as a potential incentive for legal empowerment of individuals and groups.

A crucial underlying assumption for all arguments expressed is the awareness and desire for individuals in today's world to achieve 'reason, equality, and liberty not just in the public sphere, but also in the private spheres of religion, culture, and family'.[26] Obstacles, in some cases, are placed from the law's own perception and treatment of religion.

Connected to this point, as religion becomes more relevant within fragmented societies, law is required to intervene, in order to determine the boundaries of religion, religious jurisdiction(s), individual autonomy and equality. A very common situation, especially for the more vulnerable groups in society, requires individuals to choose between religious freedom (and identity) and equality and respect for their fundamental rights. This volume addresses this recurring question but dares to ask one more: under what conditions, if at all, can the exercise of religious freedom, privately or in public, lead to the legal empowerment of individuals and groups?

In a sense, the book appears to adopt an 'instrumentalized' understanding of law and rights as a tool to assess modernity and cultural evolution. This is true to some extent but because it is difficult to imagine the total absence of law from religion,[27]

25 On this question, see Sunder (2003).
26 Sunder (2003: 1403).
27 Sunder (2003: 1409).

we have opted to reflect on ways that law can facilitate and promote modernity and change within religious communities. We are accepting that it is increasingly difficult to ignore that commitment to rights is not incompatible with commitment to religion and its expression through the exercise of religious rights. Religion is, therefore, not constructed as the law's past.[28] The law's understanding, however, of religion has shifted: law should reflect and take account of religion as a social expression that is not static, homogenous or unchanging. This point resonates well Sudipta Kaviraj's observation, quoted in Sunder, that 'the more modernity unfolds [the more] it seems inescapably plural'.[29] Neither law nor religion has escaped this plurality. And as these two internally complex entities overlap and thus are connected, they cannot be neatly separated. This then generates struggles over power.

A fundamental question, at this point, requires us to address our understanding of the notion of legal empowerment. In today's secular framework of discourse, we do not even reflect on the fact that we put the law above religion and thus operate within what is commonly called a 'secular' framework, in other words, not a theocratic context. Legal empowerment essentially pursues a liberal approach to religious rights that protects a religious person's capacity to choose his/her faith and beliefs but does not extend to the respect for any religion and its content.[30] Furthermore, as several of the contributions in this volume demonstrate, legal empowerment becomes a complex process due to the intersectionality affecting the status of individuals as believers, with existing combinations increasing their vulnerability due to gender, race/ethnic origin or religion.

The general framework for the consideration of religious rights, as human rights, relies on the context that Reva Siegel described in the late 1990s: the ways that legal systems enforce social stratification are diverse and tend to evolve over time.[31] The context for that proposition was racial and gender equality but, looking back, it is arguable that the same process may be applied to the recognition and enforcement of religious rights, especially for minority groups.

As mentioned, we consider (and ultimately reject) the notion that law is static and homogenous. Quite the opposite, the voices expressed in this volume assert that law is complex, multi-layered and evolving. Religious freedom norms, just like gender, race and class relationships, rely on legal systems that perpetuate, often, former systems in hierarchical terms.[32] In that sense, it is highly contestable that we have indeed reached the 'end of history'. The following question becomes then relevant: if we accept that the role of the law is to afford formal, *de jure* equality, what about de facto social equality?

An easy answer that Siegel provides (and then deconstructs) would resonate that 'social relations cannot be regulated by law. They are beyond its power. They are not the legitimate subject of legal regulation. Social equality is a matter of taste,

28 Sunder (2003: 1415).
29 Sunder (2003: 1414).
30 Gal-Or (2011: 324).
31 Siegel (1997: 1113).
32 Siegel (1997: 1116).

of feeling, of every man's unfettered sense of propriety'.[33] Yet, can we rule out all possibility that the exercise of religious rights can bring more social equality (through legal empowerment) to those that are for various reasons at the margins of contemporary societies or simply belong to minorities? Uncontestably, current definitions of equality have allowed our social practices to evolve but the level of inquiry that is most relevant for this collection of contributions is whether and how (if at all) these social changes can lead to established discriminatory systems and perceptions of status.[34]

Legal empowerment becomes an interesting approach and trajectory for the study of religious rights in multicultural settings because it provides a solution against the essentialism of religious minorities. Religion cannot be portrayed in homogenizing terms, nor can the discourse against religious rights for all be instrumentalized to pursue an anti-immigration agenda. The real concern, nevertheless, remains how to assess the impact of targeted legislation on these issues. There is a widespread observation that data is lacking. Towards a remedy to this gap, a number of contributions to this volume are taking a more empirical approach in an attempt to understand better how religious identity affects or may enforce one's exercise of rights.

Legal empowerment is especially relevant in contexts where language, dress and behaviour, connected to religious identity, are no longer a private matter but become publicly and at times violently contested.[35] Religion is largely also the triggering factor for the emergence of 'parallel societies' or 'parallel lives' in several European countries,[36] as well as elsewhere. This fact reinforces the demonstration that difference can be problematic, and remains problematic for many analysts (this is again the problem of the glass being half full or half empty: does one start from a presumption that difference is a fact, or a presumption that equality is a fact or a desirable end fact?).

Law can assist in articulating 'multi-dimensional and hyphenated identities'[37] but it is not self-sufficient. 'Culture-specific' legislation (e.g. burqa bans) furthers the representation of some religious groups in society, both internally and externally, as less worthy of the same legal protection afforded to others. The law clearly sets itself up as a higher authority than religion. Part of the complexity of the situation is linked to the overlap between culture and religion. Due to the lack of clarity and agreement as to whether it is law or religion that is problematic towards the exercise of such rights, legal empowerment of individuals and groups becomes important, especially in circumstances where culture is to give 'agency'. At the same time, by focusing on culture, one tends to neglect socio-economic

33 Quote belonging to US Sen. Waitman T. Willey, CONG. GLOBE, 39th Cong. 1st Sess. 34, 3437 (1866), borrowed from Siegel (1997: 1126).

34 For a similar qustions cf. Siegel (1997: 1148).

35 Dustin (2006: 4).

36 Dustin (2006: 7–8) gives the examples of Germany, Austria and the UK. The equivalent term in German describes the phenomenon as 'parallelgesellschaften'.

37 Dustin (2006: 28).

factors, leading to sustained marginalization of groups, often along religious (and ethnic) lines.[38] Ultimately, we are aiming at problematizing the paths that lead individuals as believers, but also as members of religious groups and communities, to acquire the right to shape and challenge, whenever needed, their normative community,[39] both as citizens and as believers. It is this right that reflects best our understanding of legal empowerment.

Traditional human rights appear occasionally insufficient to protect individuals from religious claims, hence any notion of legal empowerment may seem unlikely. Accordingly, legal empowerment is presented as a possibility only outside the religious and cultural community. With the contribution of evolving notions of human rights, that are at the same time culturally relevant and representative of traditional and more liberal interpretations of the exercise and practice of faith, the aim of legal empowerment can begin to be considered in a more sophisticated manner than before.

Some chapters, nevertheless, place emphasis on the ways that law has contributed towards the preservation of traditional, legal disempowering practices within religious communities. Indeed, there are various accounts in this book and elsewhere that demonstrate how legal norms through cultural relativism and multiculturalism policies have re-made religious communities in strikingly more fundamentalist terms.[40]

Reva Siegel's 'preservation through transformation' strategy describes well the quest for law, as a system of norms, to service the rights of all, without losing sight of its regulatory effects on the social stratification of persons and entire groups.[41] Deference to religious leaders in this respect, who shape the norms applicant to the group, is needed but is no longer self-sufficient.

The structure of the volume

In the light of all the above, the book is structured in two parts: the first part addresses the role played in religion as a separate, yet fully-fledged, system of law, operating side by side with state law. In other words, religion AS law. The second part focuses more on the ways that religion influences the normative content of contemporary legal systems, i.e. religion IN law. Both parts contain chapters that ultimately reflect on the potential and conditionality surrounding the exercise of religious rights towards the legal empowerment of right-holders.

Evidently, the various contributions in this volume come to their analysis from different disciplinary and methodological trajectories. The question of religion as a factor of legal empowerment is therefore approached from a variety of 'starting points' both in terms of geography but also concerning the foci of analysis of each account on the interaction between law and religion offered.

38 Dustin (2006: 29–30).
39 Expression borrowed from Sunder (2003: 1440).
40 See Sunder (2003), in particular footnote 22.
41 Siegel (1997).

In the first part, Federica Sona chooses to look at the role played by Islamic religious identity and belonging in shaping the socio-legal conducts of Muslim intended spouses within the context of the Italian legal system. The question of legal empowerment is addressed in her work through the lens of the dynamic interplay between Italian civil law legal provisions and sharia-compliant norms. She argues that Islam can potentially empower or disempower Muslim fiancé(e)s wishing to marry in compliance with Italian laws, depending on the techniques used by Muslim intended spouses. Through a detailed legal classification and explanation of situations in which Islamic and/or Muslim marriages can be (and are) recognized as valid under Italian law, Sona notices the existence of grey zones when superimposing sharia-compliant norms to Italian laws. It is within this space that the author reaches the conclusion that the interaction between the Italian legal system and Muslim norms on marriages remains a fluid one, requiring reciprocal adjustments and allowing individual navigation, either in the search for empowerment, or in efforts to control diversity and difference. Depending therefore on the legal strategic path used by Muslim intended spouses, Islam can become an effective tool for legal empowerment or a tool of discrimination against them.

A similar question, with a broader remit, is taken on by Waheeda Amien in the South African context within the next chapter. Amien chooses to focus on the issue of lack of recognition of Muslim personal law in South Africa and how this affects Muslim women who are married only by Muslim rites and are placed in a situation of struggle when attempting to access Islamic law rights related to marriage and divorce and other civil benefits available to spouses married under the secular South African Marriage Act of 1961.

Amien's trajectory on the subject utilizes case-law analysis and collected narratives from her consultations as an attorney to demonstrate the difficulties faced by these women in accessing their rights. Interestingly, in the South African context, the judiciary has come to the rescue of these women, often in order to implement constitutional expectations rather than out of respect for religion. Furthermore, legal adjudication rules allow South African Muslims to access their Islamic law rights if they can prove the terms and customs of their Muslim marriage contracts. These purely legal strategic considerations, however, do not seem to 'compensate' for the reluctance of Muslim women to enter into marriage contracts, as a result of what Amien labels 'a lack of agency or not . . . asserting agency'. Inevitably, this choice leads often to their legal disempowerment. This last point is well illustrated in the second part of Amien's chapter, which provides accounts drawn from real-life situations that seem to confirm the persistence of power imbalances when entering into Muslim marriage in South Africa. Ultimately, the chapter concludes by noting the gendered nature of power in the context of Muslim family law in South Africa as an indication that in her case the interplay of religion with law tends to lead to legal disempowerment, understood as lack (or refusal) to exercise agency.

In continuation of Amien's inquiry on the use(s) of Muslim personal law, the next chapter by Kalindi Kokal takes the discussion to the Indian legal context. Kokal's contribution is also linked to an empirical study, conducted in the lower courts of Maharashtra, in the western part of India. On the basis of her observations and interactions with litigants, lawyers and judges, Kokal discusses the characteristics of civil litigation initiated by members of religious minorities, particularly when involving the application of personal laws.

The limited number of such cases is the concurrent result of lack of awareness of right-holders, their preference for alternative fora for dispute resolution managed by their own religious community and/or the reluctance of the members of the judiciary sitting in those courts to make use and application of personal law, as provided for by the Indian constitution. Kokal's viewpoint focuses on understanding how personal law is experienced by lawyers, judges and litigants and on the basis of her findings reflects on the broader concepts of secularism, religious identity and cultural pluralism. Her analysis is critical of essentialist practices towards religion(s) and puts an accent on the need to adjust decision-making processes to appreciate the context arising from religious plurality, instead of focusing on the task of ascertaining the essential practices of a particular religion.

The centre of gravity of this chapter clearly is the use of personal laws. This consideration alone, given also the limited data available, does not allow the author to conclude on the level of (dis-)empowerment of individuals when using personal law (containing religious rights) in the context she studies. In that sense, similarly to Amien's South African Muslim personal law analysis, there is a clear need for further research. However, the mere presumption that the presence and/or application of personal laws is necessarily damaging for empowerment becomes increasingly questionable.

The next chapter takes readers back to South Africa but offers a completely different account of the layers of interaction between law and religion. Dennis Xulu discusses how courts do not bring closure to contentions among individuals, families and society. He argues that in some cases religious systems of laws are better positioned to provide 'closure' to contentious causes by virtue of their dealing with the human person more holistically. By balancing justice, caritas, mercy, dignity of the person and human rights Xulu argues for a different type of empowerment: one that accepts the complementarity of law and religion towards legal and cultural pluralism. To do so, he employs Canon law of the Catholic Church in showcasing the existence (and relevance) of religious laws, as non-state laws, as well as their contribution in healing contentions in society.

Xulu's starting point is the assumption that religious communities try to exercise and promote justice and as such produce their own legal system. With the help of the example of the South African experience with the Truth and Reconciliation Commission, Xulu discusses the role and influence of religion in South African society. Like all previous contributions of the volume to varying degrees, Xulu acknowledges the presence and influence of legally pluralistic environments as well as their importance in empowering individuals or entire societies, when operating in synergy with the state. The essence of his analysis looks at religious laws as instruments to better understand the human person and her relationship with others and the environment. Ultimately, to Xulu religious laws have emancipatory power over individuals, which should not be denied a presence and a voice on mere secular grounds. They need to be balanced, rather than excluding one and favouring or privileging the other.

The last chapter of the first part of the volume considers the concept of Islamic constitutionalism as an empowering tool to limit arbitrariness in the exercise of power by the executive, the legislative and the judiciary in constitutional settings of modern democracies that recognise sharia as a source of law.

Based on general principles contained in sharia that regulate the relationship of individuals in the public sphere, Pietro Longo discusses the notion of the conduct of politics within the boundaries of Islamic religious law. At the same time, Pietro Longo shows how these 'political principles' can contribute towards the better conceptualisation of Islamic constitutionalism per se. This last concept is treated and described in this contribution as an ongoing and evolving project, which constitutional courts in countries of the Arab world play a role in shaping, when using sharia as a source of law within their decision-making processes.

Longo's chapter concludes that the use of sharia as a *grundnorm* highlights the possibility that far from constituting a threat to rights and freedoms of citizens, could be transformed, under favourable conditions, to a new instrument of legal empowerment. Like others in this volume, however, Longo is cautious to draw attention to the plurality within sharia and the variety in the methods of its interpretation. Nevertheless, its constitutional recognition offers a window of opportunity to consider the characteristics of this unique normative universe.

The second part of the book, on religion within law, begins with a theoretical contribution on possible options for religious laws, communities and players to serve as empowerment tools for individuals and communities. Addressing the heart of the matter of this volume, Amos Israel-Vleeschhouwer, with the help of Jewish law, spells out the necessary conditions for religious empowerment and empowerment through religion, with special focus on the role of international law and international legal players.

The author's initial point is one shared by most authors contributing to this book: religion does not 'speak' with one voice when addressing the law(s) and it quickly becomes a disempowering factor if it is related or perceived to be related only to the hegemonic voice within each religion. In his analysis, he treats religions as complex legal systems, focuses on the structures of the relationships within and between these systems of faith and international law and finally comes up with a concrete proposal materialising the dynamic processes described. Relying on a multi-player system, Israel-Vleeschhouwer introduces exciting arguments about the merits of such a system of religious leaders and its implications. He explains how religious communities may (and will) strive for inter-communal bottom-up agreements, even without being state-supported organizations. Variation and adaptation within these communities ensure the preservation of diversity through a bottom-up empowering approach that offers options to individuals and groups to share their religious and social experiences. Finally, the author concludes that knowledge of law is useful but not self-sufficient to a path towards empowerment, simply because it represents a partial and limited form of engagement. It is precisely this gap that his work seeks to address.

The next chapter takes the discussion of the interactions between law and religion to Indonesia. Supriyanto Abdi looks at the Ahmadiyah controversy within the context of struggles over religion–state relations. He specifically locates the presence and treatment of a minority Muslim faith community in post-Suharto Indonesia in order to highlight the ways the current discourse on religious freedom is shaped in this Muslim-majority democracy.

The author especially focuses on the recently strengthened concept of religious orthodoxy as the red line of his analysis to analyse the continuing struggles between different interpretations of Islam and competing constructions of national identities in contemporary Indonesia. In that sense, he echoes Israel-Vleeschhouwer's point on the need to continue to acknowledge a multitude of religious voices to fulfil the perspective of legal empowerment. Abdi, however, adds another layer to his analysis when he criticizes the ambiguous nature of the Indonesian state and the constitutional parameters of the construction of religious freedom. He shows the risk that any empowering balance may be taken away again, and thus illustrates the well-known basic principle that all laws are highly dynamic.

In his account, the author does not leave out the discussion of the country's contentious politics of religion–state relations, with emphasis on Muslim liberal political actors. He concludes that the deeper factor justifying the ambiguity on the conception and activation of religious freedoms, as mirrored in the case of Ahmadiyah, lies in the specificities of the ambiguous nature of the Indonesian state, with a tendency for the state to intervene in religious matters when there is a perception that core values are at risk. In this case, the core value is outwardly the doctrinal element of the finality of the Prophet, but the power shifts in local societies when people adhere to different forms of Muslim sectarian orientations should not be overlooked.

From Indonesia, the following chapter moves to Switzerland and offers a Swiss perspective on the much-debated issue of women's rights within religious communities. Adrian Loretan looks at gender equality from the perspective of the debate on universalism versus cultural relativism. His departing point is one that accepts that human rights are a culturally loaded normative construction. He chooses then to focus on the question on whether the state should – and can truthfully claim to – promote human rights within religious groups. With the help of human dignity, Loretan describes how religious group rights often conflict with other individual human rights, particularly equality. A crucial part of his account looks at the right of exit from religious communities, the notion of consent to certain religious practices and the overarching state's duty from a gender perspective. He then adds the Swiss dimension to this debate, with emphasis on the role of the state in this context.

The second level of Loretan's discussion turns to the exercise of collective religious freedom and how it is connected to legal pluralism. He proposes four approaches to the situation of conflict between a member and his/her religious community, namely the communitarian one, the feminist, the liberal and finally one that looks at group rights as derivative rights. Loretan concludes that the 'reconciliation' of religious freedom with gender equality remains a challenging enterprise in need of contextualization. Human dignity, in his view, could be one way to reflect better the needs for further protection of the more vulnerable segments of society, in particular women.

Lauren Fielder's chapter retains a gendered perspective on the relationship between law and religion and looks at polygyny in sub-Saharan Africa. Reflecting the book's central question, Fielder asks pointedly whether polygyny is a practice that empowers or disempowers women. Following a brief account of the historical evolution of polygyny in Africa, the author explores the living realities of women living in polygynous marriages in order to assess whether the practice is (dis-)empowering. Methodologically, the chapter relies on a dual account of how polygyny is situated within the legal pluralist African landscape and the role that constitutional courts play vis-à-vis the practice. Without dismissing the cultural dimensions of polygyny, the analysis focuses on the ways that it tends or works to disempower African women. The personal, economic and health dimensions are addressed side-by-side with the response from legal systems, at different levels (from local to international). Fielder, similarly to Loretan, advocates a careful balancing of the rights of women with the right to religion and culture. She also resonates Xulu's South African discussion earlier in the book, when she considers in her conclusion the multi-faceted role that religious associations can undertake in empowering African women. Given that women are half of humanity, no religion can simply ignore the legitimate claims of women to fair and equitable treatment. As elsewhere, the challenge for our understanding of these complex issues lies in the value-based assessments of what is fair, reasonable and ultimately empowering.

The chapter by Bogdan Mihai Radu and Cosmina Paul discusses attitudes towards abortion in Romania and how these attitudes are shaped by the work of religious non-governmental organizations. Their arguments are premised against a background discussion on the role of religion in post-communist Romania and Central and Eastern Europe more broadly. They posit what we seem to know, namely that there is a very delicate relationship between religion and democracy, which often shows that religion can be a source and influence towards value formation also in contexts where it is officially not present. With the help of a partly qualitative, partly quantitative methodological approach, the authors demonstrate an asymmetrical attachment to different values in Romania: homosexuality is decreasingly contested, while abortion (and divorce) remain steadily rejected.

The new post-communist framework of discussion on abortion continues, therefore, to be affected by religious discourses. This occurs partly as a result of the fact that religious organizations are increasingly involved in education and development services. This chapter focuses, therefore, on the question of how one may understand the shift in the church's focus to development projects and poverty alleviation, in lieu of individual rights issues, leading to its re-discovery and legitimization, utilizing the potential of civil society mobilization.

At the same time, the chapter insists on the discussion of abortion through the illumination of religious aspects that come to play a formative role. The authors conclude their analysis by finding the need to reconsider the alignment of women's rights with the internal norms of values of the Church of Romania, echoing Loretan's query on the compatibility between the right to equality and that to freedom of religion.

The last chapter of the volume examines the expression of religious freedoms in public education classrooms from a legal comparative basis. Kyriaki Topidi sets her account against the main legal concepts of secularism, post-secularism and state neutrality in order to then study their effects and implications with an eye to the aim of promotion of religious diversity in schools. She effectively reflects on the protection of diversity in public education in Europe, as evidenced in European Court of Human Rights decisions, and contrasts the findings with similar cases in Canada and South Africa. Following this comparative exercise, Topidi returns to a more macroscopic, policy level by transposing her observations to both multicultural and post-multicultural policy frames. The main inquiry in that respect focuses on how students in these schools can indeed become empowered agents and subjects of law, depending on the legal and policy environment under which their public schooling is organized. In parallel with most chapters in the book, Topidi's analysis is assuming that in contemporary states and legal systems, legal plurality has become a fact which the legal discipline is called to account for. In that respect, the role of law, however, cannot be conceived as independent, detached or insulated from social movements surrounding the debate on religious diversity in any given legal system and context.

In analysing the conflicts and tensions in the power relations between law and religion, and seeking to open spaces for individual empowerment, this book collectively argues that neither of the main two competitors can simply be banned or sidelined – they have to engage in an elaborate discourse that first of all respects the existence of the other and thus allows for scope of a level of trust that will not make distrust evaporate or vanish, but will result in a guarded relationship of mutual supervision and scrutiny, ultimately designed to protect the core value of individual choice. This would then serve as a basis for empowerment of that individual to make decisions that may not be accepted by all others who are more or less closely connected to that individual, but preserves the crucial freedom of conscience that both religious and constitutional systems claim to protect in their own different ways. If at the end of the day, every individual has basic constitutional rights as a human being, but every individual is also believed to be accountable to a higher 'religious' entity, of whatever kind, then this balancing of competing perceptions of empowerment through religion becomes an integral part of the key challenges of life. In late modernity, to claim to rescue vulnerable individuals by guiding them away from, protecting them from, or even banning them from access to religious forms of power is all too clearly one particular Western type of prescription. It may have become rather dominant in the minds of many 'modern' people, but is not a realistic reflection of the complexities of human experience in the interface of law and religion.

References

Borradori, G. (2003) *Philosophy in a time of terror: Dialogues with Jürgen Habermas and Jacques Derrida*. Chicago and London: University of Chicago Press.

Chiba, Masaji (1989) *Legal pluralism: Towards a general theory through Japanese legal culture*. Tokyo: Tokai University Press.

Cotterrell, Roger and Maksymilian del Mar (eds) (2015) *Authority in transnational legal theory: Theorising across disciplines. Dedicated to the memory of Professor Patrick Glenn*. Cheltenham: Edward Elgar.

Degiorgis, Nicoló (2014) *Hidden Islam: Islamic nakeshift places of worship in North East Italy, 2009–2013*. Bolzano: Rorhof.

Dustin, Moira (2006) Gender equality, cultural diversity: European comparisons and lessons. Gender Institute, LSE, available at www.lse.ac.uk/genderInstitute/pdf/NuffieldReport_final.pdf.

Gal-Or, Noemi (2011) Is the law empowering or patronizing women? The dilemma in the French burqa decision as the tip of the secular law iceberg. *Religion and Human Rights* 6, 315–333.

Grillo, Ralph (2015) *Muslim families, politics and the law: A legal industry in multicultural Britain*. Farnham: Ashgate

Habermas, Jürgen (2008) *Between naturalism and religion*. Cambridge: Polity Press.

Habermas, Jürgen (2010) *An awareness of what is missing: Faith and reason in a post-secular age*. Cambridge, MA: Polity Press.

Khair, Sumaiya (2008) *Legal empowerment for the poor and disadvantaged: Strategies, achievements and challenges. Experiences from Bangladesh*. Dhaka: Colorline.

Menski, Werner (2003) *Hindu law: Beyond tradition and modernity*. New Delhi: Oxford University Press.

Menski, Werner (2006) *Comparative law in a global context: The legal systems of Asia and Africa*. Second edition. Cambridge: Cambridge University Press.

Menski, Werner (2008) The Uniform Civil Code debate in Indian law: New developments and changing agenda. *German Law Journal* 9(3), 211–250. Available at: http://www.germanlawjournal.com/submissions.php (last visited 1 April 2015).

Menski, Werner (2014) Remembering and applying legal pluralism: Law as kite flying. In Séan Patrick Donlan and Lukas Heckendorn Urscheler (eds) *Concepts of law: Comparative, jurisprudential, and social science perspectives*. Farnham: Ashgate, pp. 91–108.

Pearl, David and Werner Menski (1998) *Muslim family law*. Third edition. London: Sweet and Maxwell.

Robertson, Robbie (2003) *The three waves of globalization: A hisory of a developing global consciousness*. Nova Scotia and London: Fernwood Publishing and Zed Books.

Siegel, Reva B. (1997)Why equal protection no longer protects: The evolving forms of status-enforcing state action. *Stan L. Rev.* 49, 1113.

Sunder, Madhavi (2003) Piercing the veil. UC Davis Legal Studies Research Paper Series, Research Paper No.112, available at: http://ssrn.com/abstract=413982.

Tamanaha, B.Z., S. Sage and M. Woolcock (eds) (2012) *Legal pluralism and development: Scholars and practitioners in dialogue*. Cambridge: Cambridge University Press.

Twining, William (ed.) (2009) *Human rights, southern voices*. Cambridge: Cambridge University Press.

Ventura, Marco (2014) *From your gods to our gods: A history of religion in Indian, South African, and British courts*. Eugene: Cascade Books.

Wacquant, Loïc (2014) Marginality, ethnicity and penality in the neo-liberal city: An analytic cartography. *Ethnic and Racial Studies* 37(10), 1687–1711.

Part I

Religion AS law

2 Islām as legal (dis-)empowerment

The dynamic interplay between Italian legal provisions and *sharī'ah*-compliant norms

Federica Sona

Introduction

This chapter discusses the role played by 'Islamic belonging' in moulding the socio-legal conducts of Muslim intended spouses and the response of the Italian legal system.[1] Islām is thus investigated as a tool for legal (dis-)empowerment.[2]

Legal empowerment is currently understood as the process of 'strengthening the capacity of all people to exercise their rights, either as individuals or as members of a community'.[3] As explained by Cotula (2007: 10), originally defined as 'the use of legal services and other development activities to increase disadvantaged populations' control over their lives';[4] legal empowerment gradually became a core concept, partly as a result of the establishment of the UN-hosted Commission on the Legal Empowerment of the Poor. Emerging from a critique of the 'rule of law orthodoxy', legal empowerment is nowadays interested in the 'agency and priorities of marginalised people'.[5] Whereas the idea of legal empowerment remains per se largely borrowed from development studies, and it tends to be linked to poor and disadvantaged legal subjects mostly settled in non-Western countries,[6] this analysis focuses on a sort of 'new' legal empowerment,[7] namely the agency of Muslims settled in Europe who face discrimination.

1 The expression 'Islamic belonging' is here used when referring to practicing Muslims as well as nationals of Muslim-majority countries.

2 A shorter version of this chapter was presented at the UNILU Doctoral Programme on *Culture and Law*, 14–15 November 2014, SICL, Lausanne (Switzerland). I am very grateful to Dr Kyriaki Topidi for giving me the opportunity to contribute to the very interesting debate and I thank all the participants for helpful and thought-provoking discussion.

3 See Open Society Institute (2014).

4 This definition was given by Golub (2005: 304).

5 See Domingo and O'Neil (2014: 4).

6 See, for instance, the definition of legal empowerment as 'the use of law to specifically strengthen the disadvantaged' as recently suggested by Golub (2010: 6).

7 I am here echoing the vocabulary chosen by Merry (1988) when identifying 'classical' and 'new' legal pluralism and describing the second as the study of coexisting multiple legal systems in 'advanced industrial countries of Europe and the United States'. Similarly, in this chapter the idea of legal empowerment of disadvantaged legal subjects belonging to a religious minority (i.e. Muslim fiancé/es and spouses) is analysed with respect to Italy.

A general point first: religion generally can either empower or disempower. As a key point, the present analysis clarifies that Islām can either disempower or empower Muslim fiancé/es wishing to marry or to register their marriage in compliance with Italian laws. Focusing on multi-folded marriage routes followed by Muslim partners settled on the Italian soil, the partly overlooked dynamic interplay between domestic legal provisions and *sharīʿah*-compliant norms is brought to light.

It is often properly assumed that 'Islamic belonging' can imply discrimination of a legal subject and, with respect to civilly valid nuptial unions of Muslim fiancées, this happens on a daily basis.[8] Nonetheless, relying upon a decade of extensive empirical investigations,[9] this study shows that – in some situations – Muslim fiancé/es actually benefit from more room for manoeuvre when compared to non-Muslim (non-European national or immigrant) intended spouses. This broader spectrum of nuptial possibilities contemplates strategic countermeasures and loopholes. Clever tactics tend to be elaborated by European Islamic bodies and/or Muslim diplomatic premises as a result of (religious) discriminatory norms enacted by European domestic legal systems. Grey areas come into existence when superimposing *sharīʿah*-compliant and/or foreign norms to Italian laws. A strategic use of legal provisions can thus either empower or disempower a purported spouse and/or a nation state.

In this field, issues of public and private international laws intertwine with legal pluralism, in particular with religious-Islamic and customary-Muslim norms.[10]

8 Further to dramatic international events, the number of academic publications and media coverage debating Islamophobia and discrimination of Muslims in Western countries exponentially grew in the last three decades. Discussing these issues is beyond the scope of the present work, I shall thus refer to some relevant literature. Among the others, see R. Richardson (1997, 2004); Vertovec (2002); Halliday (2002); Allen and Nielsen (2004); J. Richardson (2004); Helly and Césari (2005); Choudhury *et al.* (2006); Bloul (2008); Allen (2010); Sayyid and Vakil (2010); ADGC (2011); Esposito and Kalin (2011); Ansari and Hafez (2012); Taras (2012); Petrley and Richardson (2013); Kaya (2014).

9 Relying upon socio-legal deductive-inductive methods, qualitative data were collected from 2004 to 2014 through a combination of field observations, oral and written surveys. Methodological triangulation techniques – such as semi-structured interviewees, self-designed questionnaires, observational techniques, and documents analysis (including unpublished court materials, spouses' private official papers, confidential legal administrative certificates) – were variously combined accordingly to the field peculiarities. For further details on the employed research methodology, see *inter alia* Weber (1949); Denzin (1989); Gray and Guppy (1994); Ringer (1997); Denzin and Lincoln (1994; 1998); Flick (1998); Hollway and Jefferson (2000); Bryman (2001); Patton (2002); Bulmer (2003); Huff (2003); Banakar and Travers (2005); Yanow and Schwartz-Shea (2006); Walliman (2006); McConville and Chui (2007); Jeldtoft and Nielsen (2012).

10 It is worth mentioning that the adjectives 'Muslim' and 'Islamic' are frequently used as synonyms; nonetheless, their meaning is slightly different. The adjective Islamic comes from the word *Islām*, which derives from the Arabic verb *sallama li* . . . that means 'to submit to . . . [God's will]'. The word *Muslim* is the participle of the same Arabic verb, therefore the meaning of the word Muslim is 'the submitter'. Accordingly, the adjective Islamic identifies the religion and its sources; whereas the adjective Muslim identifies the believers and also *sharīʿah* as interpreted and lived in light of local customs and family traditions. On this see also Sona (2014: 116).

Accordingly, the proposed analysis aims to disentangle these overlapping socio-legal sources in order to investigate the fluid reciprocal adjustments between clever empowerment techniques developed by (foreign) Muslim intended spouses and discriminative provisions enacted by the domestic legal systems of Italy and Muslim-majority countries.

Marrying in Italy

In Italy, purported spouses can contract three types of marriages: civil, religious, and religious with civil effects. Muslim fiancé/es can thus marry in compliance with Italian laws and/or *sharīʿah*. In particular, Muslim purported spouses can choose either to contract a civil-only marriage as regulated by Italian laws, or they may favour a *sharīʿah*-compliant nuptial union, which might be acknowledged as civilly valid by the Italian legal system. An Islamic and/or Muslim marriage can be recognized and recorded by the Italian legal systems in three scenarios. This happens when:

1 the wedding is celebrated by an appointed religious minister;
2 the nuptial union is perfected in compliance with the laws of a foreign country;
3 the competent foreign authorities and/or diplomatic premises of a foreign country recognize as valid and register a Muslim-only and/or Islamic-only marriage.

In the above listed cases, a *sharīʿah*-compliant marriage is also valid with civil effects on the Italian soil. Whereas the former two case scenarios are well-known, the last hypothesis seems to be frequently overlooked by scholarship and judiciary alike. It involves the operation of private international law rules.

Similarly, another neglected aspect concerns the actual possibility not to disclose a potentially civilly valid Islamic and/or Muslim nuptial union to the state authorities. Accordingly, some spouses can be regarded as cohabitees by the Italian legal system, whilst being considered husband and wife by the national laws of some Muslim-majority countries, and/or from an Islamic religious perspective. The nuptial status of these partners therefore differs in different legal systems. The choice not to disclose an Islamic/Muslim marriage might stem from the legal character's personal will (e.g. in case of polygynous marriage), or it could be the result of power imbalances, social constraints, group coercion, poor legal advice and/or irregular (im)migration status in European countries. Superimposing *sharīʿah*-compliant and/or foreign norms to Italian laws creates grey areas in which multiple nuptial statuses can be hidden. As a result, Muslim fiancé/es may *de facto* benefit from more room for manoeuvre when compared to non-Muslim European national or immigrant intended spouses. In these situations, Islām becomes a tool for legal empowerment of legal subjects.

A layer of further complexity is added by the fact that – independently from the Muslim parties' willingness to do so – the 'Islamic belonging' of an intended Muslim foreign spouse can affect the spectrum of his/her rights to contract a marriage with civil effects in Italy. In effect, foreign spouses-to-be are asked to satisfy further requirements and some of them might be particularly problematic for citizens of Muslim-majority countries. Under the latter circumstances, Islām becomes a tool for discrimination and legal disempowerment of intended (foreign) Muslim spouses.

The following three sections focus on the three cases in which Islamic and/or Muslim marriages can be recognized and recorded as valid nuptial union with civil effects by the Italian legal systems; the fourth section addresses civil marriages contracted by non-Italian Muslim spouses.

Sharīʿah-compliant marriages with civil effects

In Italy, a marriage solemnized in compliance with state and (some) religious laws can be recognized and have civil effects. The following two sub-sections revolve around marriages solemnized by appointed religious ministers and the partly concealed unfavorable conditions faced by Muslim intended spouses when trying to contract a *sharīʿah*-compliant civilly valid marriage.

Marriages solemnized by appointed religious ministers

On Italian soil, religious denominations are acknowledged to have different hierarchical positions, and their capacity to solemnize valid marriages with civil effects may vary. From a constitutional perspective, a special position is recognized to the Catholic Church (art. 7 Italian Constitution).[11] 'Denominations other than Catholicism' have the right to self-organization according to their own statutes, provided these do not conflict with Italian law (art. 8(2) Italian Constitution).

'Other religions permitted within the state'[12] are recognized the right to sign *ad hoc* bilateral agreements with the state in order to regulate their relations with the Italian legal system.[13] These agreements are called *intese* and are a reflection of the Concordat signed between the state and the Catholic Church.[14] Religions

11 Italian Constitution, 'Costituzione della Repubblica Italiana', 22.12.1947, in *Gazzetta Ufficiale* 27.12.1947 No. 298.

12 The adjective 'permitted' is employed in the translation of art. 83 of the Italian Civil Code suggested by the English version of the Italian Civil Code (Beltramo *et al.*, 1969–2007). For an introduction on the Italian legal system in English language and from a Common law perspective, see Cappelletti *et al.* (1967).

13 Casuscelli (2008: 292) identifies further internal differentiation among confessions: religions with a proper *intesa*, religions with an inferior *intesa*, religions with a non-approved *intesa*, religions recognized as 'admitted cult', religions recognized by international law treaties, otherwise known religions, and *de facto* religions.

14 In 1929, a Treaty was signed by the Kingdom of Italy and the Holy See. In 1948, the *Lateranensia Pacta* were incorporated into art. 7 of the Italian Constitution. In 1984, a Concordat amended the 1929 Pacts. See Law 27.05.1929 No. 810, 'Esecuzione del Trattato, dei quattro allegati annessi, e del Concordato, sottoscritti in Roma, tra la Santa Sede e l'Italia, l'11.02.1929', in *Gazzetta Ufficiale* 05.06.1929 No. 130; Law 27.05.1929 No. 847, 'Disposizioni per l'applicazione del

without an *intesa* are regulated by general norms on 'admitted cults'.[15] During the 1990s, three associations of Italian Muslims submitted four proposals of a draft-agreement;[16] nonetheless, none of these *bozza d'intesa* was eventually signed. As a consequence, nowadays Islām finds itself amongst the 'admitted' and 'permitted cults' in Italy.

Ministers of denominations other than Catholicism can solemnize marriages according to their religious rite; these nuptial unions are civilly valid when they abide by the provisions of the Italian Civil Code and some special norms.[17] An appointed religious minister can thus celebrate religious marriages with civil effects, provided s/he is an Italian citizen, is fluent in the Italian language and does not practise a public function. In particular, these religious ministers cannot be elected as mayor; provincial president; communal, provincial and district councillor (Legal Decree No. 267 of 2000); juryman (art. 12, Law No. 287 of 1951); justice of the peace (art. 8, Law No. 374 of 1991); associated honorary judge (art. 8, Law No. 276 of 1997); notary public (art. 2, Law No. 89 of 1913) and tax collector (art. 17, Royal Decree No. 1401 of 1922).[18] Additionally, the community of believers should meet for worship activities in the commune of residence of

Concordato del 11.02.1929 fra la Santa Sede e l'Italia, nella parte relativa al matrimonio', in *Gazzetta Ufficiale* 08.06.1929 No. 133; Law 25.03.1985 No. 121, 'Ratifica ed esecuzione dell'accordo con protocollo addizionale, firmato a Roma il 18 febbraio 1984, che apporta modifiche al Concordato lateranense dell'11 febbraio 1929, tra la Repubblica italiana e la Santa Sede', in *Gazzetta Ufficiale* 10.04.1985 No. 85 SO.

15 Law No. 1159 of 1929 and Royal Decree No. 289 of 1930 employ the words *culti ammessi*. See Law 24.06.1929 No. 1159, 'Disposizioni sull'esercizio dei culti ammessi nello Stato e sul matrimonio celebrato davanti ai ministri dei culti medesimi', in *Gazzetta Ufficiale* 16.07.1929 No. 164; and Royal Decree 28.02.1930 No. 289, 'Norme per l'attuazione della L. 24 giugno 1929, n. 1159, sui culti ammessi nello Stato e per coordinamento di essa con le altre leggi dello Stato', in *Gazzetta Ufficiale* 12.04.1930 No. 87.

16 The four draft agreements were submitted for approval by the Unione delle Comunità e Organizzazioni Islamiche in Italia (UCOII) in 1990 and 1992, by the Associazione Musulmani italiani (AMI) in 1993, and by the Comunità Religiosa Islamica italiana (CoReIs) in 1998. For a discussion on these *bozze d'intese*, see for instance Ricca (1996); Cilardo (2001); D'Andrea (2004); Spreafico and Coppi (2006); Casuscelli (2008). For a summary of the the main Islamic and Muslim organizations, see Coglievina (2013: 354–356).

17 Italian Civil Code, Royal Decree 16.03.1942, No. 262, 'Approvazione del testo del Codice Civile', in *Gazzetta Ufficiale,* Edizione Straordinaria 04.04.1942 No. 79. See also Law No. 1159 of 1929 and Royal Decree No. 289 of 1930. For a comparison with the religions that signed a bilateral agreements with the state, see for instance Di Marzio (2005).

18 See respectively Legal Decree No. 18.08.2000 No. 267, 'Testo unico delle leggi sull'ordinamento degli enti locali', in *Gazzetta Ufficiale* 28.09.2000 No. 227 SO No. 162; Law 10.04.1951 No. 287, 'Riordinamento dei giudizi di assise', in *Gazzetta Ufficiale* 07.05.1951 No. 102; Law 21.11.1991 No. 374, 'Istituzione del giudice di pace', in *Gazzetta Ufficiale* 27.11.1991 No. 278 SO No. 76; Law 22.07.1997 No. 276, 'Disposizioni per la definizione del contenzioso civile pendente: nomina di giudici onorari aggregati e istituzione delle sezioni stralcio nei tribunali ordinari', in *Gazzetta Ufficiale* 19.08.1997 No. 192; Law 16.02.1913 No. 89, 'Ordinamento del natariato e degli archivi notarili', in *Gazzetta Ufficiale* 07.03.1913 No. 55; Royal Decree 17.10.1922 No. 1401, 'Approvazione del nuovo Testo Unico delle leggi per la riscossione delle imposte diriette', in *Gazzetta Ufficiale* 17.11.1922 No. 269.

the appointed religious minister.[19] As a further requirement, the locally competent vital statistics officer (*ufficiale di stato civile*) shall provide a written authorization to the spouses-to-be. This authorization specifies the place and the time for the marriage to take place, and it identifies the competent religious minister, whose appointment was formerly approved by the Ministry of the Interior.[20]

With respect to the procedure of religious marriages with civil effects, Italian laws impel appointed religious ministers to follow the same procedure as the vital statistics officer. An appointed religious minister shall thus read the arts. 143, 144, 147 of the Italian Civil Code, and receive declarations of the bride's and the groom's intent to take each other as husband and wife before two witnesses. Immediately after the wedding celebration the marriage deed shall be completed in the Italian language.[21] The original copy of this marriage deed shall be sent to the competent vital statistics officer, who shall then register such religious marriage in the vital statistics records.

Religious discriminatory disempowerment

Although relying upon what can be identified as a controversial lexicon,[22] and requiring the enactment of a complex and detailed procedure, the above examined provisions on registered religious marriages appear to accommodate religious needs within the Italian legal system. Additionally, these norms do not conflict per se with constitutional principles.[23]

19 Ministero dell'Interno (undated).

20 In the Ministry of Interior, the Direzione Centrale degli Affari dei Culti shall approve the appointment of religious ministers (arts. 20–22, Royal Decree No. 289 of 1930).

21 Art. 10, Law No. 1159 of 1929. The list of details to be reported in the marriage deed is quite dated; this provision is to be co-ordinated with arts. 63(2a) and 64 of the Decree of the President of the Republic 03.11.2000 No. 396, 'Regolamento per la revisione e la semplificazione dell'ordinamento dello stato civile a norma dell'art.2(12) della Legge 15.05.1997 No. 127', in *Gazzetta Ufficiale* 30.12.2000 No. 303, SO No. 223/L.

22 See *infra* and the following footnote. See also art. 8(2) Italian Constitution; art. 83 Italian Civil Code; Law No. 1159 of 1929; Royal Decree No. 289 of 1930. It should be pinpointed that the Italian Parliament has been debating the abrogation of the law on admitted cults since 1997. A number of Bills exists. See for instance, Bill (*disegno di legge*) No. 36/2006 submitted by Boato (www.uaar.it/6laicita/osservatorio-parlamentare/xv-legislatura/proposte-legge/pdl-2006-36.html), 28.04.2006, XV Legislatura; Bill (*disegno di legge*) No. 134/2006 submitted by Spini *et al.* (www.uaar.it/ laicita/osser vatorio-parlamentare/xv-legislatura/proposte-legge/pdl-2006-134.html), 28.04.2006, XV Legislatura; Bill (*disegno di legge*) No. 48/2008 submitted on 29.04.2008 by Zaccaria *et al.*, XVI Legislatura; Bill (*disegno di legge*) No. 618/2008 submitted on 20.05.2008 by Negri, XVI Legislatura; Bill (*disegno di legge*) No. 3613/2010 submitted by Miglioli, (http://parlamento16.openpolis.it/singolo_atto/56076), 07.07.2010, XVI Legislatura. For an interesting discussion, see *inter alia* Colaianni (2006, 2008); Casuscelli (2008); Ferrari (2008); De Gregorio (2012).

23 The arts. 7 and 19 Italian Constitution grant religious freedom and protect against discrimination any persons, also stressing that all religious denominations are free before the law. The expression 'admitted cults' is regarded as being compatible with art. 8 Italian Constitution since Italy recognizes the same freedom to all religions; nonetheless, this does not imply that all religions are equal in an absolute sense, and different norms can regulate their relations with the state.

An effective discriminatory disempowerment tool was, however, hidden in the bureaucratic implementation of these provisions on civilly valid marriages solemnized by appointed religious ministers of 'admitted' and 'permitted' faiths. The civil validity as well as the registration of a religious nuptial union perfected by an appointed minister could indeed be easily denied in case of minor flaws. In some cases, registered religious marriages were deprived of their civil effects simply on the ground of bureaucratic errors. In other situations, registration issues arose. This happened when a marriage was celebrated in a place outside the appointed religious minister's allocated area as precisely identified by the minister's appointment decree. As a result, these marriages were not registered in the official nuptial record by the competent vital statistics officer; and – if registered – such nuptial unions were to be cancelled under art. 100 of the Decree of the President of the Republic No. 369 of 2000.[24] As a result, a number of couples, who intended to contract a religious marriage with civil effects and were thus married by their religious ministers, were then told that their nuptial union was religious-only and not valid in the Italian legal system.

This discrimination based on the intended spouses' religious belonging was manifest and the Council of State's opinions were repeatedly pleaded. In September 2009, in counter-tendency with its previous statements,[25] the Council of State clarified that no legal reason could be identified in order to limit the territorial competence of the functions with civil effects of the minister of cults other than Catholicism.[26] Accordingly, in contrast with the recent past, a registered religious marriage cannot be deprived of its validity with civil effects on the ground of bureaucratic errors. The manifest procedural impartiality against marriages solemnized by appointed religious ministers of 'admitted' and 'permitted' faiths was thus eventually amended.

Field-collected evidence nonetheless indicates that an idea of insecurity continues to characterize the status of the nuptial unions solemnized by appointed religious ministers on Italian soil. Italian Muslim communities, in particular, appear not to rely upon these provisions to contract civilly valid religious marriages. In more than ten years of empirical investigations, I never met Muslim spouses who chose this form of registered religious marriage, or examined a *sharīʿah*-compliant nuptial certificate issued by an appointed Muslim minister.

With respect to Muslim partners, additional explanations to this trend may be found and these are to be scrutinized. Whereas the above-mentioned bureaucratic discriminations of registered religious marriages were dealt with by the Italian competent authorities, the norms on civilly valid religious nuptial unions

24 Memorandum (*circolare*) of the Ministry of Interior No. 46, 11.11.2007. See also Costanzo (2008: 50).

25 The former opinions were always negative since the personal status of authorized celebrant was confined to a territorial jurisdiction. See *inter alia* Opinion (*parere*) of the State Council, S.I., No. 853, 01.06.1954; Opinion (*parere*) of the State Council, S.I., No. 1332, 28.08.1959; Opinion (*parere*) of the State Council, S.I., No. 377, 27.02.1970; Opinion (*parere*) of the State Council, S.I., No. 435, 16.03.1984.

26 Opinion (*parere*) of the State Council, S.I., No. 2758. 22.10.2009.

still conceal further disempowerment attitudes with specific reference to Muslim fiancé/es. In particular, in order to effectively enact the formula of appointed ministers of admitted/permitted religions with regard to Italian Muslim communities, two additional obstacles can be identified.

First, the above examined appointed religious ministers' requirements of citizenship/naturalization and fluency in the Italian language[27] might be difficult to satisfy in the case of first generation Muslim migrants. Second, religious ministers of associations with non-official legal status – i.e. non-profit organizations of social utility or non-recognized associations – are compelled to provide the competent state authorities with additional information regarding the 'cult'.[28] It should be pinpointed that in Italy religious groups can be acknowledged as religious legal entities,[29] or as recognized or non-recognized associations.[30] Islamic and Muslim associations tend to appear predominantly as *onlus*[31] or as non-recognized associations in compliance with art. 36 Italian Civil Code.[32] Non-profit corporations are instead less common:[33] among the 40 non-profit religious organizations recognized by the state, only one is an Islamic centre.[34] As a result, the vast majority of Islamic and Muslim associations in Italy has non-official legal status and therefore the appointment of a Muslim minister appears to be a slow and laborious process.

In the aftermath of this disguised indirect discrimination of Islamic and Muslim associations, no Muslims are listed amongst the religious ministers authorized to celebrate marriages with civil effects in Italy. The statistical data published by the Minister of the Interior confirm that from 2003 to 2013 no Muslims were appointed

27 See pp. 000–000.

28 Art. 20(3), Royal Decree No. 289 of 1930.

29 Law No. 1159 of 1929; Royal Decree No. 289 of 1930.

30 Decree of the President of the Republic 10.02.2000 No. 361 'Regolamento recante norme per la semplificazione dei procedimenti di riconoscimento di persone giuridiche private e di approvazione delle modifiche dell'atto costitutivo e dello statuto (n. 17 dell'allegato 1 della L 15.03.1997 No. 59)', in *Gazzetta Ufficiale* 07.12.2000 No. 286.

31 This acronym identifies a 'non-profit organisation of social utility'.

32 Aluffi Beck-Peccoz (2004a, 2004b); Allievi and Castro (2000: 173–176); Coglievina (2013: 352–356).

33 Colaianni (2008: 267–277) explains that religion and culture are frequently intertwined, especially in Islām. Consequently, Islamic associations cannot limit themselves to a non-profit corporation; the confession is instead a preferable model. Ferrari (2006a: 48–50) suggests that Islamic associations should try to be recognized as non-profit corporations, analogous to other religious denominations. Similarly, Casuscelli (2008: 287–292) elucidates that the law does not assure an unconditional right to an *intesa*, although a principle of justice would suggest so.

34 Ministero dell'Interno (2009c, 2006d–2012d). Indeed, the Centro Islamico Culturale d'Italia (CICI) is the sole Islamic organization recognized as a religious legal entity (*ente morale di culto*). See Decree of the President of the Republic 21.12.1974 No. 712, 'Riconoscimento della personalità giuridica dell'ente "Centro Islamico culturale d'Italia" con sede in Roma Via A. Casella n. 51', *Gazzetta Ufficiale* 10–11.01.1975 No. 10, p. I. This privileged position implies that the *sharīʿah*-compliant nuptial contracts perfected in this centre used to be the sole recognized as valid by foreign diplomatic premises in Italy; my evidence however reveals a different outcome.

or revoked as 'minister of cults', and no refusal to Muslim ministers was issued.[35] Additionally, no Muslim actually applied to be recognized as a minister of cult in the last decade. Remarkably, Muslim ministers were not mentioned even in an official report published in 2007, which clarified that 1,220 'ministers of cults' were appointed or revoked in Italy by 31.12.2005. The only data concerning Islām elucidate that by December 2005, a total of 57 orders (*provvedimenti*) and opinions (*pareri*) were issued to grant religious assistance to Muslim prisoners.[36] The lack of Muslim ministers in Italy is further confirmed by the fact that previous ministerial *memoranda* were issued as remedies to the absence of any officially listed Muslim ministers.[37] In real terms, it is not even clear if a Muslim minister ever applied to be appointed as an authorized person to celebrate marriages with civil effects in Italy.

Three considerations can be advanced. First of all, we can wonder whether Italian Muslim communities are not conforming to the 'admitted cults' law since they are aspiring to sign an *intesa* with the state and thus obtain *ad hoc* provisions, also with respect to Islamic and Muslim marriage forms. Second, it is doubtful whether Italian Islamic/Muslim associations followed, and eventually abandoned, the path of the admitted/permitted cults' ministers on the ground of refusals to earlier claims. Lastly, it is not clear whether Islamic scholars in Italy are conversant with the norms regulating appointed religious ministers in the Italian legal system. Empirical evidence indeed indicates that leaders of Muslim associations and Islamic worship centres are rather confused regarding civilly valid *sharīʿah*-compliant marriages.

The absence of authorized Muslim religious ministers implies that *de facto* Islamic and/or Muslim marriages in Italy remain religious-only and/or customary-only marriages with no civil effects. As formerly elucidated, a *sharīʿah*-compliant marriage can be recognized and recorded as civilly valid by the Italian legal system when the Islamic and/or Muslim marriage is perfected in compliance with foreign *sharīʿah*-compliant laws, or a foreign embassy/consulate recognizes as valid and thus records a marriage celebrated in an Italian Islamic worship centre or mosque. The following sections address these two scenarios.

Foreign Muslim intended spouses

In case Muslim fiancé/es are (also) nationals of a foreign country, their marriage can be perfected in compliance with Italian laws as well as with the (*sharīʿah*-compliant) laws of the country they are nationals of. Accordingly, these intended spouses can

35 See http://politichepersonale.interno.it/dcds/compendio04/file06/culti-34.pdf; http://politichepersonale.interno.it/dcds/compendio04/file07/21_culti.pdf; http://politichepersonale.interno.it/dcds/compendio04/file08/15%20culti%20int34.pdf (05.04.2009); http://ssai.interno.it/download/allegati1/annuario2010indice.pdf (10.01.2010). See also Ministero dell'Interno (2006d–2012d); Ufficio Centrale di Statistica and Scuola Superiore delle Statistiche Ufficiali dell'Amministrazione dell'Interno (2009: 209–214; 2010: 217–222; 2011: 213–218; 2012: 201–215; 2013: 153–166). See also Sona (2014: 121).

36 Ministero dell'Interno (2007d).

37 See Memorandum (*circolare*) of the Ministry of Justice No. 5354554, 06.05.1997; Memorandum (*circolare*) of the Ministry of Justice No. 508110, 02.01.2002.

either marry abroad, or marry in compliance with foreign national laws while being on Italian soil. The latter hypothesis includes telephone and proxy marriages, as well as nuptial unions perfected in the competent diplomatic premises of a foreign country. As a third facilitative option, some Muslim-majority countries recognize as valid and thus record Italian civil marriages. These civilly valid and *sharīʿah*-compliant multiple nuptial routes are analysed in the following sub-sections.

Transnational marriages and empowered Muslim spouses

European Muslim spouses can claim recognition of a *sharīʿah*-compliant marriage that is recognized as valid with civil effects by foreign legal systems. In effect, European nationals (with or without foreign origins) and aliens can also demand the recognition of their nuptial union celebrated abroad.

International principles are enshrined in the Hague Convention of 12.06.1902 relating to the Settlement of the Conflict of the Laws Concerning Marriage,[38] and in the scarcely ratified[39] XXVI Hague Convention of 14.03.1978 on Celebration and Recognition of the Validity of Marriages.[40] In European countries, domestic provisions echo the international principles; however, the same (*sharīʿah*-compliant) foreign nuptial union can be recognized as civilly valid in a European national legal system, whilst being regarded as invalid in another one.[41]

In Italy, a transnational marriage is valid in three hypotheses. The nuptial form must be valid according to the *lex loci celebrationis*, or compliant with one of the spouses' national law, or in accordance with the law of the country of the parties' common residence at the time of the marriage.[42] Nationality is thus regarded as a second criterion by the Italian legal system.[43] The *lex loci celebrationis* and spouses' national laws are to be considered at the time of the wedding celebration. The criterion of public policy can, however, be applied by Italian tribunals as a justification not to acknowledge the existence of 'particularly problematic' marriages.

In European legal systems, issues can be raised with regard to some *sharīʿah*-compliant nuptial unions perfected in foreign countries. In particular, the validity of proxy and telephone marriages is proven to be highly controversial. In Italy,

38 Available at www.hcch.net/index_en.php?act=text.display&tid=13 (last accessed 24.10.2104). Italy signed this Hague Convention on 12.06.1902 and it entered into force on 14.09.1905.

39 According to the website of the Hague Conference on Private International Law, Australia, Luxembourg and the Netherlands are the only States Parties of the XXVI Hague Convention. This important factor is sometimes overlooked by international family law books. For instance, Stark (2005: 18–19) explains that the Hague Conventions are binding on State parties, where these international treaties become enforceable in national courts and tribunal through implementing legislation; nonetheless, the list of the signatory countries is not reported.

40 Available at www.hcch.net/upload/conventions/txt26en.pdf (last accessed 24.10.2014).

41 For instance, the recognition of a proxy marriage can be more difficult in the United Kingdom when compared to Italy. See *infra*.

42 Art. 28, Law 31.05.1995 No. 218, 'Riforma del sistema italiano di diritto internazionale privato', in *Gazzetta Ufficiale* 03.06.1995 No. 128 SO.

43 Arts. 27–28, Law No. 218 of 1995.

the case law on *sharīʿah*-compliant nuptial unions is scarce and sparse, and the judiciary seems to prefer to issue *ad hoc* decisions. However, some specific nuptial form – such as proxy marriages – are expressly regulated by the Italian Civil Code.[44] Proxy marriages can take place if one of the future spouses resides abroad and 'serious conditions' exist.[45] Few formal requirements must be satisfied. A tribunal's authorization is needed. In addition, the proxy shall be made in the form of a public act and indicate the person with whom the marriage is to be contracted. The Ministry of Interior's Instructions clarify that, in case the formal requirements stated in art. 111 Italian Civil Code are not fulfilled by the parties, the marriage is nonetheless valid by virtue of the principle of *favor marimonii*, unless a dirimant impediment exists and a tribunal declares such marriage null and void.[46] European Muslim fiancé/es can thus validly marry by proxy an intended spouse settled abroad and then obtain the recognition of their marriage in Italy as well as a spouse's visa.

Telephone (*sharīʿah*-compliant) marriages are similarly recognized as valid nuptial unions on whose ground a spouse's entry visa can be claimed in Italy. In 2007, the Milan Tribunal clarified that, when a telephone marriage is celebrated in compliance with the laws of the spouses' country/ies of origin, that nuptial union is valid with civil effects in the Italian legal system. In this case, the Italian judge was asked to examine the validity of the nuptial union of two Pakistani nationals who married over the phone while the fiancé was resident in Italy.[47] It should be mentioned that, in a former similar proceeding, the Court of Appeal of Milan stated its incompetence to determine the validity of a polygynous telephone marriage. As a result, the appellate court did not authorize the telephone-married polygynous spouses on the ground that the husband and wife never lived together and probably had never met in person before.[48] Nonetheless, the above-mentioned Court of Appeal case concerned a foreign *sharīʿah*-compliant matrimony, which was not only a telephone marriage, but also a polygynous nuptial union of Pakistani nationals. It can thus be inferred that a number of problematic and controversial elements characterized this nuptial union and affected the court's decision.[49]

In both proceedings, the Italian judiciary analogously stressed that the Italian diplomatic premises are not authorized to evaluate the formal validity of a marriage

44 This form of marriage was actually widely adopted by Italians when marrying across the Italian peninsula or abroad being migrants. See Pugliese (2002); Zincone (2006); Sanfilippo and Corti (2009).

45 Art. 111(2) Italian Civil Code. In compliance with the Legal Decree No. 71 of 2011 (art. 16 (1,2)), proxy marriages can also be perfected by Italian consuls provided that the intended spouse is not resident in Italy.

46 See Ministero dell'Interno (2011a: 112–113; 2012a: 119). On dirimant impediments see further footnote 72.

47 Tribunal of Milano, 02.02.2007, *Rivista di Diritto Internazionale Privato Processuale*, 2007, XLIV (1), 137; *Diritto di Famiglia e delle Persone*, XXXVII, 2008, 155. For a comment, see Bianchini (2008).

48 Court of Appeal of Milano, 24.09.2003, unpublished, Campiglio (2008: 54). For a comment, see Campiglio (2008).

49 For a discussion on the recognition of Islamic marriages in Italy, see *inter alia* Campiglio (1999, 2008) and Mancini (2003, 2006).

in compliance with the art. 29 of the Legal Decree No. 286 of 1998.[50] A non-Italian Muslim spouse settled in Italy can therefore validly contract a *sharīʿah*-compliant telephone marriage with a fiancé/e domiciled abroad and then submit to the Italian competent authorities an application for entry clearance as a validly married spouse.

In the two scenarios examined, foreign (Muslim) fiancé/es settled in Italy thus benefit from more room for manoeuvre when compared to (non-Muslim) immigrant intended spouses whose national legal systems do not recognize proxy and telephone marriages as valid nuptial unions. As a result, a spouse's visa can be more easily obtained when the parties are nationals of countries whose (Islamic and/or Muslim) nuptial forms tend to be recognized as valid by the Italian legal system.

Diplomatic premises and nationality-based discrimination

On Italian soil, Muslim fiancé/es can also contract a *sharīʿah*-compliant marriage in the Muslim-majority country's diplomatic premises of an intended foreign spouse. These nuptial unions are simultaneously civil and religious, being based on *sharīʿah* as well as conforming with state law requirements.

Highly ratified international private law rules establish that consulates can act 'as notary and civil registrar and in capacities of a similar kind, and performing certain functions of an administrative nature'.[51] Accordingly, diplomatic premises can perfect, record and legalize marriages. Two requisites are to be satisfied: embassies and consulates must not interfere in the internal affairs of the receiving state, and they shall respect the laws and regulations of the host country.[52]

In Italy, the appointed personnel of foreign embassies and consulates can perform marriages.[53] These nuptial unions are perfected in compliance with foreign domestic laws; nonetheless, empirical evidence reveals that foreign *sharīʿah*-compliant law can be adjusted to suit the needs of migrant communities. For instance, marriages between a Muslim woman and a non-Muslim man can be solemnized provided that some requisites are satisfied.[54]

Italian laws are not necessarily implemented by foreign embassies and consulates. On the one hand, Italian law is respected and enacted by foreign diplomatic premises in the sense that when the purported spouse's valid permit

50 In effect, in both the above-mentioned cases, the Italian embassy in Islamabad denied the family reunification permit on the ground of an invalid telephone marriage.

51 Art. 5(1F) of the Vienna Convention on Consular Relations (Vienna, 24.04.1963), *United Nations Treaty Series*, Vol. 596, p. 261.

52 Arts. 5(1F) and 55(1), Vienna Convention on Consular Relations. Building upon this provision, Galoppini (2005: 984) notes that diplomatic premises are also compelled not to dissolve marriages between their nationals. My fieldwork however indicates that marriages and dissolutions of marriages are widely enacted in some diplomatic premise of Muslim-majority countries in Italy.

53 Art. 28, Law No. 218 of 1995 can be interpreted as authorizing the recognition of marriages celebrated in diplomatic premises.

54 By way of illustration, the mentioned nuptial union is not to be recorded in the Muslim-majority country of origin of the Muslim wife who married a non-Muslim man.

to stay was regarded as a condition to validly marry in Italy, the same document was requested by some consulates.[55] At that time, the personnel of the competent diplomatic premise of the Muslim-majority country national fiancé/e used to require the valid permit to stay of the intended spouse, in case s/he was an alien settled in Italy. If a party was not able to produce this document, the certificate of no impediment to the marriage (*nulla osta*) required by the Italian vital statistics officer was not released to the alien purported spouse by the foreign diplomatic premise.[56] Accordingly, from 2009 to 2011, some foreign authorities partook in implementing Italian discriminative laws. In particular, some diplomatic premises of Muslim-majority countries were actually providing a sort of 'first test' on the regular settlement status of non-Italian purported spouses wishing to marry aliens settled in Italy. In this case, embassies and consulates of Muslim-majority countries were *de facto* enforcing an Italian discriminatory provision that manifestly affected their nationals settled abroad.

On the other hand, a number of foreign embassies and consulates do not implement Italian law. In effect, empirical evidence and document examination reveal that some Muslim-majority countries' diplomatic premises celebrate marriages also when one party is an Italian national.[57] This happens despite the fact that an Italian citizen is subject to the law of his/her own country, even when s/he contracts marriage in a foreign country according to the formalities there established.[58]

Perfecting nuptial unions between nationals of Muslim-majority countries and Italian nationals in Muslim-majority countries' diplomatic premises on Italian soil implies serious consequences. First of all, international and national provisions on territorial sovereignty are violated.[59] Italian case law is consistent in considering these nuptial unions as null and void.[60] The Ministry of the Interior's Instructions similarly stress that the marriage of Italian citizens perfected in foreign diplomatic premises on Italian soil cannot be acknowledged as

55 This was confirmed by field-collected data.

56 On the *nulla osta*, see *infra* pp. 000–000.

57 Amongst the studied nuptial contracts perfected in Muslim-majority countries' diplomatic premises, I identified four types of marriages: two nationals of the same Muslim-majority country; two nationals of different Muslim-majority countries; a non-Italian citizen (either European national or non-European national) and a national of a Muslim-majority country; an Italian citizen and a national of a Muslim-majority country.

58 Art. 115 Italian Civil Code.

59 Hague Convention of 12.06.1902 (art. 6); Law 07.09.1905 No. 523, 'Legge colla quale si dà piena ed intera esecuzione alle Convenzioni riguardanti i conflitti di leggi in materia di matrimonio, di divorzio e di tutela di minorenni tra l'Italia e vari Stati d'Europa', in *Gazzetta Ufficiale* 09.11.1905 No. 261.

60 Tribunal of Milano, 16.05.1963, *Monitore dei Tribunali*, 1963, 1136; Tribunal of Milano, 25.07.1963, *Monitore dei Tribunali*, 1963, 1389; Tribunal of Napoli 05.04.1982, *Diritto di Famiglia e delle Persone*, 1982, 1334. Cf. Court of Cassation, 09.06.2000 No. 7877, *Diritto Internazionale Privato e Processuale*, XXXVII, 2001, 409. This last case regarded a religious marriage celebrated in Italy and recognized as valid by a foreign state.

a valid nuptial union.[61] Therefore, these Italian nationals' marriages cannot be recorded by the vital statistics officer in the marriage record.[62]

Second, limping marriages are *de facto* resulting from this practice. Accordingly, the Italian spouse has different status in two countries: s/he is not married in his/her own national country, but is married in the partner's Muslim-majority country of origin. Additionally, they cannot remarry in Italy since the foreign spouse's diplomatic premise cannot release the *nulla osta* to the foreign husband or wife, given the couple is already married according to the respective Muslim-majority country's nuptial record. The Italian party is thus prejudiced and remains chained in a marriage whose existence is recognized only by *sharīʿah* and by the Muslim-majority country legal system of his/her spouse.

Fieldwork evidence indicates that these Italian nationals' limping marriages tend to remain in the shadow until the couple discovers not to be legally married, or problems arise between the partners. Unfortunately, the above-mentioned limping nuptial statuses are not as rare as one may expect (and hope) them to be. During a decade of empirical investigations, I have examined a consistent number of these marriages (irregularly) perfected in the diplomatic premises of Muslim-majority countries on European soil. Entering this type of *sharīʿah*-compliant nuptial union thus highly discriminates and disempowers the Italian party, whether Muslim or non-Muslim. In this scenario, the tool for empowerment is not represented by Islām per se, rather by the Muslim-majority country's nationality of the spouse.

In case of foreign fiancé/es, a third facilitative option is granted by some Muslim-majority countries to their citizens. In effect, the validity of European administrative procedures regarding marriages can be acknowledged by some Muslim-majority countries. Although the above-mentioned foreign *sharīʿah*-compliant provisions are particularly relevant for Muslims settled in European states, this possibility is frequently overlooked and rarely analysed by scholarship.

In real terms, nationals of Muslim-majority countries can marry abroad following the procedure of the non-Muslim country of settlement, provided that the Muslim-majority country's conditions established for a valid union are respected.[63] These nuptial unions can then be registered in the foreign diplomatic premises on Italian soil. Foreign provisions of a non-*sharīʿah*-compliant legal system can thus have some effects in Muslim-majority countries.

The Moroccan *Moudawwanah* represents a good example of this approach.[64] Articles 14 and 15 of the Moroccan Family Code detail the procedure to be followed by Moroccans settled abroad. Additionally, the preamble of the law

61 Ministero dell'Interno (2011a: 101; 2012a: 106).

62 Law No. 523 of 1905 (art. 6); Decree of the President of the Republic No. 396 of 2000 (art. 63(2(d))); Law No. 218 of 1995 (art. 28). See Ministero dell'Interno (2011a: 101; 2012a: 106).

63 The rules regard the spouse's nuptial impediments and the necessary elements of the marriage contract and depend upon the different Islamic belonging of the parties.

64 Moroccan Family Code, 05.02.2004, Royal Edict (*Sherifyan Dahir*) No. 1/04/22 issued on 03.02.2004 (12 *Dou Al Hijja* 1424) to implement the law No. 70/03 as the 'Family Code' on the *Official Gazette, General Provisions*.

of 05.02.2004 clearly indicates the simplification of marriage procedures for citizens settled abroad as one of the fundamental reforms of the Moroccan Family Code. The fifth point states:

> [a]s a token of our royal concern for our dear subjects residing abroad, marriage procedures are to be simplified for them: the marriage contract is to be drawn up in the presence of two Muslim witnesses and in accordance with the procedures in effect in the country of residence, and then registered with the proper Moroccan consular or judicial authorities, according to *al-ḥadīth*: 'Seek ease, not hardship'.

This approach *de facto* empowers foreign Muslim nationals whose European civil nuptial union is recognized as valid and also 'upgraded' as being *sharīʿah*-compliant by the legal systems of some Muslim-majority countries. A broader spectrum of possible marriage routes is thus granted to Muslim spouses whose national laws can record European/Western civil marriage certificates. As a result, these couples may decide to benefit from such provisions, or – at the opposite – may intentionally choose not to disclose their civil marriage to the competent authorities of their Muslim-majority country of origin, thus acquiring a diverse nuptial status in different legal systems.[65]

Muslim and Islamic marriages through the back door

In the previous sections we have seen that Muslim fiancé/es can contract an Islamic and/or Muslim marriage with civil effects in Italy when married before an authorized Muslim religious minister, or in compliance with foreign *sharīʿah*-compliant laws. This last marriage route encompasses three options:

i *sharīʿah*-compliant nuptial unions perfected abroad;
ii marriages contracted in the diplomatic premises of Muslim-majority countries;
iii Italian civil marriages acknowledged and recorded as valid by Muslim-majority countries.

A further option does exist. Muslim purported spouses can contract a religious and/or customary marriage in Europe or abroad. The Islamic-only and/or Muslim-only marriage may be 'upgraded' as a nuptial union with civil effects in case it is recognized as valid and registered by foreign authorities and/or diplomatic premises of a Muslim-majority country. Unfortunately, similarly to the above discussed case of European civil nuptial unions recorded as *sharīʿah*-compliant by a Muslim-majority country, also this marriage route is left unnoticed by academic literature and judicial authorities.

65 Empirical evidence indicates that this can be a profitable and advantageous choice in case of polygamously married spouses.

Superimposing Islamic and Muslim provisions to European domestic norms, grey areas come into existence. These extra civilly valid *sharīʿah*-compliant marriage alternatives tend to remain in the shadow unless unveiled by field-collected data. My empirical investigation indeed discloses that European Muslims actually do marry in mosques and worship centres whose Islamic and/or Muslim nuptial contracts are recognized as valid and recorded by Muslim-majority countries and their diplomatic premises.

In Italy, an uncounted number of Islamic/Muslim worship centres solemnize religious-only marriages.[66] Theoretically, only the nuptial contracts perfected in the Rome mosque are and should be recognized as valid by the diplomatic premises of Muslim-majority countries.[67] The Rome mosque indeed is the seat of the Centro Islamico Culturale d'Italia (CICI), the sole Muslim organization in Italy which has recognized status as a non-profit corporation.[68] Additionally, the CICI board of directors is constituted predominantly by ambassadors of Muslim-majority countries accredited to the Holy See and/or the Italian state; accordingly this centre is considered the 'official Italian Islām'.[69]

Nonetheless, empirical evidence discloses that *sharīʿah*-compliant nuptial contracts solemnized in other Islamic/Muslim centres have been recorded with civil effects in some Muslim-majority countries as well as in their diplomatic premises in Italy. The diplomatic personnel I interviewed described this behaviour partly as a reaction to the discriminative Italian immigration laws and partly as result of a mistake. Nonetheless, when foreign legal systems legitimize nuptial unions which are otherwise religious-only and/or customary-only, notable implications arise for European legal systems. In effect, in case foreign *sharīʿah*-compliant legal systems recognize as civilly valid Muslim-only and/or Islamic-only marriages, these nuptial unions can have civil effects on European soil as well.[70]

With respect to the issue of power, it is clear that the recognition of religious-only (Islamic) and/or customary-only (Muslim) marriages by some Muslim-majority countries and/or their diplomatic premises empowers Muslim spouses. In real terms, this implies that Muslim partners benefit from a broader spectrum of possible alternative marriage routes and nuptial statuses. As further explored in the following section, some of these empowerment strategies are

66 In 2007, the Chamber of Representatives reported 774 Islamic worship centres (Camera dei Deputati, 2008: 69). The research conducted by Allievi and Ethnobarometer (2009: 33) counted 661 non-purpose-built mosques and three purpose-built mosques in 2009. Cf. Coglievina (2013: 357).

67 Recently, anecdotal evidence suggested that the recently built Turin mosque can also release Islamic marriage certificates which can be recognized as valid with civil effects by some Muslim-majority countries and/or some diplomatic premises on European soil. This information is to be verified by the author.

68 See *supra* pp. 000–000 and *infra* pp. 000–000.

69 See *inter alia* Roggero (2002: 136–137); Allievi (2002: 87; 2003: 73–79); Aluffi Beck-Peccoz (2004a: 136; 2004b: 184).

70 In European legal systems, a foreign *sharīʿah*-compliant marriage is not recognized as valid when it is against the public order and morality.

however to be understood as counter-reactions of European Islamic bodies and/or Muslim diplomatic premises against (religious) discriminative practices enacted by European domestic legal systems.

Civil marriage of non-Italian Muslim fiancé/es

Earlier sections examined the implications of potentially recognizable Islamic and/or Muslim marriages. When on Italian soil, Muslim fiancé/es can also opt for an additional nuptial route and choose a civil-only marriage. As seen earlier, this form of European civilly valid marriage can be acknowledged and recorded by some Muslim-majority countries and thus it can become *sharī'ah*-compliant.

The last sections of this chapter specifically address Muslim purported spouses who choose to contract a civil-only marriage.[71] Although this union is perfected in compliance with Italian laws, Islām can become a tool for legal discrimination and disempowerment for Muslim intended spouses. In-depth investigations, however, reveal that Muslim communities may rapidly adjust and elaborate successful anti-prejudicial techniques.

Italian civil marriage and religious discrimination

The necessary conditions to contract a civil marriage are listed in Section I, Chapter III, Title VI of the Italian Civil Code. The purported spouses must satisfy some legal requirements in order to have their marriage celebrated by the vital statistics officer. In case the intended spouses do not meet the prescribed legal requirements, nuptial impediments arise. These impediments can be dirimant or impedient.[72]

In Italy, the wedding celebration shall be preceded by the publication (*pubblicazioni*)[73] by the vital statistics officer.[74] The publication is an impediment to the celebration of a valid marriage.[75] Both intended spouses, or a person specially appointed by them for that purpose, are compelled to apply for the publication of matrimony to the vital statistics officer of the commune where one of the future spouses resides.[76] When one party is resident (not only domiciled) in a

71 The issues examined in this section are also addressed in Sona (2015).

72 This lexicon is borrowed from Canon law. In case of a dirimant impediment, the marriage is invalid, when the impediment is impedient, the parties may be impelled to pay an administrative penalty.

73 The *pubblicazioni* are nuptial preliminaries required by arts. 93–96, 106 Italian Civil Code.

74 Arts. 93–101 Italian Civil Code; arts. 50–53, Decree of the President of the Republic No. 396 of 2000. From 01.01.2011, the publication is made online in compliance with Memorandum (*circolare*) of the Ministry of Interior No. 1, 05.01.2011; Memorandum (*circolare*) of the Ministry of Interior No. 13, 21.04.2011; Memorandum (*circolare*) of the Ministry of Interior No. 26, 28.10.2011.

75 The spouses and the vital statistics officer who celebrate the marriage without prior publication are punishable by an administrative penalty (art. 134 Italian Civil Code).

76 If the purported spouses live in two different communes, the approached vital statistics officer shall apply for the publication also in the other fiancé/e's commune of residence.

foreign country, and the parties wish to marry in a foreign diplomatic premise, the vital statistics officer shall request the foreign diplomatic premise to proceed with the publication,[77] but the publication is not necessary in case the parties marry abroad before foreign authorities.[78]

The Italian legal system requires the intended spouses to provide their personal details to the vital statistics officer.[79] In compliance with the Ministry of Interior's Instructions, the mention of the purported spouse's identity seeks to ascertain that no impediment to the marriage exists according to the involved Italian and foreign laws.[80] The fiancé/es shall also give assurance that their marriage is not prevented by the nuptial impediments specified by arts. 85–89 Italian Civil Code.[81] The vital statistics officer can ask them to produce some additional documents.[82] In particular, non-Italian intended spouses are compelled to satisfy further requirements.

Once the spouses submit their request for publication, the vital statistics officer compiles a public record.[83] In case the vital statistics officer deems that s/he cannot proceed with the publication, s/he issues a certificate reporting the reasons for the denial. Against the denial, a complaint may be brought before the tribunal. The judiciary can be involved also in case of reduction or omission of publication.[84] In effect, if serious reasons occur, the parties may request a reduction of the publication period.[85] The tribunal may authorize the omission of publication for more serious reasons, and only when the purported spouses give assurances (on their own responsibility) that the marriage is not prevented by any impediments specified by arts. 85–89 Italian Civil Code. Additionally, the publication may be missing in case of imminent danger of death of one future spouse.[86] As explained

77 Art. 11 of the Decree of the President of the Republic 05.01.1967 No. 200 (1), 'Disposizioni sulle funzioni e sui poteri consolari' (1/circ), *Gazzetta Ufficiale* 19.04.1967 No. 98 SO. See also Legal Decree 03.02.2011 No. 71, 'Ordinamento e funzioni degli Uffici consolari', *Gazzetta Ufficiale* 13.05.2011 No. 110.

78 Art. 13(2), Legal Decree No. 71 of 2011.

79 They shall declare their names, surnames, dates of birth, citizenships, residences, matrimonial status.

80 See Ministero dell'Interno (2011a: 113; 2012a: 119–120).

81 These regards the fiancé/es' minor age, interdiction for mental incapacity, already married status, prohibited degrees of relations (art. 51(1), Decree of the President of the Republic No. 396 of 2000).

82 Art. 110, Decree of the President of the Republic No. 396 of 2000 repealed art. 97 Italian Civil Code; a formal comprehensive list of the necessary documents is not provided by the Italian Civil Code.

83 This shall be displayed on the commune's main door for at least eight consecutive days (arts. 54–58, Decree of the President of the Republic No. 396 of 2000).

84 Art. 100 Italian Civil Code.

85 The tribunal, having heard the public prosecutor, may reduce the period required for publications by a decree non susceptible of appeal and issued in chambers (art. 100(1) Italian Civil Code).

86 In these cases, the vital statistics officer can proceed with the celebration of marriage without the publication and without the tribunal's assent to the marriage, when the parties swear that there are no impediments susceptible of dispensation between them. In this case, a marriage celebrated without publication is valid even if the spouses falsely declared the imminent danger of death of one future spouse (Court of Cassation, 24.01.1967 No. 216, *Foro Italiano* 1967, I, 230).

in the next section, the provision of art. 100 Italian Civil Code may thus represent an effective remedy for foreign Muslim fiancées who cannot produce the requested *nulla osta* to the vital statistics officer.

Nulla osta and discrimination of Muslim fiancé/es

In order to contract a valid marriage with civil effects in the Italian legal system, alien intended spouses must satisfy two further requirements. First of all, the foreign purported spouse is impelled to submit to the vital statistics officer a certificate of no impediment to the marriage. This important document is called *nulla osta*.[87] It is issued by the foreign fiancé/e's diplomatic premises and it must prove that no impediments to the marriage exist 'under the laws to which he is subject'.[88]

This requirement is highly controversial for Muslim intended spouses since *sharīʿah* limits inter-religious marriages. Accordingly, problems may arise when a Muslim fiancé/e wishes to marry a non-Muslim partner.[89] In practice, Muslim-majority countries' embassies and consulates insist on issuing the *nulla osta* on condition that the purported groom converts to Islām, or that the intended bride belongs to one of the 'religions of the Book'.[90] In some situations, Jewish or Christian brides-to-be can similarly be required or advised to embrace Islām.

In the Italian legal scenario, the second hypothesis is marginal; the former case instead regards a significant percentage of inter-religious marriages. A Muslim-majority country national whose parents are Muslim[91] could thus be denied his/her right to marry by the Italian authorities on the ground that s/he cannot produce the certificate of no impediment to his/her marriage from his/her diplomatic premise.[92]

My empirical investigation unveils two patterns that can be followed by the embassies and consulates of Muslim-majority countries. First, the diplomatic authorization for an Italian civil marriage is provided only when the act of conversion to Islām of the non-Muslim partner is submitted. Additionally, diplomatic

87 This is the Italian version of the Latin expression *nihil obstat*.

88 Art. 116 Italian Civil Code, and Royal Decree 16.03.1942 No. 262, 'Approvazione del testo del Codice Civile', in *Gazzetta Ufficiale* 04.04.1942 No. 79. This provision does not necessarily refer to the foreign citizen's national laws, due to the principle of *renvoi* (Ballarino, 2008: 136).

89 According to the *Qur'ān* (2: 221; 5: 5; 60: 10), Muslims cannot validly marry idolaters and unbelievers. A Muslim man can validly marry a Muslim, Jewish or Christian woman; whilst a Muslim woman can marry a Muslim man only. According to a more restrictive interpretation, a Muslim man cannot validly marry a 'woman of the Book' unless they live in a *sharīʿah*-compliant environment such as a Muslim-majority country.

90 The *Qur'ān* refers to Jews and Christians with the expression *ahl al-kitāb* which means 'people of the book'. A Christian or Jewish bride is thus called *kitābiyyah*.

91 It should be mentioned that a situation is frequently neglected. This regards the case of a citizen of a Muslim-majority country who abandons Islām and therefore is a non-Muslim, although his/her parents are Muslim. The peculiar position of Muslim-majority country nationals who are atheist or embraced other religions are relevant also in relation to same-sex unions. Researchers are much needed in this field.

92 See also Sona (2014: 124–125).

premises may recognize as valid only the *shahādah*[93] released by some selected Italian worship centres or Muslim-majority countries' religious authorities.[94] The listed centres vary depending upon the Muslim-majority country and the Consul's interpretation of the national Muslim legal system.[95] In Italy, the Rome mosque is usually addressed as the proper place where to officially embrace Islām by the majority of Muslim-majority countries' diplomatic premises.[96] Aspiring converts may nonetheless be asked to follow different procedures in compliance to diverse religious authorities. In some cases, a course and a pre-exam are compulsorily requested; whereas, in other places obtaining a *shahādah* certificate may be easier.

Second, the *nulla osta* is released under some conditions. In some cases, the diplomatic premises of Muslim-majority countries can issue a negative *nulla osta* on the ground of the religious belonging of the non-Muslim purported spouse. In other situations, a consulate or embassy may nonetheless issue a certificate of no nuptial impediments, but in the same document a clause of conversion to Islām of the non-Muslim fiancé/e is inserted as a condition for validity.

As a third option, some consulates release the *nulla osta* although the conversion to Islām of its national's purported groom is not submitted. This happens when a further condition is fulfilled: such marriage would never be acknowledged and registered in the bride's Muslim-majority country of origin. Therefore, once a wife agrees not to register her marriage with a non-Muslim fiancée in the nuptial record of her Muslim-majority country of origin and its foreign diplomatic premises, her certificate of no nuptial impediment is released. This choice naturally implies consequences regarding this family member's inheritance rights and the status of the couple's offspring in Muslim-majority countries. Additionally, a *décollement* of the same person's nuptial status is created: the Muslim-majority country national is 'married' in the settlement country, whilst she remains 'unmarried' in the country of origin. Accordingly, she would be able to marry again in compliance with *sharīʿah*. In case this woman (re)marries, she would be a polyandrous wife only in the eyes of the (European and possibly Western) legal systems that recognize as valid her marriage to a non-Muslim man. The described controversial situations are not only hypothetical cases, as my fieldwork revealed. Analogously to the previously discussed marriage routes concealed in legal grey areas, these cases lie in the shadow of *sharīʿah* and European domestic provisions and thus remained concealed.

93 This word comes from the Arabic verb *shahida* which means 'to witness, to testify'; *shahādah* can thus be translated as 'profession of faith', and it is one of the five pillars of Islām. This word is also used to identify a person's conversion to Islām.

94 The professions of faith of *Sunnī* and *Shīʿī* Muslims slightly differ. The former states 'There is no God but God, and Muḥammad is His messenger'; *Shīʿī* Muslims add that 'and Ali is the *walī* of God'.

95 Different diplomatic premises can either accept or refuse a *shahādah* released by the same authority.

96 As mentioned above, this is the seat of the Centro Islamico Culturale d'Italia (CICI), the sole Muslim organization in Italy which has been recognized as a non-profit corporation (*ente morale di culto*) by the Decree of the President of the Republic No. 712 of 1974.

Interviews with diplomatic personnel disclose that a significant percentage of Muslim-majority country nationals do not register their marriage in their country of origin. Clear-cut evidence is however impossible to achieve. Once the *nulla osta* is released, diplomatic premises have no actual possibilities to verify whether the couple marries in compliance with Italian laws, and if the spouse registers his/her Italian civil marriage in his/her Muslim-majority country of origin. The only exception is represented by a personal communication given by the Italian vital statistics officer to the diplomatic premise/s that realized the spouse's certificate of no nuptial impediments. Empirical evidence indicates that this rarely happens. A further layer of complexity is represented by the fact that foreign intended spouses – who need the *nulla osta* to marry in Italy – may be nationals of two different Muslim-majority countries, and thus they can register their marriage in only one of their countries of origin.

The *nulla osta* required by Italian authorities raises controversial issues. In effect, Muslim intended spouses are *de facto* disempowered by the religious belonging of their family. In other words, the fulfillment of this legal prescription may lead to religious prejudice of the Muslim fiancé/e wishing to marry in compliance with Italian laws.

In order to tackle this form of religious discrimination, administrative and judicial remedies have been created. The Italian judiciary can thus be asked to recognize that the *nulla osta* limits the nuptial right of non-nationals and therefore this requirement can be against the Italian public order.[97] The relevant Italian case law dates back to the mid-1980s/1990s and it is rather consistent. In these situations, the Italian judge orders the vital statistics officer to proceed with the publication without the *nulla osta* on the ground that the capacity to contract marriage of the non-Italian Muslim purported spouse has been made subject to the religious belonging of his/her fiancé/e.[98]

Religiously discriminated foreign intended spouses are, however, not impelled to bring their cases before the Italian judiciary. The Ministry of the

97 Nonetheless, the Constitutional Court clarified that the requirement of a *nulla osta* does not per se infringe the inviolable rights of the person as protected by art. 2 Italian Constitution. The Court order clarifies that the *nulla osta* is a 'document that in the majority of cases does not limit but rather facilitates the enactment of the freedom of marriage' (Constitutional Court, 16–30.01.2003 No. 14, *Gazzetta Ufficiale* 05.02.2003; *Diritto di Famiglia e delle Persone*, 2003, 331).

98 See *inter alia* Tribunal of Reggio Emilia, 29.09.1986, *Diritto di Famiglia e delle Persone* 1987, 268; Tribunal of Verona, 06.03.1987, *Foro Italiano*, Rep. 1987, Matrimonio, 152; Tribunal of Potenza, 30.11.1989, *Diritto di Famiglia e delle Persone*, XXX, 2001, 558; Tribunal of Camerino, 12.04.1990, *Diritto Internazionale Privato e Processuale*, XXVII, 1991, 800–801; *Rivista di Diritto Internazionale Privato Processuale* 1991, 750; Tribunal of Genova, 04.04.1990, *Giurisprudenza di Merito*, 1992, 1195; Tribunal of Torino, 24.02.1992, *Rivista di Diritto Internazionale Privato Processuale* 1992, 985; Tribunal of Torino, 24.06.1993, *Diritto di Famiglia e delle Persone*, 1993, 1181; Tribunal of Barcellona 09.03.1995, *Diritto di Famiglia e delle Persone*, 1996, 164; *Giurisprudenza di Merito*, 1996, 702; Tribunal of Napoli, 29.04.1996, *Famiglia e Diritto*, 5/1996, 454; Tribunal of Taranto, 13.07.1996, *Famiglia e Diritto*, 5/1996, 444. The majority of cases concerns non-Italian Muslim women wishing to marry non-Muslim men; in some cases, foreign men have been denied the *nulla osta* by their diplomatic premises on the ground that they were non-Muslims. See also Sona (2014: 125).

Interior underlines that any conditions inserted by Muslim-majority countries' diplomatic premises regarding the purported spouses' religious belonging are against Italian public order, and thus do not prevent the marriage celebration between the parties.[99] The Ministry of Interior's Instructions also clarify that, for the same public order reasons, the marriage can nonetheless be celebrated when the parties cannot produce a valid *nulla osta* in case it has been denied on the ground of the fiancé/e's religious belonging, or the certificate is negative or conditional to the party's conversion.[100] Additionally, the more recent version of the Ministry of the Interior's Instructions explicitly states that 'the lack of publication does not nullify the validity of the marriage deed'.[101]

Empirical evidence nevertheless indicates that some Italian communes still assume not to be authorized to proceed with the nuptial publication when a foreign purported spouse submits a *nulla osta* that is against the Italian public order. Accordingly, this remains a case-by-case solution-seeking situation.[102] Muslims, who are less familiar with the dynamics of the Italian legal system, might be victims of this religious discrimination and thus opt for an Islamic-only and/or Muslim-only marriage.

Strategic countermeasures and legal empowerment

In addition to the *nulla osta*, the Italian legal system used to require non-nationals wishing to contract civil marriage in Italy to provide a regular residence permit to the vital statistics officer. From 2009 to 2011, the capacity of a non-European national Muslim fiancé/e to contract a marriage in Italy was subordinated not only to the religion of his/her purported spouse, but also to his/her own valid permit to stay in a European country.[103]

Art. 1(15) of the Law No. 94 of 2009 modified art. 116(1) of the Italian Civil Code inserting a blanket prohibition to civilly marry for non-European nationals irregularly settled in Italy.[104] In July 2011, the Italian Constitutional Court declared this provision unconstitutional.[105] The request of a document attesting the regularity of the non-European fiancé/e's stay in Europe was indeed regarded as violating constitutional and international norms, as endorsed by the

99 See Memorandum (*circolare*) of the Ministry of Interior No. 46, 11.11.2007 and Ministero dell'Interno (2009a: 96; 2011a: 109; 2012a: 115–116, 119).

100 Ministero dell'Interno (2011a: 109; 2012a: 115–116).

101 Ministero dell'Interno (2012a: 119).

102 See for instance Tribunal of Milano, 13.03.2007, *Quaderni di Diritto e Politica Ecclesiastica*, 2007, 829, and Tribunal of Piacenza, 05.05.2011, Sez. II, July, 2011, available online at www.stranieriinitalia.it/briguglio/immigrazione-e-asilo/2011/luglio/trib-pc-nullaosta-nozze.pdf (last accessed 01.02.3013).

103 On this, see also Sona (2014: 125–126).

104 The Directive of the Ministry of Interior No. 2, 28.01.2010 clarified that European nationals were exempted from that provision.

105 Constitutional Court, 20-25.07.2011 No. 245, *Gazzetta Ufficiale* 27.07.2011. See also Memorandum (*circolare*) of the Ministry of Interior No. 21 of 26.07.2011.

Italian legal system. The right granted by art. 2 of the Italian Constitution,[106] the constraints deriving from European and international obligations,[107] and the balance of interest criterion[108] lead all to the mentioned judgment. In particular, the Constitutional Court underlined the violation of constraints deriving from international obligations as recognized by art. 117(1) of the Italian Constitution. A blanket prohibition on the exercise of the right to marry violates also art. 12 of the European Convention on Human Rights.[109] From Summer 2011, thus, a Muslim foreign who is irregularly settled in Europe can marry on Italian soil without submitting to the vital statistics officer 'a document attesting the regularity of his/her stay in the Italian territory'.[110]

During the years in which the valid permit to stay was a condition to obtain any administrative act in Italy, empirical investigations disclosed that temporary strategic tactics were cleverly elaborated by Muslim purported spouses. As a first remedy, the intended spouses tended to contract an Islamic-only and/or Muslim-only marriage in the shadow of European domestic legal systems. Some of these *sharīʿah*-compliant marriages were then recognized and recorded by some Muslim-majority countries or their diplomatic premises in Europe, as discussed in the sections above. As a result, privately solemnized Islamic and/or Muslim marriages may become valid nuptial unions with civil effects on European soil.

As a second option, the non-European national Muslim fiancé/es tended to contract a civil marriage in compliance with a legal system other than the Italian one. Field-collected data unveiled three alternative non-Italian nuptial routes, which were *de facto* followed by Muslim intended spouses in the examined period. The couple would either marry in the competent Muslim-majority country's embassy/consulate, or in another European country whose laws did not require a valid residence permit to contract a valid marriage. The third possible alternative nuptial

106 The Constitutional Court elucidates that 'the inviolable rights of art. 2 Italian Constitution are owed to any person not since s/he may belong to a particular political community, but to human beings as such' (para 3.1). Relying upon former decisions, this court also clarifies that citizens and foreign persons differ since the alien has a merely 'acquired and temporary' relation with the Italian state; the foreign legal status should however not be regarded as 'a justification allowing diversified or pejorative treatments'. See Constitutional Court, 19–26.06.1969 No. 104, *Gazzetta Ufficiale* 02.07.1969 No. 165; Constitutional Court, 10–24.02.1994 No. 62, *Gazzetta Ufficiale* 02.03.1994; Constitutional Court, 05–08.07.2010 No. 249, *Gazzetta Ufficiale* 14.07.2010.

107 Art. 117(1) Italian Constitution.

108 On one hand, the need 'to ensure defense and protection of the borders and the control of migration flows' is acknowledged, on the other hand, the imposed sacrifice of the matrimonial freedom should not be disproportionate (para 3.1). In effect, both the rights of the irregularly settled foreign fiancé/es and the Italian citizens wishing to marry an alien person without a permit to stay are compressed by art. 116(1) Italian Civil Code.

109 Quoting *O'Donoghue and Others* v. *the United Kingdom* [Application No. 34848/07, 14.12.2010 – 14.03.2011, [2011] All ER (D) 46 (Jan)], the Italian Constitution Court stressed that 'the States' margin of appreciation cannot be so wide to imply a general, automatic and indiscriminate restriction of a fundamental right granted by the [European] Convention' (para 3.2).

110 Art. 116(1) Italian Civil Code as amended by art. 1(15), Law 15.07.2009 No. 94, 'Disposizioni in materia di sicurezza pubblica', in *Gazzetta Ufficiale* 24.07.2009 No. 170 SO No. 128.

route was to marry in compliance with the laws of a Muslim-majority country. Since travelling abroad was a risky alternative for Muslim migrants irregularly settled in Europe, evidence indicates that in this case the purported spouses would increasingly choose to marry through proxy/ies.[111]

In the examined alternative nuptial options, the 'Islamic belonging' of the intended spouses empowered irregularly settled Muslim fiancé/es, when compared to non-Muslim immigrants. The Muslim partners married in compliance with one of the two above-mentioned procedures were indeed entitled to claim the recognition of their foreign marriage certificate through private international law principles. Therefore, the Muslim fiancé/e – who was originally irregularly settled in Europe – was then entitled to claim a spouse's visa in Italy on the ground of a civil marriage, which was originally prevented by Italian law but perfected abroad.

Among the three concurrent possible categories of alternative legal systems – a Muslim-majority country, the fiancé/e's foreign diplomatic premises, or a European state characterized by less demanding nuptial provisions – the latter appears to be the favourite countermeasure chosen by irregularly settled Muslim partners. Among European domestic legal systems, San Marino was soon identified as the best option. From 2009 to 2011, thus, Muslim communities rapidly identified and skilfully learned how to take advance of a loophole in the Italian legislation.

In San Marino, the intended spouses are requested to satisfy conditions that are almost analogous to the Italian ones;[112] nonetheless, the foreign spouse's valid permit to stay is not listed amongst the requested documents. Additionally, the marriage deed is automatically transmitted between Italy and San Marino, and the marriage act is instantly valid in the other country.[113] Consequently, spouses married in San Marino are almost immediately regarded as civilly married also in the Italian legal system. Strategically circumnavigating an Italian religious discriminative provision, Muslim intended spouses empowered themselves in legitimising the spouse's reunification claim on the ground of the very same marriage that was forbidden by Italian authorities but recognized as valid if celebrated in San Marino.

Conclusion

The analysis focused on the multi-folded marriage routes – religious-only, customary-only, religious with civil effects, civil and *sharīʿah*-compliant – followed by Muslim partners settled on the Italian soil.

111 See pp. 000–000.

112 A notarial act signed by the purported spouses and four Italian national witnesses are also requested.

113 Arts. 38(1) and 39(1) of the Law 06.06.1939 No. 1320, 'Esecutorietà della Convenzione di amicizia e buon vicinato stipulata in Roma, fra l'Italia e la Repubblica di San Marino il 31 marzo 1939', in *Gazzetta Ufficiale* 16.09.1939 No. 217. Accordingly, the marriage act is not further examined by the Italian administrative when recording it.

The situations in which Islamic and/or Muslim marriages can be recognized and recorded as valid nuptial union with civil effects by the Italian legal systems were explored. It was clarified that *sharī'ah*-compliant marriages can be celebrated by an appointed religious minister (case 1). Additionally, the Italian legal system can acknowledge the validity of Islamic and/or Muslim marriages perfected in compliance with the laws of Muslim-majority countries (case 2). In the last scenario, *sharī'ah*-compliant nuptial unions can be solemnized abroad (point i), or Muslim marriages can be contracted in the diplomatic premises of Muslim-majority countries (point ii). Furthermore, the competent foreign authorities and/or diplomatic premises of Muslim-majority countries may recognize as valid and register Muslim-only and/or Islamic-only marriages (case 3). The last sections of the chapter investigated an additional nuptial route. Muslims can indeed opt to contract a (non-religious) civil marriage in compliance with Italian laws. This union can then become *sharī'ah*-compliant when recognized as valid by the laws of Muslim-majority countries (point iii).

As illustrated by the proposed analysis, a number of these situations – such as the above-mentioned case 3 and point iii, as well as marriages strategically undisclosed to some domestic legal systems – tend to remain unnoticed by both scholarship and judiciary. In effect, grey areas come into existence only when superimposing *sharī'ah*-compliant and/or foreign norms to Italian laws. Therefore, light was shed upon the partly neglected dynamic interplay between domestic legal provisions and *sharī'ah*-compliant norms. On the one hand, this chapter explored the role played by 'Islamic belonging' in moulding the socio-legal conducts of Muslim intended spouses. On the other hand, the attitude of the domestic European and Muslim-majority countries' legal system was analysed with respect to Muslim fiancé/es.

Building upon a decade of extensive empirical evidence, the chapter considered Islām as a tool for legal (dis-)empowerment. Three main considerations were drawn. First, the study revealed that Muslim intended spouses can be either disempowered or empowered by *sharī'ah* and/or European domestic norms. Second, the *sharī'ah*-compliant laws of Muslim-majority countries are to be carefully considered when dealing with Muslim migrant fiancé/es. Third, the interaction between the Italian legal system and Muslim intended spouses is fluid and constantly changing. Reciprocal adjustments are repeatedly negotiated. A strategic use of legal provisions, loopholes and discriminatory norms can indeed (dis-) empower an intended (Muslim or non-Muslim, Italian or foreign) spouse as well as a state's legal system.

In particular, the discussion indicated that some (partly concealed) discriminatory tools against Muslim purported spouses may be eventually amended by the Italian legal system, as happened in the case of the manifest procedural impartiality of marriages perfected by appointed religious ministers and the blanket prohibition to civilly marry for non-European nationals irregularly settled in Italy. Nonetheless, other disempowerment attitudes may persist and specifically affect Muslim purported spouses. Further obstacles indeed exist in the appointment of Muslim religious ministers and in the celebration of a civil marriage in case of foreign Muslim fiancé/es. Case-by-case judicial solutions and administrative remedies may be elaborated and implemented; however fieldwork evidence suggested that an idea of insecurity might continue to characterize civilly valid religious nuptial unions. As a result, Muslim partners may choose a different form of marriage.

Muslim (foreign) intended spouses, in effect, benefit from a number of alternative marriage routes. Alien (Muslim) fiancé/es settled in Italy can, for instance, have more room for manoeuvre when compared to (non-Muslim) immigrant intended spouses, whose national legal systems do not recognize proxy and telephone marriages as valid nuptial unions. Similarly, Islamic-only and/or Muslim-only marriages may be 'upgraded' as nuptial unions with civil effects in case they are recognized – through the back door – as civilly valid and registered by foreign authorities and/or diplomatic premises of a Muslim-majority country. In these situations, a spouse's visa can be easily claimed in Italy relying upon private international law principles. Attention should also be paid to the mirroring option. Alien Muslim nationals, whose Italian civil marriage is recognized as valid and also 'upgraded' as being *sharīʿah*-compliant by the legal systems of some Muslim-majority countries, are *de facto* granted a broader spectrum of possible alternative nuptial options.

The study also illustrated that Islām can be an effective tool for legal empowerment of Muslim intended spouses. Muslim spouses can indeed decide not to disclose (and thus record at civil effects) their Islamic and/or Muslim marriage to the legal systems of European and/or Muslim-majority countries. Muslim partners can thus benefit from different nuptial statuses in diverse legal systems. The choice not to disclose an Islamic/Muslim marriage might stem from the legal character's personal will: the spouses may for instance be part of a polygynous nuptial union. Muslim spouses can also be nationals of different European and/or Muslim-majority countries therefore they might register their marriage in only one of their countries of origin.

Conversely, a (Muslim) spouse can be impelled not to register his/her marriage in a European state or Muslim-majority country. As pinpointed, Islamic-only and Muslim-only marriages may not be acknowledged as valid nuptial unions with civil effects by some Muslim-majority countries as well as by European states. The marriage of a foreign national Muslim woman, who civilly married a non-Muslim man, cannot be recorded by some Muslim-majority countries; others record this nuptial union only when certain conditions are met. The *sharīʿah*-compliant marriage of an Italian national cannot be recognized as valid by the Italian legal system in case it was celebrated in foreign diplomatic premises on Italian soil.

It becomes thus evident that discriminatory practices can be enacted not only by European domestic legal systems, but also by Muslim-majority countries' diplomatic premises. Empirical data indicates that the latter may actually discriminate against their national citizens as well as Italian nationals. On the one hand, Muslim-majority countries' embassies/consulates can enforce Italian discriminatory immigration provisions; or record as valid Islamic-only and/or

Muslim-only marriages; or refuse to release a certificate of nuptial impediment on the ground of the religious belonging of the Muslim citizen's fiancé/e. On the other hand, Muslim-majority countries' embassies/consulates can violate international and national laws perfecting limping marriages of Italian nationals. As a result, a foreign *sharīʿah*-compliant law can disempower Italian (Muslim or non-Muslim) spouses.

As a key point, this study uncovered that Muslim partners are not passive victims of discriminatory state legal systems. On the contrary, in the aftermath of manifestly disempowering practices, creative solutions may be invented and legislative loopholes may be found. In particular, it has been highlighted that anti-prejudicial techniques may be rapidly elaborated as successful countermeasures against discriminatory laws.

With respect to the Italian legal system, empirical investigations disclosed that when a document attesting the regularity of the non-European fiancé/e's stay in Europe was requested for the celebration of a civil marriage, temporary strategic tactics were cleverly elaborated by Muslim purported spouses. In some cases, Islamic-only and/or Muslim-only marriages were recognized and recorded by some Muslim-majority countries or their diplomatic premises in Europe. As a result, privately solemnized *sharīʿah*-compliant nuptial unions became valid with civil effects on European soil. In other cases, non-European national Muslim fiancé/es opted to contract a civil marriage according to the laws of Muslim-majority countries, or to European domestic legal systems characterized by less demanding nuptial provisions. When following these alternative nuptial routes, the 'Islamic belonging' of the intended spouses empowered irregularly settled Muslim fiancé/es, when compared to non-Muslim immigrants. By virtue of international treaties and private international laws, originally irregularly settled Muslim fiancé/es were entitled to claim a spouse's visa in Italy on the ground of a civil marriage which was originally prevented by Italian laws but validly recorded at civil effects once perfected abroad.

The proposed analysis thus demonstrated that grey areas exist in the dynamic interplay between Italian legal provisions and *sharīʿah*-compliant norms. In these hidden domains, nationality-based discrimination techniques and religious disempowerment provisions can enfold themselves into new opportunities and multiple nuptial paths for Muslim intended spouses.

References

Abu Dhabi Gallup Center (ADGC). *Islamophobia: Understanding anti-Muslim sentiment in the West*. Abu Dhabi: Gallup, 2011.

Allen, Chris. *Islamophobia*. Farnham: Ashgate, 2010.

Allen, Christopher and Jørgen S. Nielsen. *Islamophobia in the EU after 11 September 2001: A summary report*. On behalf of the European Monitoring Centre on Racism and Xenophobia (EUMC), Luxembourg: Office for Official Publications of the European Communities, 2004.

Allievi, Stefano. *Islam italiano. Viaggio nella seconda religione del paese*. Torino: Einaudi, 2003.

Allievi, Stefano. *Musulmani d'Occidente. Tendenze dell'Islam europeo.* Roma: Carocci, 2002.

Allievi, Stefano and Francesco Castro. 'The Islamic presence in Italy: Social rootedness and legal questions'. In *Islam and European legal systems*, edited by Silvio Ferrari and Antony Bradney, 155–180. Dartmouth: Ashgate, 2000.

Allievi, Stefano and Ethnobarometer. *Conflicts over mosques in Europe: Policy issues and trends*. London: Alliance Publishing Trust, 2009.

Aluffi Beck-Peccoz, Roberta. 'The legal treatment of the Muslim minority in Italy'. In *The legal treatment of Islamic minorities in Europe*, edited by Roberta Aluffi Beck-Peccoz and Giovanna Zincone, 133–158. Leuven: Peeters, 2004a.

Aluffi Beck-Peccoz, Roberta. 'Islam in the European Union: Italy'. In *Islam and the European Union*, edited by Richard Potz and Wolfgang Wieshaider, 181–198. Leuven: Peeters, 2004b.

Ansari, Humayun and Farid Hafez (eds). *From the far right to the mainstream: Islamophobia in party politics and the media*. Birkach: Cambus Verlag, 2012.

Ballarino, Tito. *Manuale breve di diritto internazionale privato* (3rd ed.). Padova: CEDAM, 2008.

Banakar, Reza and Max Travers (eds). *Theory and method in socio-legal research*. Oxford and Portland: Hart, 2005.

Beltramo, Mario, Giovanni E. Longo, John H. Merryman and Susanna Beltramo (eds). *The Italian Civil Code*. Dobbs Ferry: Oceana, 1969–2007.

Bianchini, Daniela. 'Matrimonio per telefono e ricongiungimento familiare: il tribunale di Milano asserisce la validità del vincolo "telefonico"'. *Diritto di Famiglia* 37, No. I (2008): 155–164.

Bloul, Rachel A.D. 'Anti-discrimination laws, Islamophobia, and ethnicization of Muslim identities in Europe and Australia'. *Journal of Muslim Minority Affairs* 28, Issue 1 (2008): 7–25.

Bryman, Alan. *Social research methods*. Oxford and New York: Oxford University Press, 2001.

Bulmer, Martin (ed.). *Sociological research methods: An introduction* (2nd ed.). Piscataway: Macmillan Press, 2003.

Camera dei Deputati. *Relazione sulla politica dell'informazione per la sicurezza. Anno 2007*. Doc. XXXIII No. 4, 29.02.2008. Roma: Tipografia del Senato.

Campiglio, Cristina. 'Il diritto di famiglia islamico nella prassi italiana'. *Rivista di Diritto Internazionale Privato e Processuale* XLIV, No. 1 (2008): 343–376.

Campiglio, Cristina. 'La famiglia islamica nel diritto internazionale privato italiano'. *Rivista di Diritto Internazionale Privato e Processuale* XXXV (1999): 21–42.

Cappelletti, Mauro, John Henry Merryman and Joseph M. Perillo. *The Italian legal system*. Stanford: Stanford University Press, 1967.

Casuscelli, Giuseppe. 'La laicità e le democrazie: La laicità della Repubblica democratica secondo la Costituziona italiana'. *Quaderni di Diritto e Politica Ecclesiastica* I (2007): 170–202.

Casuscelli, Giuseppe. 'La rappresentanza e l'intesa'. In *Islam in Europa / Islam in Italia tra diritto e società*, edited by Alessandro Ferrari, 285–322. Bologna: Il Mulino, 2008.

Choudhury, Tufyal, Mohammed Aziz, Duaa Izzidien, Intissar Khreeji and Dilwar Hussain. *Perceptions of discrimination and Islamophobia: Voices from members of Muslim communities in the European Union*. Vienna: European Monitoring Centre on Racism and Xenophobia (EUMC), 2006.

Cilardo, Agostino. *Il diritto islamico e il sistema giuridico italiano: le bozze di intesa tra la Repubblica Italiana e le associazioni islamiche italiane*. Napoli: ESI, 2001.

Coglievina, Stella. 'Italy'. In *Yearbook of Muslims in Europe*, Vol. 5, edited by Jørgen Nielsen, Samim Akgönül, Ahmet Alibašić and Egdunas Racius, 351–367. Leiden: Brill, 2013.

Colaianni, Nicola. *Eguaglianza e diversità culturali e religiose. Un percorso costituzionale*. Bologna: Il Mulino, 2006.

Colaianni, Nicola. 'I nuovi confini del diritto matrimoniale tra istanze religiose e secolarizzazione: la giurisdizione'. *Rivista di Diritto Privato* No. 3–4 (2009): 7–31.

Colaianni, Nicola. 'L'ente di culto e gli statuti nell'islam'. In *Islam in Europa / Islam in Italia tra diritto e società*, edited by Alessandro Ferrari, 259–283. Bologna: Il Mulino, 2008.

Costanzo, Antonio. 'Stato civile'. In *Famiglia e Persone*, Vol. I, edited by Rita Rossi, 3–74. Lavis: UTET, 2008.

Cotula, Lorenzo. *Legal empowerment for local resource control: Securing local resource rights within foreign investment projects in Africa*. London: International Institute for Environment and Development (IIED), 2007.

D'Andrea, Luigi. 'Eguale libertà ed interesse alle intese delle Confessioni religiose: brevi note a margine della sentenza della Corte Costituzionale n. 346 del 2002'. *Il diritto ecclesiastico* Fasc. II (2004): 480–497.

De Gregorio, Laura. *La legge generale sulla lbertà religiosa. Disegni e dibattiti parlamentari.* Quaderni del Dipartimento di Scienze Giuridiche, Università Cattolica del Sacro Cuore, No. 4. Milano: Università Cattolica del Sacro Cuore, 2012.

Denzin, K. Norman. *The research act: A theoretical introduction to sociological methods*. Englewood Cliffs: Prentice Hall, 1989.

Denzin, Norman K. and Yvonna S. Lincoln (eds). *Collecting and interpreting qualitative materials*. Thousand Oaks and London: Sage Publications, 1998.

Denzin, Norman K. and Yvonna S. Lincoln (eds). *The handbook of qualitative research*. London: Sage Publications, 1994.

Di Marzio, Paolo. 'La disciplina del matrimonio celebrato davanti ad un ministro di culto di confessione religiosa dotata di intesa'. *Il Diritto di Famiglia e delle Persone* XXXIV, No. 1 (2005): 264–280.

Domingo, Pilar and Tam O'Neil. *The politics of legal empowerment: Legal mobilisation strategies and implications for development*. London: Overseas Development Institute (ODI), 2014.

Esposito, John and L. Ibrahim Kalin (eds). *Islamophobia: The challenge of pluralism in the 21st century*. Oxford: Oxford University Press, 2011.

Ferrari, Silvio. 'Introduction'. In *Islam and European legal systems*, edited by Silvio Ferrari, and Anthony Bradney, 1–9. Aldershot: Ashgate, 2000.

Ferrari, Silvio. 'Islam and the European system of Church-State relation: A (false) problem?' *Derecho y Religión* I, El Islam en Europa (2006b): 87–115.

Ferrari, Silvio. 'Islam in Europe: An introduction to legal problems and perspectives'. In *The legal treatment of Islamic minorities in Europe*, edited by Roberta Aluffi Beck-Peccoz and Giovanna Zincone, 1–9. Leuven: Peeters, 2004.

Ferrari, Silvio. 'Le questioni normative'. In *Islam in Europa / Islam in Italia tra diritto e società*, edited by Alessandro Ferrari, 77–87. Bologna: Il Mulino, 2008.

Ferrari, Silvio. 'Lo statuto giuridico dell'islam in Europa occidentale'. In *Islam ed Europa. I simboli religiosi nei diritti del vecchio continente*, edited by Silvio Ferrari, 17–61. Roma: Carocci, 2006a.

Flick, Uwe. *An introduction to qualitative research: Theory, method and applications*. London: Sage Publications, 1998.

Galoppini, Anna Maria. 'Il ripudio e la sua rilevanza nell'ordinamento italiano'. *Il Diritto di Famiglia e delle Persone* 34, Fasc. 3, Part 2 (2005): 969–989.

Golub, Stephen. 'Less law and reform, more politics and enforcement: A civil society approach to integrating rights and development.' In *Human rights and development: Towards mutual reinforcement*, edited by Philip Alston and Mary Robinson, 297–324. Oxford: Oxford University Press, 2005.

Golub, Stephen. 'What is legal empowerment? An introduction'. In *Legal empowerment: Practitioners' perspectives. Legal and governance reform: Lessons learned*, No. 2/2010, edited by Stephen Golub, 1–12. Rome: International Development Law Organization (IDLO), 2010.

Gray, George and Neil Guppy. *Successful surveys: Research methods and practice*. Toronto: Harcourt Brace, 1994.

Halliday, Fred. 'West encountering Islam: Islamophobia reconsidered'. In *Islam encountering globalisation*, edited by Ali Mohammadi, 14–35. London and New York: Routledge Curzon, 2002.

Helly, Denise and Jocelyne Césari. 'Ostracisme, tolérance ou reconnaissance: les musulmans en Europe'. In *Reconnaissance de l'islam dans les communes d'Europe. Actions contre les discriminations religieuses*, Collection compétences intercuturelles, edited by Altay Manço and Spyros Amoranitis, 163–182. Paris: l'Harmattan, 2005.

Hollway, Wendy and Tony Jefferson. *Doing qualitative research differently: Free association, narrative, and the interview method*. London: Sage Publications, 2000.

Huff, Toby E. *Max Weber and the methodology of the social sciences*. New Brunswick: Transaction Publishers, 2003.

Jeldtoft, Nadia and Jørgen Nielsen (eds). *Methods and contexts in the study of Muslim minorities: Visible and invisible Muslims*. London: Routledge, 2012.

Kaya, Ayhan. 'Islamophobia'. In *The Oxford handbook of European Islam*, edited by Jocelyne Césari, 745–768. Oxford: Oxford University Press, 2014.

Mancini, Letizia. 'Il matrimonio islamico in Italia'. In *Sposare l'altro. Matrimoni e matrimoni misti nell'ordinamento italiano e nel diritto islamico*, edited by Ida Zilio-Grandi, 105–118. Venezia: Marsilio, 2006.

Mancini, Letizia. 'Società multiculturale, pluralismo normativo e diritto: il caso del matrimonio islamico'. In *Elementi di etica pratica. Argomento normativi e spazi del diritto*, edited by Gianfrancesco Zanetti, 47–58. Roma: Carocci, 2003.

McConville, Michael and Wing Hong Chui (eds). *Research methods for law*. Edinburgh: Edinburgh University Press, 2007.

Merry, Sally Engle. 'Legal pluralism'. *Law and Society Review*, Vol. 22 (1988): 869–896.

Ministero dell'Interno. 'Le nomine dei ministri di culto'. *Ministero dell'Interno, Religioni e Stato* (undated): available at www.interno.gov.it/mininterno/export/233sites/default/it/temi/religioni/scheda_17631.html (last accessed 12.03.2013).

Ministero dell'Interno. *Enti di culto diversi dal Cattolico dotati di personalità giuridica*. Rome: www.interno.gov.it/mininterno/site/it/assets/files/ 14/0853_enti_di_culto_riconosciuti_D.P.R.pdf (last accessed 12.03.2013), 2009c.

Ministero dell'Interno. *Il Regolamento dello stato civile: guida all'applicazione. Massimario per l'ufficiale di stato civile 2009/4*. Authored by Mazza, Rosalia, Fabio De Fanti, Federico Vitali, Donato Berloco and Renzo Calvigioni. Roma: Ministero dell'Interno, 2009a.

Ministero dell'Interno. *Il Regolamento dello stato civile: guida all'applicazione. Massimario per l'ufficiale di stato civile. Edizione 2011*. Authored by Mazza, Rosalia, Anna La Marca, Federico Vitali, Donato Berloco, and Renzo Calvigioni. Roma: Ministero dell'Interno, 2011a.

Ministero dell'Interno. *Il Regolamento dello stato civile: guida all'applicazione. Massimario per l'ufficiale di stato civile. Edizione 2012*. Authored by Mazza, Rosalia, Anna La Marca, Federico Vitali, Donato Berloco, and Renzo Calvigioni. Roma: Ministero dell'Interno, 2012a.

Ministero dell'Interno. *Provvedimenti emanati in materia di culti*. INT00034. Settore di interesse: Famiglie e comportamenti sociali. Roma: Direzione Centrale degli Affari dei Culti. Available at http://ssai.interno.it/download/allegati1/int_34_2006.pdf (last accessed 12.10.2014), 2006d.

Ministero dell'Interno. *Provvedimenti emanati in materia di culti*. INT00034. Settore di interesse: Famiglie e comportamenti sociali. Roma: Direzione Centrale degli Affari dei Culti. Available at http://ssai.interno.it/download/allegati1/int_34_2007.pdf (last accessed 12.10.2014), 2007d.

Ministero dell'Interno. *Provvedimenti emanati in materia di culti*. INT00034. Settore di interesse: Famiglie e comportamenti sociali. Roma: Direzione Centrale degli Affari dei Culti. Available at http://ssai.interno.it/download/allegati1/int_34_2008.pdf (last accessed 12.10.2014), 2008d.

Ministero dell'Interno. *Provvedimenti emanati in materia di culti*. INT00034. Settore di interesse: Famiglie e comportamenti sociali. Roma: Direzione Centrale degli Affari dei Culti. Available at http://ssai.interno.it/download/allegati1/int_34_2009.pdf (last accessed 12.10.2014), 2009d.

Ministero dell'Interno. *Provvedimenti emanati in materia di culti*. INT00034. Settore di interesse: Famiglie e comportamenti sociali. Roma: Direzione Centrale degli Affari dei Culti. Available at http://ssai.interno.it/download/allegati1/int_34_2010.pdf (last accessed 12.10.2014), 2010d.

Ministero dell'Interno. *Provvedimenti emanati in materia di culti*. INT00034. Settore di interesse: Famiglie e comportamenti sociali. Roma: Direzione Centrale degli Affari dei Culti. Available at http://ssai.interno.it/download/allegati1/int_34_2011a.pdf (last accessed 12.10.2014), 2011d.

Ministero dell'Interno. *Provvedimenti emanati in materia di culti*. INT00034. Settore di interesse: Famiglie e comportamenti sociali. Roma: Direzione Centrale degli Affari dei Culti. Available at http://ssai.interno.it/download/allegati1/int_34_2012.pdf (last accessed 12.10.2014), 2012d.

Open Society Institute (OSI). 'Project legal empowerment'. In *Open Society Justice Initiative & Public Health Program*, [15 September], 2014. Available at www.opensocietyfoundations.org/projects/legal-empowerment (last accessed 12.12.2014).

Open Society Institute (OSI). "The situation of Muslims in Italy." In *Monitoring the EU accession process: Minority protection*, edited by Silvio Ferrari, Filippo Corbetta and Gianluca Parolin, 225–279. New York and London: OSI, 2002.

Patton, Michael Quinn. *Qualitative research and evaluation methods* (3rd ed.). London: Sage, 2002.

Petrley, Julian and Richardson Robin (eds). *Pointing the finger: Islam and Muslims in the British media*. London: Oneworld, 2013 [2011].

Pugliese, Enrico. *L'Italia tra migrazioni internazionali e migrazioni interne*. Bologna: Il Mulino, 2002.

Ricca, Mario. *Legge e intesa con le confessioni religiose*. Torino: Giappichelli, 1996.

Richardson, John E. *(Mis)representing Islam: The racism and rhetoric of British broadsheet newspapers*. Amsterdam and Philadelphia: John Benjamins Pub, 2004.

Richardson, Robin (ed.). *Islamophobia: A challenge for us all*. Report of the Runnymede Trust Commission on British Muslims and Islamophobia. London: Runnymede Trust, 1997.

Richardson, Robin, (ed.). *Islamophobia: Issues, challenges and action.* A Report by the Commission on British Muslims and Islamophobia Research (chaired by Richard Stone; research by Hugh Muir and Laura Smith; advised by Abduljalil Sajid). Stoke on Trent and Sterling: Trentham Books, in association with the Uniting Britain Trust, London, 2004.

Ringer, Fritz K. *Max Weber's methodology: The unification of the cultural and social sciences*. Cambridge, MA: Harvard University Press, 1997.

Roggero, Maria Adele. 'Muslims in Italy'. In *Muslims in the West: From sojourners to citizens*, edited by Yvonne Yazbeck Haddad, 131–143. Oxford and New York: Oxford University Press, 2002.

Sanfilippo, Matteo and Paola Corti (eds). *Storia d'Italia. Annali 24. Migrazioni*. Torino: Einaudi, 2009.

Sayyid, S. and Abdoolkarim Vakil (eds). *Thinking through Islamophobia: Global perspectives*. London: C. Hurst & Co, 2010.

Sona, Federica. 'Defending the family treasure-chest: Navigating Muslim families and secured positivistic islands of European legal systems'. In *Family, religion, and law: Cultural encounters in Europe*, edited by Prakash Shah, with Marie-Claire Foblets and Mathias Rohe, 115–141. Farnham: Asghate in association with Religare, 2014.

Sona, Federica. 'Overcoming obstacles through hidden nuptial paths: Muslim foreign purported spouses marrying in Italy'. *The Review of Social Studies* 2, No. 1 (2015): 25–53.

Spreafico, Andrea and Andrea Coppi. *La rappresentanza dei musulmani in Italia*. Roma: Edizioni XL, 2006.

Stark, Barbara. *International family law: An introduction*. Burlington: Ashgate, 2005.

Taras, Ray. *Xenophobia and Islamophobia in Europe*. Edinburgh: Edinburgh University Press, 2012.

Ufficio Centrale di Statistica and Scuola Superiore delle Statistiche Ufficiali dell'-Amministrazione dell'Interno. *Annuario delle statistiche ufficiali dell'amministrazione dell'interno*. Roma: SISTAN, 2009.

Ufficio Centrale di Statistica and Scuola Superiore delle Statistiche Ufficiali dell'-Amministrazione dell'Interno. *Annuario delle statistiche ufficiali dell'amministrazione dell'interno*. Roma: SISTAN, 2010.

Ufficio Centrale di Statistica and Scuola Superiore delle Statistiche Ufficiali dell'-Amministrazione dell'Interno. *Annuario delle statistiche ufficiali dell'amministrazione dell'interno*. Roma: SISTAN, 2011.

Ufficio Centrale di Statistica and Scuola Superiore delle Statistiche Ufficiali dell'-Amministrazione dell'Interno. *Annuario delle statistiche ufficiali dell'amministrazione dell'interno*. Roma: SISTAN, 2012.

Ufficio Centrale di Statistica and Scuola Superiore delle Statistiche Ufficiali dell'-Amministrazione dell'Interno. *Annuario delle statistiche ufficiali dell'amministrazione dell'interno*. Roma: SISTAN, 2013.

Vertovec, Steven. 'Islamophobia and Muslim recognition in Britain'. In *Muslims in the West: From sojourners to citizens*, edited by Yvonne Yazbeck Haddad, 19–35. Oxford and New York: Oxford University Press, 2002.

Walliman, Nicholas S.R. *Social research methods*. London: Sage Publications, 2006.

Weber, Max. *The methodology of the social sciences* (translated and edited by Edward A. Shils and Henry A. Finch; forward by Edward A. Shils). New York: Free Press, 1949.

Yanow, Dvora and Peregrine Schwartz-Shea (eds). *Interpretation and method: Empirical research methods and the interpretive turn*. New York, Armonk and London: M.E. Sharp, 2006.

Zincone, Giovanna (ed.). *Familismo legale. Come (non) diventare italiani*. Bari: Laterza, 2006.

3 South African women's legal experiences of Muslim personal law

*Waheeda Amien**

Introduction

Although the South African Constitution makes it possible for legislation to be enacted to afford legal recognition to religious or traditional marriages or family or personal law systems,[1] Muslim personal law[2] has not yet been legally recognised in South Africa. This has had a disparate effect on Muslim women who are married only by Muslim rites and struggle to access Islamic law rights related to Muslim marriage and divorce as well as civil law benefits that are available to spouses married under the secular Marriage Act 25 of 1961. In the absence of legislation to recognise Muslim marriages or Muslim personal law, the South African judiciary has found creative ways of providing relief to Muslim women. One of these ways is recognition of the Muslim marriage as a contract so that proven terms and customs arising from the contract can be legally enforced.

The aim of this chapter is to illustrate, through selected judgments, the creative ways in which the South African judiciary has come to the aid of Muslim women. These judgments are discussed in the second of this chapter. However, through a presentation of selected narratives in the third part of the chapter, I also show that while South African Muslims can access their Islamic law rights if they can prove the terms and customs of their Muslim marriage contracts, they do not all utilise the opportunity to enter into marriage contracts. The narratives are acquired from consultations that I conducted with clients who sought advice about Muslim marriage contracts. To protect lawyer/client confidentiality, significant details of the cases and the true identity of the clients are not disclosed in this chapter.

I suggest that one of the reasons that Muslim women do not insist on entering into marriage contracts may be related to a lack of agency or not asserting their agency. Sally Engle Merry defines agency as 'the capacity to act, [which]

* BA LLB (Cape Town) LLM (Western Cape) PhD (Ghent). Associate Professor, Department of Public Law, University of Cape Town. Email: waheeda.amien@uct.ac.za.

1 Section 15(3) of the Constitution of South Africa, 1996.

2 Muslim personal law refers to a system of Islamic-based private laws that include family law and inheritance. D. Pearl and W. Menski, *Muslim Family Law*, 3rd edn (London: Sweet & Maxwell, 1998) 29.

is demonstrated in the ability of people to orient themselves or align themselves with particular relationships'.[3] So, in the fourth part of the chapter, I attempt to analyse the narratives within the paradigm of women's agency. I do not, however, explore the reasons that they fail to do so. That research needs to be undertaken in a follow-up project involving empirical methodologies.

South African law: background and evolution

In 1994, South Africa was faced with the colonial and apartheid legacies of not affording recognition to marriages that did not conform to Christian expectations of marriage. So marriages that were potentially polygynous such as Muslim, Hindu, Jewish and African customary marriages were not recognised as legally valid.[4]

With the introduction of a constitutional democracy, there was commitment to address and eradicate all forms of unfair discrimination that had plagued South African society for several centuries and to ensure that such discrimination would never again be repeated. This included religious discrimination since historically, Christianity had been the favoured religion of the colonial and apartheid states, which resulted in the marginalisation of the remaining religions.[5]

Sections 15 and 31(1) of the Constitution[6] are the main constitutional provisions that protect and promote the rights of individuals and communities to respectively maintain, manifest and propagate their religious beliefs individually and in association with each other. In particular, section 15(3)(a) creates the possibility for legislation to be enacted to afford recognition to customary and religious marriages or customary and religious personal law systems. To prevent the sanctioning of *inter alia* harmful religious practices, such legislation and the collective right of religious communities to practise their religion and maintain religious associations are internally limited to the extent that they must not be inconsistent with other provisions of the Constitution including the right to not be unfairly discriminated against on the basis of gender or sex.[7]

In accordance with section 15(3)(a) of the Constitution, the Recognition of Customary Marriages Act[8] was enacted, so that African customary marriages

3 Sally Engle Merry, 'Relating to the Subjects of Human Rights: The Culture of Agency in Human Rights Discourse', in Michael Freeman and David Napier (eds), *Law and Anthropology: Current Legal Issues* Vol. 12 (Oxford Scholarship Online, 2010), 385–407, 388.

4 *Bronn* v. *Frits Bronn's Executors and Others* 1860 3 Searle 313; *Seedat's Executors* v. *The Master (Natal)* 1917 A.D. 302; *Estate Mehta* v. *Acting Master, High Court* 1958 (4) SA 252 (F.C); *Kader* v. *Kader* 1972 (3) SA 203 (R.,A.D.); *Ismail* v. *Ismail* 1983 (1) SA 1006 (AD).

5 *S* v. *Lawrence, Negal, Solberg* 1997 (10) BCLR 1348 (CC) at para 123. Census 2001 reveals that South Africa comprises 80 per cent Christians, 1.5 per cent Muslims, 1.2 per cent Hindus, 0.3 per cent African traditional beliefs, 0.2 per cent Judaism, and 0.6 per cent unidentified faiths. www.statssa.gov.za/census01/html/RSAPrimary.pdf (accessed 11 January 2011).

6 The Constitution of the Republic of South Africa, 1996.

7 Sections 15(3)(b), 31(2) and 9(3) of the Constitution.

8 120 of 1998.

are now legally recognised. Attempts have also been made since 1994 to enact legislation to recognise Muslim marriages but the government and the Muslim community have not been able to sufficiently get their act together to ensure that the legislation is passed.[9] In the meantime, the only recourse that Muslims have to assert their Islamic law rights relating to their Muslim marriage is through the secular court system.

Since 1997, the South African judiciary has come to the aid of Muslim parties, particularly women, and has shaped groundbreaking jurisprudence for the recognition of certain aspects of Muslim personal law, namely, the elements and consequences arising from the Muslim marriage contract including *mahr* (dower),[10] spousal *nafaqah* (maintenance)[11] and *mata'a* (compensatory gift).[12] The judiciary

9 For a discussion of the draft legislation ('Muslim Marriages Bill'), see Waheeda Amien, 'Overcoming the Conflict between the Right to Religious Freedom and Women's Rights to Equality – a South African Case Study of Muslim Marriages', *Human Rights Quarterly* 28 (2006) 729–754: 741–746. Waheeda Amien, 'A South African Case Study for the Recognition and Regulation of Muslim Family Law in a Minority Muslim Secular Context', *International Journal of Law, Policy and the Family* 24:3 (2010) 361–396: 373–380.

10 Most Muslim scholars suggest that *mahr* is given to the bride/wife by the groom/husband as an obligation arising out of the marriage. If the marriage contract does not specify *mahr*, it is considered void by the *Māliki madhhab*. In contrast, the *Hanafī madhhab* does not regard *mahr* as a necessary component of the marriage contract. *Mahr* is anything of value that is permissible according to Islamic law and agreed upon between the bride and groom at the date of marriage. Once agreement is reached on the nature and amount of *mahr*, it belongs exclusively to the wife. If the nature and amount of *mahr* is not stipulated, the *Shāfi'ī* and *Hanafī madhāhib* adopt the view that a woman is entitled to *mahr al-mithl*, which is calculated as an average *mahr*. If *mahr* is not paid to the wife, it accrues to her estate as a debt owed by the husband. The parties can agree that *mahr* is either paid promptly at the date of marriage or that payment will be deferred until a stipulated time or at the end of the marriage. *Qur'ān* 4:4, 2:236. Ibn Rushd, *The Distinguished Jurist's Primer: A Translation of Bidayat Al-Mujtahid* (transl) Imran Ahsan Khan Nyazee (UK: Center for Muslim Contribution to Civilization, Garnet Publishing Limited, 1996), 23. Joseph Schacht, *An Introduction to Islamic Law* (London: Oxford University Press, 1964),167. A.D. Ajijola, *Introduction to Islamic Law* (Karachi: International Islamic Publishers, 1981), 117, 154–155. David Pearl, *A Textbook on Muslim Law* (London: Croom Helm Ltd, 1979), 57. K.N. Ahmad, *Muslim Law of Divorce* (New Delhi: Kitab Bhavan, 1978), 21. Sayyid Sabiq, *Fiqh Us-Sunnah: Doctrine of Sunnah of the Holy Prophet* (New Delhi: Millat Book Centre, undated), 51, 105. Ziba Mir-Hosseini, 'The Construction of Gender in Islamic Legal Thought and Strategies for Reform', *Journal of Women in the Middle East and the Islamic World* 1:1 (2003) 1–28: 13. Abdur Rahman I. Doi, *Shariah: The Islamic Law* (Jeddah: Abul Qasim Bookstore, 1984), 158–166. John L. Esposito and Natana J. DeLong-Bas, *Women in Muslim Family Law*, 2nd edn (New York: Syracuse University Press, 2001), 24. Asaf A.A. Fyzee, *Outlines of Muhammadan Law* (London: Oxford University Press, 1949), 133.

11 Under a traditional understanding of Islamic law, men have a unilateral obligation to provide reasonable *nafaqah* to their wives and children. The minimum form of reasonable *nafaqah* consists of food, clothing and accommodation and may also include health care. The extent of the *nafaqah* depends on what the man can afford. *Qur'ān* 4:34, 65:7. Ibn Rushd, 63. Sabiq, 51, 363. Schacht, 167–168. Esposito and DeLong-Bas, 25. Fyzee, 205. Ajijola, 192. Ahmad, 21, 711, 715.

12 When a Muslim marriage terminates at the unjustified behest of the husband, the latter is required to give a compensatory gift (*mata'a*) to the wife. This could take the form of financial compensation. See *Ryland* v. *Edros* 1997 (2) SA 690 (C).

has also intervened to provide relief to surviving Muslim spouses whose deceased spouses had died without leaving wills and who had not been permitted to inherit intestate due to their marriages not being legally recognised. In the next section, I present these cases that have shaped South African law relating to Muslim marriages and the ability of Muslim spouses to inherit in circumstances of intestacy.

Judicial recognition of aspects of Muslim personal law

At the outset, it is important to note that the South African judiciary has clearly indicated that it will not recognise Muslim marriages because it sees this as a function of the legislature.[13] This is not an altogether undesirable approach since recognition will involve some form of regulation and to achieve that effectively, consultations with relevant stakeholders are necessary; the legislature is better equipped to undertake such consultations.

Nevertheless, by recognising the Muslim marriage as a contract, the judiciary is able to creatively provide some measure of protection to Muslim parties because this enables proven terms, conditions and customs of a Muslim marriage contract to be legally enforceable.[14] For instance, claims for *mahr*, spousal *nafaqah* and *mata'a* could not be previously asserted. Under the constitutional dispensation, however, this type of negative effect of non-recognition of Muslim marriages has become a thing of the past.[15] Since 1994, the High Courts, Supreme Court of Appeal and Constitutional Court adjudicated several cases involving claims related to the non-recognition of Muslim marriages, which I discuss in the following paragraphs, namely, *Ryland* v. *Edros* ('*Ryland*'),[16] *Khan* v. *Khan* ('*Khan*'),[17] *Cassim* v. *Cassim and Others* ('*Cassim*'),[18] *Amod* v. *Multilateral Motor Vehicle Accidents Fund (Commission for Gender Equality Intervening)*,[19] *Mahomed* v. *Mahomed* ('*Mahomed*'),[20] *Hoosain* v. *Dangor* ('*Hoosain*'),[21] *Arendse* v. *Arendse*

13 *Amod* v. *Multilateral Motor Vehicle Accidents Fund (Commission for Gender Equality Intervening)* 1999 (4) SA 1319 (SCA) at para 28.

14 *Ryland* v. *Edros* 1997 (2) SA 690 (C) at 707E-H, 708J.

15 *Mahr* was recognised in *Arendse* v. *Arendse and Others* (Reportable judgment Case No: 1659/2009 (WCC). Judgment delivered on 20 August 2012). *Mata'a* was recognised in *Ryland* v. *Edros*. Spousal *nafaqah* was also recognised in *Ryland* v. *Edros*; *Khan* v. *Khan* 2005 (2) SA 272 (T); *Cassim* v. *Cassim and Others* (Part A) (TPD) (Unreported 15 December 2006, Case No: 3954/06); *Mahomed* v. *Mahomed* (Case No: 2154/08, Judgment delivered 29 May 2009 (ECP)); and *Hoosain* v. *Dangor* (Case No: 18141/09, Judgment delivered 18 November 2009 (WCC)). The right of a Muslim spouse to inherit on an intestate basis was recognised in *Daniels* v. *Campbell NO and Others* 2004 (5) SA 331 (CC) and *Fatima Gabie Hassam* v. *Johan Hermanus Jacobs NO and Others* 2009 (5) SA 572 (CC).

16 1997 (2) SA 690 (C).

17 2005 (2) SA 272 (T).

18 (Part A) (TPD) (Unreported 15 December 2006, Case No: 3954/06).

19 1999 (4) SA 1319 (SCA).

20 Case No: 2154/08, Judgment delivered 29 May 2009 (ECP). Also cited as *AM* v. *RAM*. Available online at www.saflii.org/za/cases/ZAECPEHC/2009/31.pdf. Accessed on 19 December 2014.

21 Case No: 18141/09, Judgment delivered 18 November 2009 (WCC).

and Others (*'Arendse'*),[22] *Isaacs* v. *Isaacs and Another*,[23] *Faro* v. *Bingham*,[24] *Daniels* v. *Campbell NO and Others* (*'Daniels'*)[25] and *Hassam* v. *Jacobs NO and Others* (*'Hassam'*).[26] In all of these cases, the parties had not entered into written marriage contracts. Except for *Khan* and *Hassam*, all the marriages in the remaining cases had been *de facto* monogamous and except for *Arendse*, all the parties in the other cases had not concluded a civil marriage.

Ryland v. Edros

As noted above, in *Ryland*, the parties had concluded a *de facto* monogamous Muslim marriage only. After 16 years of marriage, the husband (hereafter referred to as the 'ex-husband') had irrevocably *talāqed* his wife (hereafter referred to as the 'ex-wife').[27] In this case, the ex-wife had claimed arrear *nafaqah* for the duration of the marriage, which included the three-month *iddah* period;[28] *mata'a* on the basis that her ex-husband had unjustifiably divorced her; and an equitable share of his estate on the basis that she had directly and indirectly contributed to the growth of his estate through her labour, effort and money.[29]

Ryland was the first case in which the South African judiciary had departed from the racist decisions of its colonial and apartheid predecessors as they pertained to Muslim marriages. On the basis of the constitutional values of equality and tolerance of diversity,[30] the Cape Provincial Division (as it then was) recognised that the proven terms, conditions and customs of a Muslim marriage contract are legally enforceable.[31] Since the parties had not entered into a written marriage contract, the Court relied on the default mainstream Islamic law position relating to Muslim marriages as enunciated by Islamic law experts who were called upon to testify.

22 Reportable judgment Case No: 1659/2009 (WCC). Judgment delivered on 20 August 2012.

23 Case No: 2807/14.

24 (4466/2013) [2013] ZAWCHC 159 (25 October 2130).

25 2004 (5) SA 331 (CC).

26 2009 (5) SA 572 (CC).

27 *Ryland* at 701C-G. *Talāq* is the exclusive right of a man to divorce his wife by unilaterally repudiating her through up to three utterances of divorce without having to provide any grounds. It is exercised at the husband's discretion who is seldom held accountable to an external forum for applying his right to *talāq*. *Qur'ān* 2:229. Joseph Schacht, *An Introduction to Islamic Law* (London: Oxford University Press, 1964), 163. Esposito and DeLong-Bas, 28–29. Ibn Rushd, 72, 97, 119. Sabiq, 51. Fyzee, 142–143. Pearl, 89.

28 *Iddah* is the waiting period that is observed by a wife following termination of the marriage by death or divorce. In the case of death, the widow is required to observe an *iddah* of four months and ten days. In the case of dissolution of the marriage by *talāq*, the wife is expected to observe *iddah* of three months. During the *iddah* period, a wife/widow is expected to remain housebound and may only leave her abode to attend to necessities such as work, grocery shopping etc. She may also not marry or engage in a romantic relationship. Ibn Rushd, 54, 106, 115–16; Doi, 198–203; *Qur'an* 2:228, 2:234, 33:49, 65:4.

29 *Ryland* at 696G-I.

30 *Ryland* at 708J.

31 *Ryland* at 707E-H.

In this instance, the Court accepted the experts' undisputed testimony that the wife is entitled to *nafaqah* for the subsistence of the marriage until the end of her *iddah* period and *mata'a* since the marriage had been terminated at the unjustified behest of the husband. Consequently, the Court granted the ex-wife's claims for *nafaqah* and *mata'a*.[32] However, the Court subjected the claims to the South African law of prescription,[33] even though the Islamic law experts had also agreed that prescription does not apply to Islamic-based claims. This meant that the ex-wife was entitled to only receive *nafaqah* for no more than three years.[34] So while the Court attempted to accommodate religious diversity, it simultaneously expected the ex-wife's claims to assimilate to the civil law standard for civil claims.

When faced with conflicting Islamic opinions relating to the ex-wife's claim for an equitable distribution of her husband's estate, the Court favoured the one that appeared to conform to local custom.[35] To illustrate: Dr Ebrahim Moosa testified on behalf of the ex-wife that members of the Muslim community in the Western Cape did not know what the true Islamic law position is relating to the parties' estates. In his opinion, the Court should have been guided by the Malaysian custom of *harta sepencarian* ('jointly acquired property'), which is codified into Malaysian family law.[36] Moosa presumably referred to the Malaysian custom because Malaysia is primarily a *Shāfi'ī* jurisdiction and the Islamic law experts for the ex-husband and ex-wife agreed that the *Shāfi'ī madhhab* (school of thought) applied in this case.[37] The custom enables a spouse who does not acquire assets but has made tangible and intangible contributions to the growth of the other spouse's estate to be compensated for those contributions. Tangible contributions could comprise money and property. Intangible contributions could consist of labour extended in the acquisition of assets or taking care of the home and/or family.[38] In contrast, Moulana Mohamed Allie Moosajee of the Muslim Judicial Council testified on behalf of the ex-husband that the Western Cape Muslim community does not practise the Malaysian custom of *harta sepencarian*.[39] The Court found that Dr Moosa had not adduced evidence to show that *harta sepencarian* is practised within the Western Cape Muslim community. Accordingly, it did not grant the ex-wife's claim for an equitable distribution of her ex-husband's estate.[40]

One might argue that the Court's rejection of *harta sepencarian* for the purpose of the Western Cape Muslim community inadvertently gave effect

32 *Ryland* at 718I-J.

33 Section 12(5) of the Prescription Act 68 of 1969 places a three-year prescription period on civil claims, which means that civil claims have to be instituted within three years from the date that the cause arose, failing which they are no longer enforceable.

34 *Ryland* at 713F.

35 *Ryland* at 717D-E.

36 The Malaysian Islamic Family Law (Federal Territory) Act of 1984.

37 *Ryland* at 698H-I, 715B-716D.

38 Section 58(2)(a) and (4)(a) of the Malaysian Islamic Family Law (Federal Territory) Act of 1984.

39 *Ryland* at 717D.

40 *Ryland* at 717D-E.

to a subsidiary source of Islamic law namely, *'urf*, which refers to a custom that the community accepts and practises in the course of their daily lives and as a result becomes part of the Islamic law of that community.[41] Since the Court indicated an inclination to accept the Muslim rules and practices of the Western Cape Muslim community, it might have been more useful for the ex-wife's legal counsel to inform the Court that the *'ulamā* (Muslim clergy) in the Western Cape acknowledges the Islamic law rule that enables a wife to be compensated for her unpaid labour in the home even though they do not pro-actively encourage the implementation of the rule within the community. The ex-wife's claim for an equitable distribution of her ex-husband's estate might then have been fortified.

The issue of the husband's unilateral Islamic law obligation to maintain his wife arose again the cases of *Amod, Khan* and *Cassim*. In *Amod*, the wife based her claim on the Multilateral Motor Vehicle Accidents Fund (MMVAF) Act 93 of 1989 while in *Khan* and *Cassim*, the wives asserted their claims *inter alia* in terms of the Maintenance Act 99 of 1998.

Amod v. Multilateral Motor Vehicle Accidents Fund (Commission for Gender Equality Intervening)

In *Amod*, the parties had been married to each other by Muslim rites only, and the marriage had been *de facto* monogamous for its duration. The husband had been killed in a motor vehicle collision, which had resulted from the negligent driving of a third party.[42] The compensation provided for in the MMVAF Act is based on a common law remedy to compensate dependants who suffer loss resulting from the death of a breadwinner who had a duty to support her or his dependants.[43] The Muslim widow therefore claimed compensation from the Multilateral Motor Vehicle Accidents Fund in terms of the MMVAF Act, for loss of support arising from her husband's death.[44]

The SCA recognised the widow's claim on the basis that her right as a dependant to receive support was worthy of recognition and protection under the law because the Muslim marriage had been contracted according to the tenets of a major religion; had involved a public ceremony that required the observance of special formalities; and placed onerous obligations on the husband and wife.[45] Moreover, the SCA found that recognition and protection of the Islamic law duty of support is consistent with the *boni mores* of our society, which reflects the constitutional values of tolerance, pluralism and respect for religious freedom.[46]

41 Ayman Shabana, *Custom in Islamic Law and Legal Theory: The Development of the Concepts of 'Urf and 'Ādah in the Islamic Legal Tradition* (New York: Palgrave Macmillan, 2010).

42 *Amod* at 1323A.

43 *Amod* at 1324B.

44 *Amod* at 1323D.

45 *Amod* at 1327G-H.

46 *Amod* at 1328B.

In both the *Ryland* and *Amod* cases, the judiciary's recognition of aspects of a Muslim marriage was limited to *de facto* Muslim marriages.[47]

The SCA decision in *Amod* recognising the Islamic law duty of support along with the *Ryland* decision that recognised *nafaqah* as an enforceable term of a Muslim marriage contract, laid the basis for the South African judiciary to later enable Muslim wives to access their husbands' unilateral obligation to maintain them during the marriage through the secular Maintenance Act. This is evident in the cases of *Khan* and *Cassim*.

Khan v. Khan, Cassim v. Cassim and Others

The *Khan* case involved a *de facto* polygynous Muslim marriage while in the *Cassim* case the parties were in a *de facto* monogamous Muslim marriage. Both *Khan* and *Cassim* were adjudicated in the Transvaal Provincial Division ('TPD' as it then was), and in both cases, the claimants were Muslim wives who had instituted their *nafaqah* claims *inter alia* under section 2(1) of the Maintenance Act 99 of 1998, which reads:

> The provisions of [the Maintenance] Act shall apply in respect of the legal duty of any person to maintain another person irrespective of the nature of the relationship between those persons giving rise to that duty.

Since the SCA in *Amod* had recognised a Muslim husband's duty of support vis-à-vis his wife, the TPD in *Khan* and *Cassim* concluded that the duty could be enforced through the Maintenance Act.[48]

In particular, the TPD in *Khan* was of the view that it would be discriminatory to not recognise the duty of support within the context of a *de facto* polygynous Muslim marriage since it had already been recognised in a *de facto* monogamous Muslim marriage.[49] Moreover, the TPD held that not affording legal recognition to the duty of support in a *de facto* polygynous Muslim marriage would obstruct the aim of social and economic justice that the Maintenance Act seeks to achieve.[50]

The TPD therefore expanded on the decisions in *Ryland* and *Amod* by enabling a Muslim wife's *nafaqah* claim to be accessed through the Maintenance Act and by extending recognition of the claim to *de facto* polygynous Muslim marriages.[51]

47 *Ryland* at 92C; *Amod* at para 24.

48 *Khan* at 283A-B; *Cassim* at paras 3 and 4.

49 *Khan* at 283A-B.

50 *Khan* at 283C. See part of the Preamble of the Maintenance Act 99 of 1998, which provides: 'WHEREAS the Constitution of the Republic of South Africa, 1996, as the supreme law of the Republic, was adopted so as to establish a society based on democratic values, social and economic justice, equality and fundamental human rights and to improve the quality of life of all citizens and to free the potential of all persons by every means possible, including, amongst others, by the establishment of a fair and equitable maintenance system.'

51 *Khan* at 283D.

In particular, by allowing Muslim wives in *de facto* monogamous and polygynous Muslim marriages to assert their spousal *nafaqah* claims through the Maintenance Act, the judiciary may have increased their access to justice because they can now simply approach a maintenance court, which is more time- and cost effective than approaching an ordinary magistrates court.

The decisions of *Ryland*, *Amod*, *Khan* and *Cassim* led to the ambit of Muslim wives' maintenance claims being extended even further. This is illustrated below in the cases of *Mahomed* and *Hoosain.*

Mahomed v. Mahomed and Hoosain v. Dangor

The facts in *Mahomed* and *Hoosain* were similar. In these two cases, the parties had been married to each other by Muslim rites only and for the duration of their marriages, they had been *de facto* monogamous. In *Hoosain*, the marriage had ended in Muslim divorce. In *Mahomed*, there was a dispute between the parties as to whether or not the Muslim divorce was valid: the ex-wife contended that it was not while the ex-husband claimed that it was.[52]

In each case, the Muslim ex-wives had applied for interim spousal maintenance within the context of Rule 43 applications.[53] In *Mahomed*, the ex-wife also claimed interim maintenance under Rule 43 for the daughter born of the marriage.[54] An application based on Rule 43 of the Uniform Rules of Court involves a claim for interim maintenance, custody and/or access to minor children pending the finalisation of a matrimonial action and/or a contribution towards the costs of a pending matrimonial action.

Until 2009, only parties who were lawfully married to each other had invoked Rule 43 applications. However, this pattern changed in the cases of *Mahomed* and *Hoosain.* In both instances, the Rule 43 applications preceded a divorce action, which included requests for declaratory orders where the ex-wives asked among others that their Muslim marriages be declared valid under the Marriage Act 25 of 1961 and that the Divorce Act 70 of 1979 should govern the termination of their marriages.[55]

In the two cases under discussion in this section, the ex-husbands argued that their marriages to their ex-wives did not constitute lawful marriages, therefore the actions preceding the Rule 43 applications were not 'matrimonial' and the word 'spouse' referred to in Rule 43 did not include parties who were married to each other by Muslim rites only.[56] The ex-husband in *Hoosain* further argued

52 *Mahomed* at para 2.

53 Rule 43(1) of the Uniform Rules of Court reads: 'This rule shall apply whenever a spouse seeks relief from the court in respect of one or more of the following matters: *(a)* Maintenance *pendente lite*; *(b)* a contribution towards the costs of a pending matrimonial action; *(c)* interim custody of any child; *(d)* interim access to any child.'

54 *Mahomed* at para 1.

55 *Mahomed* at para 3; *Hoosain* at para 2.

56 *Mahomed* at para 2. *Hoosain* at para 3.

that the appropriate course of action should have been for his ex-wife to apply for maintenance under section 2(1) of the Maintenance Act.[57]

The High Courts in both cases disagreed with the views extended by the ex-husbands. The Eastern Cape High Court in *Mahomed* held that since the ex-wife had instituted a divorce action against her ex-husband, that fact located her application within the parameters of a 'matrimonial action' as envisioned in Rule 43. The Court reasoned:

> The fact that a Muslim divorce has been concluded, is no obstacle for the divorce trial, and the constitutional challenges raised therein, to proceed. Once there is a constitutional challenge in the context of relief sought under the Divorce Act, not only the status and effect of the nikah but also the status and effect of the *talaq*, will be under scrutiny. The constitutional challenge pending in the trial court, clearly encompasses a challenge to the legal effect of a *talaq*. By virtue of the main action for divorce, its effect is suspended for all practical purposes. Therefore, when a court has to decide whether or not to grant maintenance pending the outcome of the divorce action, where there is a constitutional challenge to the status of the marriage, it does not matter whether or not the parties were divorced in accordance with Muslim rites or not.[58]

The Western Cape High Court in *Hoosain* held that even though the legality of Muslim marriages was being disputed in the preceding action between the parties, the word 'spouse' as it appears in Rule 43 includes a spouse in a Muslim marriage.[59] The Western Cape High Court built on the precedent that had been set by the Constitutional Court in *Daniels* where the latter Court found that the word 'spouse' in the Intestate Succession Act 81 of 1987 and the Maintenance of Surviving Spouses Act 27 of 1990 includes spouses married by Muslim rites only.[60] The *Daniels* case is discussed in greater detail later in this chapter.

The Western Cape High Court in *Hoosain* further found that although a right of recourse to the maintenance court is recognised in the context of parties married by Muslim rites only; this did not make the discrimination that arises from a failure to access Rule 43 any fairer.[61] Consequently, the ex-wives in the *Mahomed* and *Hoosain* cases succeeded in their applications for interim maintenance pending the finalisation of their divorce actions.[62] The latter, however, were settled out of court. So the question whether or not a Muslim marriage is a legal marriage for the purpose of the Marriage Act was not answered.

57 *Hoosain* at para 22.
58 *Mahomed* at para 10.
59 *Hoosain* at para 28.
60 *Daniels* at para 19.
61 *Hoosain* at *para* 25.
62 *Mahomed* at paras 13, 15 *Hoosain* at para 31. This precedent was followed in the case of *AM* v. *RM* 2010 (2) SA 223 (ECP).

Apart from spousal *nafaqah* and *mata'a*, the South African judiciary has also recognised *mahr* as a relevant consideration in legal proceedings, as is illustrated in the next case under discussion, namely, *Arendse*.

Arendse v. Arendse and Others

In *Arendse*, the matter revolved around a review of an eviction order granted by the Goodwood Magistrate's Court that the ex-husband had obtained against his ex-wife in terms of the Prevention of Illegal Eviction from and Unlawful Occupation of Land Act 19 of 1998 (PIE).[63]

The parties in this case had been married to each other by Muslim rites in 1995.[64] Their Muslim marriage certificate reflected that the husband had undertaken to give *mahr* comprising a house to his wife.[65] A year later, in 1996, the parties had also concluded a civil marriage, which was in community of property.[66] Three children, still minors, were born to the parties. After about five years of marriage, the parties obtained a civil divorce and a Muslim divorce.[67] The ex-wife averred that her ex-husband had not fulfilled his *mahr* obligation and approached the Muslim Judicial Council (MJC) to assist her in claiming her *mahr*.[68] The MJC is one of the *ulamā* bodies in South Africa, which among others, adjudicates and/or mediates Muslim-related disputes between parties. The MJC agreed that the ex-husband had not fulfilled his *mahr* obligation.[69]

The eviction order required the ex-wife to be evicted from their family home. The ex-wife was unemployed as a result of her doctor's advice that she should not work because she suffered from epilepsy and had been diagnosed with bipolar mood disorder.[70] The practical implication of the order was that the ex-wife as a single, unemployed mother would have had to move out along with the parties' children and be rendered homeless.[71]

In reviewing the eviction order, the Western Cape High Court had regard to sections 4(6) and 4(7) of the PIE, which provide:

> Section 4(6):
>
> If an unlawful occupier has occupied the land in question for less than six months at the time when the proceedings are initiated, the Court may grant

63 *Arendse* at para 1.

64 *Arendse* at para 9.

65 *Arendse* at para 9.

66 *Arendse* at para 9. A marriage in community of property entails a joint estate, comprising both spouses' assets and liabilities, which they accrue prior to marriage and during the marriage. Each spouse has a 50 per cent share in the joint estate (Chapter III of the Matrimonial Property Act 88 of 1984).

67 *Arendse* at paras 11, 13.

68 *Arendse* at para 15.

69 *Arendse* at para 15.

70 *Arendse* at para 8.

71 *Arendse* at paras 1, 40.

> an order for eviction if it is of the opinion that it is just and equitable to do so after considering all the relevant circumstances, including the rights and needs of the elderly, children, disabled persons and households headed by women.
>
> Section 4(7):
>
> If an unlawful occupier has occupied the land in question for more than six months at the time when the proceedings are initiated, a Court may grant an order for eviction if it is of the opinion that it is just and equitable to do so, after considering all the relevant circumstances including, except where the land is sold in a sale of execution pursuant to a mortgage, whether land has been made available or can reasonably be made available by a municipality or other organ of state or another land owner for the relocation of the unlawful occupier, and including the rights and needs of the elderly, children, disabled persons and households headed by women.

Although the ex-wife could be considered an unlawful occupier in terms of the PIE, the Western Cape High Court found that the magistrate had failed to consider the rights and needs of the children, the fact that the ex-wife was disabled and headed the household as a single woman, and that the ex-husband had failed to provide them with alternative accommodation.[72] Of particular importance to this analysis is the fact that the Western Cape High Court noted that the agreement between the parties regarding *mahr* was a relevant circumstance to also be considered in the eviction proceedings, which it found the magistrate's court had failed to do.[73] Accordingly, the Western Cape High Court held that it was not just and equitable to evict the ex-wife along with the children and set the eviction order aside.[74]

The *Arendse* case did not recognise *mahr* as a legally enforceable component of the Muslim marriage contract but in all fairness to the Western Cape High Court, it was not required to do so, given the circumstances of the case. The important thing is that the Western Cape High Court accepted *mahr* as a significant consideration that weighs in during the balancing of considerations when determining whether or not an eviction order should be granted. It displays a meaningful awareness and appreciation of religious diversity, the impact of which was considerable in the life of the wife and the parties' children. Should a court be faced with an action to enforce a *mahr* obligation, there is little doubt that given the principles relating to religious diversity that the judiciary have accepted thus far and in light of precedent that has been set regarding the enforceability of terms, customs and conditions of a Muslim marriage contract, such an action would succeed if sufficient evidence is adduced.

More recently in the case of *Isaacs*, a Muslim ex-husband again tried to use the PIE to evict his ex-wife from their marital home. The facts in *Isaacs* were similar

72 *Arendse* at para 36.
73 *Arendse* at para 44.
74 *Arendse* at para 36.

to those in *Arendse*, and with the precedent set by *Arendse* and a whole body of cases in which the jurisprudence in respect of the PIE has been developed,[75] which are not pertinent to the analysis in this chapter, the ex-husband did not enjoy any success at the magistrate's court level.

Isaacs v. Isaacs

In *Isaacs*, the parties were married to each other in June 2000 by Muslim rites only.[76] Two children were born during the marriage.[77] The parties were divorced under Muslim law in August 2013.[78] Subsequent to the Muslim divorce, the ex-wife continued living in the marital home with the two children. Due to the ill-health of one of the children, the ex-wife discontinued her employment to take care of the child and the household on a full-time basis.[79] Thereafter, the ex-husband married someone else and sought to evict his ex-wife from what was their marital home so that he could live there with his new wife and the two children from his previous marriage to his ex-wife.[80]

The marital home from which the ex-husband wished to evict his ex-wife was purchased from the proceeds of property (hereafter referred to as the 'first property') that had been jointly acquired by the parties. However, because the parties were not regarded as being legally married to each other, the housing policy of the Cape Town City Council at that time precluded the first property from being registered in both their names; it could only be registered in the ex-husband's name.

After considering sections 4(6) and 4(7) of the PIE, the Goodwood Magistrate's Court decided that although the ex-wife was an unlawful occupier in terms of the PIE, her eviction was not just and equitable because she was 'a single mother heading the household singlehandedly', she had been discriminated against on the basis of gender and religion when the first property had been purchased, 'the consequences of the divorce according to Muslim Rights [was] . . . unfair and discriminatory', and it would not be in the best interests of the children to evict her.

This time, the Goodwood Magistrate's Court interpreted sections 4(6) and 4(7) correctly. However, it did not provide any information to explain its view that the Muslim divorce had discriminated against the ex-wife so it is unclear how it came to that position. Nevertheless, the fact that it regarded the Muslim divorce as being discriminatory against the ex-wife as a consideration for sections 4(6) and 4(7) of the PIE is significant because along with the consideration of *mahr* as explicated in the *Arendse* matter, it may serve as a deterrent to Muslim men against using the PIE to attempt to evict their ex-wives from their marital or family homes.

75 *Arendse* at paras 31–35, 45.
76 *Isaacs* at p1.
77 *Isaacs* at p1.
78 *Isaacs* at p1.
79 *Isaacs* at p2.
80 *Isaacs* at p1–2.

In addition to the circumstances described thus far in all of the aforementioned cases where the South African judiciary has attempted to provide relief to marginalised and vulnerable women who were married by Muslim rites, the judiciary has also intervened in the domain of succession to come to the aid of Muslim widows who were previously denied the right to inherit from their deceased spouses' estates in circumstances where the deceased had died without a will. In this respect, two seminal cases, namely, *Daniels* and *Hassam*, must be considered.

Daniels v. Campbell NO and Others and Hassam v. Jacobs NO and Others

In both *Daniels* and *Hassam*, the parties had been married to their deceased husbands by Muslim rites. The main distinguishing feature between *Daniels* and *Hassam* was that the parties' Muslim marriage in *Daniels* had been *de facto* monogamous while the marriage between the parties in *Hassam* had been *de facto* polygynous. In both cases, the Muslim widows had asked the Master of the High Court to recognise them as 'surviving spouses' for the purposes of the Intestate Succession Act (ISA) 81 of 1987 and the Maintenance of Surviving Spouses Act (MSSA) 27 of 1990 so that they could respectively inherit intestate and be maintained from their deceased husbands' estates. However, since Muslim marriages are not recognised as legally valid, the Master of the High Court did not regard a Muslim widow or widower as a 'surviving spouse' for the purposes of the ISA and the MSSA.[81] The two cases were adjudicated separately where the Muslim widows respectively challenged the constitutionality of the aforementioned statutes on the basis that they unfairly discriminated against parties within Muslim marriages.[82]

The Constitutional Court in *Daniels*, decided prior to *Hassam*, found that the legislation was not unconstitutional because the word 'spouse' within its ordinary meaning (as it appears in the ISA and the MSSA) includes parties to a Muslim marriage.[83] The Court found that their previous exclusion from the word 'spouse':

> emanated from a linguistically strained use of the word flowing from a culturally and racially hegemonic appropriation of it. Such interpretation owed more to the artifice of prejudice than to the dictates of the English language. Both in intent and impact the restricted interpretation was discriminatory, expressly exalting a particular concept of marriage, flowing initially from a particular world-view, as the ideal against which Muslim marriages were measured and found to be wanting. Discriminatory interpretations deeply injurious to those negatively affected were in the conditions of the time widely accepted in the court. They are no longer sustainable in the light of our

81 *Daniels* at para 8; *Hassam* at para 3.

82 *Daniels* at para 8; *Hassam* at paras 6, 9.

83 *Daniels* at para 19.

> Constitution . . . In the present matter the constitutional values of equality, tolerance and respect for diversity point strongly in favour of giving the word 'spouse' a broad and inclusive construction, the more so when it corresponds with the ordinary meaning of the word. The issue is not whether to impose some degree of strain on the language in order to achieve a constitutionally acceptable result. It is whether to remove the strain imposed by past discriminatory interpretations in favour of its ordinary meaning.[84]

In contrast, the Constitutional Court in *Hassam* found that the ordinary meaning of the word 'spouse' as it appears in the statutes is incapable of being understood to include more than one spouse presumably because the original intent behind the usage of the word denotes a spouse in a monogamous marriage.[85] Notably, the Court observed that existing wives who find themselves in polygynous marriages often lack the power to influence their husbands' decisions to take a subsequent wife.[86]

The Court held that the exclusion of Muslim polygynous widows from the ambit of the statutes constituted unjustifiably unfair discrimination on the grounds of gender, marital status and religion vis-à-vis spouses who are able to benefit from the statutes.[87] The gendered nature of the unfair discrimination relates to Muslim widowers being permitted to benefit from the legislation since their wives are not allowed under Islamic law to have multiple spouses hence only wives in polygynous Muslim marriages are excluded from benefitting.[88] Marital status as a ground for unfair discrimination was recognised since wives in polygynous Muslim marriages did not receive the same protection as wives in civil marriages, polygynous customary marriages and monogamous Muslim marriages.[89] Religion was identified as a ground for unfair discrimination since Islam was historically marginalised in South Africa as a religion that was not considered worthy of respect.[90]

In particular, the Court held that the purpose of the legislation would be frustrated and the achievement of substantive equality would be negated if Muslim polygynous widows continued to be excluded from the ambit of the legislation.[91] In the Court's opinion:

> The effect of the failure to afford the benefits of the Act to widows of polygynous Muslim marriages will generally cause widows significant and material disadvantage of the sort which it is the express purpose of our equality provision to avoid . . . refusing appropriate protection to those women who are

84 *Daniels* at paras 19–21.
85 *Hassam* at para 48.
86 *Hassam* at para 38.
87 *Hassam* at paras 6, 9.
88 *Hassam* at paras 34, 36.
89 *Hassam* at para 34.
90 *Hassam* at para 34.
91 *Hassam* at para 38.

> parties to such marriages . . . would be to lose sight of a key message of our Constitution: each person is of equal worth and must be treated accordingly . . . By discriminating against women in polygynous Muslim marriages on the grounds of religion, gender and marital status, the Act clearly reinforces a pattern of stereotyping and patriarchal practices that relegates women in these marriages to being unworthy of protection.[92]

Without expressing an opinion on the constitutionality of polygyny per se,[93] the Court decided that the statutes were unconstitutional and read in the word 'spouses' after each appearance of the word 'spouse' to cure the legislative defect.[94] *Hassam* and *Daniels* therefore set the precedent for monogamous and polygynous Muslim widows to inherit from and be maintained by their deceased spouses' intestate estates.

The issue of intestate succession for a Muslim widow arose again in the context of the *Faro* case but this time the determining issue related to the validity of the *talāq*, which had been issued against the Muslim widow by her deceased husband while he was alive.

Faro v. Bingham

In *Faro*, the parties had been married to each other by Muslim rites only.[95] Two minor children were involved; one born prior to their marriage and one during the course of their marriage.[96] The deceased had also had an adult son and an adult daughter from a previous marriage.[97] While the widow was pregnant with their second child, the deceased had obtained a *talāq* certificate from the Muslim Judicial Council (MJC).[98] The widow claimed that during her *iddah* period, the parties reconciled, which revoked the *talāq* and allowed the marriage to remain intact.[99] After the deceased's death, the widow was appointed executrix of her deceased husband's estate and considered herself to be a surviving spouse in terms of the Intestate Succession Act (ISA) 81 of 1987 and the Maintenance of Surviving Spouses Act (MSSA) 27 of 1990.[100] What followed was a sequence of events that could have been taken directly from a television soap opera.

In an attempt to prevent the widow from inheriting as an intestate spouse, the deceased's adult daughter approached the MJC for an affidavit declaring that the marriage between the widow and her deceased husband had been annulled and

92 *Hassam* at paras 34–35, 37.
93 *Hassam* at para 35.
94 *Hassam* at paras 48, 53.
95 *Faro* at para 2.
96 *Faro* at para 2.
97 *Faro* at para 2.
98 *Faro* at para 3.
99 *Faro* at para 4.
100 *Faro* at para 6.

that they were therefore not married at the date of the deceased's death.[101] On the basis of the *talāq* certificate that the MJC had issued to the deceased husband while the latter was alive, the MJC provided the affidavit as requested by the deceased's adult daughter.[102] Subsequently, the widow, the deceased's adult son and a social worker provided affidavits to the MJC confirming that the parties had reconciled during the widow's *iddah* period.[103] Consequently, the MJC withdrew its previous affidavit and provided a letter indicating that the parties had still been married to each other when the deceased had died.[104] However, the deceased's adult son then changed his position and provided further affidavits to the MJC, in which he claimed that the parties had not reconciled during the widow's *iddah* period.[105] As a result, the MJC reconfirmed its former position that the marriage between the parties had been irrevocably terminated through the *talāq*.[106] In the meantime, the widow and her two minor children were forcibly removed from the marital home by the deceased's adult children with the result that the minor children were taken into state care and the widow was homeless and living on the streets and in shelters.[107] On the basis of the MJC's confirmation that the marriage had been annulled at the time of the deceased's death, the Master of the High Court did not regard the widow to be a surviving spouse and required her to furnish security for the administration of the deceased's estate.[108] The widow was unable to provide the security and was therefore removed as executrix of her deceased husband's estate.[109]

The widow challenged the Master's decision in the Western Cape High Court and also asked for a declaratory order that her Muslim marriage be recognised as legally valid. The Court assessed the factual evidence that had been placed before it and decided that the Muslim marriage had not been annulled at the date of the deceased's death. It therefore confirmed her status as a surviving spouse, especially for the purposes of the ISA and the MSSA. With regard to the widow's declaratory order, the Court decided to postpone judgment pending a report from the South African government on the progress of the Muslim Marriages Bill.[110] The latter was drafted by the South African Law Reform Commission and submitted to the Ministry of Justice and Constitutional Development in 2003. It was amended by the Department of Justice and Constitutional Development in 2009 and approved by Cabinet in 2010. To date, however, the Bill has not yet

101 *Faro* at para 5.
102 *Faro* at para 5.
103 *Faro* at para 6.
104 *Faro* at para 6.
105 *Faro* at para 7.
106 *Faro* at para 7.
107 *Faro* at para 9.
108 *Faro* at para 10.
109 *Faro* at para 10.
110 The Muslim Marriages Bill is available at www.justice.gov.za/legislation/bills/2010_muslim-marriages-bill.pdf. Accessed on 18 December 2014.

been enacted.[111] Judgment regarding the legal validity of the widow's Muslim marriage to her deceased husband is also still pending.

Two pertinent issues arise from the *Faro* case,[112] which are relevant for the analysis in this chapter. First, the case confirms anecdotal evidence that prevails within the Cape Town Muslim community that the MJC functions in an arbitrary manner, which 'usually militates against Muslim women'.[113] Second, by substituting its own judgment above that of the MJC regarding the validity of the *talāq*, the Court indicated a willingness to enter the religious arena, which the South African judiciary has thus far been hesitant to do.[114] It would be interesting to see with future cases if the *Faro* case has created a precedent for the departure by the South African judiciary from its approach of non-entanglement with religious doctrine.

From the perusal of the case law discussed thus far, it is clear that the judiciary has, since the advent of democracy and the introduction of constitutional principles and human rights law in South Africa in 1994, been proactive about providing relief to women who suffer marginalisation as a result of their Muslim marriages not being legally recognised. Yet, judicial intervention is limited to the extent that relief can only be sought and granted on a case-by-case basis. So for those women who do not have the financial and emotional resources to pursue legal action for their Muslim marriage related claims, access to justice becomes a pipedream. The enactment of legislation to recognise and regulate Muslim marriages is therefore necessary. Until then, however, Muslim parties should utilise the opportunity created by *Ryland* when, as indicated previously, the Court recognised the Muslim marriage as a contract and was willing to enforce proven terms and customs arising from the contract.

The unfortunate reality in South Africa is that parties seldom enter into written Muslim marriage contracts. Usually, only a marriage certificate is issued by the officiating *imām*, which records the parties' names, the names of the bride's *wali* (guardian) and/or *waqīl* (representative), the date and place of the marriage and the particulars of the *mahr*. So essentially, *mahr* is the only term of the contract that is specifically recorded. That means that provisions of the marriage contract that are not recorded are regulated by the default Islamic law position, many of which militate against women. For instance, while the obligation of the husband

111 For a discussion about the Muslim Marriages Bill, see Waheeda Amien, 'Overcoming the Conflict between the Right to Religious Freedom and Women's Rights to Equality – a South African Case Study of Muslim Marriages', *Human Rights Quarterly* 28 (2006) 729–754; Waheeda Amien, 'A South African Case Study for the Recognition and Regulation of Muslim Family Law in a Minority Muslim Secular Context', *International Journal of Law, Policy and the Family* 24:3 (2010) 361–396.

112 For a more detailed analysis of the *Faro* judgment, see Waheeda Amien, 'The Viability for Women's Rights of Incorporating Islamic Inheritance Laws into the South African Legal System', *Acta Juridica* (2014) 192–218, 213–217.

113 Waheeda Amien, 'The Viability for Women's Rights of Incorporating Islamic Inheritance Laws into the South African Legal System', *Acta Juridica* (2014) 192–218, 216.

114 See *Taylor* v. *Kurtstag NO and Others* 2005 (1) SA 362 (W) at para 61.

to provide *mahr* and *nafaqah* might be of financial benefit to the wife, they elicit concomitant obligations by the wife to be sexually subservient and obedient to her husband.[115] Polygyny is also permitted by the South African *ulamā* and practised without regulation within the Muslim community. While divorce options are available to women under Islamic law, it is very difficult for South African women to access those options mainly due to patriarchal approaches of religious bodies and religious leaders to Islamic law, whereby women are seldom able to exit their marriages without their husbands' permission or the authorisation of religious leaders or religious bodies. Furthermore, upon dissolution of the marriage, a conservative understanding of Islamic law does not afford equal rights of guardianship, custody and access of minor children born of the marriage to women.[116]

Women could thus protect themselves against potentially harmful Islamic law rules and practices by incorporating provisions that exclude or amend the default Islamic law position as understood by most religious leaders in the community. For example, they could stipulate that the payment of *mahr* and *nafaqah* does not require their sexual subservience and obedience and that they be permitted to work outside the home and engage in academic studies of their choosing without requiring their husbands' permission, failing which they would have grounds for being released from the marriage. They could

115 Mir-Hosseini observes that when agreement is reached regarding the payment of *mahr*, the husband has a right to *tamkin* (submission), which is unimpeded sexual access to his wife. In other words, the wife has a duty to make herself sexually available to her husband unless his sexual demands are made at an Islamically impermissible time, for example when she is menstruating. If a wife exercises *nushūz* (disobedience), her husband may chastise her and she may lose her right to receive *nafaqah*. Mir-Hosseini, 13. See also *Qur'ān* 2:222: 'They ask thee concerning women's courses. Say: They are a hurt and a pollution: So keep away from women in their courses, and do not approach them until they are clean. But when they have purified themselves, ye may approach them in any manner, time, or place ordained for you by God.' *Qur'ān* 2:223: 'Your wives are as a tilth unto you: So approach your tilth when or how ye will.' *Qur'ān* 4:34: 'Men are the protectors and maintainers of women, because God has given the one more (strength) than the other, and because they support them from their means. Therefore the righteous women are devoutly obedient, and guard in (the husband's) absence what God would have them guard. As to those women on whose part ye fear disloyalty and ill-conduct, admonish them (first), (next), refuse to share their beds, (and last) beat them lightly; but if they return to obedience, seek not against them means (of annoyance).' Sabiq suggests that *ahadīth* records the following two sayings of Prophet Muhammad: 'The best of the women is that, if you look at her she pleases you, and if you command her she obeys you, and if you are away from her she safeguards you in her soul and in your property.' And: 'If the woman prays five times, and she fasts her month, protects her vulva, and she obeys her husband, it was said to her: Enter the Paradise from any door of the doors of Paradise you desire.' Sabiq, 105.

116 The husband has sole guardianship rights during marriage and upon dissolution of the marriage. In the latter case, the wife has custodial rights in certain circumstances depending on the sex and age of the child. For instance, a wife has custody over a male child until he is seven or pubescent and over a female child until she is pubescent or married, depending on which Islamic *madhhab* applies. Sabiq, 219–220. Schacht, 35, 167. Esposito and DeLong-Bas, 35. Fyzee, 189. Tahir Mahmood, 'Islamic Family Law: Latest Developments in India', in Chibli Mallat and Jane Connors (eds) *Islamic Family Law* (USA: Kluwer Academic Publishers Group, 1990) 295–311: 301.

similarly include equal divorce options for themselves that do not require their husbands' and/or the *ulamā*'s permission. The marriage contract could also regulate polygyny and enable women to exit the marriage in the event that their husbands enter into polygynous marriages. If a contract contains a provision that entitles a woman to be released from the marriage in the event that her husband enters into a subsequent marriage, religious leaders would be obliged to enforce it and recognise an Islamic divorce for the woman. Women like the ex-wife in *Ryland* would further be able to claim for an equitable division of their husbands' estates if a clause making provision for that were included in a marriage contract. Moreover, the contract could stipulate that a woman would have equal rights to guardianship, custody and access of the minor children during the subsistence of the marriage and upon its dissolution. At a time when sexually transmitted diseases are rife and in light of the HIV/AIDS pandemic, parties (particularly in polygynous marriages) may additionally want to consider including an undertaking to undergo regular testing for STDs. Should the husband fail to honour that undertaking, the contract could afford the wife the right to exit the marriage.[117]

Despite the option afforded by Islamic law for parties to enter into written marriage contracts and to regulate their marriages through agreement and in accordance with their own wishes, as mentioned previously, it is uncommon for South African Muslims to enter into written marriage contracts. As indicated in the introduction to this chapter, this is partly due to a lack of agency on the part of women, which is sometimes depicted by women tending to more easily sacrifice their expectations of marriage than men do. This observation is illustrated in the next section, which relays a few personal narratives of some women who were contemplating entering into a Muslim marriage.

Personal narratives

The following narratives are derived from discussions that I have had with Muslim women in South Africa through my lectures and consultations. Each narrative depicts the significance of agency for women.

Fatima

Fatima was raised in a lower middle class family. After completing high school, she had been employed for a number of years and continued to enjoy a lower middle class lifestyle before she met her fiancé, Zain. They were due to be wed so Fatima approached me to draft a Muslim marriage contract on their behalf. Since they were both living in another city, I engaged in telephonic consultations with Fatima. I advised her of their civil and Islamic law rights and then proceeded to draft the contract according to her instructions, which provided various measures

117 See a draft Muslim marriage contract compiled by the author available at https://uct.academia.edu/WaheedaAmien/Papers. Accessed on 19 December 2014.

of protection for Fatima including in the event that Zain took a subsequent wife. Fatima advised that Zain had had insight into the provisions of the contract and was in agreement with all of them.

Unfortunately, on the morning of the wedding day, the contract did not reach the mosque for signature by Zain before the *nikāh* was performed. There appeared to be no untoward reason for the contract having being left behind while everyone had made her or his way to the mosque. After all the wedding festivities were concluded for the day, the contract surfaced and was presented to Zain for signature to which he duly responded: 'I do not need to sign that anymore; I'm already married to her.'

Rukayya

Rukayya was raised in a working class family and found employment immediately after completing her high school education. A few years later, she met and became engaged to Fu'aad who similarly grew up in a working class family. Rukayya was encouraged by her mother to approach me for assistance with drafting a Muslim marriage contract because she (Rukayya's mother) had experienced the rigours of a Muslim divorce. I informed Rukayya about how the marriage contract could protect her and what the possible consequences could be if she were to find herself in a situation without a marriage contract and the marriage did not work out. After listening quite attentively to all the options I put to her, Rukayya conveyed the information to Fu'aad. He refused to enter into a written agreement and the marriage commenced without a written contract.

Layla

Layla was raised in a middle class family. After completing her tertiary education, she worked for a few years during which time she amassed a sizeable estate. On the other hand, her fiancé, Usman, was raised in a working class family and hardly had any estate attached to his name.

Layla convinced Usman that they needed to enter into a Muslim marriage contract and approached me to draft one for them. After advising her of the options available under Islamic law as well as civil law, I took instructions from her and proceeded to draft a contract, which I presented to both of them for feedback. Although the contract included provisions that recognised and protected Layla's rights and benefits under Islamic law, Usman felt that it was weighted heavily in her favour. They re-negotiated the contract and agreed that the maintenance obligations should be reciprocal since both would be working and contributing to the maintenance of their household.

Hashim

Hashim's future father-in-law had had a Muslim marriage contract drawn up to ensure that his daughter, Sadia, would be protected. Hashim's mother had been concerned that the contract had been weighted too heavily in Sadia's favour and had asked me to provide a legal opinion on the contract. After perusing the contract, I advised Hashim's mother that the contract had simply set out Sadia's rights under Islamic law and that Hashim had not been disadvantaged in any way. Still not satisfied, Hashim's mother advised him not to sign the contract and informed Sadia's family that the marriage would have to proceed without the written contract. Sadia then decided to go ahead with the marriage ceremony in the absence of a signed marriage contract.

Farhana

One evening after having delivered a lecture on Muslim marriages within the Cape Town Muslim community, I was approached by one of the attendees, Farhana, who told me the following story: She had been party to a very unhappy marriage for several years and had tried unsuccessfully to get her husband to *talāq* her. She had also failed to obtain *faskh*[118] from members of the *ulamā* despite having approached them many times. During the course of her marriage, she came across *hādīth* in which a woman had approached Prophet Muhammad and informed him that she no longer wished to be married to her husband. The Prophet required her to give back her *mahr* and instructed her husband to divorce her.[119]

The above *hādīth* describes the process of *khul'a*, which is an extra-judicial form of dissolving a marriage at the instance of a wife.[120] There is a dispute about whether or not a lawful *khul'a* requires the husband's consent. Muslim-majority countries such as Egypt, Nigeria, Bangladesh, Pakistan and the Philippines do not

118 *Faskh* is a fault-based judicial (*tafriq*) form of dissolution of the marriage that requires either a husband or wife to apply to a *qadi* (judge) for an order of divorce by proving some fault on the part of her or his spouse e.g. failure of the husband to comply with his maintenance obligations; impotence; desertion; imprisonment; mental illness; apostasy; discord etc. In the case of a wife, she runs the risk of having to pay some form of financial compensation such as forfeiting her *mahr* claim in order to be released from the marriage. Neither spouse requires the other's consent to be granted a *faskh*. Doi, 170–172. Sabiq, 51. John L. Esposito, *Islam, the Straight Path* (New York and Oxford: Oxford University Press), 78, 83. Pearl, 108–109.

119 The *hādīth* that Farhana referred to is cited in Bukhari, *Book of Divorce. The Sahih Collection of al-Bukhari* at 4971 as follows: 'It is related from Ibn 'Abbas that the wife of Thabit ibn Qays came to the Prophet, may Allah bless him and grant him peace, and said, "I not do criticise Thabit ibn Qays for his character or his *deen*, but I dislike ingratitude in Islam." The Messenger of Allah, may Allah bless him and grant him peace, said, "Will you return his garden to him?" "Yes," she answered. The Messenger of Allah, may Allah bless him and grant him peace, said, "Accept your garden and divorce her once." Abu 'Abdullah [al-Bukhari] said, "It is uninterrupted from Ibn 'Abbas."' Translated by Aisha Bewley. www.sunnipath.com/library/Hadith/H0002P0071.aspx. Accessed 11 November 2012.

120 Sabiq, 51. Ibn Rushd, 75. Pearl, 102. Doi, 192. Schacht, 164. Ahmad, 219–220. Vijay Malik, *Muslim Law of Marriage, Divorce and Maintenance* (Lucknow: Eastern Book Company, 1961), 99.

require his consent.[121] But most members of the South African *ulamā* adopt the interpretation that his consent is required.[122]

However, Farhana explained that after reading the *hādīth*, her understanding was that she did not need anyone's permission to exit the marriage. So she gave back her *mahr* to her husband, left the marital home and proceeded to move on with her life. In her mind, she had affected a lawful dissolution of her marriage.

Discussion

Farhana's story is a powerful one of a woman who, through self-education about her Islamic law options, claimed and asserted her agency. In this way, she was able to exit her marriage without feeling the need to obtain her husband's or *imām*'s permission. This seems to suggest that an important component of accessing agency is being educated about one's Islamic law rights and options. This is especially true since in the face of differing interpretations of religious law, religious leaders usually adopt the interpretation that most favours men in an attempt to maintain patriarchal control over the religious community.[123] Hence, Fareeda Shaheed observes:

> It is by opening doors to a multiplicity of possible alternatives that the WLUML [Women Living Under Muslim Laws] network hopes to make its most important contribution, by furnishing women with information and the tangible and less tangible support they need to think the unthinkable, to question what is taken for granted, and to start assuming the right to define for themselves the parameters of their own identity and thereby that of their community.[124]

Although education is an important mechanism to make women (and men) aware that multiple interpretations of Islamic law exist, I have found through my awareness-raising initiatives and consultations with women that education itself is not enough to enable them to assert their agency. Rukayya's story exemplifies this point. Despite having been informed about all her rights under South African law and Islamic law, she still chose to proceed without a marriage contract simply because her husband-to-be objected to having one. She had witnessed the difficulties and abuse that her mother had experienced in her own marriage and while undergoing her divorce. So at some level, Rukayya was aware of the need for a marriage contract. Yet, it was more important to her to be married to her fiancé

121 Women Living Under Muslim Laws, *Knowing our Rights: Women, Family, Laws and Customs in the Muslim World* (London: Women Living Under Muslim Laws, 2003), 278–279.

122 This is evident in the definition of *khul'a* that is adopted in clause 1 of the Muslim Marriages Bill, 2010.

123 Fareeda Shaheed, 'Constructing Identities: Culture, Women's Agency and the Muslim World', 51 (1999) *International Social Science Journal* 159, 61–73: 69.

124 Shaheed, 72.

than to ensure that she had a marriage contract that protected her rights. I have heard many women on countless occasions say that they trust that God will ensure that their marital rights are protected. In reality, this view camouflages the fact that they have submitted to a flagrant exercise of power by men who will eventually become their husbands.

Being able to claim one's power must therefore be another component of agency. In the context of marriage, a woman's negotiating power is strongest before the marriage contract is signed as indicated by Fatima's story where the husband's incentive to enter into the marriage contract disappeared after the *nikāh* was concluded. At the same time, Layla's story demonstrates that even when the male is willing to enter into a marriage contract prior to the *nikāh*, he could insist that it be on his terms. For all intents and purposes, Layla was the financially stronger one in the relationship and although she had initiated the drafting process for a marriage contract, she was willing to forfeit her expectations to make her fiancé happy. Some would say that demonstrates the extent of her love for him. But surely his acquiescence of her expectations would have demonstrated his love for her? Why was she expected to compromise her expectations of the contract and he was not similarly expected to do so?

External forces in the form of the older generation could also determine if and to what extent women assert agency. For instance, Sadia's father recognised a need for his daughter's Islamic law marital rights to be explicitly protected in a written marriage contract and forwarded a contract that he had had drafted to Hashim for signature. Sadia's father had therefore assumed agency on behalf of his daughter. However, Hashim's mother decided that the contract incorporated too many Islamic law rights for her future daughter-in-law and prevented her son from signing it. This is also an example of the way in which women (and not just men) are capable of reinforcing the oppression of other women.

Merry distinguishes between an autonomous self and a relational self. She suggests that when a person asserts her or his autonomous self, in other words, asserts her or his agency, she or he runs the risk of being rejected from relationships. In contrast, reliance on the relational self affords a person the opportunity to stay connected to 'a network of relationships' but that simultaneously 'requires compliance with the obligations of [those] relationships'.[125] In Farhana's case, she chose to assert her autonomous self even though she ran the risk of being isolated from her community. In the other examples described above, the women sacrificed their autonomous selves in favour of their relational selves because the option of being married under circumstances that they may not have been entirely satisfied with outweighed the prospect of not being married at all. Such an outcome was the result of empowerment being overshadowed by paternalism thereby negating agency to the women.[126]

125 Engle Merry, 404.
126 Engle Merry, 400.

Conclusion

Although a process has been initiated for legislation to be enacted to recognise Muslim marriages, it is unclear whether or not such legislation will ever see the light of day. In the absence of legislation that can provide automatic protection for women's Muslim marital rights, the only other option to enforce those rights is through written marriage contracts given that the South African judiciary has appropriately seen fit to recognise them. Yet, few South African Muslims appear to avail themselves of this option. In those instances where they do, it seems that the bridegroom and/or his family generally dictate the terms of the contract.

Although this study highlights the gendered nature of power in the context of Muslim family law in South Africa, it raises more questions than it has the potential to answer. For instance, why does entering Muslim marriage contracts appear to be the exception rather than the norm for South African Muslims? What are the reasons that women do not assert their agency for the purposes of entering into marriage contracts? What informs the negotiating power between couples before they enter marriage? For these questions to be answered, follow-up research is required within the South African Muslim community. It is my hope that this chapter has at least laid the foundation for such comprehensive research to be undertaken.

4 Decoding diversity

Experiences with personal law in the lower courts of Maharashtra

*Kalindi Kokal**

Introduction

This study evolves out of a pilot empirical study conducted in the lower tier of courts of Maharashtra. Maharashtra is located in the Western part of India. It has a total population of 112 million people.[1] According to the 2001 census, 10.6 per cent of the population comprised Muslims, 1.1 per cent are Christians, 0.056 per cent are Parsis, 6 per cent are Buddhists and 0.2 per cent are Sikhs.[2] The 2011 census figures concerning religion-wise distribution of population at the state level are yet to be made available.

Data collected through ground level observation and interactions with litigants and lawyers in three *taluka*[3] courts and with sitting and retired judges of different lower courts reveals that the proportion of civil litigation initiated by members of religious minorities and particularly that involving application of the personal law is significantly small in the lower courts.[4] Judges and lawyers broadly define the

* The author is presently a PhD candidate at the Max Planck Institute for Social Anthropology in Halle (Saale), Germany. The author would like to thank Prof. Werner Menski for motivating the pursuit of this research; and Prof. Marie-Claire Foblets, Dr Shirish Kavadi and Mr Prafulla Parekh, for their encouragement and support. All of their comments were crucial to the development of this chapter. The author would also like to acknowledge the support she received from all the judges, lawyers and litigants who spared time from their busy schedules to share their experience and insights for the purpose of this research study.

1 'Maharashtra Population Census Data 2011', accessed 19 January 2014, www.census2011.co.in/census/state/maharashtra.html.

2 National Commission for Minorities, *Proportion and Growth Rate of Population by Religious Communities, India, 1961–2001*, accessed 19 January 2014, http://ncm.nic.in/minority_population.pdf.

3 States in India are divided into districts, which are further sub-divided into sub-district or *talukas*. Districts and *talukas* are administrative divisions within a district. Every *taluka* – administrative block – has a court. In some instances, where a *taluka* may not have a large population, it shares a court with the neighbouring *taluka*. The *talukas* studied here have a fair population of religious minorities and particularly Muslims.

4 The Family Courts Act, 1984 provides for family courts to be established in every town that has a population of more than one million. However, family courts are most often not the court of first instance because they are usually located at the district headquarter and litigants may be deterred from a filing cases in such a court because of the expenditure of time and money that would result from pursuing a case located at a far distance. Since the family court was not studied as a part of

quantity of litigation initiated by religious minority groups in a particular court to be determined by the population of a religious minority group in the said jurisdiction of the court concerned, the levels of literacy within such a group and the extent of their financial means.[5] While the amount of litigation involving application of the personal law can be said to be dependent on the above factors, there are also other elements of political and social nature as well as the dynamics of the working of a particular court that influence such choices.

Based on the empirical evidence, it is observed that *taluka* courts in Maharashtra seem to be struggling with the effective application of personal laws of religious minorities. I perceive that the low instances of litigation in the lower court requiring application of personal laws of religious minority groups is a cause as well as a result of why judges and lawyers (both from within and outside religious minority groups) in the *taluka* courts remain wary of using and applying the personal law. This situation is quite paradoxical considering that the Constitution provides for citizens of India, including religious minorities, to be governed by their respective personal laws in the broader realm of the goals of justice and equality.

There is evidence that litigants from religious minority groups do access, sometimes in the first and many times in the only instance, alternate fora of dispute resolution which are often run and managed by members from their own religious community.[6] These alternate fora more often than not are known to resolve disputes within the broader cultural precincts of their respective communities. They innovatively and strategically use and interpret personal laws, customs and norms to conciliate between the parties.[7] On gaining an insight into the experiences of litigants who have approached both the court and such alternative forums, it comes to light that these fora are perceived to be easily accessible because they are inexpensive, but more importantly because of the methods they adopt to process disputes and the familiarity of their presiding members with the socio-cultural contexts of such disputes.[8] These factors make such alternative fora more appealing. However, due to structural problems including the lack of legal recognition of their awards/decisions and the fear of conservative biases or prejudices overshadowing their decision-making processes, many members of religious minority groups are inclined to approach the formal judiciary as a second resort; women being the largest of such a section.

this study, we cannot over rule the possibility that where, in a jurisdiction that comprises of both a *taluka* court and a family court, the reason for a low number of family related disputes to be filed in the *taluka* court, may be due to the overlapping jurisdiction of the family court, where such cases may have been filed.

5 Research interview with a judge, 24.12.2011.

6 Gopika Solanki, *Adjudication in Religious Family Laws: Cultural Accommodation, Legal Pluralism, and Gender Equality in India* (Cambridge: Cambridge University Press, 2011); Yüksel Sezgin, *Human Rights under State-Enforced Religious Family Laws in Israel, Egypt and India* (Cambridge: Cambridge University Press, 2013).

7 Sezgin, *Human Rights under State-Enforced Religious Family Laws in Israel, Egypt and India.*

8 Ibid., 196.

In light of this evidence it is argued that there is a need for an appropriate structural balance to ensure more effective application of personal laws, while taking care to do so without fossilising them. I, therefore, submit that in the present scenario it is important that the formal judiciary establishes a dialogue with non-state alternative fora being managed by religious minorities in order to work out a dynamic approach of applying personal laws in the correct spirit of justice and pluralism. As to whether such an approach will actually result in more creative interpretations of the state enforced personal law[9] and enable decision-makers to view the codified personal law in their dynamic contexts remains to be established through further research, particularly focusing in an in-depth manner on dispute resolution processes of informal dispute resolution forums run by religious minority communities.

This chapter explores how personal law – one of the most central and dynamic interfaces between religion and law in India – is handled by actors in the district and *taluka* courts. The first section of this chapter probes into the history of personal law in India, how it developed and gauges its importance in the socio-cultural context of Indian society. In the second part, the focus lies on understanding how personal law is experienced by lawyers, judges and litigants in the *taluka* courts through the empirical evidence that has been collected. The third part sums up an analysis and conclusion based on the empirical evidence, which is scrutinised in the context of broader concepts such as secularism, religious identity and cultural pluralism.

Methodological background

The data presented in this study are based on fieldwork carried out in two parts. The first part of the fieldwork consisted of preliminary interviews with judges, lawyers and litigants in *taluka* courts located in *taluka*s with a substantial Muslim population. These interviews were initiated on the basis of observations in the field where it was found that even in the courts of *taluka*s comprising a substantial population of religious minorities, the numbers of litigants in that court from such religious minority group were relatively small; in the then case it was Muslims. Additionally, it also came to light that instances involving application of personal law in the *taluka* courts were very rare. This first part of fieldwork was carried out as part of a larger study that focused on access to economic and social rights in the lower courts of India.[10]

Data collected through the preliminary fieldwork called for further enquiry which was undertaken through part two of the fieldwork which was based on a guideline of questions dedicated solely towards understanding the experiences with personal law of litigants, lawyers and judges in *taluka* courts. Since the focus of this study was limited to experiences in *taluka* courts, an attempt has

9 For a better understanding of this term see ibid.

10 For a full report of this study, see Jayanth K. Krishnan *et al.*, 'Grappling at the Grassroots: Access to Justice in India's Lower Tier', *Harvard Human Rights Journal* 27, no. 1 (May 2014): 151 –189.

been made to focus on such *talukas*[11] where the *taluka* court is accessed widely. The empirical evidence presented here is drawn from interactions with about 20 respondents carried out over a total duration of six months. The respondents interviewed included lawyers and litigants in the three *taluka* courts and sitting and retired judges with experiences from postings in several different *taluka* courts.

This study is limited to the extent that it focuses only on litigants who have approached the court; as a result of which the magnitude of experiences of people using personal law outside the scope of the formal judiciary remains to be studied. This study hopes to raise questions that initiate such research in order to gather a more holistic perspective, which at the same time is also comparative.

1. Personal laws in India: a background

In the colonial era

Personal law, in a particular sense, was always a feature of the governance system within Indian society, in that, prior to the Muslim invasions, the Hindus lived under the broad guidance of the *shastras* – which was partly a result of customs systematised, compared and summarily set down. Additionally people were also governed by local customs, which overruled written texts to the extent that they were proved and were still within the rather wide fundamental tenets of the Hindu socio-religious system as expounded by the *shastra*.[12] During the reign of the Muslim rulers, the population of Hindus and Muslims in the subcontinent considered themselves bound by their respective laws, which included religious laws, customs, norms and sometimes a combination of all three. While Shariat was declared as the law of the land, Hindus were more or less left free to be governed by their own religious law except for certain criminal matters. The law governing the individual was not the law of the locality, rather – in the case of Muslims – the law of the *Kazi* to whom s/he applied for resolution of his/her dispute and in the case of Hindus, the principles of the dominant school of law recognized in the region from which such individual originally came.[13] When the British came, even though they claimed to be following the practice of the Muslim rulers, they ensured the administration of personal laws by

11 The terms 'urban' and 'rural' taluka have been used throughout the study. I use the terms urban and rural *talukas* in a very broad sense. In the manner that they are used here, urban *talukas* refer to *talukas* with a high population density, substantial industrialization and many features of development including schools and banks. Rural *talukas* on the other hand, refer to *talukas* that have a low population density, industrialization that may vary from very low scale to nil and mostly lack the presence of the development features that may be noticed in urban areas. It is important to understand these terms in the context that in rural areas, *taluka* courts are mostly the only formally established courts, as against in urban *talukas* where there may be more formally established alternative courts as well.

12 John Duncan Martin Derrett, *Religion, Law and the State in India* (New York: Free Press, 1968), chap. 6.

13 Ibid., 54–55; Archana Parashar, 'Religious Personal Laws as Non-State Laws: Implications for Gender Justice', *The Journal of Legal Pluralism and Unofficial Law* 45, no. 1 (2013): 5–23.

a secular judiciary rather than by members of the religious group themselves like in the time of the Muslim rulers. To enable the European judges to cope with the flood of petitions brought to them by the public, the Administration of Justice regulation of 11 April 1780 was brought into force. This scheme provided for European judges to consult religious scholars of the religion concerned on subjects of inheritance, marriage, caste and other religious usages or institutions. For instance, amongst Hindus, the *shastri-s*, that is, those conversant with the *shastras*, were to be consulted.[14]

Diversity in customary practices motivated continuous attempts towards codification of the natives' laws based on translations of scriptural texts. The works that resulted oftentimes were at variance with the prevailing customs, which led to a divergence in the decisions of the formal courts and customary dispute-resolution forums. Two situations resulted therefrom: where the colonial-era judges realized that the religious laws of the communities were not necessarily scriptural rules, the judges began giving effect to the customs of people. In other instances, since there was no coherent scheme of identifying the religious practices that could be the basis for effective dispute-resolution, the secular judges – who were eventually trained in Common Law – began invoking the doctrine of 'Justice, Equity and Good Conscience' to decide cases where they were faced with uncertainty while choosing between scriptural interpretation and actual customs.[15] Thus the application of Hindu and Islamic laws was transformed through the processes of translation, interpretation and adjudication by British judges and came to be described as Anglo-Hindu and Anglo Mohammadan laws.[16]

Personal laws after independence

The recognition of difference appeared crucial in India after independence due to the complex and cross-cutting variations along the lines of religion, language and caste. The main ways in which cultural specificity was accommodated in India were through the formation of states primarily along linguistic lines; recognition of different official languages by the national and state governments, the introduction and later expansion of preferential policies (and in some states through affirmative action which extended even to religious and linguistic minorities) in higher education and government employment largely based on caste membership (perhaps suggested by income); the provision of political representation and special civil rights protections to the lower castes and tribal groups; the restriction of land rights to the members of certain scheduled tribe groups in the regions of their prolonged habitation; and the continued use of distinct personal laws governing the major religious groups.[17]

14 Derrett, *Religion, Law and the State in India*, chap. 8.

15 K. Balakrishnan, 'Individual Rights in India: A Perspective from the Supreme Court', 2009.

16 Rohit De, 'Personal Laws: A Reality Check', *Frontline*, 21 August 2013.

17 Narendra Subramanian, 'Myths of the Nation, Cultural Recognition and Personal Law in India', in *Whither National Myths? Reflections on the Present and Future of National Myths*, edited

Today, India still recognizes the personal laws of the various religious communities that reside in the country. Consequently, each individual has a right to be governed by his/her personal law in matters of marriage and divorce, infants and minors, adoptions, wills, intestacy and succession. Personal laws reflect a multicultural rule of law giving religious/cultural minorities an opportunity to be governed by their own customs, norms and religious laws. Minorities, defined either numerically or from the point of view of power, stand in special need of having their cultures affirmed by the state. Their sense of worth may be fragile and, understandably, they may be sceptical of the ordinary political process. A system of personal laws helps to affirm the distinct identities of cultural and religious groups, and this is a positive advantage. It is an advantage because in affirming the identities of these groups, the state contributes to the wellbeing of the individuals who compose them.[18] According to Mansfield,[19] the argument that 'pluralism' is the best antidote to alienation and secessionist tendencies may be especially persuasive in the case of minorities.

Along with allowing people in the country to be governed by personal laws, the Constitution of India in Article 44 also directs the state to secure a uniform civil code for the citizens throughout the territory of India.[20] A review of the debates of the Constituent Assembly reveals that there was no intention to force a uniform civil code upon any community that was opposed to it. The hope was rather that change would take place within communities, particularly the Muslim community, so that would bring the members to feel that their own interests would best be served by a uniform civil code. Consequently, the Constitution did not abolish the system of personal laws, but only held forth a uniform civil code as an ideal towards which the state should strive.[21] As it stands today, the Constitution recognizes the existence and permits the continuation of the various personal laws, pending the realization of the goal of a uniform civil code, for which it does not prescribe any time limit. However, there is also increasing secular legislative intervention in the field of family laws and related subjects, as identified in the next section.

Many of the personal laws in India are state made in the sense that modern state institutions, mainly legislatures and courts, have been responsible for the codification of these laws out of a diversity of religious practices and their application to the different communities. In India and elsewhere, personal laws have

by Gérard Bouchard (New York: Routledge, 2013), 9–11, http://nsubramanian.files.wordpress.com/2009/11/myths-of-the-nation-cultural-recognition-and-personal-law-in-india-bouchard-volume-version-ii-docx.pdf.

18 John Mansfield, 'Personal Laws or a Uniform Civil Code?', in *Sociology of Law*, edited by Indra Deva (Oxford University Press, 2005), 180.

19 Ibid., 180.

20 Tahir Mahmood, *Muslim Personal Law: Role of the State in the Subcontinent* (New Delhi: Vikas Pub. House, 1977), chap. 1, http://catalog.hathitrust.org/Record/007848061.

21 Mansfield, 'Personal Laws or a Uniform Civil Code?', 175.

both historically facilitated the consolidation of religious groups, and come to be an important component of their identities.[22]

Personal laws: the grassroots experience

The experience of the judges and lawyers in the lower courts and of the litigants from small *taluka* places is extremely varied with regard to the use and application of personal laws. Personal 'law', which exists more as a legal reality than a lived reality for members of religious minority groups, is used extremely strategically and sometimes conveniently to further personal claims under marriage and succession laws, but more frequently to promote causes related to religious identity in the political spheres.

This section gathers the experiences of people with personal law, the manner in which the concept of personal laws is approached and handled by the lawyers and judges and assesses how it is perceived and negotiated by litigants from religious minority groups.

On the whole the extent of litigation invoking application of the personal law is very small in the *taluka* courts. To begin with, members of religious minority groups do not bring a large number of cases to the formal courts. While members of religious communities may be defendants in criminal litigation, a very small quantity of civil litigation is initiated by members of religious minority communities.[23] In the experience of judges and lawyers, the largest minority community that litigates in the lower court is the Muslim community.

The type of litigation initiated by members of religious communities is observed to be dependent on a variety of factors including the population of a specific religious minority group in a particular jurisdiction, the level of their awareness, their financial circumstances and occupational trends. A senior civil judge has observed that it is men from the Christian and Parsi communities that file petitions for divorce and restitution of conjugal rights. Women from all religious minority groups usually resort to applications for maintenance under Section 125 of the Criminal Procedure Code (CrPC), or suits regarding cruelty under Section 498 of the Indian Penal Code (IPC) or applications under the recent Protection of Women from Domestic Violence Act, 2005 (Domestic Violence Act).[24] According to the observation of a retired district court judge who had been posted to *taluka*s with a large Muslim population, the Muslims who approached the civil court under the general[25] law were usually economically well-established Muslim traders or businessmen. 'They usually come to court for breach of contract or making recovery claims', he explained.[26] These would then not be family law matters.

22 Rochana Bajpai, *Debating Difference: Group Rights and Liberal Democracy in India* (New Delhi: Oxford University Press, 2011), 182.

23 Research interview with judges,23.10.2013; 24.12.2013. Research interview with a lawyer, 03.10.2013.

24 Research interview with a judge, 24.12.2013.

25 By general, this judge meant laws related to company, banking, insurance and such matters.

26 Research interview with a judge, 23.10.2013.

Particular occupational patterns observed in members of certain religious minority communities and more so distinct in the rural areas, were also perceived to be a determinant of the type of litigation filed/not filed by such communities. For instance, in the rural areas that were studied, Muslims were mostly running small businesses and were not observed to be holding substantial pieces of land, if at all. As a result there were few occasions for land disputes to arise within this community, except of course in matters of succession. Similarly in the urban areas, Muslims were involved mostly in tenancy disputes. Their small representation in large corporations and government sectors was a probable factor determining lack of litigation from their community in these areas.[27]

The quantity of litigation invoking personal law, however, is essentially determined by two factors:

1 The initiative of litigants, which fact depends upon their levels of awareness.
2 The discretion of the lawyers who represent litigants belonging to religious minority groups.

How do litigants experience the personal law?

Knowledge about the personal law depends largely upon the levels of literacy and awareness within the religious minority group in an area. It is important to note here that knowledge of one's own personal law need not necessarily imply knowledge about the codified version of such a personal law or the fact that applications under such personal law can be made in the local judicial court. Again, there are differences between the religious personal laws and the customs that people live by. Not all such customs, traditions and rituals emanate from or have a connection to religious personal laws.[28] For instance, a lawyer who has extensive experience in representing litigants in the *taluka* courts of rural Maharashtra explained how, in the case of the Muslim community, people are more inclined to perpetuating rituals and customs or following local interpretations of the personal law without really trying to understand whether that is actually correct or not in strictly Islamic terms. For example:

> They [the Muslim community] are aware that there are many types of Muslim divorces. Sometimes the couple reconciliates at the instance of mediation. But at other times – and [even though] these instances are few – the husband does force the wife to enter a second marriage, consummate it and seek a divorce from the second husband, before he can marry her again. This ritual is [compelled] despite not knowing whether it was actually mandatory under the type of divorce he had given the wife.[29]

27 This was expressed by a senior practising high court lawyer. Research interview with a lawyer, 03.10.2013

28 Research interview with a lawyer, 05.10.2013.

29 Research interview with a lawyer, 05.10.2013.

But whether such need to adhere to local practices arises out of plain ignorance – as is observed by this lawyer, or whether it is rather a matter of strategy to negotiate broader social relations still remains to be studied in more detail. A senior Muslim lawyer, with a long-standing practice in a High Court and other lower courts, stated that the Muslim community shared a strong feeling that they should be free to organize their family life so as for it to be governed by the divine law that is according to the *Quran* and the *hadith*. But, he admitted: 'Often this feeling is abused and followed only conveniently, like when men want to adhere to Muslim personal law only to the extent that it allows polygamy or triple *talaq*; and that I agree is very wrong.'[30] A question that immediately comes to mind is: to what extent does such strategic non-adherence to the religious personal law, whether by actions of the litigant or by a decree of the court, transpire to be many times a dilemma for lawyers and especially for those who may be orthodox or God-fearing? On asking a lawyer in a small *taluka* court located in a largely drought-prone region of Maharashtra about how the dynamics of such a situation work for him, he said: 'It troubles my conscience, but we *have* to earn a livelihood.'[31] And the impacts of earning a livelihood are felt far more greatly; this being evident from the dockets of the few Muslim lawyers in the area who are often pleading for directions from Court that are absolutely contrary to what their religious personal law may be providing for.

In recent years, it can be observed that social institutions that are run and managed by religious minority groups have become more active in spreading awareness about the personal law amongst the members of their community.[32] For instance, between two Muslim female litigants, the one who had attended a government-run school had absolutely no knowledge about personal law and its applicability in her case; whereas the other who was schooled in an Urdu medium school not only had knowledge of Shariat law but also about its applicability in her situation. Explaining her own situation, the litigant who had been educated in the Urdu school narrated that her husband had taken another wife and deserted her for more than seven years. 'In Islam, a man can marry more than once, but only with the permission of his first wife. This usually happens when the [first] wife is infertile. And he is supposed to treat both wives equally', she said.[33] Interestingly, both these litigants were educated up to secondary school and had applications under the same law pending in the same family court.[34]

At another level, in the Muslim community, the All India Muslim Personal Law Board (AIMPLB) was also spoken of as making efforts to make people aware of

30 Research interview with a lawyer, 03.10.2013.

31 Research interview with a lawyer, 02.10.2013, emphasis added.

32 De, 'Personal Laws'.

33 Research interview with a litigant, 21.11.2013.

34 In India, the economic class that an individual belongs to is also perceived to have an impact on the levels of awareness of such an individual. This may be a result of increased exposure, better type of education and different modes of socialization that a person from a higher economic class may experience as compared to one from a lower economic class. In the said example, however, both the female litigants were brought up in an urban *taluka* and belonged to a socio-economic class of a comparable level.

the correct personal law and also trying to encourage the community to desist from actions such as the triple *talaq*. Like the lawyers have correctly observed, there are several misconceptions as regards the personal law at the grassroots level. 'For instance, in many slum areas, dominated by the Muslim community, there is a notion that triple *talaq* is the only correct method of *talaq*', shared a senior Muslim advocate, about his experience in an urban *taluka*, and continued: 'Now this is not true – there are other methods that are more humane and even allow reconciliation, if at all. Therefore the AIMPLB on its part is making an attempt to spread awareness.'[35]

Similarly, in the Christian community, churches have begun to take an initiative in spreading awareness about the personal laws that were in existence and how one could use them. An activist lawyer who is involved with the awareness drive of a Catholic church in her city said: 'The Church organises pre-marital courses for all catholic youth. These courses contain a module on Christian personal law as well.'[36] A litigant, who very reluctantly admitted that she had first approached the priest in the church for a solution to her marital problems, stated that the first time her husband began abusing her, she approached the priest for help. The priest (who is also a counsellor and has good legal knowledge) agreed to counsel her husband.

> I did not want the marriage to break. I thought that this man would improve if the priest spoke to him. A lot of people go to the priest, because there is no concept of divorce in Christianity. Many of them improve, because going against the priest, is like going against God. The priest tried to reason with my husband, but in the end even the priest felt that this man would not improve and advised that I seek divorce from him.[37]

In the end, it was the priest who referred this lady to the lawyer who was presently representing her.

With the spread of literacy and new forms of media, religious authority is being fragmented and new groups are questioning older orthodoxies. Religious institutions are becoming innovative in spreading legal awareness and doing advocacy not by using the language of secularism but by the reinterpretation of religious scriptures and the codes prescribed within them.[38]

Personal law through the eyes of the judges and lawyers

It is the awareness of the litigant on one hand, but also the initiative of the lawyer in filing applications under the personal law on the other hand, which is crucial in determining the quantity of litigation under the personal law.

35 Research interview with a lawyer, 03.10.2013.

36 Research interview with a lawyer, 05.10.2013.

37 Research interview with a litigant, 21.11.2013.

38 Sezgin, *Human Rights under State-Enforced Religious Family Laws in Israel, Egypt and India*; De, 'Personal Laws'.

Using personal law to plead a matter can be quite tricky in matrimony-related disputes. Lawyers in both rural and urban *taluka*s desisted from using personal law in such cases because the validity of a marriage according to a particular custom or ritual is difficult to prove in court. One female lawyer made the point that:

> Proving such a marriage can be quite challenging and the matter [case] can remain pending on this very point for years. In rural areas marriages may not be conducted in a uniform manner, sometime couples elope and merely garland each other in a temple. Now establishing that this marriage is valid according to the personal law under which the lady is claiming rights can be quite difficult. Therefore filing under the regular criminal code or the DV Act [Domestic Violence Act] is quicker and more efficient.[39]

Another reason that lawyers claimed to avoid filing applications under the personal law was because they felt that the judges in the lower courts were not very conversant with the personal laws of religious minorities. While the litigants from such minority communities did not share this feeling, the lawyers felt that lower court judges had very limited or sometimes absolutely no knowledge of the personal laws. Issues arising out of the cultural conditioning of judges themselves coupled with lack of awareness and sensitivity towards the varied cultural contexts of a dispute were perceived by lawyers to impact on decision-making processes and eventually execution or implementation of the decrees. Take the instance of a rural *taluka* court, where one of the reasons cited by Muslim lawyers for the low number of Muslim litigants in court was that judges tended to approach cases involving Muslim litigants and their personal law, in the 'same manner' that they handle cases of Hindu law.[40]

As an explanation of 'in the same manner', an example of succession cases was offered. Under the Muslim personal law, a son of a predeceased son has no share in the grandfather's property, in that he is not an heir to the grandfather's property. A case that was related concerned the dispute of a Muslim man (X) with his son (Y). It was a property dispute, between the man, X, and his son, Y. The son Y died while the case was still pending and the court while processing the application for bringing on record Y's heirs, insisted on adding Y's son Z as an heir, even though a son (in this case Z) does not remain an heir since his father predeceased his grandfather. Lawyers explained that even though this might have been a very technical error and that adding the son's name in the suit would not automatically entitle him to a share, such actions create confusion in further proceedings; parties may take advantage of the larger public's ignorance of Muslim law; *tahsildars* and revenue officers who tend to work very bureaucratically and

39 Research interview with a lawyer, 05.10.2013. Here, this lawyer was referring to an example from the Hindu community.

40 This data is based on various interviews with lawyers in a *taluka* court. Research interview with lawyers, 07.06.2012, 23.11.2011, 11.07.2012.

mindlessly follow the steps of the court, find a reason to add the son's name in the mutation register (similar to the way in which it is done in the majority of Hindu cases); and there is general misapplication of the law.[41]

Evidence in support of the truth in such a claim by the lawyers, comes from the statement of a judge who explained exactly with the same example of a succession dispute, how in certain instances partition disputes between Muslim families were decided in a manner similar to that in Hindu law. This senior district judge, now retired, explained how under Mohammedan law, the son is not entitled to his share in the property while his father is alive. 'But there are instances where sons file cases against their fathers for partition of the property. In such cases, according to a Supreme Court judgment, we partition the property as though it is coparcenary', explained this judge. In such instances the Mohammedan law is put aside and the situation of the family is considered as a joint Hindu family. 'The SC judgment says that where a family has been living jointly for a considerably amount of time and it is claiming joint-ness of family, partition of property be made as though it is coparcenary property', stated this judge, emphasizing the basis of this act to be case law and not his own free will.[42] Judges, like this one and some others, did acknowledge that their own cultural conditioning and awareness of the real situation at the grassroots did tint their perspectives and the manner in which they approached a case, even as they expressed almost in the same breath how this was not a correct and sustainable approach. Speaking with reference to his experience in deciding a dispute that arose out a polygamous relationship in a community where polygamy was the norm, a civil judge of the senior division said:

> We are governed by the law. I may know the ground reality that each man has two wives. But this is my personal knowledge and I have to forget my personal knowledge when I sit in court. If I hold a polygamous marriage as valid (because this is in the best interest of the parties) such a judgment will not survive. This is knowledge I have because I am at the ground level. But the superior courts will not know the situation at the grassroots and this judgment will only be reversed.

This brings us to the crucial question of how well equipped the judges of both lower and higher courts are to appreciate the culturally plural contexts in which a particular dispute may arise within the same or different geographical location.

Apart from explaining why such cases may not be brought to the formal courts in the first place, it also brings us to realize that an apprehension that their own cultural conditioning could constrain them from viewing the case at hand in an objective manner may also be a probable reason why judges do not actively

41 Research interview with a lawyer, 11.07.2012.

42 Research interview with a judge, 23.10.2013. It may be interesting to note that this judge was not a Muslim himself.

encourage parties to file under the personal law or increasingly refer such disputes to mediation proceedings.[43] A lawyer who feels that this is a less harmful approach than actually deciding a matter in a prejudiced manner stated:

> Religion is a reality and I think all judges are well aware of their cultural and religious conditioning. This is probably why they keep cases concerning questions of another personal law at bay. They refuse to comment on such cases, defer to what the lawyers from that community plead and decide. In fact, in many such cases they will openly tell the lawyers to sort the matter out between themselves. They obviously do not want either their bias or ignorance [arising out of their own religious/cultural conditioning] to impact on the situation.[44]

Moreover, since the quantity of personal law applications in lower courts is fairly small, judges rarely get an opportunity to become conversant in deciding such questions. What does happen as a result thereof is an excessive reliance on case law[45] and in some instances on the pleadings of the lawyer. A senior judge, who is presently an additional chief judicial magistrate in a district court, explained how judges do rely on the submissions of parties and lawyers regarding understanding certain terminology which may be specific to the community. 'If both parties render the same explanation and understanding of a particular term, that the judge is unfamiliar with, the judge must rely on the party's explanation', he explained. Recollecting an instance from his own tenure, he said:

> The case concerned a matrimonial dispute between two members of a tribal community in the Gondia district. They referred to a system of *path* marriage where a man could remarry if his first wife consented to such second marriage [a form of polygamy]. I had never heard of such a system, but both parties were aware of it and agreed upon the same explanation. Therefore I accepted their explanation as the correct one.[46]

But except for such instances, judges seemed to be extremely adverse to the claim that they rely extensively on the submissions made by lawyers. Lawyers were perceived to have a supporting role whereby judges were to rely on them only to the extent of understanding the relationship between the facts at hand.[47] Judges emphasized that they did not rely upon the submissions of lawyers blindly,[48] and a lot depended upon how skilfully a lawyer presented the case. Judges admitted to be more accepting of the submissions of lawyers who presented pleadings in

43 Research interview with a judge, 23.10.2013.
44 Research interview with a lawyer, 05.10.2013.
45 Research interview with judges, 23.10.2013, 25.10.2013.
46 Research interview with a judge, 24.12.2013.
47 Research interview with a judge, 15.10.2013.
48 Research interview with a judge, 25.10.2013.

a peaceful and submissive manner. 'Unfortunately, if lawyers are arrogant and aggressive, the judge tends to get annoyed and this can adversely affect his pleading and case', explained one judge, who however felt that such an attitude on the part of the judges was not proper (in the broader context of justice delivery).[49]

In the absence of frequent experience with matters covered by personal law and the reluctance to rely completely on lawyer's submissions, there exists a third option for judges that is rarely exercised by them – the liberty to invite experts to clarify complicated or culture-specific terms or explain the cultural context in which a dispute may have arisen. The lower courts being perceived to be procedural courts, the judges in these courts are more inclined towards deciding cases, to the extent that they can, only with the aid of the codified law and on the basis of the facts and evidence before them.[50] A retired district judge explained that experts, when called, were rarely called at the court's instance:

> An expert would be usually called if the validity of a particular custom, tradition or ritual is challenged. There are instances when certain communities allow marriages within the prohibited degrees of marriages. To verify such claims, religious heads or experts may be called. But this is very rare, because such disputes are rare.[51]

Application of religious personal law by religious fora: perceptions

In July 2013, it was reported that Mumbai's first official Sharia court was set up. Set up by the Bharatiya Muslim Mahila Aandolan (BMMA), this particular Sharia court will be run by women for women. Interestingly the All India Milli Council, an influential political platform for Indian Muslims, has come out in support of the initiative.[52] This Sharia court is only a latest example, but a large number of alternative fora, like this one, led by religious communities have become active over the last few years. These fora are essentially informal in nature and settle disputes arising out of matters governed by personal law, including those concerning matrimony and succession. In this chapter, such forums have been referred to as alternative fora.

Such alternative fora were perceived differently by lawyers and litigants on one hand and judges on the other. Moreover, all three sets of respondents felt that more interaction between the state and such alternative (non-state) fora would help maintain a fine balance in the application of personal law in an effective manner.

49 Research interview with a judge, 23.10.2013.

50 A retired district court judge explained: 'The laws are sufficient. The lower courts do not have to concern themselves with calling religious experts. The judge must read the law and decide the case'. Research interview with a judge, 25.10.2013. Another judge, presently posted as additional chief judicial magistrate also said something similar: 'don't think it is necessary to look at the cultural context while deciding the dispute'. Research interview with a judge, 24.12.2013.

51 Research interview with a judge,15.10.2013.

52 De, 'Personal Laws'.

Litigants from religious minority groups tend to approach either religious heads or mediation fora run by members from their own religious community before approaching the court. The Christian lady who had visited the priest before going to court felt that in matrimonial and social disputes, it was always advisable to first visit a community-run forum:

> Going to court is like creating a rift. Therefore even if there is a slight chance of couples reuniting or of parties resolving the dispute amicably; it gets destroyed if either party goes to court. There is more than counselling in community fora. I went through counselling in court as well, but the efficiency with which counselling is carried out in the Church was better. The Priests genuinely want the marriage to be saved. It is their moral duty to ensure this. But in Court, counselling is only routine and therefore, the parties don't actually get a chance to be counselled properly.[53]

A combination of efforts by state and non-state fora was perceived to be crucial so that the decision-making processes of alternative fora can be organized in order to bring them in line with the spirit of state law and natural justice and litigants would consequently feel more secure against biases and power-play, which are often alleged to be at the crux of decision-making processes by such alternative fora. A young litigant, whose husband had become transgender after marriage and joined the *hijra* community was anxious about approaching the *panchayat* because she thought her family would be shamed in the community because of her situation. '*Panchayats* usually don't get involved in family matters', she said. As a second choice the family approached the Muslim Mahila Mandal, a forum run and managed for and by Muslim women, but not within her immediate community. 'They could only conciliate matters. They helped compromise the dispute', she narrated. But then since her husband's habits never changed, she decided she would be happier if she were separated. Her family does not support the fact that she is coming to court, even though they sympathize with her situation. 'I would have liked it to be settled at the level of the *panchayat* [here she refers to the Muslim Mahila Mandal]', she confesses, but that of course did not happen. Coming to court implies expenditure in terms of time and money and litigants like this litigant, in many situations, express that it would be easier if community fora were better equipped to handle their disputes – it would mean proper dispute resolution for the litigant and in a manner that is better accepted within the community. Joint efforts by state and non-state fora may also help create structural solutions for situations such as that of another female litigant who had been a victim of domestic abuse and wanted a divorce from her husband. That, she realized, could be achieved only by coming to court:

> However this forum [Satara Mahila Mandal] stated that they couldn't help me, because they only carried out settlements or compromises. They worked

53 Research interview with a litigant, 21.11.2013.

towards bringing the husband and wife back together. But I wanted a *chod-chhitti* (divorce), my husband had harassed me so much, that I didn't want to go back to him.[54]

If one observes, this litigant also approached by choice an alternative forum in the first instance, but realized that in the present system such alternative forum could not grant her a suitable (legal) solution. Sezgin[55] also finds, similarly, how individuals who initially approached alternative fora run by religious communities had to subsequently re-file their case in a civil court because such alternate fora lacked the capacity to implement their decision.

Retention of community-led fora of dispute resolution is supported primarily because of their conciliatory approach towards dispute resolution. Mediation, according to a senior judge in a civil court, is a more final solution and better suited to the nature of Indian society:

> Mediation helps dispose of the dispute, and not just the matter at hand. Mediation is successful because the final conclusion is in the terms of both parties. In such situations there is less likelihood of the matter being appealed. The nature of our society is such that there are mediators involved from the very beginning. All the while we are negotiating.[56]

A senior Muslim lawyer, with many years of experience of having represented Muslim litigants in the lower and higher courts, felt that it would be best if the power to adjudicate social and family disputes between religious minorities is handed over to the community fora run by the minority groups concerned. Explaining his stand, he said:

> Every society and every group has its own genius towards resolving disputes and maintaining harmony, mediation is the genius of the Indian society. On the other hand the judicial system we have adopted is British. It is adversarial in nature and places one against the other. As a result, going to court in the Indian context causes a lot of bad blood and increases the disharmony in our society. Additionally, any mood to settle between the parties is banished when one of the parties goes to court. While going to court and resolving disputes is the most civilised manner of dispute resolution amongst Englishmen, it is probably the most humiliating experience for an Indian. We progressed on the notion that the western method of adjudication is the only civilised form of dispute resolution. We were unable to adopt a holistic approach, which is the reason I support community-run forums.[57]

54 Research interview with a litigant, 21.11.2013.

55 Sezgin, *Human Rights under State-Enforced Religious Family Laws in Israel, Egypt and India*, 196.

56 Research interview with a judge, 24.1.2013.

57 Research interview with a lawyer, 03.10.2013.

The common feeling articulated by this lawyer, but shared by many, is that in the re-structuring of the formal judiciary in the post-colonial period, the state failed to imbibe any of the features of the native jurisprudence.

However, there is much fear that prejudices within a community against women and certain practices could overshadow justice for these groups within the community,[58] which is why the fraternity of judges and some lawyers feels more comfortable with the idea of social and family disputes being brought within the gamut of the formal judiciary. A senior judge, now retired, did have some difficulty deciding whether community-led fora or formal courts would be the better choice for dispute resolution involving application of personal law. On one hand he felt that approaching the formal courts implied an excessive consumption of time and money which could be very frustrating for litigants. But at the same time, he was anxious that if religious fora were allowed to handle disputes involving the personal law, they would become ghetto-ized. 'People will lose their freedom – freedom to marry a person of their choice or to act in a free manner. Any act of theirs which is contrary to the personal law or culture of that community will be opposed', said this judge.[59] In light of how religious fora are portrayed popularly in the media, this judge felt that religious fora are orthodox and rigid, and therefore the state court would always be the most effective forum to decide disputes, whether it be between religious minorities or otherwise. 'Personal laws are codified. The judge is expected to read the laws. And where he is in difficulty, he may call an expert witness'[60] he said. But as we saw in an earlier section, expert witnesses are rarely called. *Taluka* and district courts are perceived as fact-finding courts where questions of law may not necessarily be pondered upon. Judges feel that they need to look at the facts and the evidence at hand and decide a matter accordingly. Judges, who are cognisant of this reality, but also understand the importance of appreciating socio-cultural contexts, suggest that in matters involving application of the personal law, the court should be assisted by a member of the community, specifically someone who has rich knowledge about the customs, religious texts and traditions of that community. 'There are such people even in the smallest *taluka*s, but they are not invited to court. Involving them in the process should be mandatory. They may assist the court in the form of social workers, mediators and conciliators. Matters of a particular community are best resolved by the community', said a retired judge who had been posted for more than half the time of his total tenure in rural *taluka* places.[61] Even while he was not in favour of religious fora entirely deciding matters involving personal laws, he realized the need for members from the concerned community to be represented in the decision-making committee. From his own experience and observation of over

58 A female lawyer voiced anxiety fear arising from the fact that 'patriarchy is far to ingrained in Indian society and informal forums if left to themselves will have a free hand'. Research interview with a lawyer, 05.10.2013.

59 Research interview with a judge, 25.10.2013.

60 Research interview with a judge, 25.10.2013.

61 Research interview with a judge, 23.10.2013.

20 years, this judge remarked that in cases involving matters of personal law, a presiding member from a different community/religion was always treated like a foreigner or, if not, then tended to act like one.[62]

It is a reality, particularly in matrimonial and family disputes, that litigants do approach in the first instance (and many times the only instance)[63] traditional, informal or alternative fora which practise a more conciliatory method of dispute resolution. Sensitivity of the decision-maker to cultural contexts and social relationships of their own community does make litigants feel more secure. This can also be seen from the manner in which litigants make a choice of lawyer. More distinct in the Muslim community, litigants usually approach a lawyer from their own community to plead their case. While litigants, interestingly, do not admit to this practice very easily, it continues to be commonly observed by lawyers and even judges.[64] Muslim lawyers expressed that this choice was determined on the basis of the fact that since the Muslim community is governed in all respects by its religion, litigants feel more secure and comfortable discussing their dispute with a lawyer from their community. The lawyers further explained: a Muslim lawyer is likely to be more familiar with the nature of the dispute brought forth by a Muslim litigant, certain terminology that the litigant is likely to use, the socio-cultural situation in which the dispute arose and the influence of the dynamics of the Muslim society.[65]

However, judges expressed that it was not appropriate for them, in their position, to be sensitive to the social and cultural contexts of the litigants or one in which the dispute might have arisen. While for some judges sensitivity to the context of a dispute meant moving away from the neutral and unbiased position they were meant to maintain, other judges felt that the nature of disputes[66] being brought before them did not require such sensitivity. A clarification in this regard comes from a retired judge. Speaking specifically with reference to Muslims, he said:

> The Muslim community in rural areas is in a very poor economic situation. They cannot afford to pay court fees or even lawyers' fees. This is why they don't even end up coming to court. Consequently the Muslim litigants who do come to court are economically well off and I don't think it is necessary to look at their cultural or social situation while deciding the dispute.

62 Research interview with a judge, 23.10.2013.

63 The concept of dissolution of a marriage being absent amongst Catholics, there are many Christian ladies who end up going only to the priest for a solution. 'Inspite of this if marriages breaks, the women usually let it go feeling that this is "how it was meant to be. (God's wish)"', explained a litigant, who however feels that this extreme is also not completely correct. Research interview with a litigant, 21.11.2013.

64 Research interview with a lawyer, 02.10.2013; Research interview with a judge, 24.12.2013.

65 Research interview with lawyers, 11.07.2012, 07.06.2012.

66 As clarification on the types of disputes that do not require an enquiry into the context of the dispute, a senior district judge provided the example of 'new age cases like those under the IT Act or cyber laws'. Research interview with a judge, 23.10.2013.

Did he think, thus, about commercial cases, as indicated earlier? But soon thereafter he continued to explain the plight of Muslim women:

> They [the Muslim women] are exploited from all ends – by their fathers and brothers at the time of marriage and then by their husbands who can divorce them anytime. They have no voice in their community. Therefore I feel that it is very important for the judge to understand this context and look at the cases brought by women from the Muslim community more liberally and sensitively. They must have the court's sympathy.[67]

Analysis of data

The approach of lower courts to personal law

Evidence from the grassroots clearly reveals that there is a need for the effective management of the application of personal laws at the level of the lower courts. Extensive reliance on case law,[68] which seems a very favoured trend, also poses a different sort of risk; especially because courts do play an essentializing role in shaping religious identities.

In ancient times, when the *dharmashastra* was still to be developed, the king – the decision-maker – would make a decision based on *dharma* (righteousness), practice, custom and reason. The king could decide with reference to either custom or the written texts. But where such an approach frustrated the science of litigation, the king could or should decide with reference to righteousness alone. This methodology clearly required textual law to be given second place to a rule of reason, where the science is contradicted by a rational principle in the point of righteousness.[69]

In the colonial times, however, when courts had to decide matters involving customs of communities with 'syncretic' practices, they would inadvertently inquire into what constituted the 'essential' religious identity of the said community. The courts preferring a definitive view on the 'essential' practices would end up inquiring into scriptural authorities and oral history. The practices commonly followed by the communities often varied from how they were provided for in the scriptures. By adopting an objective and uniform view of the essential practices of a community, the courts would confer legitimacy on such a version which in time would recast the religious identity of such a community.[70]

This trend of the colonial-era courts remains a tendency of the higher courts in India even today. Higher courts are persistent in identifying the 'essential

67 Research interview with a judge, 23.10.2013.

68 A retired district judge who felt that personal laws were in any case difficult to understand stated that 'Deciding cases of personal laws without case laws is almost impossible'. Research interview with a judge, 23.10.2013.

69 Derrett, *Religion, Law and the State in India*, 166.

70 Balakrishnan, 'Individual Rights in India: A Perspective from the Supreme Court'.

practices' of religious groups and reinforcing religious identity in public life.[71] These courts can be seen using the 'essential practices' doctrine to define what is fundamental to any religion. According to the observations of a former chief justice of India, K.G. Balakrishnan,[72] essentializing signifies preferring a distinctive version of a religious group's identity over its actual heterogeneous character. Such judicial essentializing of religious beliefs and identities is often resented by those who are subjected to it. As a result of the 'essential practices' doctrine, the courts have become involved in trying to fashion religion in a way appropriate to the working of a modernist state, rather than accepting religion as represented by its practitioners. Stripping down religion to a rationalist definition and classifying any religious practice that falls outside this grid as 'superstition' or 'accretion', the court ends up dispensing with pluralism and popular practices.[73] In a vast country and within a dynamic society such acts work towards confining societies which are rapidly changing under the pressures of modernization to fossilized forms, totally removed from their contemporary lifestyles.[74] With this approach of the higher courts, largely followed by lower courts through precedent and case law, it may of course be possible that a formally and often exceedingly well-formulated solution could be found to a particular issue or dispute. But, as has been pointed out by lower court judges themselves, such a formally resolved conflict may not forever settle the issue. The dispute would probably continue to simmer below the surface, escaping the radar of official sensors and systems and bypassing formal understandings of law, while still causing havoc in people's personal lives or in other respects. In order to avoid such situations, a combination of efforts by state and non-state fora may just be the need of the hour.

The threat of essentializing practices

There is no one form of religion. It is constantly undergoing changes and, like law, seems situation-specific. While there might be standardized notions and stereotypes surrounding certain religions and practices, on the ground level religion does not remain a static entity. It is continuously evolving and this is reflected through the manner in which people perceive it, practise it and use it. Uniformity, which was probably one of the objectives underlying codification of personal laws, is what judges admit to prefer. Just as the judges acknowledge

71 Cases such as *SST Saifudding Saheb* v. *State of Bombay* [AIR 1962 SC 853]; *Sastri Yagnapurushadji and Ors* v. *Muldas Bhudardas Vaishya and Anr* [AIR 1966 SC 1119] and *DAV College Bhatinda* v. *State of Punjab* [AIR 1971 SC 1731] are only some examples.

72 'Individual Rights in India: A Perspective from the Supreme Court', 33.

73 Ronojoy Sen, 'Legalizing Religion : The Indian Supreme Court and Secularism', *Policy Studies* 30 (2007): 10–11.

74 Flavia Agnes, 'Hindu Men. Monogamy and Uniform Civil Code', *Economic and Political Weekly*, 16 December 1995, www.epw.in/special-articles/hindu-men-monogamy-and-uniform-civil-code.html.

and understand why the implementation of a uniform civil code will not be successful in a diverse country like India, they also accept that a uniform civil code will make processes easier for them to handle.[75] Consequently, instead of moulding the decision-making processes to appreciate the contexts arising from religious and cultural plurality, the courts spend their time in ascertaining the essential practices of a particular religion. In doing so, the courts risk failing to examine a dispute – concerning an aspect governed by personal law – in its real context, which is most often intricately connected to and influenced by the manner in which religion is being practised and experienced by that religious group in that specific jurisdiction.[76]

To explain just one facet of the complex manner in which religion is experienced, I will draw upon the observations made by Tundawala[77] with respect to Bengali Muslims. Tundawala's study focuses on a comparison of literature by writers from the *ashraf* (Urdu-speaking urban Muslim aristocrats with foreign provenance and sometimes upper caste Hindu converts) and *astraf* (largely Bengali speaking indigenous rural Muslim middle and lower occupational class) through an observation of the role of religion in their literature. About the latter, she observes: 'the Bengali Muslims could not completely distance themselves from the socio-territorial realities of their life'.[78] This she says on the basis of:

> This can be seen from the literature produced by the Bengali Muslims which eschews the religious questions altogether and is certainly not Islamic in character, whether in idea or terminology. Their writing also refuses to reckon normative Islam as a powerful force in rural Bengal and allow religious dogmatism and strict discipline to dominate rural life.[79]

Tundawala further observes that as Islam's growth in Bengal progressed gradually, it took various forms and assimilated values and symbols not always in conformity with the scriptures. Its historical and cultural accommodation and integration with the local milieu brought about profound changes in the practices and modes of thinking of its adherents.[80] As a result, the ways of living of the *astraf* – that is

75 This was revealed through various interviews with different lower court judges. Research interviews with judges, 25.10.2013, 15.10.2013.

76 Here I would make a reference to Sezgin's *Human Rights under State-Enforced Religious Family Laws in Israel, Egypt and India*, 208, where he observes personal status laws to be 'multi-vocal, intersubjective and dynamic'. The knowledge (and evidence) that the effects a particular law can produce depends largely on who is allowed to interpret and manipulate the law, is also a factor that that motivates suggesting partnering of alternate forums run by religious minority communities and the formal courts Ibid., chap. 7.

77 Alefiya Tundawala, 'Multiple Representations Of Muslimhood In West Bengal: Identity Construction Through Literature', *South Asia Research* 32, no. 2 (1 July 2012): 139–163.

78 Ibid., 142.

79 Ibid., 144.

80 Ibid., 140–141.

the common Bengali Muslims – as is evident from their literature, is more assimilatory than subversive of Hindu ideas, beliefs, customs and practices.[81]

The lives of the Bengali Muslims, a largely agrarian community mostly located in rural areas, are comparable to the lives of the Muslims in rural Maharashtra as well. While this remains to be verified through extensive fieldwork, *prima facie*, it is observed that religious dogmatism and strict discipline does not dominate the rural life in these areas. At the ground level Muslim and Hindu communities live in close surroundings and sometimes community practices merge and there may not be significant differences among the practices of Hindus and Muslims; the customs of the majority may also have their impact and influence on the living styles of the minority community. Therefore, while religions may differ, the ways of living and norms governing such ways of life may be quite similar between Hindus and Muslims, a locally constructed hybrid. Therefore, even though *talaq* may be accommodated in societal ways in the local Muslim communities, Muslim women, like their Hindu counterparts, may still be bearing the brunt of social, financial and emotional consequences of divorce.[82]

This reality of how religion is positioned in people's day-to-day life, the many syncretistic forms in which it may be practised, is true of all religions in India. Essentializing practices and working towards creating uniformity within religions adversely impacts on the lives of those who are practising it, also being a probable cause for members of religious minority groups to prefer dispute resolution by forums and methods alternative to the formal structure.

Religion and legal education

In this context, a crucial question concerns understanding of how well equipped judges in the Indian courts are to appreciate, understand and incorporate the impact of such pluralities into their decision-making processes. An area which would suffice for an entire topic of research, but is worth briefly looking into in this chapter, is to what extent and in what manner is the understanding of religion and culture imparted as part of legal education and at a later stage – at the level of training for judges.

Personal laws are taught as a part of the syllabi comprising legal education. Interestingly, however, while a substantial portion of legal education focuses on personal laws and their implementation in various spheres, no part of this syllabus either lays any emphasis on or talks about the relationship between law and religion or offers any debate surrounding it.[83] The impact of such lacunae in legal education becomes obvious at much later stages when these law students – now lawyers and judges – are in the thick of their careers. For

81 Ibid., 156.

82 Solanki, *Adjudication in Religious Family Laws*.

83 Werner Menski, 'Flying Kites in a Global Sky: New Models of Jurisprudence', *Socio-Legal Review* 7, no. 0 (10 August 2011), www1.nls.ac.in/ojs-2.2.3/index.php/slr/article/view/86.

instance, at the beginning of this study, during preliminary fieldwork, it was observed that there were judges in the lower courts who were not even willing to speak of religion, and dismissed any question relating to religion and the judiciary, saying simply that everyone is equal before the law and that the judiciary was not concerned with external factors such as religion. When asked to address the issue of whether legal education provides a sufficient overview of the connection between law and other disciplines, including political science, anthropology, religious studies and their impact on the implementation of codified law, there was a common consensus among judges as well as lawyers that law as practised was very different from law in theory and that legal education did not prepare law students sufficiently to handle these dynamics. In the words of a judge with about 14 years of experience:

> After law school [when] we started practising [as lawyers] and then became judges, we realised that practically things are very different from what is taught in the college. What is taught in law-college, is hardly of any use, the syllabus is not up to the mark.[84]

Apart from the absence of an inter-disciplinary approach in legal education, the dominance of legal positivist philosophy is a disciplinary reality despite robust challenges from critical scholarship of many kinds. The dominant understanding of the concept of law within legal discourse remains positivist. A feature of positivist law, which in part was an effect of enlightenment, is that positivist law is separable *inter alia* from religion, and is therefore perceived as secular.[85] It does not come as a surprise therefore that judges did not feel the need for an emphasis on diversity-related issues on legal education. A retired judge articulated that such sort of training regarding the use and application of personal law ought to be given by the concerned district court to junior lawyers practising in the concerned court, instead of the law school level. 'This training should present graduates in law with a view of the on-ground situation of the subjects they are studying', he said.[86] This could be an effective method if carried out efficiently, as lawyers (and judges) would become more aware of and sensitive to the particular contexts arising out of the local socio-cultural diversity. One judge suggested that an amendment in the laws to better suit the socio-cultural milieu of Indian society, rather than more emphasis on religion in legal education, would improve the reach of religious minority groups to the courts.[87]

But lawyers felt differently. According to them religion and law interacted on various planes and therefore the importance of diversity and at the same time the complexities arising as result of it should be explained to law students.

84 Research interview with a judge, 24.12.2013.
85 Parashar, 'Religious Personal Laws as Non-State Laws'.
86 Research interview with a judge, 23.10.2013.
87 Research interview with a judge, 24.12.2013.

This would also help do away with the misconceptions or assumptions made on the basis of stereotypical ideas that are often held with regard to the religious minority groups. Providing clarification on this point, a female lawyer explained:

> Due to the media and many other sources, there are foolish perceptions such as if the person is Christian, s/he will speak English or that if/she is Muslim[s], s/he will speak Hindi. This is not true. In India [Maharashtra], there are several Christians and several Muslim who can and do speak only Marathi. As a result of these misconceptions, court procedures become a challenge for such litigants.[88]

Another lawyer – a senior practitioner – felt that it was the ideas of secularism that judges beheld that clouded their vision concerning the broad interaction between religion and law. The higher courts, whose primary obligation is to decide questions of 'law', are often faced with the task of interpreting the nature of interaction between law and other factors, including religion. One of the important themes emerging from the courts' descriptions of secularism is the idea that the religious can be neatly separated from the secular and that religion must be kept apart from the affairs of the state.[89] Higher courts not only play an important adjudicatory role but also shape public opinion through their discourse. And such discourse has a crucial impact on the lower court judges who are bound by the hierarchical structure of the judiciary, not just procedurally but sometimes in terms of the way they think. Consequently, as the senior lawyer correctly observed, judges prefer adopting a hands-off approach towards religion. Therefore, he felt that 'Judges must try to understand religion and therefore some explanation about the basic principles of religion must be introduced in legal education to substantiate the understanding and teaching of personal laws'.[90]

It is true that institutions of the state in India hold on to the value of secularism very dearly. Common assessments of secularism in India often rely on an overstated contrast between a 'Western' model of separation between state and religion and a distinctively 'Indian' model of equal respect for all religions. The notion of equal respect for all religions, however, has manifestly involved some forms of separation between religion and state.[91] Popularly, as is quoted by Sinha,[92] 'The word "secular" is commonly understood in contradistinction to the word "religious"'. Speaking about secularism in India, already in the 1960s, Donald E. Smith remarked: 'The indifference to religion which characterizes the

88 Research interview with a lawyer, 05.10.2013.

89 Sen, 'Legalizing Religion', 8.

90 Research interview with a lawyer, 03.10.2013.

91 Bajpai, *Debating Difference*, 179.

92 Mukul Sinha, 'Secularism in India is an Illusion', *The Milli Gazette*, 12 April 2012, www.milligazette.com/news/3479-secularism-in-india-is-an-illusion.

contemporary western outlook has already made a powerful impact on certain sections of Indian society, and the process is a continuing one.'[93] In earlier literature, Galanter[94] observed in India a disagreement about what exactly the concept of secularism implies – whether it implies severe aloofness from the religion, a benign impartiality towards religion, a corrective oversight of it, or a fond and equal indulgence of all religions. But there seems to be a general agreement that public life is not to be guided by religious doctrines or institutions. Fieldwork observations revealed that lower court judges believe that it is important to reconcile to the code that when in the chair of a judge,[95] s/he must set aside his/her personal beliefs and opinions, be objective, impartial and impersonal. In a very strict sense, s/ he is to obey the law and see to its enforcement.[96] But at the level of practice, is this really possible? In a commentary piece, Baxi[97] highlights that public officials, both elected and appointed – including judges – faced with the necessity of making decisions often find difficulty in completely dissociating their religious belief from their official task and role. And as is evident from the empirical data noted in an earlier part of this chapter, judges do acknowledge this practical truth, even though they concurrently insist that it is not a sustainable and correct approach.[98] There is a need for legal actors to accept and work with the fact that law in everyday praxis is not only linked to the amendable mechanisms of the state recognition and interpretation by the judiciary, but is also entrenched within people's intersubjectivities, defined as the shared representations and stereotypes that impact on how social actors (judges included) make sense of facts and develop arguments in the legal process.[99]

93 M. Mohsin Alam, 'Constructing Secularism: Separating "Religion" and "State" under the Indian Constitution', *Australian Journal of Asian Law* 11 (1 January 2009): 39.

94 Marc Galanter, 'Hinduism, Secularism, and the Indian Judiciary', *Philosophy East and West* 21, no. 4 (1 October 1971): 467–487.

95 A quote from a district and sessions judge with over 21 years of experience in this position accurately describes this perception. 'Maybe it [cultural conditioning] impacts at the initial stage, new recruits. But this doesn't last long. You see, a judge must practise as a lawyer before becoming a judge. He also has rigorous training before becoming a judge. In this time he adopts a new culture befitting society.' Research interview with a judge, 24.12.2013. This judge obviously feels that the culture of 'secularism' [on whether religion and the affairs of the court must be rigidly separated] is best suited for the society's welfare. He simultaneously speaks about how the cultural conditioning of a judge should not impact on his/her decision-making process. It could therefore be concluded that this judge's ideas of secularism did comprise a separation between religion and culture on one hand and implementation of law on the other.

96 S.N. Balagangadhara, 'The Platform Paper' (presented at the Rethinking Religion in India IV: Religion, Secularism and law, Mangalore, India, 2012), 1–12, www.rethinkingreligion.org/files/downloads/RRI_IV_platform_paper.pdf.

97 Upendra Baxi, 'Commentary: Savarkar and the Supreme Court', *Policy Studies* 30 (2007): 47–56.

98 Reference is made to fieldwork observations noted in the section on 'Personal law through the eyes of the judges and lawyers'.

99 Livia Holden and Azam Chaudhary, 'Daughters' Inheritance, Legal Pluralism, and Governance in Pakistan', *The Journal of Legal Pluralism and Unofficial Law* 45, no. 1 (2013): 114–115.

Some conclusions

At present we know only about the members of religious minority groups who approached the formal legal system – the courts – for the purpose of dispute resolution. And therefore we can focus only on mechanisms that can make the formal legal order more accessible for those persons from religious minority groups that are accessing it. A network of efforts making the most of the potential of both state and non-state fora and the actors within such forums could be an experiment to begin with. An improvised and more efficient version of the Parsi Chief Matrimonial Court would be one to draw inspiration from in this situation. Part III of the Parsi Marriage and Divorce Act, 1936, provided for constitution of Special Courts under this Act whereby a dispute under this Act would be presided over by a High Court or District Court judge and a team of five delegates, being members from within the Parsi community. Here, members of the same community (to which the prospective litigants would belong) would work within the structural framework of the judiciary aiding the court to understand the cultural dynamics that may be arising out of social relations within a religious minority group.

Another beginning point could be the provision for pre-litigation made under the Legal Services Authorities Act, 1987. This provision allows for parties to any dispute, before such dispute is brought to court, to make an application before a Lok Adalat or a Permanent Lok Adalat for settlement of the dispute. Emphasizing the potential of this section in the Legal Services Authorities Act, a senior civil judge stated:

> There isn't a need for additional forums. Instead, the community-run forums should settle the matter and encourage or even insist that the settlement be converted into a decree by filing a pre-litigation suit in the court. Any court can convert such a settlement into a decree. There is a provision for pre-litigation suits in the Legal Services Authority Act, but no one has paid heed to it yet.[100]

There is strength in this recommendation by the judge in that it allows the various types of dispute resolution fora to maintain a certain level of autonomy, yet retains safeguards against arbitrariness. The most important aspect of such joint efforts should be the establishment of a system that is equipped to handle the ever-evolving and plural nature of religion.

That one can be governed by his/her personal law is a right that arises from belonging to a particular religious group. The extent to which personal law is used in litigation provides a sense of whether exercise of such rights improves accessibility to the formal legal order. It is difficult to determine at this stage whether exercise of religious rights actually strengthens or limits a person's capability to access justice. By making religious minorities and the application

100 Research interview with a judge, 24.12.2013.

of personal law the focus of this study, we have only tried to understand how prepared are the *taluka* and district courts – the courts of first instance for the majority of people in India – to handle the dynamics of religious diversity. Of course, this data only provides a preliminary picture and more research in a larger number of lower courts is required to understand how empowering such a right (to be governed by one's personal law) is with respect to the formal courts. However, more importantly there is a need for research that explores (1) how the significant proportion of members of religious minority groups who do not approach the formal legal system seek dispute resolution and access justice and (2) to what extent personal law and religious rights are a part of this process. The overview that will be provided through such an exhaustive data collection in both regards will perhaps help us gauge with more certainty whether and how the rights provided by religion and/or those arising (in relation to the state) as a result of belonging to a particular religious group actually contribute to legal empowerment.

References

Agnes, Flavia. 'Hindu Men. Monogamy and Uniform Civil Code'. *Economic and Political Weekly*, 16 December 1995. Accessed 18 January 2014. www.epw.in/special-articles/hindu-men-monogamy-and-uniform-civil-code.html.

Bajpai, Rochana. *Debating Difference: Group Rights and Liberal Democracy in India.* New Delhi: Oxford University Press, 2011..

Balagangadhara, S.N. 'The Platform Paper', 1 – 12. Mangalore, India, 2012. Accessed 22 January 2013. www.rethinkingreligion.org/files/downloads/RRI_IV_platform_paper.pdf.

Balakrishnan, K. 'Individual Rights in India: A Perspective from the Supreme Court', conference paper presented at the International Roundtable Conference, University of Georgia, 2009.

Baxi, Upendra. 'Commentary: Savarkar and the Supreme Court'. *Policy Studies* 30 (2007): 47–56.

De, Rohit. 'Personal Laws: A Reality Check'. *Frontline*, 21 August 2013.

Derrett, John Duncan Martin. *Religion, Law and the State in India.* New York: Free Press, 1968.

Galanter, Marc. 'Hinduism, Secularism, and the Indian Judiciary'. *Philosophy East and West* 21, no. 4 (1 October 1971): 467–487.

Holden, Livia, and Azam Chaudhary. 'Daughters' Inheritance, Legal Pluralism, and Governance in Pakistan'. *The Journal of Legal Pluralism and Unofficial Law* 45, no. 1 (2013): 104–123.

Krishnan, Jayanth K., Shirish Naresh Kavadi, Azima Girach, Dhanaji Khupkar, Kalindi Kokal, Satyajeet Mazumdar, Ms Nupur, *et al.* 'Grappling at the Grassroots: Access to Justice in India's Lower Tier'. *Harvard Human Rights Journal* 27, no. 1 (May 2014): 151 –189.

Mohsin Alam, M. 'Constructing Secularism: Separating "Religion" and "State" under the Indian Constitution'. *Australian Journal of Asian Law* 11 (1 January 2009): 29–55.

'Maharashtra Population Census Data 2011'. Accessed 19 January 2014. www.census2011.co.in/census/state/maharashtra.html.

Mahmood, Tahir. *Muslim Personal Law: Role of the State in the Subcontinent*. New Delhi: Vikas Pub. House, 1977.

Mansfield, John. 'Personal Laws or a Uniform Civil Code?' In *Sociology of Law*, edited by Indra Deva, 174–193. New Delhi: Oxford University Press, 2005.

Menski, Werner. 'Flying Kites in a Global Sky: New Models of Jurisprudence'.." *Socio-Legal Review* 7, no. 0 (10 August 2011). Accessed 24 February 2014. www1.nls.ac.in/ojs-2.2.3/index.php/slr/article/view/86.

National Commission for Minorities. *Proportion and Growth Rate of Population by Religious Communities, India, 1961–2001*. Accessed 19 January 2014. http://ncm.nic.in/minority_population.pdf.

Parashar, Archana. "Religious Personal Laws as Non-State Laws: Implications for Gender Justice." *The Journal of Legal Pluralism and Unofficial Law* 45, no. 1 (2013): 5–23.

Sen, Ronojoy. 'Legalizing Religion : The Indian Supreme Court and Secularism'. *Policy Studies* 30 (2007). http://scholarspace.manoa.hawaii.edu/handle/10125/3499.

Sezgin, Yüksel. *Human Rights under State-Enforced Religious Family Laws in Israel, Egypt and India*. Cambridge: Cambridge University Press, 2013.

Sinha, Mukul. 'Secularism in India is an Illusion'. *The Milli Gazette*, 12 April 2012. Accessed 21 July 2014. www.milligazette.com/news/3479-secularism-in-india-is-an-illusion.

Solanki, Gopika. *Adjudication in Religious Family Laws: Cultural Accommodation, Legal Pluralism, and Gender Equality in India*. Cambridge: Cambridge University Press, 2011.

Subramanian, Narendra. 'Myths of the Nation, Cultural Recognition and Personal Law in India'. In *Whither National Myths? Reflections on the Present and Future of National Myths*, edited by Gérard Bouchard, 259–275. New York: Routledge, 2013.

Tundawala, Alefiya. 'Multiple Representations of Muslimhood in West Bengal: Identity Construction Through Literature'. *South Asia Research* 32, no. 2 (1 July 2012): 139–163.

5 When courts do not finish contentious causes

Revisiting the value of religious laws in the Rainbow Nation*

Dennis Bonginkosi Xulu

Introduction

This chapter discusses how courts do not bring closure to contentions among individuals, families and society and argues that they may sometimes have good reasons not to do so. Contentions are considered finished when an accused is given due sentence and is, for example, sent to prison. But, individuals, families and members of the society are most of the time left with psychological, emotional and spiritual scars and the relationship between them continues while the law – it claims – has done its 'work'. Due to this ongoing struggle, individuals move on to seek remedies from others, and this includes sometimes religious ministers. Religious laws, given that they are connected to theology and that they are part of broader culture, deal with the human person in its totality vis-à-vis tensions as to how individuals can cope with outcomes of court cases. Therefore the present chapter balances justice and caritas, justice and mercy, dignity of a person and human rights. Taking advantage of South Africa's TRC,[1] which leaned more towards religion and culture than international law, as most scholarship assumes, the author advances the position that religious laws are valuable in the Rainbow Nation (South Africa). These laws contribute in making people appreciate their identity as persons and at the same time promote the common good. Given the pluralism of and within religions in the country, this chapter employs canon law of the Catholic Church as a backdrop in highlighting the existence of religious laws (as non-state laws) and the role they play as an aid to healing contentions in the society.

Understanding contention

Contentio is a negative concept denoting conflict, disagreement, rivalry and discord. In legal terminology it is better understood as dispute. When we ask why people bring contentious causes to courts, the question arises whether it is only on the basis of extracting revenge, reparation and bad faith, or something else.

* The term 'Rainbow Nation' was coined by Archbishop Desmond Tutu referring to the new South Africa.

1 TRC = Truth and Reconciliation Commission, 1995–1997.

Among many reasons leading people to bring each other to court are external and internal conflicts. Tensions are emanating from unsettled financial deals, family disputes between spouses, criminal activities, infringement and compromised rights, and many more instances.

Obviously, there are expectations of closing unfinished matters in anticipation for lasting peace as people aim to start a new page in life and enlist the state's support by going to court. This is an expectation of something refreshing, similar to untying tensions in a couple who in the first place were incapable of maintaining a stable marital relationship. It would be a very different matter to answer the unanswered questions in an incident of a relative who was tragically killed or murdered; to untangle suspicion of allegations of theft of property, and of course, the list can be long. For peace to be lasting, truth telling is essential; it has to be told.

Truth telling through investigation, by assessing facts, is crucial in the protection of rights of all parties, thus due process and fair trial are central elements. The plaintiff is interrogated in order to assess the substance of the facts, causes, incidents which are crucial in the application of the law to the case submitted. Whether one is represented or not by an advocate, proceedings do have a psycho-social, physical, emotional and spiritual impact on the individual.

To illustrate, when an accused is found not guilty even though a plaintiff has all certainty of incidence leading, for example, to the death of a relative, this is severe. A case scenario is *S.* v. *Oscar Pistorius*.[2] This is a murder case involving Oscar Pistorius, whereby a verdict found Pistorius not guilty of murder, rather sentencing him for culpable homicide and contravention of section 120(3)(b) of the Firearms Control Act, 2000. An emotional case such as this clearly illustrates the impact of suits on individuals. The case had a lot of impact not only on Pistorius but on the victim's side, the Steenkamp family. They lost a beloved member of the family, but the prolongation of the case, its exhibits and tests have had an impact on the victim's family members. This is to speak of a high profile case, but what about cases involving poor people in rural areas with limited resources to meet professional support? The state may offer support to a certain degree, but healing is a process requiring highly specialised experts at times, not just a court verdict.

The point one is driving home is that individuals, family, clan, society may still experience contention after court proceedings, so people do need support after that. This is not to speak of the traumatic experience of standing in front of the judge and the public to expose secrets about one's life, whether as an accuser or as the accused. Some people return home devastated, even worse than the accused who will have to spend time being rehabilitated in prison.

Starting from the end

At the end of trial some return home to bury themselves in soaking pillows, others decide to seek professional help from psychologists and counsellors; and yet

2 *S* v. *Pistorius* 2014 sacr 589 (GP).

others would visit religious ministers, spiritual directors and pastors. Psychologist Leary and his colleagues (1998) conducted a study of 164 undergraduates as a psychological study of hurt feelings, asking how people react when they are hurt. The result came as follows:

> About 80% of people who had been hurt said they expressed their anger to the offender. About 75% said that they argued and defended themselves . . . A third cried in front of the offender. About 42% said they cried later when they were alone.[3]

When a judge has pronounced his or her last word and the court has been ordered to adjourn, the realities of emotional turmoil perhaps mixed with 'justice has been done' lie in the deepest core of a person. Justice was done, but to someone who lost a breadwinner the case is not fully closed. A dear one is no more to be seen! Some, even though they are not sent for incarceration as perpetrators, are locked in emotional prisons. True justice might have been done, but how do you ease emotional constraints? How does the society deal with close neighbours who of late have become enemies? Whilst mentioning close neighbours one cannot miss name-calling and further blaming on why the court route was taken, maybe instead of resolving the matter outside court. Such incidence might appear fictitious, but people in rural areas in some parts of South Africa do experience hardships after bringing contentious causes to courts.[4]

When a minister visits troubled individuals or families, some are broken and in tears. A contention was concluded in court, but not in the core of who the person is. Again from the study by psychologist Leary and his colleagues (1998) mentioned above one reads:

> Sixty percent said they trusted the offender less than before the incident. Almost half (44%) said they disliked the person more afterwards. Victims also reported that the event affected them psychologically in the long run. Hurt feelings lowered their self-esteem (22%), made them worry more about their hurt again (46%), and undermined their self-confidence in similar situations.[5]

In essence, this is an illustration that a person is more than body and mind. Other elements making up who and what a person becomes when he or she is internally disturbed, challenge the integrity of the whole human person. When a person as a whole is not empowered from within, and has to be assisted to transcend past pain, they suffer tremendously. When someone gets occupied by worry about their hurt

3 Everett Worthington, *Forgiveness and Reconciliation: Theory and Application*, New York: Routledge, 2006, 35–37.

4 The author reflects on instances as a minister when neighbours will approach him to solve contentions after court cases. Such contentions will not only arise from mere neighbours but between members of the church who had sued each other. Given the central focus on people, they would come asking to be reconciled with the other. And, a victim would be looking for spiritual accompaniment in order to come to terms with the self and to close the chapter well.

5 Worthington, *Forgiveness and Reconciliation*, 35–37.

again and again, precious time is wasted. When someone has their self-confidence lowered, one can imagine what impact this will have on self, family, workplace and community around. If one cannot forgive others, how can we expect to have peaceful communities?

Even though 'the lawyer has a personal moral obligation not to let a lawsuit degenerate into bitterness and revenge',[6] reality tells us that lawsuits do leave scars in the lives of people and can lead to malevolent relationships. At times, lawyers do see justice as mostly a matter of procedures, of due process, of impartial rules impersonally applied. In this case, as long as fair rules are fairly applied, they do not concern themselves much with the consequences of their actions, or whether the result is objectively true or fair.[7]

Considering the above, does the law demonstrate a moderate amount of a 'caring touch'? The answer is in the affirmative. Human laws are crafted by human beings to be applied by them as well. And, given that it is in the nature of a human person to extend care to self and others, human laws, not to mention divine law, must transmit care. If this is not obvious in state laws, religious laws do have this quality. It is actually, on this basis, that one affirms that religious laws are still of value. Encouraging the caring aspect of laws is important in enhancing empowerment of the human person holistically. Now the understanding of empowerment cannot be limited to individual's self-fulfilment and advancement or to social upliftment; there is more to empowerment of persons.

Some theoretical considerations

Prior to attempting to deal with empowering people after suits and offenders have being incarcerated, it is worthwhile to situate justice in the life of the community of believers.

Christ the Lord, indeed, did not in the least wish to destroy the very rich heritage of the law and prophets which was gradually formed from history and experience of the people of God in the Old Testament, but he brought it to completion (cf. Mt.5:17) such that in a new way and higher way it became part of the heritage of the New Testament. Therefore, although in expounding the paschal mystery St Paul teaches that justification is not obtained by the works of the law but by the means of faith (cf. Rom.3:28; Gal.2:16), he does not thereby exclude the binding force of the Decalogue (cf. Rom.13:28; Gal.5:13–25,6:2), nor does he deny the importance of discipline in the Church (cf. 1Cor.5 and 6). Thus the writings of the New Testament enable us to understand even better the importance of discipline and make us see better how it is more closely connected with the saving character of the evangelical message itself.[8]

6 Joseph Allegretti, *The Lawyers Calling: Christian Faith and Legal Practice*, New York and Mahwah: Paulist Press, 1996, at 97.

7 Ibid., at 105.

8 John Paul II, *Sacrae disciplinae leges* in Code of Canon Law 1983, Latin-English edn, Washington, DC: Canon Law Society of America, 1989, at xxix.

Law as self-controlled ordering outside the realm of the state plays a role within religious communities whether in the form of a set of rules, canons, church orders, policies and procedures. The crux of the matter is that religious communities do exercise and promote justice and in that sense produce their own legal system. What distinguishes state laws from religious laws lies in the legal sources, principles and interpretation of laws, human and divine nature, immanent and transcendent realities. Far from the religious laws emphasising punishment, they promote conciliation, that is, how people can be assisted to develop as persons and how they can be integrated in society. Religious communities further discourage litigation amongst its members on matters they themselves assisted by ministers can solve. All Christian faithful, and especially bishops, are to strive diligently to avoid litigation among the people of God as much as possible, without prejudice to justice, and to resolve peacefully. Members are encouraged and assisted to collaborate in seeking equitable solution to the controversy. Whilst conciliation and arbitration are cost-effective means to promote peace, they are at the same time avenues for the promotion of justice.[9] Of course, this position is adopted when the case was not dealt with in the court, a scenario that is not the focus of this work, which is aiming at how religion empowers people after cases have been concluded in court.

Justice and caritas

To iterate, why must some people bring others to court? In other words, why do they use state mechanisms? Is it because the religious or social dimension lacks sanctions and effectiveness? Or are we in today's world taught to use state law and its institutions? Or are people using the state to harass others? Justice makes charity concrete by establishing institutional policies and laws that express love in specific and lasting ways, thus allowing love to have a more permanent impact.[10] Love should be understood in the sense of care for the other and his/her best interests. This is more focused on individuals and societies. From a state perspective, the motivation must be the protection of public order, not necessarily because of anger and revenge. 'Justice partially fulfils love by bringing about more freedom and equality',[11] ultimately towards the common good. Essentially, common good promotes due consideration of the love of the neighbour, hence a cause of bringing perpetrators to face consequences of their wrongdoings is not about them per se, but rather to dissuade anti-social behaviour. It becomes an act of building the nation because future generations get discouraged by activities that disturb the public good.

The highest goal of justice seen from this perspective is to educate (*educare* in Latin), which means to lead someone out of the dark. Therefore justice when it is

9 Code of Canon Law 1983, canon 1446.
10 Thomas Schubeck, *Love that does Justice*, Maryknoll and New York: Orbis Books, 2007, at 131.
11 Ibid., at 205.

demanded from the *Other* or applied in court is not meant to torture, rather to send a lesson that you get punished for a wrong act you have committed. In everything, therefore, treat people the same way you want them to treat you (Mt7:12). An individual is not greater than society. Of course, the offender has to learn the hard way how to respect the common good.

Having said that, must love be sacrificed in the name of justice? The answer is negative. Promotion and protection of rights would not then make sense. Individuals who commit bad acts do not cease being human in spite of committing a wrong act. The offender also remains a human being and cannot be thrown away. He or she is still a member of society. Yet, excluding an individual from ordinary society is aimed at empowering him/her to become fit to live in society again. From this perspective, promotion of the common good is not just a responsibility of a certain portion of the population, but everybody is responsible to promote common good according to his or her capabilities as a person.

It has always been emphasised by the Catholic Church that 'the pursuit of justice must be a fundamental norm of the state and that the aim of a just social order is to guarantee to each person, according to the principle of subsidiarity, his share of the community's goods'.[12] Pope emeritus Benedict XVI observed that:

> There is no ordering of the state so that justice can eliminate the need for a service of love. Whoever wants to eliminate love is preparing to eliminate man as such. There will always be suffering which cries out for consolation and help. There will always be loneliness. There will always be situations of material need where help in the form of concrete love of neighbour is indispensable.[13]

Promotion of justice can be viewed as the love of fellow citizens based on truth. Only in truth does charity shine forth, only in truth can charity be authentically lived. Without truth love becomes an empty shell to be filled in an arbitrary way.[14] Do to others what you would like done to you. Love is in this context going beyond the erotic, or the filial, but points to the reality that every citizen is a fellow brother and sister. Love demands justice, the recognition and respect for legitimate rights of individuals and peoples.[15] This does not mean that justice must be dry bones nor should love be viewed as emotional ecstasy. Either of the two would eliminate any notion of society at all. To desire the common good and strive towards it is a requirement of justice and charity.[16] How can state and church work together in this? My suggestion, clearly, would be not by banning or excluding the other force, but by co-opting the other.

12 Benedict XVI, Encyclical *Deus Caritas est*, 25 December 2005, AAS 14 (2006), art 26.

13 Ibid., art 28. See Congregation for Bishops, Directory for the Pastoral Ministry of Bishops, *Apostolorum Successories* (22 February 2004), Vatican City, at 217.

14 Benedict XVI, Encyclical Letter, *Caritas in veritate*, 29 June 2009, AAS 73 (2009), art 3.

15 Ibid., art 6.

16 Ibid., art 7.

Justice and mercy

We have deliberated on balancing justice and love, how can we attempt striking a balance between justice and mercy? Let us reflect on the biblical story of Cain and Abel in the book of Genesis chapter 4. The story of Cain tells of the importance of justice and mercy. After Cain had committed the crime of killing his brother Abel, God had to intervene. Eventually a penalty was discharged; he was to be a wanderer (4:14). After justice has been granted, God never forgot his image and likeness in Cain. In chapter 4:15, he put a mark on Cain. God did not abandon Cain to the cycle of exclusions he himself had set in motion. Labelled by the mark of God, Cain still belonged to God and was protected by God even as he settled away from the presence of God.[17] [In African traditions, where serious offenders are exiled rather than killed, we find a similar strategy.] From a Christian perspective, Miroslav Volk further observes: 'Cain the anti-type who murdered his brother will be healed by Christ, the type who laid down his life for us, only if he sets out to walk in Christ's footsteps.'[18]

Forgiveness must be seen within the context of justice.[19] He put a seal, a sign of mercy. Religious laws approach life as not ending with justice but there is something more to it; there are possibilities of a person to become a new person. If God could come down and show mercy, those in the image of God can also mend relationships. The one wronged and the one responsible for a wrong act can reconcile. Without taking away the role of justice mercy is possible. Relationships can be mended whilst the offender is still behind bars and carries on when a sentence has been served fully. Certainly, one cannot be exclusive and claim that *only* religion can empower individuals to rise beyond the past, rather to assert that it is instrumental in balancing justice and mercy.

Human person in totality: a Christian anthropological perspective

It should not be the purpose of any law to separate a person from the self, others and society but to assist a person to realise how empowered he or she is and expand his or her being in the world. To achieve at this horizon of understanding, it is essential to embrace the following elements when one tries to deal with a human person:

1 human nature;
2 the body;
3 the soul;
4 reason;
5 affect;

17 Miroslav Volk, *Exclusion and Embrace: A Theological Exploration of Identity, Otherness and Reconciliation*, Nashville: Abingdon Press, 1996, at 98.

18 Ibid., at 98.

19 Worthington, *Forgiveness and Reconciliation*, at 39.

6 conscience;
7 free will;
8 memory;
9 the person as social being;
10 the end of the human person.[20]

Dealing with a person in his/her totality opens a new window on how laws can be fairly applied on individuals. The application of laws needs to maintain a relationship between a person as subject and the concrete basis of the law. But, more than its dealing with the victim and those disturbed by court cases, it demands more than healing emotions, and calls instead for the healing of the entire person. Religion comes to complete what occurred in courts when it journeys with both sides, perpetrator/their families and victims/their families, to reach deeper emancipation.

Certainly there is a temptation of merely treating a human person as a mind and body and of relegating other dimensions of the person. The application of laws on individuals cannot afford to avoid or exclude matters of soul or conscience. This is on the basis that disputes and conflicts have implications for the soul or 'inner being' of a person. Likewise, conscience cannot be avoided in the cause of justice because that is where the pulse of the right and wrong, good and bad, dawns.

Building from dispute resolution, religious laws try to address the person in totality. Human development concerns the whole of the person in every dimension.[21] The liberation experience involves more than simply being liberated from an externally oppressive situation: it encompasses the experience of inner freedom that comes from being emancipated.[22] One cannot speak of someone as empowered when one is not liberated from within through the 'removal of emotional barriers, the healing of the past wounds, and the coming to grips with internal forces'.[23] To speak of empowerment of a person, one needs to look beyond the merely material fulfilment into the non-material reality of a person. To speak of an empowered person is to speak of someone who is free from compulsion, someone open for genuine personal growth and that is experienced directly in human relationships.[24] This directly points to the importance of relationship between person, *Other* and God. For example:

> The believer understands canon law to express a meaning that facilitates the fulfilment of certain natural and supernatural ends. On a natural level, canon law functions as the rule of law, which aims to set optimal conditions for

20 John Coughlin, *Law, Person, and Community: Philosophical, Theological, and Comparative Perspectives on Canon Law*, New York: Oxford University Press, 2012, at 19–44.
21 Paul VI, Encyclical Letter *Populorum Progressio* (26 March 1967), AAS 22 (1967), art 14 at 268.
22 Jennifer Slater, Freedom: The Liberative Value and Ethical Credential for Christian Living in South Africa, *Journal of Theology for Southern Africa*, 148 (2014), at 50.
23 Ibid., at 52.
24 Ibid., at 53.

> justice and peace in the life of the church. On the supernatural level, canon law is intended to assist in the church's mission for the salvation of souls.[25]

Acting as a unity of body and soul, the human person constitutes the self; the integration of reason and feeling, and the formation of conscience to develop a love for self, others and God.[26] Clearly, reasoning and feeling do not represent the whole person but there is more to his/her composition. The soul as a sacred space gives humans dignity and the right to be respected as human beings irrespective of who they are or what their failings may be.[27] A human person is called to a fullness of life which far exceeds the dimensions of his/her earthly existence. After all, life on earth is not an ultimate but a penultimate reality, yet remaining a sacred reality that we are to uphold with a sense of responsibility.[28] In this way a soul is the complexity and continuity of the person-in-relationship, the soul is a work in progress, a dynamic rather than a static entity enabling us to become morally responsible human beings.[29]

The human person as an already empowered being

Scripture tells us that a human person is in the image of God (*imago dei*).[30] The root for human dignity lies in man's communion with God.[31] This is an affirmation of the endowment of a human person with divine character. In the depths of his conscience a human person detects a law which he does not impose on himself, but which holds him or her to obedience summoning him or her to love good and shun evil.[32] The overall appreciation of human dignity becomes important in human relations, care for the other and the ultimate pursuit of solidarity (common good). A human being is already empowered, yet needs awareness of this fact. Only in freedom can a human person be directed towards goodness.[33]

The theme of the dignity of a human person becomes important in transcending the past experience of victim/perpetrator discord to something greater, and that can contribute significantly to the well-being of society. True solidarity exists within a community of persons only when each member regards others as a neighbour – as having an intrinsic value simply because he or she is a unique and unrepeatable human being.[34] Re-affirming the centrality of humanity in the

25 Coughlin, *Law, Person and Community*, 26–28.

26 Ibid.

27 John de Gruchy, Retrieving the Soul: Understanding the Soul as Complex, Dynamic and Relational, *Journal of Theology for Southern Africa*, 149 (2014), 65.

28 John Paul II, Encyclical Letter, *Evangelium vitae* (25 March 1995), AAS 87 (1995), art 02.

29 de Gruchy, Retrieving the Soul.

30 Book of Genesis 1:27.

31 Paul VI, Pastoral Constitution, *Gaudium et spes*, 7 December, 1965, AAS 58 (1966), art 19.

32 Ibid., art 16.

33 Ibid., art 17.

34 Jeffrey Tranzillo, *John Paul II on the Vulnerable*, Washington, DC: The Catholic University of America Press, 2013, at 105.

study of laws can lead us far from living life in blocks, to see humanity holistically; and to understand ourselves better as human beings in relation to the other. For that reason, our need to actualise the personal property of participation, and thus relate to other people as 'I's, arises in us as a task to be fulfilled, a task that has ethical importance and whose measure is the commandment to love.[35] This, in actual fact, becomes important in the reconciliation process because, departing from a dignity platform while we assert our rights makes us see the 'I' in the other person standing in front of us. Consequently, an authentic love reflecting the mystery of God's inner life, as well as his love for humanity, is connected to the world through the interpersonal communion of every family sustained by the personal gift of God's love – that is, by the Holy Spirit poured out into the heart of the family.[36]

Rights awareness from the Church

While human rights have been defended and developed explicitly in civil society, the Church has also promoted them in the defence of the dignity of the human being.[37] Justice and Peace commissions are practical fora that enable the Church to expand its mission of protection of human rights. The Church's stance on human rights is not simply pointing to what the state must do, it tries to practise what it preaches within her borders. By taking this position, churches are like leaven within the society on how to understand the importance of rights and how to advance them as well.

As a way to illustrate how for example the Catholic Church is taking its broader stance on human rights, the Code of Canon Law of 1983 extensively considers the exercise of rights within the Church in the following:

- i All the Christian faithful have the right to be free from any kind of coercion in choosing a state in life, c.219. This canon proceeds from the exceptional dignity of the human person and the essential quality of all people to the necessity of societies (both civil and ecclesiastical) to provide means and opportunities for people to exercise their universal and inviolable rights.[38]
- ii No one is permitted to harm illegitimately the good reputation which a person possesses nor to injure the right of any person to protect his or

35 Ibid., at 106. Cf. Participation or alienation in PC, 202–204; AP, 354–355.

36 Ibid., at 136. Cf. Rm 5:5. See *Mulieris Dignitatem* (15 August 1988), 63 Vatican translation, Boston: Pauline Books and Media, 1988.

37 Peter Kanyandago, The Church's Role Regarding Education for Human Rights in AMECEA Countries, in *New Trends for the Empowerment of the people*, Proceedings of CUEA Third Interdisciplinary Session of the Faculty of Theology and the Department of Religious Studies Nairobi 1–3 April 1996, Nairobi: Paulines Publications Africa, 1997, at 147.

38 Robert Kaslyn, Book II The People of God: The Christian Faithful, in John Beal *et al.* (eds), *New Commentary on the Code of Canon Law*, New York and Mahwah: Paulist Press, 2000, at 276.

her own privacy, c.220. In the ordinary language we speak of protection from the defamation of character or character assassination. Certainly this right anchors on the very fact that a good name of a person is directly linked to the dignity of a person.

iii The Christian faithful can legitimately vindicate the rights which they are possessing in the Church in the competent ecclesiastical forum according to the norm of law, 221§1.

iv The right to due process, c.221§2.

v The Christian faithful have the right not to be punished with canonical penalties except according to the norm of law, c.221§3.

The above-mentioned canons are considered on the basis of their relevance to our discussion but there are other canons as well dealing with the rights in the church; such as rights of all Christian faithful,[39] specific rights to lay faithful,[40] rights of employees,[41] and rights to due canonical processes.[42] The 1983 Code of Canon Law has advanced rights that already exist in civil codes and constitutions as well in order to empower all the faithful. In this way, rights are not merely for the states, they are a matter of all citizens. Churches have developed alternative methods of ordering from those of the state, and at the end of the day they are often parallel and similar. So religion also claims to have power and authority and a role to play in all of this. How do we move on then? What is good must be practised by religious communities, at a right moment. The courts themselves are not the right place or the right moment, as South Africa is a secular state. So the practical application has to occur after a formal court process.

Application

Approaching aftermaths of court suits

Coping with the aftermaths of court proceedings can be dealt with through bio-psychological avenues, communal and religious fora. People who have been to court either as offended (with their family) or offenders (with their family) need a community of love. Love 'caritas' refers to agape. Members of the Christian communities contract mutual relations and obligations – ties and commitments like those of clan and family.[43] The ecclesial community becomes as it were a community that walks together with one another, interested in the good of all. Agape creates a *koinōnia*, a common life, a sharing of all in the same goods, anxiety and

39 Code of Canon Law 1983, Canon 203–223.

40 Ibid., Canon 224–231.

41 Ibid., Canon 1286.

42 Ibid., Canons 1311–1752.

43 R. Barr and José Comblin, *Retrieving the Human: A Christian Anthropology*, Maryknoll and New York: Orbis, 1990, at 12.

healing, joys and pains.[44] The experience of the agape cannot be restricted to those who come to church. As a matter of fact, members of the community do seek help from religious fellows and ministers.

Fora enhancing growth and healing of individuals, which at the same time enhance communities, are provided. Certainly, one does not claim that religion can solve all problems presented to their fora, but an avenue is affirmed. Second, individuals are helped to come to terms with the relationship between justice and love. Court cases can make people weak as persons; court cases can make people marginalised by society, therefore it has been observed that appointments with ministers have been instrumental mainly in rural parts of South Africa assisting people to regain new meaning in life. Fellowships like the *Prison Fellowship South Africa* have done so well in building bridges by practically facilitating victim–offender dialogues.[45] An encounter between NLundi who murdered Vuyo's uncle demonstrates that both the offender and victim can go beyond crime and punishment.[46] The root, the core, of Christianity is the proclamation of the new person now living among us and within us.[47] Of course, it would in many cases be better to consult priests before the court processes. Therefore, instead of running to the state, churches also offer methods of settling disputes through advising negotiation, mediation, among others, contrary to litigation. This process reflects what the modern alternative dispute resolution (ADR) model is about nowadays.

The Christian faithful have the right to receive assistance from the sacred pastors out of the spiritual goods of the Church.[48] Spiritual goods might be from the Word of God, sacraments of the Church, and counselling encounters as a way of affirming a person. The Church can never be exempted from practising charity as an organised activity of believers, and on the other hand, there will never be a situation where the charity of each individual Christian is unnecessary, because in addition to justice, man needs and will always need love.[49]

What is evident of un-forgiveness is that it remains psychological, emotional, physical and spiritually stressful. Unhealed stress ruins individuals, family and community life.[50] While one may not be pushed to forgive, spiritual accompaniment is needed, that will give way to 'gratitude, humility, contrition and hope'.[51]

Reflecting from the side of the offender, one needs to affirm that genuine repentance may be one of the most difficult acts for a person, let alone a community, to perform.[52] Conversion can be imagined as a process in which one learns to tell not

44 Ibid.

45 http://prisonfellowship.co.za/victim-offender-dialogue/ (last accessed 27.11.14).

46 Ibid.

47 Barr and Comblin, *Retrieving the Human*, at 30.

48 Code of Canon Law 1983, canon 213.

49 Benedict XVI, Encyclical *Deus Caritas est*, 25 December 2005, AAS 14 (2006), art 229.

50 Worthington, *Forgiveness and Reconciliation*, 61–77.

51 Ibid., 78–81.

52 Volk, *Exclusion and Embrace*, at 119.

just any story but a specific kind of story about oneself in which one's experience of conversion occupies a decisive place.[53] It is the converted that can embrace reconciliation with contrite heart, confession and satisfaction. Satisfaction would lead to the spirit of mending of relationships which again will need a careful minister to play this role. Avenues offered by religious communities are meant to assist individuals to a meaningful engagement with self and others.

Forgiveness can have a far enriching impetus on individuals and society. It may repair broken relationships, restore individual well-being, express love, recognition of conciliatory behaviour and can restore relational justice.[54]

> Again, forgiveness is not a substitute for justice. Forgiveness is no mere discharge of a victim's angry resentment and no mere assuaging of a perpetrator's remorseful anguish, one that demands no change of perpetrator and no righting of wrong. On the contrary: every act of forgiveness enthrones justice.[55]

A person as a social being

Religious character is also enriched with *ubuntu*[56] in the African context. *Ubuntu* became important in jurisprudence in recent years. Mokgoro J. succinctly explained *ubuntu* in *S* v. *Makwanyane and Another* in the following words:

> While it envelops the key values of group solidarity, compassion, respect, human dignity, conformity to basic norms and collective unity, in its fundamental sense it denotes humanity and morality. Its spirit emphasises respect for human dignity, marking a shift from confrontation to conciliation.[57]

Ubuntu is thus a spirit interweaving family laws, social laws and well-being of the whole community. This principle does not deny objective pluralism but directs all plurality to one source.[58]

Human reason leads to the appreciation that membership, participation and solidarity are necessary to human flourishing.[59] In this instance, communities learn to move beyond differences, past wounds and leap to new horizons.

53 Matthew Scherer, *Beyond Church and State: Democracy, Secularism and Conversion*, Cambridge: Cambridge University Press, 2013, 34.

54 Vincent Waldron and Douglas Kelley, *Communicating Forgiveness*, Los Angeles: Sage Publications, 2008, 130–132.

55 Volk, *Exclusion and Embrace*, at 123. Cf. Michael Welker, Gewaltverzicht un Feindesliebe, in Jűrgen Roloff and Hans G. Ulrich (eds), *Einfach von Got redden: eintheogischer Diskurs. Festschrift fur Friedrich Mildenbergerzum 65. Geburtstag*, Stuttgart: W. Kohlhammer, 1994, 243–247.

56 Ubuntu is an African concept meaning humanness.

57 See *S* v. *Makwanyane* 1995 (6) BCLR 665 (CC), par 308.

58 Pityana, *Being Church in South Africa Today*; Minorities in Global Society, at 176.

59 Coughlin, *Law, Person, and Community*, at 40.

These gain expression for instance in the involvement of the Church in community development and self-help projects. In recognising the social nature of the human person, canon law attempts to set the optimal conditions for participation and solidarity.[60]

We cannot and do not exist in isolation from other humans; we are locked into the society of humanity from the beginning of our lives. We are not fully conditioned or determined by our genetic make-up or sociological conditions, but responsible human beings living in relation to others in specific historical context. This does not mean that the individual has no personal identity, any more than it means the priority of the social over the personal. It means, rather, that the discovery of genuine personal identity and nurturing of the soul is only possible in community, that is, in relationship to the other.[61]

Since societies are growing even closer due to technological advancement, communion between persons leads us to a deeper understanding of the laws of social life, which the Creator has written into man's moral and spiritual nature.[62] We are led again to reflect on the development of the personality,[63] freedom[64] and vindication of rights.[65]

Learning from the TRC in South Africa

South Africa could have easily applied a notion of tooth for tooth, but rather it opted for a Truth and Reconciliation Commission (TRC) that was not led merely by a legal team, but also a religious minister, bishop emeritus Desmond Tutu. A new future could not be built on a story of fighting; justice must preserve life. We need that peace – the peace that enables us to go out and reconcile with ourselves, with our neighbours, with everybody else in our communities.[66]

In the words of the then Minister of Justice Dullah Omar, the TRC came to be seen as:

> the historic bridge of which the constitution speaks whereby our society can leave behind the past of a deeply divided society characterized by strife, conflict, untold suffering and injustice, and commence the journey towards a

60 Ibid.

61 de Gruchy, Retrieving the Soul, 66–67.

62 Paul VI, Pastoral Constitution, *Gaudium et spes*, 7 December, 1965, AAS 58 (1996), art 23.

63 Code of Canon Law 1983 canon 220 states that no one is permitted to harm illegitimately the good reputation which a person possesses nor to injure the right of any person to protect his or her privacy.

64 Ibid., canon 219 states that all the Christian faithful have the right to be free from any kind of coercion in choosing a state of life.

65 Ibid., canon 221§1 stipulates that the Christian faithful can legitimately vindicate and defend the rights which they possess in the Church in the competent ecclesiastical forum according to the norm of law.

66 Emmanuel Katongole, *The Sacrifice of Africa: A Political Theology for Africa*, Cambridge: WB Eerdmans, 2011, 162–163.

> future founded on the recognition of human rights, democracy and peaceful co-existence, and development opportunities for all South Africans irrespective of colour, race, class, belief and sex.[67]

It is essential to notice that 'forgiveness is viewed as a societal event, whereby whole peoples or nations forgive others or receive forgiveness from others'.[68] In other words, it became an event to bring a nation together as well as build a nation again (reconciliation). And, for this purpose a space, not necessarily a confessional box, had to be created. The fact is that reconciliation cannot be pursued without the alienated parties facing each other.[69]

Key in the introductory notes by Dullah Omar was the emphasis laid on the use of the phrase 'historic bridge'. It was essential that the TRC had to come into existence in order to facilitate the birth of the new nation from the dark era to a brighter future, because truth is an encounter that liberates one from being too close to one's self.[70] It is as it were a mechanism that propels transformation and healthy relationships. If the experience of truth telling were missed, the nation would not have to come to terms with the reality of its existence and its belonging together, especially at a time when the demographic majority is in charge of the rules.

The state committed itself to work hand-in-hand with other organisations and structures that are within the nation. Equally important was to witness faith communities, non-governmental organisations, community-based organisations and ordinary citizens playing a role in achieving the goal of national unity.[71] In this event the integrity of both the divine and the human partners was so carried through that the encounter was self-involving for each and all stakeholders.[72]

The TRC represented a quest for the nation to re-establish harmony; a value that would enable an integrated nation. An integrated community is one that has the capacity to know the values it needs, and the strength to obtain them.[73] South Africa could not have done better than ensuring that the constitution that was about to bind all in South Africa is coherent to the values of the peoples; cultural, social and religious ones embracing togetherness. There is a fundamental wholeness in

67 D. Omar, Minister of Justice Introducing the Promotion of National Unity and Reconciliation Act in Parliament, 17 May 1995, in *Truth and Reconciliation Commission of South Africa Report*, London and New York: Macmillan, 1999, vol. 1, at 48.

68 Anthony Da Silva, Through Nonviolence to Truth, in Raymond G. Helmick and Rodney Petersen, *Forgiveness and Reconciliation: Religion, Public Policy, and Conflict Transformation*, Philadelphia and London: Templeton Foundation Press, 2001, at 313.

69 John W. de Gruchy, *Reconciliation Restoring Justice*, Minneapolis: Fortress Press, 2002, at 148.

70 George Hunsinger, *How to Read Karl Barth: The Shape of Theology*, New York: New York University Press, 1991, at 152.

71 *Truth and Reconciliation Commission of South Africa Report*, London and New York: Macmillan, 1999, vol. 1, at 49.

72 Hunsinger, *How to Read Karl Barth*, at 154.

73 Ladislas Örsy, *Theology and Canon Law: New Horizons for Legislation and Interpretation*, Minnesota: The Liturgical Press, 1992, at 94.

the community that is contented with its laws and lives by them.[74] This of course is said without forgetting remaining challenges, of the inherent tensions between commitment to global values and international human rights principles and local cultures and traditions, in particular. The TRC became instrumental in making the nation move towards achieving its goal of national reconciliation, while avoiding expulsion of the erstwhile offenders. Today South Africa has almost three million Afrikaners who are no longer oppressors after liberation but a powerful minority of ordinary citizens, whose co-operation and goodwill was required in the reconstruction of the country.[75]

The role and influence of religion in South African society is central in its efforts to access the problems of and prospects for reconciliation in the nation.[76] To speak of religion with the prospect for reconciliation is at the same time an affirmation of relevance of religion in the sphere of justice. Law and religion, and thus law and different religions in the South Africa's context, need to work together. Faith communities enjoy a unique and privileged position in South African society. They are widely respected and have far-reaching moral influence. As such, they should play a key role in healing and reconciliation initiatives.[77]

Dullah Omar appealed to religious communities perhaps because among other factors churches that are plural within can contribute positively to the building up of the nation.

The Church recognises that worthy elements are found in today's social movements, especially an evolution towards unity, a process of wholesome socialisation and of association in civic and economic realms. The promotion of unity belongs to the innermost nature of the Church, for she is, thanks to her relationship with Christ, a sacramental sign and an instrument of intimate union with God, and of the unity of the whole human race. The Church shows the world that an authentic union, social and external, results from a union of minds and hearts, namely from that faith and charity by which her own unity is unbreakably rooted in the Holy Spirit.[78]

It is very important, especially where a pluralistic society prevails, that there be a correct notion of the relationship between the political community and the Church, and a clear distinction between the tasks which Christians undertake, individually or as a group, on their own responsibility as citizens guided by the dictates of a Christian conscience, and the activities which, in union with their pastors, they carry out in the name of the Church.[79] Yet both, under different

74 Ibid.

75 Anthony Sampson, *Mandela: The Authorised Biography*, London: HarperCollins, 1999, at 293.

76 Audrey Chapman, Introduction: Religion and Reconciliation in South Africa, in A. Chapman and B. Spong (eds), *Religion and Reconciliation in South Africa: Voices of Religious Leaders*, Philadelphia and London: Templeton Foundation Press, 2003, at 3.

77 *Truth and Reconciliation Commission of South Africa Report*, Cape Town: Juta & Co., 1998, vol. 5, at 316.

78 Pastoral Constitution on the Church in the Modern World, *Gaudium et Spes* (7 December 1965), AAS 58(1966), art 42.

79 Ibid., art 76.

titles, are devoted to the personal and social vocation of the same persons. They are interrelated out of necessity. Religion, of its essence, is wonderfully helpful to the state.[80] The more both foster sounder cooperation between themselves with due consideration for the circumstances of time and place, the more effective will their service be exercised for the good of all.[81]

In this way, the Church is ever to offer her support to the building of society and the nations:

> The body politic, whose essential duty is the implementation and administration of a just order, can be a major instrument at the service of reconciliation, justice and peace. This order, in its turn, is at the service of the 'vocation to the communion of persons'. In order to put this ideal into practice, the Church in Africa must help to build up society in cooperation with government authorities and public and private institutions that are engaged in building up the common good. Traditional chiefs have a very positive contribution to make to good governance. The Church, for her part, is committed to promoting within her own ranks and within society a culture that respects the rule of law.[82]

It is in the nature of common good that every single citizen has the right to share in it – although in different ways, depending on his or her beliefs, tasks, merits and circumstances. Hence every civil authority must strive to promote the common good in the interest of all, without favouring any individual citizen or category of citizen,[83] it is thus belonging to faith communities as well to enhance matters of common good of which rule of law is a question that cannot be avoided.

Talking of the TRC after twenty years of democracy would be hollow unless one engages in an assessment of the impact it has today in South Africa and how religion in particular has advanced the recommendation given. Why is this assessment so crucial? First and foremost, truth and reconciliation are religious concepts. When Christ says 'He is the truth', he introduced into truth a content carrying ontological implications, truth is life.[84] Put the other way round, reconciliation is life for the community.

From the very beginning of the TRC contentious claims and allegations were introduced of killings, torture and various kinds of cruelties. Life and peace had to be put back to order. Such reflections were to contribute in the future legislation as the late President Mandela in his presidential inauguration speech in 1995 exhorted: 'Never, never, never again shall it be that this beautiful land will again experience the oppression of one by another . . . Let freedom reign. God

80 Leo XIII, Encyclical Letter, *Libertas*, Acta Leonis XIII, 20 June 1888, art 22.

81 See, *Gaudium et Spes*, art 76.

82 Benedict XVI, African Synod, *Africae Munus* (19 November 2011), AAS 103 (2011), art 81.

83 John XXIII, Encyclical Letter, *Pacem in Terris* (11 April 1963), AAS 55 (1963), art 56.

84 John Zizioulas, *Being as Communion*, London: Darton, Longman and Todd Ltd, 1985, at 107.

bless Africa.'[85] To this, there was no way that the role of law could be bypassed, especially distributive justice, setting-up of policy and procedures.

Therefore the recommendations of the TRC to religious communities affirmed the importance and contribution of religious laws. 'Where reality is subject to law and thereby intelligible . . . spiritual reality has intelligibility by its native intelligence.'[86] As 'freedom is a special kind of contingence grounded in the order of the spirit, intelligent grasp, rational reflection and morally guided will'[87] the new South Africa had to be prepared in both material and spiritual means.

The beauty of legal of pluralism

Dialogue is an important characteristic of the world we live in. The whole world has become one big place where dialogue and encounter have become inevitable.[88]This is not a plea for freedom of religion within legal systems because this is already a part of many state constitutions and frameworks of international organisations like the United Nations. Likewise, informed public life may in fact be necessary to cultivate those practices of citizenship to sustain democratic governance under conditions of the deeply seated reality of pluralism in South Africa.[89]

'Whatever the rationale for the survival of deep legal pluralism in South Africa, legal pluralism is more than a simple juristic peculiarity',[90] it is a reality that is closely interwoven with the daily lives of all South Africans. The post-apartheid constitution, however, is clear that 'South Africa is a secular state with no intention to promote any one religion against another',[91] yet section 15(1)(3) of the Bill of Rights specifically allows for the statutory recognition of religious and traditional family law.[92] With such recognition, religious laws are at their rightful position in empowering individuals and achieving or finishing what could not be finished in courts. As long as religions respect the role of the state in ascertaining justice for all, in other words, as long as their effects do not contradict the constitutional aims and guarantees, there is no conflict when contentious causes land in,

85 N. Mandela, *Long Walk to Freedom: The Autobiography of Nelson Mandela*, London: Abacus, 1994, at 747.

86 F.E. Crowe and R.M. Doran, *Collected Works of Lonergan, Insight: A Study of Human Understanding*, London: Longmans, Green & Co., 1957, at 642.

87 Ibid.

88 Synod of Bishops, The Church in Africa and her Evangelisation mission towards the year 2000: You shall be my witness -Acts 1:8, Lineamenta, Vatican City, 1990, at 54.

89 Scherer, *Beyond Church and State*, at 94.

90 C. Rautenbach, Deep Legal Pluralism in South Africa: Judicial Accommodation of Non-State Law, *Journal of Legal Pluralism and Unofficial Law*, 60 *JLP* (2010),143–177, at 174.

91 J. De Gruchy and S. De Gruchy, *The Church Struggle in South Africa* (3rd edn), London: SCM Press, 2004, at 241.

92 S. Pete, The Dignity of Difference: Freedom of Religion in Post-Apartheid South Africa, in S. Du Plessis and S. Pete (eds), *Constitution Democracy in South Africa 1994–2004*, Durban: LexisNexis, 2004, 142.

and even are concluded in, religious fora. In other words, there is nothing illegal per se in a church minister dealing with dispute resolution. This is not a matter only for the state.

Concluding remarks

Pluralities are like ingredients characterising laws which one cannot afford to turn a blind eye to or deny their existence. In South Africa, this also relates to the power relationship between judges and parliament. Chief Justice Langa noted well that it is

> no longer sufficient for judges to rely on the say-so of parliament or technical readings of legislation as providing justifications for their decisions but that judges bear the ultimate responsibility to justify their decisions not only by reference to authority, but by reference to ideas and values.[93]

From this, one deduces that religious laws as well can benefit state laws. Religious laws can enable better understanding of a human person in its totality, that is in relation with the self, the *Other*, the environment and the transcendent Being. There is no contradiction, then, between state law and religious law. Such realisation is important in the empowerment of persons, and in their search for the right path. Law still has a role to play after suits; it is not only about catching people as offenders but also about emancipating people. Given canon law's relationship with theology, one is reminded that true justice is more than a matter of rules and rights. People matter. Caring also counts.[94] State and non-state laws together do have the potential to empower people when all sides acknowledge that there is value in the other. Religious laws are not the things of the past, but the future of many societies that will grow still brighter under the radiance of these laws, but never truly 'autonomous', always in a legally plural setting. This, too, confirms that in the wider context of legal pluralism debates, the potentially empowering impact of religious input must never be underplayed or simply denied on 'politically correct' secular grounds.

References

Allegretti, J., *The Lawyers Calling: Christian Faith and Legal Practice*, New York and Mahwah: Paulist Press, 1996.

Barr, R., *Retrieving the Human: A Christian Anthropology*, Maryknoll and New York: Orbis, 1990.

Beal, J., Coriden, James A. and Green, Thomas Joseph (eds), *New Commentary on the Code of Canon Law*, New York and Mahwah: Paulist Press, 2000.

93 Pius Langa, Transformative Constitutionalism, *Steell LR*, 17 (2006), 351–353.

94 Allegretti, *The Lawyers Calling*, at 108.

Chapman, A. and Spong, B. (eds), *Religion and Reconciliation in South Africa: Voices of Religious Leaders*, Philadelphia and London: Templeton Foundation Press, 2003.

Code of Canon Law 1983, Latin-English edn, Washington, DC: Canon Law Society of America, 1989.

Coughlin, J., *Law, Person, and Community: Philosophical, Theological, and Comparative Perspectives on Canon Law*, New York: Oxford University Press, 2012.

Crowe, F., and Doran, R., *Collected Works of Lonergan, Insight: A Study of Human Understanding*, London: Longmans, Green & Co., 1957.

De Gruchy, J., *Reconciliation Restoring Justice*, Minneapolis: Fortress Press, 2002.

De Gruchy, J., Retrieving the Soul: Understanding the Soul as Complex, Dynamic and Relational, *Journal of Theology for Southern Africa* 149 (2014): 56–69.

De Gruchy, J. and De Gruchy, S., *The Church Struggle in South Africa* (3rd edn), London: SCM Press, 2004.

Du Plessis, S. and Pete, S. (eds), *Constitution Democracy in South Africa 1994–2004*, Durban: LexisNexis, 2004.

Farrow, D. (ed.), *Recognising Religion in a Secular Society: Essays in Pluralism, Religion, and Public Policy*, Montreal and Kingston: McGill-Queen University Press, 2004.

Good News Bible, The Bible Societies and Collins, 2005.

Helmick, R. and Petersen, R., *Forgiveness and Reconciliation: Religion, Public Policy, and Conflict Transformation*, Philadelphia and London: Templeton Foundation Press, 2001.

Hunsinger, G., *How to Read Karl Barth: The Shape of Theology*, New York: New York University Press, 1991.

Katongole, E., *The Sacrifice of Africa: A Political Theology for Africa*, Cambridge: WB Eerdmans, 2011.

Langa, P., Transformative Constitutionalism, *Steell LR* 17(3) (2006): 351–353.

Mandela, N., *Long Walk to Freedom: The Autobiography of Nelson Mandela*, London: Abacus, 1994.

Örsy, L., *Theology and Canon Law: New Horizons for Legislation and Interpretation*, Minnesota: The Liturgical Press, 1992.

Proceedings of CUEA Third Interdisciplinary Session of the Faculty of Theology and the Department of Religious Studies Nairobi 1–3 April 1996, Nairobi, Paulines Publications Africa, 1997.

Rautenbach, C., Deep Legal Pluralism in South Africa: Judicial Accommodation of Non-State Law, Journal of Legal Pluralism and Unofficial Law 60 (2010): 143–177.

Sampson, A., *Mandela: The Authorised Biography*, London: HarperCollins, 1999.

Scherer, M., *Beyond Church and State: Democracy, Secularism and Conversion*, Cambridge: Cambridge University Press, 2013.

Schubeck, T., *Love that does Justice*, Maryknoll and New York: Orbis Books, 2007.

Slater, J., Freedom: The Liberative Value and Ethical Credential for Christian Living in South Africa, *Journal of Theology for Southern Africa* 148 (2014): 48–64.

Tranzillo, J., *John Paul II on the Vulnerable*, Washington, DC: The Catholic University of America Press, 2013.

Truth and Reconciliation Commission of South Africa Report, London and New York: Macmillan, 1999.

Villa-Vicencio, C. and Carl Niehaus, D. (eds), *Beyers Naude: A Festschrift*, Cape Town: Human & Roussow, 1995.

Volk, M., *Exclusion and Embrace: A Theological Exploration of Identity, Otherness and Reconciliation*, Nashville: Abingdon Press, 1996.

Waldron, V. and Kelley, D., *Communicating Forgiveness*, Los Angeles: Sage Publications, 2008.
Worthington, E., *Forgiveness and Reconciliation: Theory and Application*, New York: Routledge, 2006.
Zizioulas, Z., *Being as Communion*, London: Darton, Longman and Todd Ltd, 1985.

Encyclical letters and pastoral constitution

Benedict XVI, Encyclical Letter *Deus Caritas est* (25 December 2005), AAS 14 (2006).
Benedict XVI, Encyclical Letter *Caritas Veritate* (29 June 2009), AAS 73 (2009).
Benedict XVI, Post Synodal Exhortation, African Synod, *Africae Munus* (19 November 2011), AAS 103 (2011).
Leo XIII, Encyclical Letter *Libertas*, in *Acta Leonis* XIII 20 June 1888.
John XXIII, Encyclical Letter *Pacem in Terris* (11 April 1963), AAS 55 (1963).
John Paul II, Encyclical Letter *Evangelium vitae* (25 March 1995), AAS 87 (1995).
Paul VI, Encyclical Letter *Populorum Progressio* (26 March 1967), AAS 22 (1967).
Pastoral Constitution on the Church in the Modern World, *Gaudium et Spes*, AAS 58 (1966).
Synod of Bishops, The Church in Africa and her Evangelisation mission towards the year 2000: You shall be my witness – Acts 1:8, Lineamenta, Vatican City (1990).

Case law

S v. *Makwanyane* 1995 (6) BCLR 665 (CC).
S v. *Pistorius* 2014 sacr 589 (GP).

Online citation

http://prisonfellowship.co.za/victim-offender-dialogue/ (last accessed 27.11.14).

6 *Sharīʻa* deconstructed

A new definition of Islamic Constitutionalism and its enforcement through positive law

Pietro Longo

Introduction

The Islamic legal system is a complex set of laws and juridical concepts, which regulate the internal and external fora in the lives of Muslims. This set, usually referred to as the *Sharīʻa*, is taken, sometimes clearly, sometimes through deductive reasoning, from the preeminent sources of Islamic law: the Quran and the *sunna*.[1] Far from being comparable to 'codes', these sources require jurists to make legal reasoning (*iǧtihād*) to extract laws from them. Islamic law defines, at the same time, conducts between God and men (*ʻibādāt*) as well as relations between men (*muʻāmalāt*).[2] Encompassing also matters of governance, Islamic law would appear to fall more under the 'secular' domain, but it is always linked to the underlying value systems.

Aside from operational and easily inferable rules, regarding legal aspects which range from criminal law to personal status (inheritance, marriage, divorce), the *Sharīʻa* also contains a set of general principles (*qawāʻid kulliyya*) which embody its spirit and guide not only the relationships among men, but also their relations to the public sphere. The general principles, usually taken little into account by academic studies on Islamic law, are expressed as legal maxims and represent an integral part of the Islamic law. Therefore, like other rules, they could be applied in practical terms in specific cases. In the same way, the theory of *maqāṣid al-Sharīʻa*, expressing the 'purposes of divine law', could help judges or legislators of modern constitutional systems to issue sentences or guide the legislative activity. Considering the interconnections between the religious and secular spheres in the Islamic system of law, Muslim scholars elaborated the concept of *siyāsa sharʻiyya*, being politics under the boundaries of the religious law. This is akin to the *lex humana* of St Thomas Aquinas, and thus a combination of natural law plus socio-legal approach to the understanding of human obligations vis-à-vis God as well as his fellow humans.[3]

1 See in general: N. Coulson, *A History of Islamic Law*, Edinburgh University Press, Edinburgh, 1991.

2 On the difference between *ʻibādāt* and *muʻāmalāt* see: J. Schacht, *An Introduction to Islamic Law*, Clarendon, Oxford, 1982, p. 79.

3 On the concept of *Lex humana*, see: F. Kessler, 'The Philosophy of Law from St. Augustine to Thomas Aquinas', *The New Scholasticism*, vol. 20, no. 1, 1946, pp. 26–71.

Both the *qawā'id kulliyya* and *maqāṣid al-Sharī'a*, although formally and more visibly developed starting from the medieval ages, have been systematized by contemporary jurists, like Muḥammad al-Ṭāhir ibn 'Āshūr (1879–1973) and Yūsuf al-Qaraḍāwī (1926–).[4] This confirms that the underlying conceptual issues are at the same time old and very much of current relevance. In this chapter, the works of these authors, containing the analysis of such instruments of the Islamic law, will be taken into account. Basing my analysis on the most recent doctrine, I will try to deconstruct the idea of the *Sharī'a* as a fixed and immutable code of conduct.

Similarly, I demonstrate that the principles of the *Sharī'a* regarding good government or good governance, here collectively defined as 'political principles', could fundamentally contribute towards defining 'Islamic Constitutionalism' in a comprehensive way. To this end, it is useful to recall the old Greek distinction between 'material' and 'formal' Constitution. Through this distinction, Aristotle indicated how a city-state gave itself an organization apart from the existence of written rules. According to Aristotle: 'the politician and lawgiver are wholly occupied with the city-state, and the constitution is a certain way of organizing those who inhabit the city-state'.[5] The substantial aspect of the Constitution concerns a set of social and economic rules, which represent the core values of a society in a certain historical timeframe. The Constitution thus defines the governing body, which takes different forms: for example, in a democracy it is the people, and in an oligarchy it is a select few such as the wealthy.

In my analysis, Islamic Constitutionalism, the intimate values of the Islamic good government, could result from the combination of:

1 the general principles of the Islamic law;
2 the theory of the *maqāṣid al-Sharī'a*;
3 the political principles of Islam.

Once defined, my thesis concerns the possibility to put Islamic Constitutionalism in operation through the recall of the *Sharī'a* by the Constitution (i.e. article 2 of Egyptian Constitution of 1972 amended in 1980). If applied, Islamic Constitutionalism would create a substantial limit to the arbitrariness of the executive, legislative and judicial powers and could produce a significant empowerment. However, this ideal system requires institutional bodies to be enforced; otherwise Islamic Constitutionalism is likely simply to remain a dead letter.

4 Muḥammad al-Ṭāhir ibn 'Āshūr, *Maqāṣid al-Sharī'a al-Islāmiyya* [Purposes of the Islamic Law], Dār al-Nafā'is li'l-Nashr wa'l-Tawzī', 'Ammān, 2001; Yūsuf al-Qaraḍāwī, *al-Qawā'id al-ḥākima li-fiqh al-mu'āmalāt* [Dominant Principles in the Jurisprudence of Human Relationships], Dār al-Shurūq, Cairo, 2010.

5 B. Hjern and C. Hull, 'Implementation Research as Empirical Constitutionalism', *European Journal of Political Research*, vol. 10, no. 2, 1982, pp. 105–115; Aristotle, *Politics*, ed. H. Rackham, William Heinemann Ltd, Cambridge, 1932, pp. 172–276.

The general principles (*qawāʻid kulliyya*) of *Sharīʻa*

General principles (*qawāʻid kulliyya*) are legal maxims extracted from the Quran and the *sunna* that have been systematized by the jurisprudence of Muslim scholars in the medieval ages. These principles sometimes are called jurisprudential principles (*qawāʻid fiqhiyya*) because they are applied to all the Islamic law elements, which concern the relationships among men (*muʻāmalāt*). Some jurists distinguish major general principles (*qawāʻid kulliyya kubrā*) from minor ones (*qawāʻid mutafarriʻa*), so called because they are extracted from the former. Moreover, a distinction between fixed principles and disputable principles is also in use: the former are immutable and scholars tend agree on them, while the latter are not immutable and are subject indeed to interpretation.[6]

According to al-Zarqa', the general principles can be defined as 'constitutional sources of jurisprudence which supervise the general legislation'. Al-Nadwi, instead, defines general principles in the light of legality (*sharʻiyya*) excluding those principles which are not compliant with Islamic law because they are referring to something *ḥarām*.[7] Therefore, general principles are operational laws, which regulate different aspects of the life of Muslims and are applied to any legal interaction. Moreover, because they embody the spirit of the *Sharīʻa*, these principles make easier the definition of the rights and duties which Muslims must observe. According to al-Qaraḍāwī, in fact, the application of the general principles allows the full respect of the *Sharīʻa*, assuring the achievement of the highest spiritual wealth for the community. General principles, under this light, function as 'dampeners', because they temper the rigidity of some rules and make the application of the Islamic law possible.

In the case of inheritance law, for example, despite the existence of well-determined rules in the Quran and in the *sunna*, with regard to how the inheritance is distributed among the heirs, recourse to the general principles can allow a different and fairer distribution compared to what is normally ordered.[8] However, the general principles are typically applied when in the primary sources of the Islamic law there is no answer to a judicial case: lacking a reference (*naṣṣ ǧuz'ī*) in the Quran and in the *sunna*, it is possible to decide through the general principles, taking into account the *maqāṣid al-Sharīʻa*. Al-Qaraḍāwī draws an interesting hierarchy among the sources of Islamic law,

6 A fixed principle is one according to which no interpretation is allowed in the field of acts of worship (*ʻibādāt*) and in that of dogma (*ʻaqīda*). In the field of human transactions (contracts and their stipulated conditions) the basic principle is not the forbiddance but the lawfulness of the interpretation. On methodological disagreement between Muslim scholars, see: N. Coulson, *Conflicts and Tensions in Islamic Jurisprudence*, Islamic Book Trust, London, 2007.

7 In the Islamic law, the terms *Sharīʻa* and *sharʻiyya* are interrelated: if the first word actually indicates the religious and revealed law, the latter denotes what is legal on the base of the sources identified by the *Sharīʻa*. Islamic law conceptualizes all the human behaviour into five ranks: forbidden (*ḥarām*); compulsory (*farḍ*); recommended (*mustaḥabb*); recommended (*mubāḥ)*; disliked (*makrūḥ*). This also explains why politics in accordance with Islamic law is called *siyāsa sharʻiyya*.

8 Yūsuf al-Qaraḍāwī, *al-Qawāʻid al-ḥākima li-fiqh al-muʻāmalāt*, p. 13.

composed, on the top, by operational rules taken from the Quran and the *sunna*, followed by what can be decided through the *maqāṣid al-Sharīʿa* and, in third place, by what can be decided through the enforcement of the general principles.[9]

General principles are not systematic and jurists have sought to establish a way to order them. Following al-Qaraḍāwī's approach, the most general principle, and therefore the introductive one in comparison with the others, is the following: *al-aṣl fī'l-muʿāmalāt al-ibāḥa,* which implies that lawfulness (*al-ibāḥa*) must be the rule governing the relationships among men.[10] In Islamic law, all legal interactions existing among human beings are called *muʿāmalāt*. Therefore, in this domain, according to the above-mentioned principle, what is not formally forbidden by the Quran or *sunna* is allowed. The most common fields of application are that of contracts and obligations which link two or more parties. In regard to the relationship between man and God (*ʿibādāt*), on the contrary, the general rule is prohibition, not lawfulness. In fact, it must be noticed that in Islamic law not only is the public life of Muslims regulated by law, but also their private life, including the relationship to God.

General principles, then, empower the state to lay down general rules that affect the daily lives of all people present, even non-Muslims, such as the prohibition on having any food or drink during the fasting month. Speculation is not allowed over religious dogmas and acts of worship, and the attempt to introduce any change is defined as a reprehensible innovation (*bidʿa*). In the field of *muʿāmalāt*, on the contrary, the negotiation of the spaces of what is forbidden and what is compulsory is precisely what empowers or disempowers individuals.

Al-Qaraḍāwī explains that Islam was born in a tribal and 'ignorant' society (*ǧāhiliyya*), of which some aspects have been updated while others have been maintained. In the field of trade, Islamic law has allowed any kind of contracts as long as they are not based on usury or on selling uncertain goods. The aim was to prevent unjustified enrichment and maintain a fairer distribution of wealth, as is sanctioned in Quran II:275 'God has permitted trade and has forbidden interest'.[11]

From the principle discussed above, jurists have extracted the variation of *al-aṣl fī'l-ʿuqūd wa'l-shurūṭ al-ibāḥa*, which extends lawfulness from contracts to the conditions stipulated in them.[12] In fact, contractual conditions are customarily legal if they are mentioned in the sources of law. In accordance with this principle, also the contractual conditions not included in the Quran or in the *sunna* are admitted as long as they are not in conflict with the spirit of Islam. For example, under this principle a Muslim husband could be allowed to take a second wife against the wish of his wife, or without asking her permission. The higher principle here in permitting this would be the avoidance of unlawful sexual intercourse (*zinā*), it seems, a higher principle than the avoidance of harm to an existing wife.

9 Ibid., p. 14.

10 Ibid., p. 15.

11 It is important to note that the precise definition of *ribā* remains contested. For some scholars it is any form of interest. For others it regards mainly 'excessive interest'.

12 al-Qaraḍāwī, *al-Qawāʿid al-ḥākima li-fiqh al-muʿāmalāt*, p. 22.

Another principle related to the previous one is expressed by the statement *al-umūr bi-maqāṣidihā*, which implies that actions should ideally tend to their corresponding purposes.[13] The Arabic term for 'purposes' refers to the semantic root expressing the concept of wilfulness (*qaṣd*) which is related to the idea of *niyya* or intention.[14] According to a well-known *ḥadīth*, in fact, the Prophet would have said that human actions lie in their intentions, thus stressing the freedom in human behaviour.[15] In other words, man is created free and therefore Islamic law forbids all actions and obligations, which obstruct this freedom and the possibility for the worshipper to express a right and benevolent intention.

General principles do not protect men as individuals only but also their properties. The saying *taḥrīm akl amwāl al-nās bi'l-bāṭil* prohibits the illegal use of other people's property, as ordered in the Quran IV:29.[16] The principle *lā ḍirar wa-lā ḍarār*, that is the prohibition to cause personal or collective damages, obliges Muslims to take useful actions avoiding offences, or rather to prevent them. Aside from their literal meaning, these principles impose that every human action must produce individual or social wealth and does not provoke unjustified wrongs.

In the same field, the saying *al-ḍirar yuzāl* equates the damage and the tyranny, thus equating the unjust ruler acting in a harmful manner to the tyrant.[17] However, Islamic law invites Muslims to bear circumscribed damages to prevent offences that affect the whole community.[18] Another principle is expressed by the saying *al-taḥfīf wa'l-taysīr lā al-tashdīd wa'l-ta'sīr*, taken from Quran IV:28. According to it, it is possible to make legal what is generally forbidden.[19] This principle is widely applied for Muslim minorities living in non-Islamic societies where it is hard to fulfil all the duties Islamic law prescribes, but it also applies in Muslim-majority societies.

Moreover, the maxim *al-'ādāt wa'l-a'rāf fī mā lā yukhālifu al-shar'* allows to recur to customary laws if they are not in conflict with the Quran.[20] The principle *lā yankaru taghayyur al-aḥkām bi-taghayyur al-amzān* allows adaptation of rules

13 Ṣāliḥ bin Ġānim al-Sadlān, *al-Qawā'id al-fiqhiyya al-kubrā wa-ma tafarra' 'anhā* [Major Principles of Jurisprudence and What Derives from Them], Dār Balansiyya, Riyad, 1996, p. 41.

14 Ibid., p. 47. Here the *niyya* is defined by the jurist as 'the will to obey and to get closer to God through actions or abstention'.

15 See the collection of prophetic traditions by Muslim ibn Ḥaǧǧāǧ, *Ṣaḥīḥ Muslim*, Dar Tayyiba li'l-Nashr wa'l-Tawzī', Riyadh, 2006, vol. 5, p. 920.

16 Yūsuf al-Qaraḍāwī, *al-Qawā'id al-ḥākima li-fiqh al-mu'āmalāt*, p. 51. Quran IV:29 states: 'O you who have believed, do not consume one another's wealth unjustly.'

17 Ibid., p. 72.

18 This principle is applicable, for example, in the case when a sentence of death is issued for a doctor who caused the death of his patients due to his ignorance in medical sciences. Then, a minor damage is acceptable if it can prevent more serious damages.

19 Yūsuf al-Qaraḍāwī, *al-Qawā'id al-ḥākima li-fiqh al-mu'āmalāt*, pp. 105–106. Quran IV:28 states: 'And God wants to lighten for you [your difficulties]; and mankind was created weak.'

20 Customs are divided into general and particular. The latter are those followed in specific places and have a local character, while the former are common either to Muslims or to believers of other religions. Moreover, the Islamic law recognizes the difference between customs that derive from actions (*'urf 'amalī*) and those that derive from language and discourses (*'urf qawlī*).

to customs of the time, except for those regulations based on indisputable verses of the Quran. What customs acknowledge as legal can acquire the same status of what the Quran or the *sunna* clearly order. The jurists believe, in fact, that the change in the historical contingencies must cause an evolution of the norms, too.

Through the general principles, *Sharī'a* is deconstructed and becomes a system of law in continuous update. In specific cases, based on the application of the general principles, jurists are also able to make lawful what the Quran forbade, such as the prohibition of interests on economic transactions or alcohol consumption.[21] For example, while Islamic law generally prohibits drinking wine and alcohol of every kind, their consumption is allowed, under the enforcement of general principles, to safeguard a Muslim's life in precise circumstances (such as for medical purposes). Similar cases could be allowed simply because Islamic law does not forbid an action for itself but for its legal meaning, its effects and its final purpose. For example, in the Islamic law of war, women are dispensed to fight the defensive *ğihād* not because they are deemed unable to wage war compared to men but because their eventual deaths could reverberate over the future of the Muslim society.

The theory of *maqāṣid al-Sharī'a* in classical and contemporary sources

According to Islamic law, rights and freedoms are granted to man by God for the realization of general welfare (*maṣlaḥa 'amma*). This, in turn, depends on the achievement of the *maqāṣid al-Sharī'a*, the purposes of divine law.[22] In the oldest doctrinal essays, in fact, jurists used the Arabic terms for purposes and general welfare in an interchangeable way, proving their correspondence had already been assumed. The jurist al-Qārafī (d. 1285) made this relation clear, stating that: 'a purpose (*maqṣid*) is not valid unless it leads to the achievement of some kind of welfare (*maṣlaḥa*) or at least avoids damage (*mafsada*)'.[23]

The purposes of Islamic law have been systematically codified by the doctrine of the mālikite jurist Abū Isḥāq al-Shāṭibī (d. 1388), who defined them as 'the fundamental elements of religion, the basic principles of the law and the universals of the community'.[24] This jurist divided the purposes into three main levels, which determine a rigid hierarchy. In the first level, al-Shāṭibī placed the *al-maṣāliḥ al-ḍarūriyya*, compulsory aspects of human life to which Islamic law pledges a total legal protection. There are five domains: religion (*dīn*), life (*nafs*), reason (*'aql*), possessions (*māl*) and filial relationship (*nasb*). These are elements that Islamic law preserves with more care and attention because they are unavoidable

21 Yūsuf al-Qaraḍāwī, *al-Qawā'id al-ḥākima li-fiqh al-mu'āmalāt*, p. 40.

22 J. Auda, *Maqasid al-Shariah as Philosophy of Islamic Law*, The International Institute of Islamic Thought, London, 2008, p. 2.

23 Auda, *Maqasid al-Shariah as Philosophy of Islamic Law*.

24 Ibid., p. 21.

for human life. At the second level, there are the *al-maṣāliḥ al-ḥāğğiyya*, those interests of all human beings deserving protection, which can be classified as needs. Finally, the third level comprises the *al-maṣāliḥ al-taḥsīniyya*, embellishments, composed by good habits (*al-'ādāt al-ḥusnā*) and moral rules (*makārim al-akhlāq*). These three levels, however, are strictly interconnected and, according to al-Shāṭibī, each higher level must protect the lower ones.[25]

The most recent doctrine has gradually extended the purposes of revelation, following the example of Muḥammad al-Ṭāhir ibn 'Āshūr who added the general purposes of freedom and justice to the traditional theory. The classical theory of *maqāṣid al-Sharī'a* is only the starting point to develop a more comprehensive doctrine which covers religious freedoms, protection of life, right to education, freedom of thought, right to family care and protection of possessions.[26] During the twentieth century, jurists have extended its sphere of influence: for example, from the protection of women and children, modern doctrines have deduced a protection for the family, while the protection of property has been extended to assets in a broader sense.

Redefining the limits which the theory of *maqāṣid al-Sharī'a* was classically given, the jurists have distinguished three kinds of purposes of Islamic law:

1 General purposes (*maqāṣid 'āmma*), which represent the essence of the law, such as the principles of freedom, justice and integrity of human beings.
2 Particular purposes (*maqāṣid khāṣṣa*), which are applied to preserve the welfare of some peculiar contexts such as family life and the statute of women. The commitments to avoid offences to women in their private and public life or to prevent speculation in financial transactions, thus preserving the balance among social classes, fall within this group.
3 This category includes partial purposes (*maqāṣid ğuz'iyya*), which reflect those intentions which lie behind particular rules and actions, such as the will to prove the truth providing a high number of witnesses to a court or a judge.[27]

Other modernist jurists such as Rashīd Riḍā (1865–1935) and Yūsuf al-Qaraḍāwī have extended the operating range of the *maqāṣid al-Sharī'a*, coming to cover women's rights and human rights. According to Muḥammad al-Ṭāhir ibn 'Āshūr, *maqāṣid al-Sharī'a* are necessary for preserving the Muslim community and to fully achieve its welfare.[28] Therefore, it is licit to extend their limits: the protection assured to progeny can be transformed into the right to build and maintain the family since the former represents a particular aspect of the latter.[29] Moreover,

25 Ibid., p. 4.
26 Muḥammad al-Ṭāhir ibn 'Āshūr, *Maqāṣid al-Sharī'a al-Islāmiyya*, pp. 273–277.
27 J. Auda, *Maqasid al-Shariah as Philosophy of Islamic Law*, p. 5.
28 Muḥammad al-Ṭāhir ibn 'Āshūr, *Maqāṣid al-Sharī'a al-Islāmiyya*, p. 148.
29 J. Auda, *al-Iğtiḥād al-maqāṣidī. Min al-taṣawwur al-uṣūlī ilā al-tanzīl al-'amalī* [The Judicial Reasoning Based on Islamic Law's Purposes: From Theory to Practice], Arab Network for Research and Publishing, Beirut, 2013, p. 20.

protecting the right to ownership, Islamic law defends the idea of economic development and social welfare, based on the Quranic concepts of cooperation and mutual assistance. Lastly, the protection guaranteed to human reason can be extended to defend intellectual and cultural works in a broader sense. If, as seen, the *Sharīʿa* aims at protecting religion, this notion has been extended to encompass all religious freedoms, especially that of worship and proselytism.[30]

According to the most recent doctrine, in fact, Islamic law has not codified its purposes in a specific and unique way, as it is not a positive law system. Moreover, since the purposes interpret the spirit of divine law, which is eternal by its nature, they must change in every age. From this theory, some contemporary jurists have coined the expression of *iǧtihād maqāṣidī*, that is the effort to interpret the Quran and the *sunna* in the light of their purposes, also taking into account human needs and the historic context.

The general principles and the *maqāṣid al-Sharīʿa* are applicable to all the relations pertaining to human beings. Islamic law formalizes these relations as contracts (*ʿaqd*) and also the government arises from a contract, being a pact established between two parties: the community, represented by electors, and the governor (at the time called Caliph or Sultan). Therefore, the general principles and the *maqāṣid al-Sharīʿa* could find application at the political level, too. As will be demonstrated in the following section, the jurisprudence of medieval scholars contains several 'political principles' which represent, along with the general principles and the *maqāṣid al-Sharīʿa*, what I actually define as Islamic Constitutionalism.

The political principles of the *Sharīʿa*

There is no unanimous agreement, among jurists, regarding the political principles of Islamic law: for some jurists, they are restricted to the ideals of justice (*ʿadl*), consultation (*shūrā*) and equality (*musāwāt*), while according to others it is necessary to add the principle of obedience (*ṭāʿa*) of Muslims to the constituted power, except for the possibility to revoke it in particular cases.[31] A third group of jurists include freedom (*ḥurriyya*), the unity of the worshippers (*waḥda*), legality (*sharʿiyya*) and the responsibility (*masʾūliyya*) of the ruler towards those ruled.[32]

According to Maḥmaṣṣānī, the principles which regulate political life of the Muslim community are: consultation, the commitment of governments to the

30 Ibid., p. 30.

31 Farīd ʿAbd al-Khāliq, *Fī'l-fiqh al-siyāsī li'l-Islām* [Political Jurisprudence in Islam], Dar al-Shuruq, Cairo, 1998, pp. 11–12. See also: ʿAbd al-Salām Muḥammad al-Ġanāmī, *Muḥāḍarāt fī'l-qānūn al-ʿāmm al-islāmī* [Introduction to Islamic Public Law], Dar al-Qalam, Rabat, 2004, p. 7; Muḥammad Kamāl al-Dīn Imām, *al-Dustūr wa'l-sulṭa. Dirāsa fī'l-ʿurf al-dustūrī bayna al-Sharīʿa wa'l-qānūn* [Constitution and Power: A Study of Constitutional Customs between Islamic and Positive Law], Dar al-Jamiʿa al-Jadida li'l-Nashr, Alessandria, 2005.

32 Ǧamāl al-Sayyid Ḥabbād al-Murakkabī, *al-Khilāfa al-islāmiyya bayna nuẓūm al-ḥukm al-muʿāṣira* [The Islamic Caliphate among Contemporary Systems of Government], Jamaʿat Ansar al-Sunna al-Muhammadiyya, Cairo, 1993, p. 135.

welfare of the community, justice, charity, equality and brotherhood, prohibition to lead a war of conquest, prohibition of monopoly and fraud and the distinction between the rights of God and those of men.[33] Lastly, 'Yāḍ bin 'Āshūr distinguishes three categories of political principles extracted from the Quran's chapters:

1 principles directed to those who have a kind of authority, invited to judge or rule in accordance to justice, equity and right/truth (*ḥaqq*), as stated in Quran IV:58;
2 commitment of the governors to consult experts before making relevant decisions, as expressed in some verses;
3 the principle of obedience to the established powers, ordered in Quran IV:59.[34]

All of these principles were identified in the law of the Caliphate (sometimes called Imamate), which represented for many centuries the legitimate Islamic form of government. From the point of view of Islamic law, in fact, the first Caliphate, the community settled by Muḥammad in Medina, has taken the *Sharī'a* as its legal foundation and, since then, its application represents a duty for Muslims. Moreover, according to modern jurists, the first Caliphate enshrined the pillars of Western liberal Constitutionalism.[35]

The principle of sovereignty

In Islamic law, sovereignty means absolute and unlimited power, which ultimately rests only with God. The legislative function is not included in the Islamic notion of sovereignty, only executive and judicial powers are included in the concept of authority (*wilāya*). The Tunisian thinker Rāshid al-Ġannūshī (1941–) has developed a more moderate position, observing that in the Islamic political system the idea of choice (*istikhlāf*) made by God in favour of man is central. Two consequences derive from that:

1 only God is sovereign;
2 man is endowed with reason, freedom and responsibility, qualities which are necessary to enter into the contract of subordination.

33 S. Maḥmaṣṣānī, *Falsafat al-tashrī' fī'l-Islām* [Philosophy of Legislation in Islam], Dar al-'Ilm li'l-Malayin, Beirut, 1961, pp. 32–33. In Islam, rights are grouped in three varieties, according to the holder of the right: (1) absolute rights of God; (2) men's rights; (3) mixed rights concerning both God and men.

34 Yadh ben Achour, *Politique, religion et droit dans le monde arabe*, Cérès, Tunis, 1992, pp. 51–52. The two verses of the Quran IV:58–59 state: 'God commands you to render trusts to whom they are due and when you judge between people to judge with justice' and 'O you who have believed, obey God and obey the Messenger and those in authority among you'.

35 See for example: K.A. Faruki, *The Evolution of Islamic Constitutional Theory and Practice*, National Publishing House, Karachi, 1971; and more recently: N. Feldman, *The Fall and Rise of the Islamic State*, Princeton University Press, Princeton, 2008.

Drafting this contract, the community acknowledges God's absolute sovereignty but, at the same time, it becomes a source of authority.[36] Thus, while theocracy is based on the triad God–ruler–community, the Western secular democratic system is based on the dual concept of community and ruler. Lastly, Islamic democracy is based on the relationship among God–community–ruler. Therefore, in the Islamic law, the ruler and the community are bound by a social contract. The contractualistic theory, according to the Sudanese scholar Ḥasan al-Turābī (1932–), originated with Islam, because it is mentioned in Quran XLVIII:10: 'Indeed, those who pledge allegiance to you, [O Muḥammad] – they are actually pledging allegiance to God.' The governor receives his power from the people, along with the prerogative to lead the community under the provisions of Islamic law.[37]

Therefore, to Islamic public law it is possible to apply the double contract theory, developed by the German jurist Otto von Gierke (1841–1921). On one hand, individuals agree to submit to a ruler, who receives an exclusive power, taking charge of the defence and the protection of the people. On the other hand, after the formation of the society, the second contract regulates the terms and limits within which the authority can be exercised. In the Islamic model, the first contract is stipulated between human beings and God through the mediation of the Prophet, while the second one involves the community and the Caliphs who followed the example of Muḥammad.[38] The Caliph is the head of the state and having received the assignment to apply the *Sharī'a*, by which he himself is bound, renews the pact of alliance with God.[39]

From this perspective, the label of theocracy, often used to define the Islamic state, is imprecise, because it does not take into account the difference between cases where sovereignty is ascribed to God, and exercised directly or through His ministers, and those where the authority derives from a divine code applied by a ruler. It is useful to admit that there are different possibilities of defining theocracy. For this specific nature of Islam, the definition of nomocracy is more suitable, that is a political system where God does not rule directly, but through His law, which precedes the state and represents its legal basis.

Separation of powers

The theoretical notion of separation of powers arises in Western contexts where the theoretical claim is made that law and religion can be separate entities or

36 Rāshid al-Ġannūshī, *al-Ḥurriyyāt al-'āmma fī'l-dawla al-islāmiyya* [General Freedoms in the Islamic State], Markaz Dirasat al-Wahda al-'Arabiyya, Beirut, 2001, pp. 96–98 e 322.

37 Muḥammad Kāmil Layla, *al-Nuẓūm al-Siyāsiyya* [Political Systems], Dar al-Nahda al-'Arabiyya, Beirut, 1969, p. 436.

38 M. Khadduri, *War and Peace in the Islamic Law*, Johns Hopkins University Press, Baltimore, 1955, pp. 9–11. Otto von Gierke, *Natural Law and the Theory of Society*, Cambridge University Press, London, 1934.

39 For a comparison with the Byzantine law, see: D. Wagschal, *Law and Legality in the Greek East: The Byzantine Canonical Tradition, 381–883*, Oxford University Press, Oxford, 2015.

categories, and can even be autonomous. Although this principle is thus seen as a prerogative of Western Constitutionalism, Muslim jurists believe that it has been used in Islamic governance, too. It is neither a permanent feature in Islamic history, nor an idea developed since the earliest jurisprudence. This acknowledges that the Muslim community, even if it is the source of the powers, has specific limits in their execution. The community does not have any right to legislate in opposition to the Islamic law and is not entitled to administer judicial power overcoming the limits established by the Quran and *sunna.* The practice of legislation, expression of the popular sovereignty according to the Western doctrine, is the ability to establish compulsory rules in a universal way. Applied to ideal notions of Islamic government, this definition enshrines two meanings: in the strict sense the legislative power coincides with the *Sharīʻa,* that is what God ordered or prohibited; in another sense, based on Quran XVI:44 'that you may make clear to the people what was sent down to them', jurisprudence (*fiqh*) is developed by jurists and scholars to promote the application of Islamic law. In Western constitutional systems, the power to make laws is generally attributed to the parliament, a representative body, which acts in the people's place. People have the authority to legislate because they are the source of power as a collective legal entity. Therefore, people, through their representatives, guide the legislative process based on their needs and expectations. In the Islamic system of government, the *Sharīʻa* circumscribes the activity of legislation, and establishes strict boundaries, which cannot be overcome. This is merely an idealizing system, that hopes to devise good patterns but that can also be abused.

The principle of responsibility

The principle of responsibility has been codified by Islamic jurisprudence starting from the Quran and the *sunna* and also with regard to the role of the Caliph. In Islamic law, this principle implies the duty to be loyal to the governor of the community, who holds the authority and is responsible for the correct application of the *Sharīʻa.* The legal basis is represented by Quran XXVI:151–152 'And do not obey the order of the transgressors, who cause corruption in the land and do not amend'.[40] This principle, ideally, gives the community the right to escape the authority of the unjust ruler, suspending obedience.[41] Even though the community is the source of the ruler's authority and has the right to revoke the given office, a real reason such as a grave crime or sin is necessary, since the ruler is not infallible.

Jurists lean towards moderation and allow the use of coercion only when the community is certain to achieve the target of overthrowing the unjust ruler and there is no danger of civil war. According to another doctrine, if *Sharīʻa* is

40 The duty of obedience is expressed in Quran IV:80: 'He who obeys the Messenger has obeyed God, but those who turn away – We have not sent you over them as a guardian.'

41 Marwān Muḥammad Maḥrūs al-Mudarris, *Masʼūliyya raʼīs al-dawla fīʼl-niẓām al-riʼāsī waʼl-fiqh al-islāmī* [The Responsibility of the Head of the State in the Presidential System and in the Islamic Jurisprudence], Dar al-Aʻlam, ʻAmman, 2002, p. 171.

applied, the ruler who exceeds the borders of legality cannot be removed with force, but the community must tolerate him, bearing patience, giving advice and acting as a guide. When *Sharīʻa* is not applied, Muslims are obliged to root out the evil, through persuasion and good offices. If recurring to these means is not sufficient, and the illegitimacy persists, it is possible to withdraw obedience and loyalty, causing the resignation, even violent, of the ruler. Only the most influential members of the community, who nominate the ruler, have also the power to remove him.

The principle of consultation

Consultation (*shūrā*) is a general principle of the *Sharīʻa*, expressed in Quran III:159 and Quran XLII:38.[42] It is qualified as one of the government's principles by which the freedoms of expression and opinion find their application. According to some scholars, consultation is superior to the democratic principle because, while consultation is ordered by God for the material and spiritual welfare, democracy is a human concept applicable to worldly issues only. Therefore, the Islamic system of government is conditioned and not absolute in its nature, because it is practised with two limits: the principles taken from the Quran and the *sunna*, and the practice of the *shūrā* which connects the power of the ruler to the community. In its turn, consultation is subjected to three principles, which limit its range: sovereignty belongs to God, who, as a unique holistic legislator, allows men to legislate only in accordance with his law; it is not possible to modify the dogmas and key principles of Islam; and the way to implement consultation is flexible, because Islamic law does not impose a univocal model of government.[43]

Consensus (*iğmāʻ*) is, at the same time, the third source of Islamic law, after the Quran and the *sunna*, and a method that requires the practice of consultation. In every age, Muslims have considered it compulsory to consult among themselves on different matters, among which is the designation of their rulers. During the modern age, if on the one hand the application of the *shūrā* has been claimed, based on the impulses of European political philosophy, the widespread opinion among jurists is that the consent about it is not recent and was even achieved already after the death of the Prophet, on the occasion of the negotiations to designate his successor Abū Bakr. There is a mutual relation between consensus and consultation as consensus is only one way in which the consultation can take place and consultation is a way to achieve a majoritarian

42 Quran III:159 states: 'and consult them in the matter' while Quran XLII:38 states: 'and whose affair is [determined by] consultation among themselves'.

43 Muḥammad ibn Aḥmad ibn Ṣāliḥ al- Ṣāliḥ, *al-Shūrā fi'l-Kitāb wa'l-sunna wa-ʻinda ʻulamā' al-muslimīna* [The Consultation according to the Quran, the *Sunna* and the Consensus of Muslim Scholars], Maktabat al-Malik Fahd al-Wataniyya li'l-Nashr, al-Riyadh, 1999, p. 5; F. Rahman, 'The Principle of Shura and the Role of the Umma in Islam', *American Journal of Islamic Studies*, vol. 1, no. 1, 1984, pp. 1–9; P. Crone, 'Shura as an Elective Institution', in *Quaderni di Studi Arabi*, vol. 19, Università degli Studi di Venezia, Venice, 2001, pp. 3–39.

and ideally a unanimous opinion. The practice of consultation is articulated in three stages: mutual consultation, or the moment when attendants share their opinions; the confrontation and the evaluation of the conflicting opinions; the stage of the decision, when a position is chosen and a resolution is expressed. Jurists never clarified who can be part of the *shūrā*, but there is agreement on seven necessary requirements for the attendants: first of all, acceptance of Islam, because the Islamic state is based on the unity of faith. Consultation, in fact, is an instrument to exercise authority and non-Muslims cannot exercise any authority over Muslims. The second requirement is justice, which means morality and good manners. The third requirement is the ability to conduct legal reasoning. According to Quran IV:34 'Men are in charge of women', thus manhood is compulsory to attend consultation. Another requirement is the necessary knowledge to distinguish different opinions. The sixth requirement is wisdom. Lastly, the seventh requirement is the *status libertatis*, because a slave cannot exercise any authority over himself or over other people.[44]

It is not clear in which way members of the *shūrā* are elected or nominated. The prevailing opinion is based on the flexibility of the Islamic system, and according to the most widespread opinions, divine law has not imposed a univocal rule, valid in every time and place, but has given only general principles with eternal applicability. The best electoral system is also the one which is considered the most suitable by the Muslim community and that serves its public interest. Consultation has not only the aim to express popular will, but to represent God's will in the most loyal way. Therefore, the members of the consultative process represent the community, but they also have to be experts in religious sciences or those who master the means to approach the intimate meaning of *Sharīʻa*.[45] Moreover, they have to have good standing in society as well as in religious terms.

The principle of justice

Justice does not concern only the field of judgments, but, given the religious nature of Islamic law, it acquires an ethical value and is one of the fundamental principles of the Islamic political system in its entirety. In this domain, Quranic references are various, but Quran IV:58 and Quran XVI:90 are quoted above all others.[46] Justice is the first quality that a Caliph, or in general the ruler, must possess and it is required for whoever exercises a power of this kind and nature.

Islamic jurists have divided the content of justice into two main aspects: constitutive elements and the essence of justice, and the procedural norms, such as the principle of due process and principles of neutrality, coherence and regularity of

44 Muḥammad ibn Aḥmad ibn Ṣāliḥ al- Ṣāliḥ, *al-Shūrā fī'l-Kitāb wa'l-sunna wa-'inda 'ulamā' al-muslimīna*, p. 97.

45 M. Flory, R. Mantran, B. Qurany, M. Camau and P. Agate, *Les régimes politiques arabes*, Presses Universitaires de France, Paris, 1990, p. 83.

46 Quran XVI:90 states: 'Indeed, God orders justice and good conduct and giving to relatives.'

the trial.[47] Justice is one of the necessary qualities to fulfil public offices such as the judiciary. Judges were traditionally designated by the Caliph, or by a provincial governor, and after taking office, they had more or less complete autonomy in judicial matters. Islamic law does not recognize the principle of *stare decisis*, and judges were not obliged to be coherent with previous sentences.

In substantial matters, justice is defined by the opposite categories of permissible (*ḥalāl*) and prohibited (*ḥarām*): what falls in the first category is considered right and is ordered as a duty. The second category designates what is considered harmful and to be avoided.

The principles of freedom and equality

Like justice, also the idea of freedom in the Islamic law consists of many levels: on the one hand there is the philosophical and ontological dimension and on the other the political and social dimensions. A different lexical expression corresponds to each field. In the first cases the words *irāda* and *ikhtiyār* recur above all others. In the second one the term *ḥurriyya* is preferable. From the theological point of view, man's freedom derives from the dogma of divine uniqueness. Muslims are claimed to be equal because of their shared condition of subjection (*'ubūdiyya*) according to Quran XLIX:13, 'Indeed We created you from male and female and made you peoples and tribes that may know one another'.[48] Freedom in Islam is an innate right because it has divine origins. While European legal philosophy distinguishes between positive rights and negative liberties, the latter indicating those judicial conditions that come from the absence of the legislator's intervention, in Islam rights and freedoms are only positive, being possible through an act of will of God.

In the European and North American constitutional doctrines, freedoms and rights, although inalienable and fundamental, can be restricted in particular circumstances on the basis of a procedure set forth by the Constitution. On the contrary, according to the Islamic law, the human legislator can never impede or obstruct rights because they have divine origins. Thus, many scholars stress that the Islamic state acknowledges the rule of law, the principle of strict legality and all the judicial guarantees for rights and freedoms.

Freedoms of opinion, worship and thought

In the domain of freedom of worship, Quran II:256 is frequently quoted: 'There shall be no compulsion in religion.' Jurists refer to this verse as one of the most important pillars of Islamic law. It implies the absence of coercion in entering the Muslim community and, as a consequence, the impossibility for a believer to

47 M. Khadduri, *The Islamic Concept of Justice*, Johns Hopkins University Press, Baltimore, 1984, p. 3.
48 F. Rosenthal, *The Muslims Concept of Freedom Prior to the Nineteenth Century*, Brill, Leiden, 1960, pp. 2–14 e 23–25.

oblige someone to leave it. However, this rule has some limits: God created reason so that men could make use of it to examine religious matters, as long as the dogmas of Islam are not called into question. Muslims are entitled to speculate on their faith without changing the basic principles they have to believe in.

Freedom of worship consists also of a second aspect addressed to Muslims and non-Muslims. The reading of the above-mentioned verse has to be integrated with Quran CIX:6, 'For you is your religion, and for me is my religion'; this text prohibits in any case the imposition of religion. The deriving rule implies the possibility for non-Muslims to join Islam at any moment and it is also a guarantee of protection for different religious communities.[49]

Apostasy (*ridda*) is central concerning the freedom of worship. While some jurists consider the apostate responsible for a crime punishable by death, others believe that this action falls into those behaviours punishable by a discretionary punishment (*ta'zīr*) established by the judge. Leaving the community is allowed, but it causes the loss of all rights and duties connected to the condition of being a legal person under Islamic law. Moreover, according to the most moderate doctrine, the criminal status of apostasy is a historic phenomenon more than a judicial one, which was pursued at the beginning of the history of Islam when the Prophet Muḥammad struggled to preserve the newly established religion from vanishing.

Economic and social rights

The typical rights and freedoms concerning the economic sphere derive from the circumstance that God has created man, endowing him with the ability to live in a community and in very close contact with others. Therefore, Islamic law allows both private property (*tamalluk*) and socio-economic rights in a spirit of sharing. A legal cornerstone of the latter is contained in Quran LI:19, 'and from their properties was [given] the right of the [needy] petitioner and the deprived', in Quran V:2, 'And cooperate in righteousness and piety, but do not cooperate in sin and aggression'. However, formally property does not fall into man's right because the real possessor is God. It emerges as the consequence of divine favour, which makes man able to exploit material possessions. This favour must be directed towards the achievement of general welfare, because individual property is a social means. So the right to have possessions is intrinsic in Islam by virtue of the fact that they are constitutive of society. Moreover, no limits are set for the amount of money Muslims can have, as long as it is not accumulated illicitly, such as through loans with interest or usury.

Private property is not totally free, but is limited through precise conditions aimed at avoiding concentration of wealth in the hands of one social group. In general, either prodigality or unjustified parsimony is forbidden. The instrument to achieve these goals and realize the ideal social solidarity is ritual charity (*zakāt*), and other forms of purification of possessions. A second limit set on the

49 Rāshid al-Ġannūshī, *al-Ḥurriyyāt al-'āmma fi'l-dawla al-islāmiyya*, p. 44.

right to have material possessions derives from the concept of public welfare. Islam protects possessions from the interference of authorities in so far as they cannot expropriate them unlawfully. This principle can be restricted when needed or when it is the only way to guarantee public welfare.

The application of Islamic Constitutionalism through positive Constitution

After defining what I mean by Islamic Constitutionalism, this section explains how it can be applied through the Constitution and, in general, through positive law. The Constitutions of Islamic countries include many references to Islamic law as the source of legislation. These references appear in two main ways: all Constitutions of the Arabic countries, except for Lebanon, contain a confessional clause, which makes Islam the religion of the state, and in some cases the king or president's faith. The second practice is the inclusion of *Sharīʻa* among the sources of law, as in the case of the Constitutions of Libya, Egypt, Sudan, Syria, Iraq and in the countries of the Arabian Peninsula.[50] In this case, the legislative power is subject to respecting Islamic law, creating a hierarchy among the sources of legislation. Minority practices make a different use of the Islamic references, such as the Algerian Constitution, which provides for the High Islamic Council, composed of 15 members including the President of the Republic, which is exclusively in charge of the practice of legal reasoning (*iğtihād*). But its powers remain quite advisory and restricted to specific matters (arts 171–172 Const.). In the Tunisian Constitution of 1959 and in the Algerian Constitution in force today (art. 73), the requirement for the head of state to be Muslim is sought, a provision which does not restrict the legislation but limits the participation in the political life of the country to the Muslim majority. Another practice is established by the Constitution of Jordan where the *Sharīʻa* is not mentioned as a source, but the existence of religious courts, which are the only ones entitled to deal with disputes regarding personal statutes, implies that it is enforced. In this case, the reference to Islamic law reveals itself in the field of judicial power but not in legislation.

From this brief analysis, it is quite clear that the inclusion of the *Sharīʻa* among normative sources is not uniform in the Islamic systems of law. The Egyptian Constitution of 1971 established an exemplary model adopted in many other countries. This Constitution remained unchanged until 1980 when it was amended through public referendum. The change concerned Article 2, which in the original text referred to the *Sharīʻa* as 'one' of the sources of legislation. As a consequence of the reform of Article 2, *Sharīʻa* became 'the' main source. This amendment soon created a lot of ambiguity, due to the fact that the reform regulated the creation of future laws, but it was not applicable to previous ones. Moreover, the use of the adjective 'main' did not exclude the possibility of having other sources of

50 S. Lavorel, *Les Constitutions arabes et l'Islam*, Presses de l'Université du Québec, Sainte-Foy, 2005, p. 31.

law and, as suggested by the Egyptian 'Abd al-Ḥamīd Mutawallī, while it created a hierarchical super-ordination, it did not prohibit the legislator to refer to other sources of law.[51]

Therefore, in 1980 Article 2 of the Egyptian Constitution was modified to read that 'the principles of the Islamic *Sharī'a* are the main source of the legislation'.[52] According to the reading of 'Abd al-Ḥamīd Mutawallī, in this formulation the use of the term *tashrī'* is central to indicate the legislation, instead of using the word *qānūn*.[53] These two terms are comparable respectively to the French words *loi* and *droit* and also in Arabic the second one includes the first one. *Tashrī'* alludes specifically to three domains:

1 to the Constitution, which is the fundamental law;
2 to the ordinary laws issued by parliament; and
3 to what is issued by the executive in the form of legislative decrees.

In the event that *Sharī'a* is referenced as 'one' of the sources of the legislation (as in the Egyptian Constitution of 1972 before the amendment), Islamic law enjoys an intermediate position between the Constitution and other ordinary laws. This formulation, actually little used, abolishes every hierarchy among Islamic law and positive sources; rather it places them on the same level.

The current formulation of Article 2 of the Egyptian Constitution, remaining unchanged after the revolution of 2011, poses the problem of the synchronization of the positive sources of law and the *Sharī'a*, a problem that the Egyptian Supreme Constitutional Court (SCC) had taken on with determination in the past. In the decision of 4 May 1985, the court established that the amendment of Article 2, after the referendum of 1980, had introduced a limit to the legislative power represented by the principles of *Sharī'a*. Divine law was raised to the rank of supreme law, a normative universe that was given the duty to guide future legislation.[54] The SCC with the decision of 15 May 1993 has distinguished between immutable and changeable principles of Islamic law. Ordinary laws must be compliant with the former (also known in Arabic as *al-nuṣūṣ al-qāṭ'iyya al-dalāla wa'l-thubūt*) unless it will be invalid.[55] In light of the previous paragraphs, the general principles, the *maqāṣid al-Sharī'a* and the 'political

51 E. Cotran and C. Mallat (eds), *Yearbook of Islamic and Middle Eastern Law*, Kluwer Law International, London, 1994, vol. 1, p. 127; J.P. O'Kane, 'Islam in the New Egyptian Constitution: Some Discussions in al-Ahram', *Middle East Journal*, vol. 26, no. 2, 1972, pp. 137–148.

52 In Arabic: *mabādī al-Sharī'a al-Islāmiyya al-maṣdar al-ra'īsī li'l-tashrī'*.

53 'Abd al-Ḥamīd Mutawallī, *al-Sharī'a al-Islāmiyya ka-maṣdar asāsī li'l-Dustūr* [The Sharia as Fundamental Source of Constitution], Munasha'at al-Ma'arif, Alexandria, 1975, p. 15.

54 B. Dupret, 'La chari'a est la source de la législation: interprétations jurisprudentielles et théories juridiques', in A. Mahiou, *L'État de droit dans le monde arabe*, CNRS Éditios, Paris, 1997, p. 127.

55 J. Murray and M. El-Molla, 'Islamic Shari'a and Constitutional Interpretation in Egypt', in E. Cotran and A.O. Sherif, *Democracy, the Rule of Law and Islam*, CIMEL Book Series no. 6, School of Oriental and African Studies, University of London, London, 1999, p. 507.

principles' of Islamic law, could be classified as immutable principles, which may guide the activities of the legislator and the judge. Moreover, they can also limit the activity of the executive and of the other governmental bodies. This is even more evident if we consider, as the SCC said referring to the changeable principles (*al-nuṣūṣ al-ẓanniyya*), that the executive and legislative powers have a broader discretionary authority in interpreting the sources of Islamic law, but they remain bound to the preservation of religion, integrity of individuals, their reason, virtues and possessions. With the decision of 4 May 1985, the SCC also expressed the principle of non-retroactivity for the control of compliance with *Sharī'a*: it became effective for laws adopted since 22 May 1980, the date of the coming into force of the new version of Article 2, and for possible changes to laws or codes already in force.

Finally, Article 2 is put into operation by the SCC, so *Sharī'a* is applied, as is evident in decision n.8 of 18 March 1996. In this decision, the SCC rejected the request of a father to repeal an administrative decree, which prevented the wearing of the *niqāb* (female garment that veils the face and leaves only the eyes visible) for female students at school and during classes. The reasoning of judges was the following: the rules of Islamic law regarding female clothing fall into the group of changeable principles of Islamic law, not into the immutable ones. Therefore, they belong to a field that the human legislator can regulate, in accordance with the purposes of the Islamic law (*maqāṣid al-Sharī'a*). The commitment imposed on women to wear a veil over the whole face, the SCC said, is at odds with the rules of the *Sharī'a*, which do not impose a defined way of clothing on women, but, at most, impose modesty and sobriety. In this way, the sentence of the SCC aimed to protect *Sharī'a* from a too radical interpretation and also the rule of law, as stated in the Constitution which is the basis of organization of the Egyptian society. Therefore, the regulation adopted by the Ministry of Education, contested by the father who had raised the case, was judged legal and compatible with the *Sharī'a*.[56]

Conclusion

Sharī'a is often defined as a monolithic set of particular norms and rules. In reality, Islamic law is a complete system of law that, in a well-defined historical age, enjoyed an autonomous existence. It has its own sources, clear rules and hermeneutical methods to define unclear norms related to those aspects of human life on which the Quran and the *sunna* are silent. However, because jurists can and do use different methods of interpretation, there are many divergences of opinion and different positions on virtually any topic.

56 N. Brown and C. Lombardi, 'The Supreme Constitutional Court of Egypt on Islamic Law, Veiling and Civil Rights: An Annotated Translation of Supreme Constitutional Court of Egypt Case no. 8 of Judicial Year 17 (May 18, 1996)', *American University International Law Review*, vol. 21, no. 3, 2006, pp. 437–460. See also: K. Balz, 'La reconstruction séculière du droit islamique: la Haute Cour constitutionelle égyptienne et la "bataille du voile" dans les écoles publique', in *Droit et Société*, vol. 39, Lextenso Éditions, Paris, 1998, pp. 277–291.

The process of legal acculturation resulting from the contact of the Islamic world with Europe made it possible that, since the nineteenth century, the Islamic system of law was thrown into crisis, losing some of its intrinsic qualities. The codification, for example, seen by the jurists of the Ottoman Empire as a way to prevent the ruin of the state, has perverted the nature of *Sharīʻa* and has posed the problem of its inclusion in positive systems of law where the hierarchy among the sources of law is established by the Constitution. This process disempowered the Islamic law as it is no longer the true *Sharīʻa*.

The practice in use to recall the principle of *Sharīʻa* as the main or one additional source of legislation poses new questions: which part(s) of Islamic law must be included in the phrase 'principle of *Sharīʻa*'? In the opening paragraphs, in light of the notion of material Constitution suggested by Aristotle, I have defined the general principles of Islamic law, the theory of *maqāṣid al-Sharīʻa* and its political principles as part of what is referenced by Islamic Constitutionalism. I believe that these are the main elements of the Islamic law, which deal with the public sphere and good governance.

Without any doubt, Islamic Constitutionalism is 'evolving', because it can always be broadened to include new rules, as demonstrated by the gradual extension that the *maqāṣid al-Sharīʻa* have experienced in the contemporary age due to some jurists. Moreover, some general principles do not include precise and definitively closed rules, but set forth procedural norms or serve as guides for interpretation. Through them, it is possible to constantly update the positive system of law where these general principles are recalled. The reasoning of the SCC, contained in the reported rulings, demonstrates that the court, when it has to decide about a matter linked to religion, draws on *Sharīʻa* and takes into account immutable and changeable principles, and the whole spirit of Islamic law. In other words, it takes into account what has been identified here as the body of Islamic Constitutionalism. Inscribed in a system of civil law, *Sharīʻa* becomes judiciable, because among the sources of law, it occupies a prominent position both on the constitutional as well as on ordinary laws level. At the same time, formulations such as Article 2 of the Egyptian Constitution allow other normative sources, such as international treaties, to enter the picture. Through this process, *Sharīʻa* becomes a *Grundnorm*, a normative universe valid for the judge and the legislator, but one that represents a constraint on the arbitrariness of the executive power, too.

In light of this perspective, recalling to *Sharīʻa* in the Constitution, far from being a danger to citizenship rights and universal freedoms as they are commonly understood, could represent a new instrument to guarantee their application in an effective and more incisive way. In other words *Sharīʻa*, thus, can be assumed as a tool for empowerment.

Part II

Religion IN law

7 Engaging religious laws, players and communities

Confronting religious disempowerment

Amos Israel-Vleeschhouwer•

Introduction

In this chapter I will consider some ways in which smart and responsible engagement of religious law, players and communities might serve to empower individuals and communities. Most examples will come from Jewish law,[1] my field of expertise.[2] However, the argument is applicable, to various degrees, to most religions.

Religion and international law

Theorists and practitioners tend to disregard religion both ideologically and practically.[3] Their vision of enlightenment, progress, humanism and world governance regards religion in one of the following two ways:

• Email: amosthesis@gmail.com. Independent researcher, Jerusalem. Prepared for the 2010 meeting of the American Society of International Law. I thank Profs. Eyal Benvenisti, Nathan Lerner, Kyriaki Topidi and participants at the ASIL meeting, IDC Herzelia law faculty colloquium and the international law research forum at the Hebrew university, for comments.

1 The argument originates from research about Jewish law and communities for my PhD dissertation (The Attitudes of Jewish Law towards International Law, Faculty of Law, Tel Aviv University, 2012) supervised by Prof. Arye Edre'i and Prof. Orna Ben Naftali. For a historical and cultural analysis of *Jewish* law and community see my *Jewish Law in the Age of Globalization: Conceptual Impacts, Multi-Player Interaction and Halachic Re-Organization of the Jewish 'Community'*, European 18 Review of History 57–67 (2011). For a focus on community and women *empowerment*, see *Migrating from Home to Homes: Adapting to Complex Contexts and Changing to Healthier Modes of Communication*, Migration, Home and Communication: Jewish Tradition, Change & Gender in a Global World 16–40, Tania Reytan-Marincheshka (ed.); LIK Publishing House 2011.

2 The current project cannot be approached objectively (Marti Koskenniemi, The Gentle Civilizer of Nations (1999), international law tends to be ideologically biased). I'll minimise this problem by disclosure. I identify myself or am identified as Ashkenazi/white (western Jewish origin), heterosexual, Israeli, Jewish, Jewish law observant, middle class, male and 46 years old. I'm married and raise four children under a regime that denies the right (e.g. to marry) from others, based on religious grounds.

3 See, e.g., Mark W. Janis & Carolyn Evans (eds.), Religion and International Law (2004), at xiii: 'surprisingly little studied or analyzed'; ix: 'international law distanced . . . from Religion . . . the latter receives scarcely a mention in the standard treatises'; p. 155: 'little has

1 The disappearance of religion as a world force, or at least an ever-shrinking religious population;
2 an ever-enlightening religion – religion changes to endorse and embody generally accepted secular ideas.[4]

Non-enlightened religion is perceived as an oppressive regime, as disempowering individuals and using them, *inter alia*, to cause wars. No wonder that international law and all enlightened, rational and secular players sought to ensure total personal freedom from religion,[5] and to remove religion from the public sphere.

However, religion has not disappeared and has not changed in such a way. It cannot be discounted or ignored.[6] Its power is not negligible,[7] and it influences beliefs and behaviour of individuals and communities. Religion gains prominence both in states and on the international level.[8] Its law, leaders and communities are a rising power.[9]

In some cases, modern religion is disempowered and disempowering because it is either co-opted by the state or marginalised as a fundamentalist opposition to international order. My contribution will lay the necessary ground for discussing

been written – almost nothing – about the relationship between Religion and law'. There is no entry 'Religion' in most indexes of international law encyclopedias (see e.g. Max Planck Encyclopedia Of international Law; James R. Fox, Dictionary of International and Comparative Law [2003]), textbooks (e.g. Martin Dixon, Textbook on International Law [6th ed. 2007]; Malcolm N. Shaw, International Law [5th ed. 2003]) and case collections. Classic international law literature stresses the influence religion and religious sources *had* upon the creation and establishment of International law, and goes on to stress the importance of the secularization of international law to its development, and discusses religious rights. See Mark W. Janis, *Religion and International Law*, ASIL Insights, November 2002 (www.asil.org/insigh93.cfm). For secularisation see Leo Gross, *The Peace of Westphalia, 1648–1948*, 42 AJIL 20 (1948). But see David Kennedy, *Images of Religion in International Legal Theory*, Religion and International Law 145 (1999).

4 See Fredrick M. Gedicks, *Spirituality, Fundamentalism, Liberty: Religion at the End of Modernity*, 54 DePaul L. Rev. 1193 (2005).

5 Nathan Lerner, Religion, Beliefs, and International Human Rights (2000).

6 For data on (organised) religions, see www.adherents.com. For critique and discussion see David Chidester, Global Citizenship, Cultural Citizenship and World Religions in Religion Education (2002), 10–11 (www.hsrcpress.ac.za/product.php?productid=1976).

7 Jose Casanova, Public Religions in the Modern World (1994); Johnston Douglas & Cynthia Sampson, Religion, The Missing Dimension of Statecraft (1994); Jef Haynes, Religion in Global Politics (1998).

8 Scott Thomas, The Global Resurgence of Religion and the Transformation of International Relations: The Struggle for the Soul of the Twenty-First Century (2005); Hugh Heclo & Wilfred M. McClay, Religion Returns to the Public Sphere: Faith and Policy in America (2003). Gabriel Motzkin & Yochi Fischer (eds.), Religion and Democracy in Contemporary Europe (2008).

9 Susane Hoeber Rudolph & James Piscatori, Transnational Religion and Fading States (1997). Compare A. Claire Cutler, *Critical Reflections on the Westphalian Assumptions of International Law and Organization: A Crisis of Legitimacy*, 27 Rev. Int. Stud. 133 (2001). Noah Feldman, The Fall and Rise of the Islamic State (2012).

the necessary conditions for religious empowerment and empowerment through religion, and the role of international law and international legal players.

Religious laws, players and communities vs 'religion'

The definition of religion in general, as well as when related to specific religions, is debatable, diverse, elusive[10] and problematic.[11] We can, however, gain some relevant insights from the various definitions: a lot of religions are total or holistic systems and see themselves as being alternative comprehensive *weltanschauungs*;[12] community,[13] commitment and non-rational sincere belief are central and important.[14] The religious phenomenon is complex and is expressed in 'recognizable human conduct'.[15] Religion is a private, but also a public, communal and political, matter and practice.[16] It is a spiritual, cultural and legal system. Religions are not rigid, as seems, and generally adapt well to changing realities. Specifically, they react to processes – e.g. globalisation[17] and technology – that changed the theory and practice of international law.[18]

'Religion', as a general term, implicates a belief that all religions are, in some sense, 'the same thing'.[19] That is however just *one* possible theory about religiosity.[20] The differences between religions are vast. In each religion, religions seem simple,

10 John Witte Jr., *Introduction, in* RELIGIOUS HUMAN RIGHTS IN A GLOBAL PERSPECTIVE: RELIGIOUS PERSPECTIVES XXIV (John Witte Jr. & Johan D. Van der Vyver (eds.), 1996): 'bewildering array of definitions of Religion'. Lerner, *supra* note 5, 3–5; Winnifred F. Sullivan, *Judging Religion*, 81 MARQ. L. REV. 443 (1998).

11 Definition may conflict with the first amendment or with freedom of Religion, see *Wisconsin v. Yoder*, 406 U.S. 205 (1972) at 205; James A.R. Nafziger, *The Functions of Religion in the International Legal System*, RELIGION AND INTERNATIONAL LAW 155 (1999); Winnifred Jonathan Weiss, *Priviledge, Posture and Protection: 'Religion' in the Law*, 73 YALE L. REV. 604 (1964).

12 David A. Westerbrook, *Islamic International Law and Public International Law: Separate Expressions of World Order*, 33 VIRG. J. INT. L. 819 (1993). Compare JOHN RAWLS, POLITICAL LIBERALISM (2002).

13 BRYAN A. GARNER (ED. IN CHIEF), BLACK'S LAW DICTIONARY 7TH ED. (1999).

14 Dmitry N. Feofanov, *Defining Religion: An Immodest Proposal*, 23 HOFSTRA L. REV. 309, 385 (1994). See Lerner, *supra* note 5, 4–5.

15 G. MACGREGOR, INTRODUCTION TO RELIGIOUS PHILOSOPHY (1959).

16 JACOB NEUSNER (ED.), GOD'S RULE: THE POLITICS OF WORLD RELIGIONS (2003) (religions are inherently political and have public power, political will and action).

17 PETER BEYER, RELIGION AND GLOBALIZATION (2000).

18 See P. Radhakrishnan, *Religion under Globalisation*, ECO. AND POL. WEEKLY March 27, 2004, 1403 (www.scribd.com/doc/198823655) ('Globalisation of religions is qualitatively different from what is understood as globalisation today'); David Smock, *Religion in World Affairs*, www.usip.org/pubs/specialreports/sr201.pdf (2008). MAHJABEEN KHALED, GLOBALIZATION AND RELIGION (2007), http://ihmsaw.org/resourcefiles/1260067215.pdf.

19 From the internal point of view of one religion (however defined) the existence of another legitimate religion is rarely acknowledged (even if it answers to the same criteria). All the above definitions are not self-definitions of religion. Indeed, some clerics would not define their belief or practice system as 'religion' at all.

20 MacGregor, *supra* note 15.

rigid and extreme because we tend to relate to each religion by its hegemonic voice. One could of course say the same about law! Professor Sunder stresses the need to give voice to many voices in each religion.[21] Empowerment depends on recognising that one should engage multiple religious law*s*, as well as various religious players and communities, instead of just engaging the simple singular amorphous 'religion' and its hegemonic representative(s).

Engagement and empowerment

I use the term 'engage'[22] in a very broad sense. Engagement includes recognition and acceptance of religion as relevant; it implies curiosity about it, interest in it and knowledge of and about it; it includes considering religion, to be involved with it and interact, acknowledge, enable participation, conduct negotiations, co-opt and cooperate. It also includes competition, inhibition, obstruction and confrontation.[23] This proposed non-binaric rich matrix of possibilities promotes empowering engagements.

Empowerment is also a broad concept,[24] meaning 'the process of enhancing the capacity of individuals or groups to make choices and to transform those choices into desired actions and outcomes', or 'enhancing freedom of choice and actions'.[25] In the context of international law it can be best understood as accompanying the concept of subsidiarity. If a matter ought to be handled by the smallest, least centralised authority capable of addressing that matter effectively,[26] then empowerment of individuals, communities and agents is essential to address major issues in international law,[27] such as poverty[28] or women's rights.[29]

21 Madhavi Sunder, *Piercing the Veil*, 112 Yale L. J. 1399 (2003). Peter Danchin, *Between Rogues and Liberals: Towards Value Pluralism as a Theory of Freedom of Religion in International Law*, ASIL Proceedings 2006 414 (2007); www.christianhegemony.org.

22 Edith Brown-Weiss & Harold Jacobson, Engaging Countries: Strengthening Compliance with International Environmental Accords (2000).

23 I will not discuss the engagement of 'others' by religion, but engagement is, creates and is always part of interactive, mutual, two-sided dynamics.

24 For empowerment in international law in related contexts see: Estelle Fach, *Legal Empowerment of Local Communities: A Role for International Environmental Law?*, www.scps.nyu.edu/export/sites/scps/pdf/global-affairs/estelle-fach.pdf; Kas Raustiala, *The Architecture of International Cooperation; Transgovernmental Networks and the Future of International Law*, 43 Va. J. Int'l L. 1 (2002).

25 *What is Empowerment?*, at http://go.worldbank.org/VELLT7XGR0; see also http://go.worldbank.org/U72REYP4F0.

26 For subsidiary see e.g. Art. 5(3) of the treaty of the EU.

27 Stephan Golub, *Beyond the Rule of Law Orthodoxy: The Legal Empowerment Alternative* (2003) at www.carnegieendowment.org/files/wp41.pdf ('potential benefits of legal empowerment work are . . . the importance of civil society capacity building, organization, or political influence . . . vibrant NGOs' roles in successful development efforts, especially when they are able to engage or collaborate with government').

28 M. Stephens,*The Commission on Legal Empowerment of the Poor: An Opportunity Missed.* 1 Hague J. on the Rule of Law 132–157 (2009); *Report of the Secretary-General; Legal Empowerment of the Poor and Eradication of Poverty,* GA A/64/133 (3 July 2009), at www.unrol.org/doc.aspx?d=2315.

29 Hilary Charlesworth and C. Chinkin, *The Boundaries of International Law. A Feminist Analysis*, 69 Nordic J. Int'l Law 523 (2000).

I argue that the prevalent understanding of the structure and nature of contemporary church–state relations on the international level disempowers religious communities and fosters religious hegemonies that disempower individuals and communities.

Why engage religious players and communities?

Religious motivation can influence voluntary compliance to international norms, promote human rights and better the human condition. It can also motivate conflict and competition with the international law project.[30] I will argue for engaging religious laws, players or communities in both cases.

Religious communities are transnational players that can enhance democratic aspects of international law and governance, because they have strong grassroots power. Religions are like organisations with vast membership, resources, spread, influence and power – but at the same time they behave like small, highly ideological, intense organisations which can inform, organise, galvanise and act effectively.[31]

Religions have a role in forming public opinion at communal, national and international levels.[32] Religious leaders and institutions collect, analyse, frame, edit and disseminate information to their constituencies on a permanent and continued basis. The religious mediation forms private and communal consciousness, identity, knowledge, opinions, values and political choices. News, opinions and possible public choices are routinely translated into religious language and contexts.[33] In addition to the translation,[34] a moral, judgmental addendum accompanies many of these communications, promoting some options over others.

Churches, synagogues and mosques are life-long educational, recreational and communal centres. They can be used to organise, disband, hinder or enhance political activities, as well as civil and personal awareness. They may act as interest groups or cooperate with existing ones.

Religious texts, institutions and communities are major tools for mobilising public opinion and actions around the world. These religious information

30 Westerbrook, *supra* note 12; Janis, *supra* note 3; Courtenay W. Howland, *The Challenge of Religious Fundamentalism to the Liberty and Equality Rights of Women: An Analysis Under the United Nations Charter*, 35 Colom. J. Int. L. 271 (1997) ('Religious fundamentalism is an inherently transnational movement . . . that confront and challenge the international law system'). Religious players encouraged violations of human rights and of international peace and law. For religious backing of regimes conducting atrocities see Mark J. Osiel, Mass atrocity, Ordinary Evil and Hannah Arendt: Criminal Consciousness in Argentina's Dirty war (2001).

31 Eyal Benvenisti, *Exit and Voice in the Age of Globalization*, 98 Mich. L. Rev. 167 (1999).

32 Howland, *supra* note 30. Religions can also serve to measure and assess public opinion (see pp. 000–000,below).

33 Data may be censored, withheld, altered and manipulated as well as enhanced, nuanced, critically analysed, and made user-friendly during this process.

34 Maximo Langer, *From Legal Transplants to Legal Translations*, 45 Harv. Int. L. J. 1 (2004).

pathways and grassroots organisational features may empower individuals and communities, and they might be used to disempower them. Following the legal materials and analysing the discursive systems and processes might shed some light on these processes. Engaging the religious laws, players and communities smartly and responsibly can serve to contradict disempowering forces and promote processes of empowerment.[35]

In the following two sections of the chapter I will suggest to recognise religions as complex legal *systems*, and engage them. The second section will focus on the structure of the relations, while the third section will deal with the dynamic processes. Moving from theory to praxis in the fourth section, I will propose to create the RILM (= Religious International Legal Materials) database project.

Religion and international law revisited: the multiplayer paradigm

What status do religions have in the inter*national* arena? Religions' existence pre-dates the state. The authority and legitimacy of religious communities, players and laws in the eyes of the religious constituency is independent of their legal form of organisation, whether national or international.[36] Therefore one could expect religious players to strive for an independent state-like status (self-determination).[37] But religions mostly chose other paths – influencing domestic politics,[38] or going global.

In the Westphalian tradition, the only subject is the state. Interactions between religion and international law are always mediated by states, in a linear-hierarchical model. Religion influences the state and vice versa (but only within church–state relations):

international law >> nation state >> religion

35 Engagement is enriching religion, esp. the human rights empowering aspect: see Hilary Charlsworth, *The Challenges of Human Rights Law for Religious Traditions,* RELIGION AND INTERNATIONAL LAW 401 (1999).

36 This internal view is thus different from the authority and legitimacy as it is perceived from 'outside'. Some of the religious constituency might share this 'outside' view, and some of the outside players are actually conscious of this different source of power. No customary law exists about religion as a reason for self-determination (ANTONIO CASSESE, SELF DETERMINATION OF PEOPLES at 121 [1995]). 'Old' religions pre-date the state system, and may therefore prefer to exist outside, and independent of, the system. Continuous documentation of religious international law (see below) can reveal change in religion's will to seek self-determination.

37 Religion can be a reason for self-determination. DOV RONEN, THE QUEST FOR SELF DETERMINATION 9–12, 24–52 (1979) (minorities as deserving independence). Cassese (op. cit., at 119) counts religion as one kind of such minority. The classic example is the Holy See.

38 Gerald Frug, *The City as a Legal Concept*, 93 HARV. L. REV. 1057 (1980) (religion is an intermediate level of organisation between the individual and the state). Compare PACEM IN TERRIS (1963) (emphasises the importance of 'intermediate groups or societies').

Since in modern nation states religion has been confined to the private sphere, religion can be presented as internalised by individuals within states (see Figure 7.1).[39]

I note that what is missing in this picture is society or communities as an entity.

This concentric paradigm is hierarchical. All relations in the model are two-sided, placing an emphasis on the 'us–them' – either 'in' or 'out' – dichotomy (see p. 155).

But this model is problematic.[40] Hierarchy and dichotomies are disempowering. They seek to restrict creativity, choices and courses of action. But first and foremost – it is simply wrong as a description of reality and wrong as a prescription for reality. A more exact model would include religion, state and international law and others in a multiplayer model where all constantly interact and are taken into account.

Some communities actually overlap. Real people can be individuals, citizens, international NGO members, supporters and members of religious communities. The ideals, concepts, interests and representation might also overlap (see Figure 7.2).

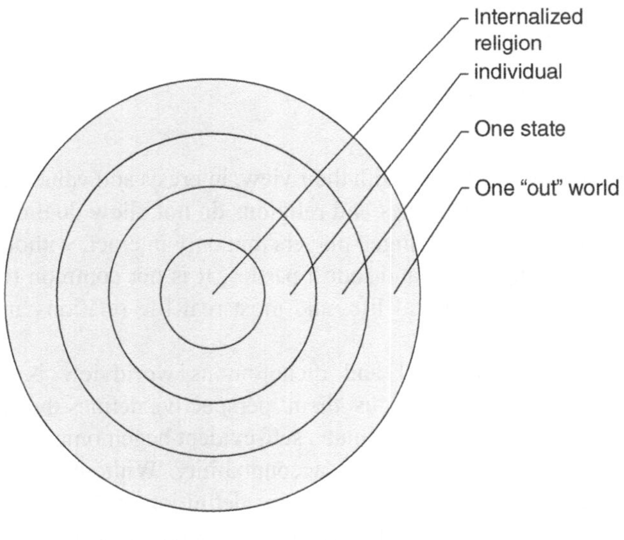

Figure 7.1 The us–them, hierarchal Westphalian paradigm

39 The parallel religious view would be a hierarchy of Religion >> world/state (human law) >> community >> individual. The concentric hierarchal structure is the same, with religion supreme or all-encompassing. Article 18 of the universal declaration of human rights ensures freedom of religion but also '*the primacy of international law over national law and religious codes*, of individual minority and collective rights and of the relationship between rights, duties and community'. Boyle Kevin & Sheen Juliet (eds.), Freedom of Religion and Belief: A World Report 4 (1997); Lerner, *supra* note 5; R.W. Garnett, *Changing Minds: Proselytism, Religious Freedom and the First Amendment*, 2 U. of st. Thomas L. J. 453 (2005).

40 Samuel N. Eisenstadt, *Multiple Modernities,* 129 Deadalus J. of the Am. Ac. of Arts and Sciences 1 *(2000)* challenges these basic assumptions; Cutler, *supra* note 9; See further Israel-Vleeschhouwer, *Jewish Law*, *Supra* note 1. The Ven model is illustrative and inexact. For example, one rarely is member of two religions at once (even though it happens).

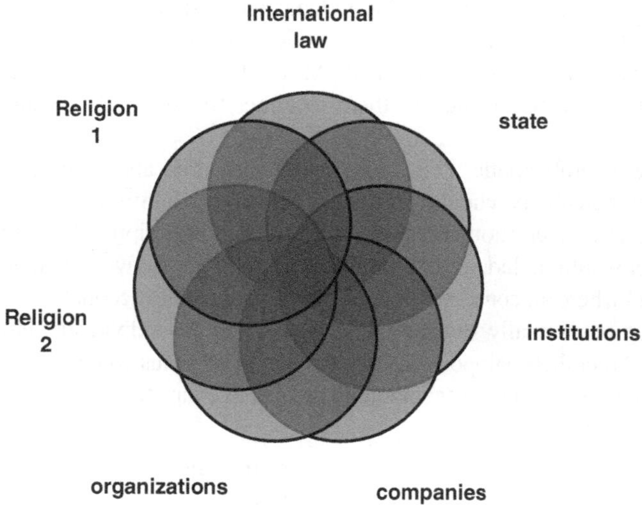

Figure 7.2 Multiplayer network paradigm

Multiple players are involved, each with their view, interests and values. Some 'circles' might not overlap – most states and religions do not allow dual citizenship, but it is rare to find totally enstranged players that only interact, without any overlap or connection through third and fourth parties. It is not common to find clear and dichotomous borders in real life, and most real life relations are not cleanly two-sided and hierarchical.

However, this untrue hierarchical and dichotomous worldview is maintained because it serves a purpose. The 'us–them' perspective defines the issues, restricts the options and suggests the legitimate, self-evident hegemonic outcome. Hierarchy restricts responsibility and skews accountability. Without clear hierarchy it is more difficult to restrict the debate to one definition of the problem or enforce a solution. Therefore empowerment requires a paradigm shift.

The multiplayer model suggested above is best portrayed (and researched) as interacting networks with hubs (see Figure 7.3).[41] Currently, the *state* is a more centrally connected hub – interfering, influencing and mediating even in bilateral relations of other players.

Actually, there are numerous coexisting networks – e.g. for commerce, power relations, legal and social interactions – which are different but interdependent. A more exact model would superimpose them into one complex structure.

Note also that most players in the model are themselves a miniature multiplayer system. Especially, each 'religion' is better thought of as a matrix of

41 Hub – a (relative) convergence point of a network. As in a lot of networks, some hubs (e.g. the nation states) are (relative) 'hotspots' in terms of power, number of interactions, etc.

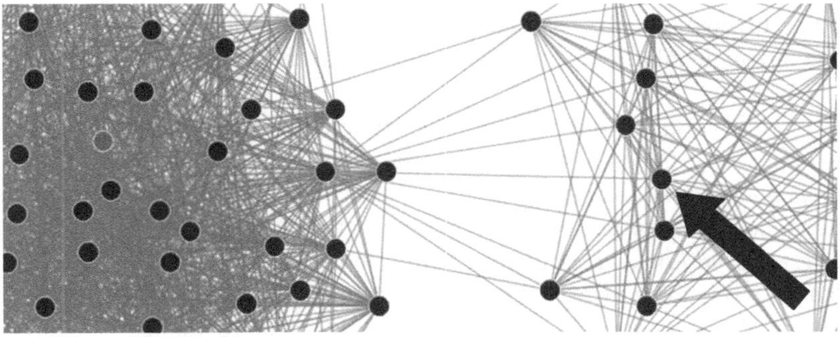

Figure 7.3 A network of relations

Source: 'Social Network Diagram (segment)' by DarwinPeacock, Maklaan. Licensed under CC BY 3.0 via Wikimedia Commons https://commons.wikimedia.org/wiki/File:Social_Network_Diagram_(segment).svg#/media/File:Social_Network_Diagram_(segment).svg

Taken from http://en.wikipedia.org/wiki/Social_network (accessed 28 April 2013).

religious legal options, players and communities. Each one is a network, and they are all interconnected so that various components from each religion, state or player interact with other players, both independently and interdependently. Thus, this presentation acknowledges the power of individuals and of multiple players while at the same time showing the futility of any single execution of hegemonic power. Only aggregated efforts can influence the matrix as a whole – thus inviting debates about bottom-up communal power and institutionalised religious powers.

In the proposed complex view of multiple relations and interactions, similarities and differences between players play a role. Surprisingly enough, international law and religion have a lot in common,[42] including the promotion of empowerment by a lot of religions and by international legal players (at least *de jure*).

Relations: coalitions, interaction, cooperations

In the multiplayer system all players continuously form coalitions, cooperate, co-opt, interact, consider, recognise and acknowledge each other (as well as hinder, boycott, kill, etc.). Thus each player tries to create and maintain an 'ideal' position in the relations matrix and influence others' positions in and for expected future interactions. These relations and interactions influence and sometimes define the positions of the players.

42 Both thrive more on legitimacy and law than on power/violence; reliance on voluntary compliance and on activity of subjects (peer control) more than on institutional enforcement. I hope to discuss these similarities elsewhere.

Coalitions

Examples of coalitions are abundant,[43] and they influence religious attitudes towards international law as well as attitudes of players towards religion:[44]

1 *Religion and state vs international law* – religious players and state cooperate to oppose international norms or influence them.[45]
2 *State and international law vs religion* – states might cooperate with international bodies to enforce norms on religious groups.[46]
3 *International law and religion vs state* – International law and religion collaborate to influence (promote, inhibit, change) a state's policies.[47]
4 *Other players, complex relations* – Kehillat Cha'are Shalom VeTsedek sued the state of France at the European Court of Human Rights against the monopoly of the established Jewish French community on ritual slaughter (*religious sub-community and regional law vs state and state recognised religious community*).[48] Consider also the relative new phenomenon of interfaith cooperations, which almost always occur in relation (or opposition) to other players (*faith 1 and faith 2 etc. vs state and/or international law*).[49]

43 Coalitions can be formal (e.g. established religions or state-funded religious groups) or informal; they can be public or hidden and denied; ad hoc or strategic and long-term; for certain purposes (a vote, an issue) or across the board. Each mix of the above influences the overall system's structure differently. For example, in 2010 President Obama nominated a permanent American representative to the organisation of the Islamic Conference (www.oic-oci.org/home.asp).

44 Silvio Ferrari, *Models of State-Religion Relations in Western Europe*, *in* The Future of Religious Freedom (Allen D. Hertzeke, ed., 2013), 202–214.

45 For example, religious groups influence states to exempt religious communities from eradicating discrimination against women. CEDAW has the highest number of reservations, most of them on religious grounds. About children's rights, see Jeremy T. Gunn, *The Religious Right and the Opposition to U.S. Ratification of the Convention on the Rights of the Child*, 20 Emory Int. L. Rev. 111 (2006). The state might use a religious community or religious norm as a reason to decline or postpone compliance with international law (e.g. declaring land as holy and therefore not compromising on territory). The lack of latitude strengthens the state's position in negotiation, and weakens the ability to compromise.

46 (1) States enforce laws upon religious communities claiming pressure from international law. See an example in Isaac Herzog, Legislation for Israel I, 18–19 (1989, Hebrew). (2) International legal players use existing church–state relations to introduce norms and values into religious discourse. (3) In 2009 the Vatican changed its 80-year-old semi-automatic acceptance of Italian law, submitting future laws to papal review. This is probably partly due to the influence of the EU, feminist, gay and human rights groups on Italian law. See article from 2 January 2009, http://news.bbc.co.uk/go/pr/fr/-/2/hi/Europe/7807501.stm.

47 For example, three early Jewish reactions to international law employ international law to restrict the power and sovereignty of the state (documented in my PhD, *supra* note 1, ch. 1).

48 See *Cha'are Shalom VeTsedek* v. *France*, ECHR 27417/95 (2000).

49 For example, cooperation between fundamentalist Muslims, Christians and Jews opposing the gay pride parade in Jerusalem, http://web.israelinsider.com/Articles/ Culture/ 5258.htm (31 March 2005); the Archbishop of Canterbury challenged the state (England) in favour of Islamic law and rights, www.timesonline.co.uk/tol/comment/faith/article3328024. See also religious feminist interfaith enrichment, www.wfu.edu/news/release/2008.02.12.t.php.

Will the religious legal opinion of a religious leader be influenced by the pattern of his relations with his surroundings? Can one imagine a lack of influence? The more empowered players are, the more choices they have the more (counter-intuitively) they are prone to external, indirect and non-specific influence.

Coalitions and adversity with international actors are part of what shapes the worldview of religious actors. It is the *sum of all relations* that deeply influences the structure of the world in which the religious players and communities exist. That structure shapes the culture and reality of the communities – influencing education, the intra-community discourse, the form and content of legal questions and the possible solutions. As well, they directly influence the considerations of the religious (political and/or legal) decision-maker, the available religious legal terms and the conceivable outcomes. It influences the attitude towards international law and the issues at hand.[50]

Relations beyond coalitions

Players or communities might cooperate without being in coalition[51] and vice versa.[52] Relations in the system do not have to be mutual in order to influence. Mere one-sided consideration of one player can influence an outcome, future interactions and the overall structure.[53] Multiple and even contradictory coalitions and interactions are not only possible – but very common. The matrix of relationships is not uniform (all relations being the same or compatible), and not random (effects cancelling each other out) – they constitute a complex system that influences outcomes. Religions have interests and maintain relations in many countries and with multiple organisations – so interesting relations are formed on a daily basis.[54] These relations can enrich the dynamics, empower the processes and institutions and strengthen voluntary compliance (and vice versa).[55]

50 It is arguably the total opposition to any outgroup, and lack of all contacts (except war) with other players which defines religious violent extremism.

51 A legal coalition might be – civilly or religiously – forbidden (or perceived as counterproductive), for example, between two religions, or between state and religion. Cooperating or even only coordinating for the environment with an abhorred 'other' is a good example.

52 Players which do not cooperate may create coalitions in multiplayer negotiations.

53 For example, presenting a religious consideration (even if afterwards it is rejected), offering a voice, vote or ensuring exit (without request or expecting reciprocity).

54 Religions have interests in specific countries – e.g. the organising of the Haj (Saudi Arabia) or managing the holy area in Jerusalem (Israel [and PA]). Religions have interest in diverse international negotiations and agreements – e.g. ethics (cloning, war), health (procreation, vaccination), NAFTA (commerce), law (conventions) and institutions.

55 International Relations literature should be utilised but also re-examined. For example, does broad participation (religious players and communities and other NSAs) in conventions or coalitions, enhance compliance, like in Brown Weiss & Jacobson, *supra* note 22, 529.

Relations with whom?

The multiplayer network paradigm enables to engage multiple players in various ways.[56] It encourages states and players to empower and engage[57] multiple religious actors and not only the current hegemonic representatives.[58]

Opposing hegemonic religion, promoting plurality and variation

Engaging only the hegemonic representatives of religion gives them excessive recognition, positions and power.[59] This should be prevented. In order to explain why, let's go back to the dichotomous aspect of the prevailing concentric model.

The hierarchal concentric worldview goes together with a cognitive, cultural and legal 'us–them' paradigm.[60] In it, for each player in each interaction all external cultural, legal or political forces are mainly 'external' (the 'other').[61] The interaction is shaped by the definition of the relationship as being either with a player who is part of 'us' or one of 'them'. This not only influences the definition of the groups and the relations with the 'out-group'. The paradigm also has various impacts on the *in-group*.

Differences in the 'they' category seem insignificant. In this dichotomic view, different dilemmas[62] are all seen as one and the same dilemma, solved by one principled policy decision between different adaptation mechanisms (integration, rejection or assimilation).[63] This single coping strategy is then applied, by individuals and communities, to all dilemmas in all contexts.

This worldview is reinforced by most states and NGOs which relate to religion, religious and religious law as 'others'. Instead of breaking the 'us–them' paradigm, everybody argues where the border between the 'in' and the 'out' should be. These questions are important,[64] but serve to hide the inherent disempowering force of the model itself.

56 E.g. Brown Weiss & Jacobson, *supra* n. 22, 554 (engaging all relevant actors).

57 One could argue that the order is reversed. The text should read: 'engage and empower'.

58 Engagement of religion is commonly perceived to be counterproductive – promoting and strengthening reactive, fundamentalist, religious positions.

59 I am against delegitimising the hegemonic religious legal option, player or community and against replacing one hegemony with another (more progressive) one.

60 David Berreby, Us and Them: The Science of Identity (2005).

61 For the religious players this might include seculars, the state and the world. For the state or NGOs all religious variations, individuals and communities are labelled together as one.

62 Feminism vs traditionalism, church vs state, open vs closed, modernity vs tradition, Enlightenment vs fundamentalism, religious vs national identity.

63 The subtitle of Jacob J. Schacter (ed.), Judaism's Encounter with other Cultures (1997) is: 'Rejection or integration'.

64 How to place this single border and how strong or permeable it should be. When there is only one meaning to *us* and to *them*, the criteria, strategies and decision process of setting the border are crucial. The stakes were (and are) high. Are women, children, gays and invalids in or out of the community? What is the impact of religious dissent? And what should the attitude be towards converts and enstranged communities?

In the 'us–them' paradigm, the nation state and international players view the religious 'other' as a one-faceted, shallow, uni-dimensional continuum. When engaging this 'religion' in this paradigm, the state identifies the 'most religious' representative on that continuum with whom business 'can still be done'. The state then gives that hegemonic representative non-proportional power,[65] thereby suppressing pluralism. Players at large (including in the religious constituency) identify 'religious' with that representative agent. The dichotomous worldview ignites internal struggles – a zero-sum, all-or-nothing fight[66] – for representing the in-group, and leads to coercion of in-group opposition to enhance cohesiveness (and extremism).[67] Such a struggle does not enable cooperative communication or democratic, communal, bottom-up coalition building.[68] It is also dangerous for the winner, who constantly represses dissent. Both the voices of religions and the voices of individuals and players are thus dangerously disempowered.[69]

The state and the hegemonic religious leaders externalise the costs of their 'compromises' on those who they can agree upon as 'others' (e.g. women, foreigners).[70] These others can be both inside and outside the relevant religious community.[71] The externalisation is tolerated by the state or international law in order to engage hegemonic 'religion'.[72]

Engagement in the multiplayer model strives to weaken this dynamic. It emphasises the need for empowerment due to the fading of the state, the ensuing multiplicity of external agents, the multiplicity and variety in each religion and the need for players to internalise costs.[73] To promote empowerment I advocate

65 The hegemonic representative moves towards those who were left out, thereby becoming more and more extreme. Sunder, *supra* note 21; Sunstein and Berman, note 69, below. I offer that the portrayal of any position as *the* religious position is detrimental, as is the 'shallow', uni-dimensional portrayal of religious law and community.

66 For any sub-community, the zero-sum game is more of a threat than an opportunity. Compare Rawls, *supra* note 12. Religions reject paradigms that include an option to lose all.

67 Whenever there is one 'true' religion with one authoritative voice, there is a struggle for power. What will that one religious standpoint be? Who will speak for it and who controls it?

68 Co-opting the state, forcing and subduing are common strategies to gain power.

69 According to this account, it is external non-religious agents which reinforce internal dynamics which in turn enhance extremism and fundamentalism and violence in religions. See e.g. Cass R. Sunstein, Why Societies Need Dissent (2003); Idem, *Deliberative Trouble? Why Groups Go to Extremes*, 110 Yale L. J. 71 (2000): 71–119; and the brilliant Eli Berman, Radical, Religious, and Violent: The New Economics of Terrorism (2009); Neusner, *supra* note 16; Meir Litbak and Ora Limor (eds.), Religious Extremism (Hebrew, 2008).

70 Thus some external players which object to religious extremism and warn from its dangers, are tolerating, enabling and actively encouraging it by co-option and cooperation.

71 *Outside of religion*: members of other religions, non-believers or foreigners. *Inside religious communities*: women, dissenting religious leaders and communities, minorities.

72 Sometimes the state and the secular society 'gain' from religious extremism, by portraying the religious option as less attractive and oppressive (and simultaneously co-opting it).

73 This argument is supported by the ideas of Sunder, *supra* note 21; Blank, note 132 below; Israel-Vleeschhouwer, *supra* note 1 and e.g. Ralph Michaels, *Global Legal Pluralism*, 5 Ann. Rev. L. and Soc. Sc. 243 (2009) (ssrn=1430395); For an application to church–state relations see Yuksel Sezgin, *A Political Account for Legal Confrontation Between State and Society*, 32 Stud. L. Pol. and Soc. 199 (2004).

to diminish the excessive powers of established religions, and demolish the structures that uphold the hegemony artificially. There are various ways to do that. Professor Sunder suggested giving voice and power to multiple community based, bottom-up religious players – an international affirmative action policy. In this engagement, hegemonic laws, players and communities would be heard only as part of a symphonic voice (or not heard at all). In the second stage, players can engage the influence of the coalitions and incentives on the internal relations in the religious network. Direct engagement of the religious constituency and players is another major way to enable internal diversity and engage.

Players and communities

It is important to engage a variety of leaders, especially those that grew from local, domestic processes, and draw legitimacy from them:[74] political leaders, alternative minority/local/'other' leaders, legal theorists, tradition carriers (e.g. elderly, educators, women), legal decision-makers (e.g. Rabbis, Kadis), artists, clergy.[75] It is also crucial to recognise the power of the community and its institutions as socialisation agents and as realisations of religious life that have no less power than leaders.[76] Engagement should also extend to individuals and to the constituency as a whole.[77]

The actual picture is more complex. Players (e.g. the state) can influence the size of communities; the nature of organised membership; the extent of services the community provides and increase or decrease the attractiveness of membership and activity in communities. Players can influence the relations between communities (in each state and internationally). Players can strive to communicate directly with the constituency 'over the heads' of the religious players, through e.g. media and administrative acts. One should remember that some players will tend to create disempowering incentives, and only continuous, conscious and informed efforts can ensure a responsible and smart empowering engagement.

But the structure of the relations is but one part of the empowering engagement of religious players and communities. The second part is incentives.

Incentives

In a conscious multiplayer system, players which know the religious laws (of others) and deeply understand the relevant communities can influence processes

74 E.g. Brown Weiss & Jacobson, supra note 22, e.g. at 542.

75 Of course some persons can serve in more than one form of leadership, and they should be engaged in all their capacities.

76 This seems probable when the various players contradict each other and cancel each others' influence. But, this is true even in opposition to most players' combined efforts (e.g. laity vs clergy and leaders in the sexual abuse scandals). This 'unseen' power is codified in Jewish law (BT Pesahim 66) and is also incorporated in canon law in Vatican II.

77 Charles Sabel and Michael C. Dorf, A Constitution of Democratic Experimentalism (2006) (emergent importance of broad democratic participation)

by employing general and specific incentives/sanctions. Incentives, which play a subtle but central role, can include e.g. recognition, access, participation, power (voice/vote), assistance, resources, influence and rights (e.g. freedom). Sanctions include penalties, sanctions and withdrawal of privileges.

Incentives and sanctions are part of the overall engagement.[78] As stated, religious players seem to want an international status in regional and international interactions.[79] Realising that the structure of relations is not given and fixed[80] (the multiplayer paradigm), we can enrich the toolbox of engagement and add unique forms of incentives and sanctions: giving/withdrawing legal status can be part of negotiations, as can the extent, depth and nature of relations with them (offering, denying and cancelling).[81] In some cases, just offering minority or dissenting groups a status similar to the hegemonic player can activate systematic dynamics between the offering party, the hegemonic player and these new players. The status and relations are not, and should not be considered to be, given or static. It should depend on responsibility, accountability, contributions and empowerment. A detailed model should discuss if, and under what conditions, international players and institutions might *offer* various kinds of international status to currently unrecognised religious players or take it away.

Soft power incentives

Incentives form a strong component of the empowering engagement. The economist Eli Berman showed that incentives work on even the most fundamental religious sects.[82] Together with the other components, incentives have the power to influence across borders and boundaries.[83]

78 The goals of the RILM suggested below and its suggested form (promoting multiplicity, sanctioning delegitimising an opinion, encouraging engagement) are structured to facilitate the creation and usage of incentives and sanctions. In some cases, when domestic or international players engage religious law, they influence internal religious legal discourse.

79 Religious organisations, institutions and communities sought and achieved international status as observers at UN institutions and are international players, independent of their official status, in addition to the various forms of semi-independent status in the decision processes of states.

80 *When* Brown-Weiss and Jacobson, supra note 22 discuss engagement of states vis-à-vis the environment, they didn't discuss structure and relations, because they assumed that the international system is a given.

81 Such an offer is not dependent on the religious players wanting the offer or its consequences. International law has been doing this all the time with its current members. States are invited and pressured to join conventions (see e.g. art. 155 of the fourth Geneva protocol), institutions and legal obligations. Legal recognition, participation and status are thus used as incentives (either offered or denied). Some legal interactions (customary law, part of ICC jurisdiction) also don't rely on consent.

82 Berman, *supra* note 69.

83 See Lori F. Damrosch, *Politics Across Borders: Nonintervention and Nonforcible influence over Domestic Affairs*, 83 AJIL 1 (1989); Compare Amnon Reichman, *When We Sit To Judge We Are Being Judged: The Israeli GSS Case, Ex Parte Pinochet and Domestic/Global Deliberation*, 9 Cardozo J. Int'l & Comp. L. 41 (2001).

Incentives are easier to change than official status or structures of relations. Players can adjust, refine and re-refine the incentive matrix as the legal opinions, relations and other factors change, as well as adapt it to different players, issues and situations.

Religions' ancient and well tested mechanisms for adaptation, their concern with their (and god's) reputation, their need to attract members and prevent their exit in an age of permeable borders of communities and multiple identities make religion good targets for 'soft power' strategies.[84] The impact of 'soft' incentives and sanctions on any decision-making process is profound. Soft power creates a new reality in which the internal religious processes are impacted or stressed, but not forced. The reality shapes the questions and the attitudes towards the issues at hand; they portray the relevant players, accentuate possible options and influence the religious legal argumentation in support of the ruling – internally and towards external players.[85] The religious players, communities and laws might change, integrate, compromise, develop, interpret or innovate. They might also object, reject or manipulate. In all these cases, empowering engagement has been achieved.[86] Soft power influences in a less disempowering way than straight coercion of a foreign norm on religious laws, players and community. Indeed, the possibility to reject and suffer the consequences (inherent in soft power, but not in coercion) ensures that any decision to accept the foreign norm will be the result of an internal legal process, not externally imposed – and therefore legitimate.

The structure of relations and the incentives are not created to induce a certain, specific change. The motivations and considerations are much more broad and complex. It is hard to imagine an external player influencing a religious decision by coarse force, or even just because it found the 'correct lever' and pushed with 'enough power'. Therefore the external engagements leave space for intra-communal debates, tend to *add* options to them, thereby *increasing* choice.

The impact of soft power depends on intimate knowledge of the legal system targeted, its dynamics and constrains, and its long-term engagement of multiple players and communities. Effective agents construct relations and incentives with all the players and interests in mind.[87] They can attempt to use structure, relations and incentives to shape the world in such a way that religious players will be more

84 Joseph Nye, Soft Power: The Mean to success in World Politics (2004).

85 In some cases, various versions of the same ruling will be published. In different venues and forms of publication, the actual ruling or its argumentation might be different. Informed players can use these versions to reshape the coalitions and incentives accordingly for future engagement. Thus, the coalitions and incentives join tradition and communities to shape the religious world-views and even legal argumentation. This is another goal for the RILM suggested below.

86 Initial rejection is even sometimes counted as the most crucial phase in engagement. It signifies the stage in which the external influence cannot be ignored and has to be internalised in the domestic discourse. A consequent change of attitude to e.g. adaptation or integration is then a legitimate next phase. Harold H. Koh *Why do Nations Obey International Law*, 106 Yale L. J. 2599 (1997)

87 Compare Blu Greenberg in her book On Women and Judaism: A View from Tradition (1981) (coining the expression: 'Where there is a rabbinic will, there is a Jewish legal way').

likely to voluntarily choose for a certain course of action. The incentives can thus be changed by each player and by coalitions of players.

Consider the following demonstration: Under one plausible interpretation of article 19(c) of the 1969 Vienna Convention on the Law of Treaties, international conventions do not allow reservations in favour of religious groups that oppose the conventions' goal.[88] Today, a state can gain international status and reputation by signing a convention (e.g. CEDAW), and submit reservations to accommodate the perceived needs of a religious group – externalising the costs on 'others' (women). If article 19(c) would be implemented together with article 28(2) in the CEDAW itself, a state cannot have both, but has to choose, changing the prevalent state–religion dynamics. For example, before choosing, the state will pressure the religious group to innovate or accommodate.[89] Within such a process, the costs will be more likely to be internalised.

Also sanctions, or threat of sanctions, can be effective. Consider what would happen if the reaction to a certain religious legal ruling would be to cancel that community's protected right of freedom of religion, or to lose an international status or 'voice'.[90]

Brown-Weiss and Jacobson point out that incentives and sanctions can be unilateral or part of negotiations and agreements.[91] They note that the various aspects of engagement are interrelated. They mostly empower each other but might also contradict. They warn that different players might react differently and respond optimally to different mixes of measures.[92] This is certainly true for religious players and communities.[93] Note that the imperative of equal treatment in state actions is a major constraint on players' ability to engage religions differently.[94]

88 See articles 20–23 of the convention.

89 See General Recommendation No. 4 (reservations), Report of the Committee on the EDAW (sixth session), 1987, para. 579; General Recommendation No. 20 (reservations), Report of the Committee on the CEDAW (eleventh session), 1992, p. 1; and in Statement on reservations to the CEDAW, Report of the Committee (eighteenth and nineteenth sessions), 1998, II, ch. I A.

90 For a discussion of such incentives in the relations between the Security Council, Europe, the US and European states, see Erika De Wet, *The Emergence of International and Regional Value Systems as a Manifestation of the Emerging International Constitutional Order*, 19 Leiden J. Int. L. 611, at 618 (2006). Rabbi Chalfon from Gerba urged for sanctions against free riders in international law (circa 1924, as I discuss in my PhD, *supra* note 1, ch. 2, Hebrew).

91 Empowered religious players might negotiate a price for an encyclical, Fatwa or Halachic ruling incorporating international criminal law or human rights in the religious legal codes. This is especially true if we hold that the obligation of international organisations to international law is not self-evident (see Benvenisti, *supra* note 31, 178–179). Players would probably pay differently for (1) compliance with the exact international norm, (2) incorporation into the religious thought and narrative; than they would pay for (3) creation of an adapted and nuanced compatible norm that is not similar to the international norm through translation into religious terms and norms.

92 Brown Weiss & Jacobson, *supra* note 22, 550.

93 I do not hold that in engaging religion there is a clear and agreed upon optimum.

94 But see the differential treatment in France of religious garments of Jews and Hindus versus the treatment of the Hijab and Burka.

Considering counterproductive effects

The proposed empowering engagement will probably cause states and hegemonic religious players to use their current power and connections for countermeasures.

The system analysis provided above predicts that the initial strongest reactions are to be expected from the hegemonic, extreme and fundamentalist representatives, communities and individuals, together with initial weak impact. One needs a lot of power to move a system away from an equilibrium point, especially one supported by strong structural elements. The power of the organised, hegemonic community might grow and become more extreme in the initial phases. However, consistent action to engage multiple players and communities can change the equilibrium.[95] A good example for an empowering change is the Second Vatican Council. Note the crucial empowering role of the invitation of observers from outside, the engagement of outside players and the recognition and engagement of the laity.[96] Also note that these decentralising measures did not weaken the church and its leaders Pope John Paul II and Pope Francis.

From theory to practice

I will now reflect on the theoretical model proposed above, in order to lead to the practical proposal of an empowering engagement of religious laws and communities.

Discussion of objections to the multiplayer model

The suggested multiplayer system is complex and is perceived to be chaotic and non-predictable. Therefore it may seem profitable to ignore the described 'reality' and stay with the simpler 'us–them' system.[97] This is a known basic objection to empowerment. I object to this critique.

I argue that these multiple pluralistic, multiplayer systems will not lead to a non-stable, chaotic and unpredictable reality.[98] Economic theory teaches that certain goods are network products, whose worth grows as the number of their users grows, ensuring the system's motivation to organise itself.[99] Law, certainly

95 When such a new equilibrium will be reached, any return to the now existent equilibrium will seem no less farfetched and need no less power.

96 The documents www.vatican.va/archive/hist_councils/ii_vatican_council/index.htm; see e.g. John W. O'Malley, What Happened at Vatican II (2008); Ian Linden, Global Catholicism: Diversity and Change since Vatican II (2009).

97 According to this argument, additional powers contradict each other and will eventually cancel each other out, or are weak enough to ignore. Or, an extensive multiplicity of considerations is not practical in the legal or political process.

98 The following argument is based on Talia Fisher, Hafradat hamishpat mehamedina [Separation of Law and State] (PhD Diss. Hebrew Univ., Jerusalem, 2002).

99 The first user of the telephone couldn't use it. Its worth grows with its dispersion. Laws regarding certified commercial food (Kosher, Halal), family laws or religious conversion (and even parish laws, pubic ritual or holydays) are senseless for a lone individual. These laws suppose a considerable constituency.

religious law, is such a network-product. Therefore, religion does not need a state-supported organisation and leader. Even without intervention by the state, religious communities will strive for inter-communal bottom-up agreements to achieve a broad constituency – as they did in the pre-state-era past. These agreements will create a limited set of united communities, regulated by common laws. At any given time, there are a restricted number of stable (equilibrium) solutions, achievable by a limited set of viable coalitions.[100] Each religion organises itself internally, and posits itself vis-à-vis external actors, in any of a few limited possible options. A coherent system emerges.

The same analysis assures us that no single universal united law can be achieved and maintained (even in the hierarchical Catholic Church). Competition will always arise, and ensure variation.[101] Their structural dynamics encourage variation and adaptation and enable positive legal, spiritual, cultural and intellectual tension. Networks (as opposed to an 'us–them' paradigm) enable different forms, thereby reflecting, creating and enhancing different communal and individual self-identities.

The options and the dynamics to realise equilibria are predictable and prone to influence.[102] Other players can influence the communal organisation of each player and the consequent legal development – by interactions, coalitions and incentives.[103]

From any equilibrium point, the overall 'map' can change in a limited number of ways. We can imagine a change of policy by one or more of the coalitions, a minor change in the structure of the coalitions or a restructuring

100 This argument can be based on evolution theories, on system analysis and on legal research. GUNTHER TEUBNER, GLOBAL LAW WITHOUT A STATE (1997); Sally Engle Merry, *International Law and Sociolegal Scholarship: Toward a Spatial Global Legal Pluralism*, 41 STU. L. POL. SOC. 149 (2008); Anthony D'Amato, *International law as an Autopoietic System*, DEVELOPMENTS OF INTERNATIONAL LAW IN TREATY MAKING 335 (2005); Paul Schiff Berman, *A Pluralist Approach to International Law*, 32 YALE J. OF INT. L. 301 (2007) (briefly mentions religion at p. 312); Sally Merry and Balakrishnan Rajagopal, *International Law and Global Legal Pluralism*, PAPER PRESENTED AT TEL AVIV UNIVERSITY GLOBALIZATION SEMINAR (http://citation.allacademic.com/meta/p177966_index.html); William W. Burke-White, *International Legal Pluralism*, 25 MICHIGAN J. OF INT. L. 962 (2004); Peer Zumbansen, *Transnational Legal Pluralism*, 1:2 TRANSNATIONAL LEGAL THEORY 141–189 (2010) (religion as a cultural, not as a legal, system); Nico Krisch, *The Case for Pluralism in Postnational Law*, LSE SOCIETY AND ECONOMY WORKING PAPER, ssrn=1418707. for complex systems see ALBERT-LASZLO BARABASI, LINKED: HOW EVERYTHING IS CONNECTED TO EVERYTHING IS CONNECTED TO EVERYTHING ELSE AND WHAT IT MEANS FOR BUSINESS, SCIENCE, AND EVERYDAY LIFE (2002).

101 This part of the analysis is crucial for undermining any dichotomous zero-sum game worldview.

102 Structural factors (language, geography, demography) have a strong influence.

103 E.g. consider a state that gives voice or power only to a religion with over million adherents. This will reduce the tendency to split over theological or organizational tensions and the inner relations and fundamentalist communities will have to compromise with less strict ones. If the minimum is 250,000 such alliances are discouraged. Religious laws and practices will be influenced differently in either case.

of the overall map.[104] Note, however, that in the first two options the cultural picture, overall image and power of each player is relatively stable. Thereby the proposed system presents a structural win–win strategy for religions and other players alike: preserving the advantages of diversity with the multiple advantages of a unified voice.[105]

Advantages of the proposed model: networks, identity and praxis

Contemporary individuals are members of multiple communities, associations or organisations, which are all important to the individual's identity.[106] Religious communities currently cope with this tendency by either allowing members to have dual or multiple member/citizen-ship or by internalising aspects of multiple identities.[107]

Acknowledging and internalising the multiplayer paradigm offers a third way. Each community may pursue a complex set of relations, agreements and cooperations with multiple organisations inside and outside of the religious community. A community may share the burden of local religious services with some communities, while initiating educational endeavours with others. It may cooperate with authorities on recycling, but with local faith groups on shaping the public space.

This bottom-up empowering approach creates a multiple diversity, or double plurality. On one level there are differences between communities in daily practice, culture and law. On the second level *similar* congregations will be able to offer a *different* form and experience of religious life by their different set of connections to the religious and general surroundings. As well, very *different* congregations (even from two religions) can offer a very *similar* (and even coordinated) 'package' of services. Thus, individuals and communities have more options how to shape their religious and social experience, more political possibilities and complex identities. Even the hegemonic players and communities have more options, even if not wanted.

The voluntary community and its leaders

Every community decides what the definitions of the religious legal dilemmas are; which authority or authorities is/are consulted; what the available facts are and how they are presented. Communal discourse defines the religious legal

104 Others say that this multiplayer system will most of the time be in non-equilibrium states. However, the dynamics of this kind of fluid systems are also, to some extent, predictable and controllable. See *Embodying Discontinuity: Order Through Chaos*, Encyclopedia of World Problems and Human Potential, 4th ed. Vol. II, commentaries chapter 11.2 (1994–1995) (www.uia.be/en/node/159?kap=50).

105 Interactions between players are reduced to a manageable number of participants.

106 *E.g.* Jonathan Sacks, The Persistence of Faith *(1991: 2005).*

107 They then try to cater to the members' need by providing exactly the expected complicated identity in and by the community.

categorisations and the precedents which seem relevant. The constituency and political leaders shape the context – coalitions, previous interactions, internal and external incentives – and influence the way these are perceived. Various audiences influence what form of argument is expected and will be considered to be convincing. These factors are part of the *weltanschauung* of the decision-makers that both decide religious law and react to decisions of others. As well, they influence compliance which influences the decisions' legitimacy. Thus, the communal structure influences religious law and has a central role in the model.

Individual identities interact with communities *and* with their networks. Some of these individuals will become political and religious leaders, so communities influence leaders even before any issue arises.

Political leadership can be in the community, outside of it or leading the community's external relations. Religious leadership can be through teaching, education or legal decision-making. These leaders, shaped by the community and its surroundings, will then *influence the future coalitions and relations of their community, according to their opinion.*[108] In extreme cases the leader may threaten to leave his/her post to in order to enforce his/her will on others, but usually she will influence by teaching, arguing and ruling according to her view, using personal credit and charisma (this is her 'soft power').[109] As such, both the religious leader and her interpretive community are strong players that employ mainly soft power.

Non-religious players should engage both all players and communities separately but simultaneously. Neglecting one of them makes empowering engagement almost impossible, because intra-community interaction is stronger than relations with outside players. The intra-community interactions are themselves a goal for engagement.

Engaging religion by co-opting and tolerating coercive, externalising, hegemonic players is counterproductive. Coerced membership in religious communities (like established religions) should be abolished, and the possibility of cheap exit options should be ensured and encouraged. The resulting voluntary communities, where acceptance of authority and services by religious congregation members and surrounding non-members (constituency) is voluntary, enhances the power of the individuals and communities, and empowers the religious legal process.

On differences between religions

The present model is based on research in Jewish law and initial research in monotheistic religions. The model and suggestions partially apply to more religious laws, players and communities, with the following three differences between religions in mind.

108 This is very clear in the Catholic Church (Benedict the 16th replacing John Paul the 2nd). But even there, the pope's election is influenced by bottom-up processes.

109 In addition, tradition, politics, legal theory, religious practice and personal relations place constrains on the structural influence and on the leader's activities.

Personal vs communal religions

The communal and leadership dynamics are mainly true for religions that place emphasis on the community – for worship, social support or control, socialisation and more. The community is also where the various forms of leadership are created, exist and act. More personal religions that are not based in or on communities will need separate treatment. These religions also tend to have less laws and texts.

Hierarchy and institutionalisation

Islam, Judaism and Protestant Christianity differ from the Catholic Church in their (lack of) form of institutionalisation, influencing the textual culture,[110] the relations and the incentives. This is not to say that existing hierarchy or institutionalisation (or lack of it) has to be accepted by all players, but it has to be recognised and taken into account (even if only to undermine or manipulate it).[111]

Stage of legal development regarding international law

The maturity of philosophical, legal and political discourse in the religious community is of importance. For example, Jewish law and society are in a preparadigmatic state regarding its attitude towards international law, and one can find a vast range of attitudes.[112] Therefore the prospective influence of players on Jewish law and society in this area is much higher than on religious laws that have an accepted hegemonic legal attitude (that is not to say that the influence will be high, cheap or easy).

Consequences for action and research

The model is descriptive, and holds even for ultra-orthodox, fundamentalist disempowered and disempowering communities, for whom this analysis is relevant but will probably remain opaque.[113] It raises new strategic and political options which require normative debates in the religious and international communities.

110 How can one determine the relative status of a religious text without official status?

111 Coalitions and incentives play out differently when employed towards horizontal or hierarchal religions. Leeway of players at the top and in the middle of the hierarchy is different. There are also differences in the access to players; the interaction between them and differences in the interaction between them and their (lay) communities.

112 Amos Israel-Vleeschhouwer, *When the World Changes: International Law in the Philosophy of Jewish Law*, New Frontiers in the Philosophy of Jewish Law 151–186 (Avinoam Rosnak (ed.), 2011, Hebrew). There is disagreement as to the perception of international reality and law, the questions that arise from the phenomenon of international law, the legal tools to answer these questions and the criteria to decide about the better answers. However, in certain areas of law, there is a dominant legal position, a dominant player or a community of central importance.

113 Even in cases where its operation can be recognised, it is rarely explicitly expressed and might even not be accessible to the community members or to some players.

These debates will hopefully challenge the proposed model, and enrich it. The model's testable predictions open it to quantitative and qualitative research, enabling refutation, modification and refinement. I personally recommend more research into the structural options, the points of equilibrium, the incentives and the system dynamics.

I emphasise the need for elaborate consideration before implementing any of the suggestions in actual social action. As in any complex system, interventions in the system seldom have (only) their intended effect.[114] I stress the short-term prediction of enhanced extremism and oppression, as actual human beings will be influenced by the suggested engagement.[115]

I call upon interested colleagues to join multi-confessional international research groups. One group might want to create a Religious International Legal Materials database, proposed below. Other groups might want to map networks, to create multiple matrixes of incentives and sanctions for various religious laws, players and communities or suggest other empowering modes of engaging religious players not included in the present chapter. As promised, I will now turn to one project which will demonstrate how I envision to put the suggested model into practice.

RILM: Religious International Legal Materials database

Religious laws are meaningful to their constituency. They influence transnational, regional and international communities, as well as specific, religiously identified, nations. However, most international players and the majority of religious constituencies are ignorant about religious laws (including their own, certainly of others). This enables manipulations which are inherently disempowering. Part of engaging religions (at least those which include a meaningful legal system) is engaging its laws. I offer to foster a rich perception of religious laws – actively promote the proliferation of knowledge of religious legal diversity, its institutional richness and its dynamic and innovative potential. In order to do that I propose to actively document religious legal materials which pertain to international law, analyse and publicise them. A comprehensive discussion, focused on dis/empowerment, will follow the proposal.

Religious International Legal Materials database: a practical proposal

I propose to create an online RILM database, documenting all religious materials regarding international law and relations. The database's comprehensiveness, openness and will be evident in the content as well as in the interface.

114 See Peter Coleman, The Five Percent (2011).

115 Maximum responsibility includes engaging in the broadest form possible. Document, study and acknowledge all relevant jurisprudence; engage multiple players; strive for direct feedback and engagement of the constituency and communities and finally – internalise costs and be accountable for any costs that are externalised.

The basis of the database will be reports by special rapporteurs – consisting of at least a leading hegemonic voice, a number of dissenting religious voices[116] (from or through NGOs) and leading academic researchers. They will be encouraged to portray full original texts and materials beside their analyses. The report will appear as such, but the collected sources will appear in full text in the database (with connection to the report or reports that discuss them).[117] Another major source will be more democratic – inviting users and players to contribute, together with crowd-sourcing. Special place will be given to the actual application of religious law – documenting practices, institutional events, communal activities, religiously-based lay opinions and public statements in various forms (including video, etc.).[118]

Citation of materials will be in the original language, with multiple translations and translation tools offered and encouraged. Discussions will too be multilingual.

The communal, domestic, national and international contexts of each religious legal system for each religious ruling or text are crucial. RILM will therefore strive to provide contextual data for all materials – e.g. date; place; original publication data; sociological, historical, political (and economical) contexts; and legal context.

A special interreligious team proficient in international law and religious jurisprudence will work with the reporters and the materials, to provide optimal accessibility, connectivity and maximum heuristic potential. Special effort will be needed in the initial phase to connect to existing texts and research.[119]

As an incentive, the reporters will be encouraged to shape a religiously appropriate format for the database, and given editorial power – e.g. the authorisation

116 For strong support of documenting dissenting voices and empowering them alongside hegemonic ones, see Christine Chinkin, *Women's Human Rights and Religion: How do they Coexist?* JAVAID REHMAN AND SUSAN C. BREAU (EDS.) RELIGION, HUMAN RIGHTS AND INTERNATIONAL LAW: A CRITICAL EXAMINATION OF ISLAMIC STATE PRACTICES 53 (2007)

117 Note the similarities and differences between the proposal and the ILDC database, as well as existing religious legal databases: See e.g. www.islamonline.net; www.vatican.va; www.jlaw.com; www.responsa.co.il etc.

118 For an interesting example see JOHN L. ESPOSITO AND , DALIA MOGAHED, WHO SPEAKS FOR ISLAM? WHAT A BILLION MUSLIMS REALLY THINK (2008). The following questions arise:

First, what constitutes a legal religious text? What constitutes customary religious law? How should hegemonic, dissenting, and minority opinions be presented?

These questions have an institutional aspect: Who should decide about these questions? Who should have the authority and the power? Does the authority have to be from inside or outside of the religion itself? Are the criteria to be the same in all religions or adjusted to each religion, topic or even text?

Second, questions of representation: are laws/codes, cases and other religious materials to be presented together? There are major differences between materials (theoretical works, political statements, codifications, sermons and essays) and actual (mostly specific) decisions in cases. This difference is extenuated in some religious systems and less important in others.

119 E.g. HENRY J. STEINER, PHILIP ALSTON AND RYAN GOODMAN, INTERNATIONAL HUMAN RIGHTS IN CONTEXT: LAW, POLITICS, MORALS (2008); W. COLE DURHAM & BRETT G. SCHARFFS, LAW AND RELIGION: NATIONAL, INTERNATIONAL, AND COMPARATIVE PERSPECTIVES (2010).

to comment without review (but not to censor), thereby attracting multiple contributors. Discussion and exploration of sources, options and consequences will be encouraged.

The technological platform will enable multiple forms of organisation, documentation and discussion, organising the materials according to religions, countries, issues, chronology – like the *religion and law consortium*[120] website's structure, and better.[121]

The website will enable creating personalised (sub-)divisions, as well as adding new ways of organising. Hyperlinking by end-users to other sources in the database, to research and to other sources will be technologically easy, and encouraged. These links will then be suggested, as an option, for other users.

Each religion's sub-site will have its own portal and URL,[122] which will enable and encourage its use by lay members, experts and leaders of the community without enforcing foreign options on them.[123] Permanent tools (on the page: search engines, suggested links; side by side viewing) will enable easy access to alternative opinions in each religion, commentaries, annotated sources, research about the relevant religion and the issue at hand. Other tools will enable addition of sources, commentaries, discussions, relevant ILM, state constitutions, comparative religious laws (in and out of RILM). Discussions will be encouraged in various ways (forums, blogs).

RILM will include the online promotion of multiple competing[124] religious International Law experts, who may qualify as experts of (religious) international law.

120 http://beta.religlaw.org. The site currently has three main portals: country, organisation and topic; it supports 24 languages, has a powerful search engine and a user friendly user guide. It does notably not document the *religious* legal perspective (and texts). As well, some of the features suggested below do not exist.

121 My original suggestion was simply to create 'missing volume of religious international legal materials' (see below) by creating such a volume. I went over to the proposed format, because:

1 A volume of religious materials implies that all religious sources should be in one volume because they are some common religiousity is the crucial aspect of these sources (this is the exact rational of the ILM project for *national* domestic jurisprudence). This fallacy had to be omitted. Therefore I considered other forms of organisation (and various internal divisions):

A Separate volumes for 'different' religions; monotheistic and others; 'new' and 'old'; universal and local; or maybe for each religion – without classification.

B Add religious texts to the overview of the country in which the texts were issued. This form would (1) emphasise the variety in global religions and (2) the impact of local policies and conditions upon religious sources.

C Add religious texts to thematic (criminal, labour) cases and materials volumes.

D A chronological form of organisation (like the ILM).

E Check the ways in which religions now organise their international legal material (which may or may not be compatible to any of the above), respect them and consider using them.

122 With similar addresses, like Catholic/Hindu/Islamic-internationallaw.RILM.org.

123 The main site will include all materials submitted or connected to the relevant criteria. However, the platform will enable creating mirror sites with less options.

124 E.g. competing for nominations to report; inviting competing opinions; indexing and documenting contributions to the corpus, soliciting CVs, book reviews all connected to an open expert database.

The RILM will encourage the proliferation of other databases and sources by linking to them, reviewing them and engaging their participants and contributors. It will offer the technological platform free of charge to any organisation that wants to create an independent database, demanding in return only a connection with the RILM. Part of the RILM platform could be in an open source form – to encourage development of new features. This has, however, to be balanced with concerns about abuse (see below).

Hardcopy editions of the reports and the collected texts could be mandated on a periodical schedule. The RILM will technologically encourage the possibility to publish texts, and text collections from the database (publishing on demand). The project will collect data about such publications and their (apparent) content.

Finally, the use of RILM materials in international law will be documented. Ideally, the RILM will become strongly intertwined with various tools of (other) international law documentation; legal databases; international courts and organisations. A permanent technological feature will record the ways individuals (and communities, as far as can be identified) use the website. This data will be utilised in subsequent development and analysed in the frame of comparative research. Multinational, denominational and interdisciplinary research groups will be invited to use the database, contribute to it, and participate in directing its operation.

Justifying RILM

In the Westphalian system the ILM (International Legal Materials) is the main tool for documenting state jurisprudence in order to facilitate their contributions to international jurisprudence. Prof. Lauterpacht pointed out the following contributions of national decisions; they (a) constitute an expert opinion as to international law regarding the issue at question; (b) contribute to establishing customary international law by deciding the law for their country; and (c) are used as proof for the actual norm in their countries.[125] Others offered reasons to be interested in national decisions which are inherently connected to empowerment in international law and the empowerment of its subjects: (d) national judicial decisions are one of the main tools for implementing international law in a fine-tuned, culturally adaptable way;[126] (e) national tribunals enhance the democratic basis of international law by enabling a broader participation in criticising, limiting, invoking, interpreting, and implementing international law;[127] (f) national tribunals have greater educational influence upon local population and agents than international fora, through their institutional power and cultural influence and

125 Hersch Lauterpacht, *Decisions of Municipal Courts as a Source of International Law*, 10 Brit. Y. B. Int. L. 65 (1929).

126 As such their existence is more important than recording them (see (h) below).

127 Eyal Benvenisti, *Judges and Foreign Affairs: A Comment on the Institute de Droit International's Resolution on 'The Activities of National Courts and the International Relations of their State'*, 5 EJIL 423 (1994) (The only opportunity for individuals [to] participate in the democracy-deficient process of shaping international law).

by shaping better matrixes of incentives to encourage compliance; (g) national fora are where new issues for international law arise, as well as innovative solutions and important considerations not taken into account in the international law agenda; (h) seriously taking national rulings into account will amplify and accentuate international law's diversity.[128]

Most of these motivations for documenting national law seem to be also relevant to religious law.[129] However, international law is initiated, exists and develops not only in and from inter*national* agreements, acts and fora.[130] It explicitly recognises domestic[131] and regional[132] sources which are culturally dependent,[133] and acknowledges the importance of diversity of attitudes in international law.[134]

128 Developing and researching international law through domestic rulings emphasises the legitimate diversity in interpretation of international law, as opposed to trying in vain to find one correct interpretation. Compare in Jewish law NOAM ZOHAR, ALTERNATIVES IN JEWISH BIOETHICS, introduction (1998); DAVID HARTMAN, A HEART WITH MANY ROOMS (1999). This reason contradicts (a) above, which emphasises IL's singular 'nature and content'.

129 The focus on states stems from the Westphalian paradigm of inter*national* law. LOUIS HENKIN, INTERNATIONAL LAW: POLITICS AND VALUES 16–17, 160–161 (1995). However, as many have noted, this is more mythology than methodology. *De facto* international law is not anymore (and probably never purely was) solely inter*national.* Beside the diverse non-national sources discussed above, international law relies on organisational dynamics that enable and encourage representatives of states to transgress national guidelines and policies (Benvenisti, *supra* n. 31). As well, the influence of Non-State Actors (NSA) is growing (e.g. corporations and organizations). Bass Arts, *Non-State Actors in Global Environmental Governance – New Arrangements beyond the State*, NEW MODES OF GOVERNANCE IN THE GLOBAL SYSTEM – EXPLORING PUBLICNESS, DELEGATION AND INCLUSIVENESS 177 (2006). We should also document NSA's texts. However, religious law has unique aspects that make it the best *first* candidate for joining the ILM corpus.

130 E.g. International custom and general principles (Art. 38 (1) (b)(c), ICJ Statute). The weight of customary law is diminishing in international law, but is still important (Eyal Benvenisiti, *Customary Law as a Judicial Tool for Promoting Efficiency, in* THE IMPACT OF INTERNATIONAL LAW ON INTERNATIONAL COOPERATION (Idem & M. Hirsch, eds., 2004).

131 Lauterpacht, *supra* note 125; Eyal Benvenisti, *The Attitude of the Supreme Court of Israel Towards the Implementation of the International Law of Human Rights, in* THE ROLE OF DOMESTIC COURTS IN THE ENFORCEMENT OF INTERNATIONAL HUMAN RIGHTS 207 (Francesco Francioni & Benedetto Conforti, eds., 1997); Idem, *National Courts and the 'War on Terrorism', in* INTERNATIONAL LAW AND TERRORISM 307 (A. Bianchi, ed., 2004).

132 For regional courts note the growing importance of ECHR rulings. For municipal decisions see Yishai Blank, *The City and the World*, 44 COLU. J. TRANS. L. 875 (2006); Idem, *Localism in a Global Legal Order*, 47 HARV. INT. L. J. 263 (2006).

133 'Publicists of *the various nations*'. Art. 38 (1) (d), ICJ statute. Expert opinions are influenced by national interests (e.g. the debate of Grotius v. Selden). On the role of publicists, intellectuals, lawyers and scholars, see Koskenniemi, *supra* note 2. RE'UT YAEL PAZ, A GATEWAY BETWEEN A DISTANT GOD AND A CRUEL WORLD; THE CONTRIBUTION OF 20TH CENTURY JEWISH GERMAN SPEAKING SCHOLARS ERICH KAUFMANN, HANS KELSEN, HERSCH LAUTERPACHT AND HANS J. MORGENTHAU TO THE PROFESSIONALISATION OF INTERNATIONAL LAW AND INTERNATIONAL RELATIONS (Ph.D. Dissertation, Bar Ilan University, 2008).

134 In an alternative account, all strive for a 'just world under (one) law'. See David G. Goldman, *Historical Aspects of Globalization and Law, in* JURISPRUDENCE FOR AN INTERCONNECTED GLOBE (Catherine Dauvergne, ed., 2003); Martha J. Finnemore and Stephen J. Toope, *Alternatives to 'Legalisation': Richer Views of Laws and Politics*, 5 INT. ORG. 743 (2001).

Statutes of all international institutions call for a broad and diverse representation of regions, cultures, legal systems and states, encouraging multicultural influence upon international law.[135] The RILM will contribute to this empowering enrichment of international law.

All five of Nafziger's positive functions of religion in international law[136] are good reasons for documenting religious legal texts.[137] Note that the same holds if religion has negative influences and functions for the international law project.

There are at least two structural considerations to document religious law.

1 As religions are not situated within the same territorial boundaries as countries, religious materials necessarily voice a unique set of interests. The power relations between the government and religious leaders and legal institutes are different than with the national judicial system.[138] As well, the ways in which religious communities accommodate domestic and intrinsic (legal, organisational or religious) interests are not similar.
2 Religious law may give insight into peoples' attitude towards issues of international law that are inaccessible through national jurisprudence. It may reveal the extent of internalisation of international law in the community and its interpretations of it.

The lack of RILM

The ILM project,[139] now supplemented by the ILDC project which informed our proposal,[140] omitted and still omits religious materials. Thus, important

135 Art. 9, ICJ statute ('representation of the main forms of civilization and of the principal legal systems of the world should be assured'); see same formula in Art. 8, ILC statute. Article 36(7), ICC statute states: 'No two judges may be nationals of the same state' (but they may be from the same religion). Paragraph 8, ICC statute, promotes '(i) The representation of the principal legal systems of the world; (ii) Equitable geographical representation'. Note the usage of 'legal systems' (thereby not meaning religious systems).

136 Nafziger, *supra* n. 11. (*Mediation* in conflicts; Being the *custodian* of international law; strengthening the *aspirational* aspects (vs. enforcing) of international law; contributing to *creating* and developing the law and finally *educating* about international law). In all functions, language and texts are important.

137 Compare Paz, *supra* note 133; Janis & Evans, *supra* note 3. Falk says that religious motivation (broadly defined) is needed for global governance to succeed (Richard Falk, Religion and Humane Global Governance 25, 29 (2001)). For critique of the reliance on spirituality and religion, see Jeremy Rabkin, Law Without Nations 242–243 (2005).

138 Religious rulings take their domestic governments politics into account, just like 'International organization will generally track the interplay of interests and power among the relevant state actors . . . a structural problem rooted in the lack of autonomy on the part of international organizations vis-a-vis member states'. S. James Anaya, *Book Reviews and Notes: International Organizations and Ethnic Conflict. Edited by Miton J, Esman and Shilbey Telhami*, 91 AJIL 566 (1997); Sam A. Muller, International Organizations and their Host States: Aspects of their Legal Relationship (1995).

139 See e.g. in Lauterpacht & Greenwood's index to the *International Law Reports*.

140 'ILDC creates a network of reporters and researchers who analyze domestic cases and conduct research on the internationalization of law and its development in domestic jurisdictions.

documents like Pope John's 23rd Encyclical *Pacem in Terris* (1963)[141] and Ayatullah Khoumeini's Rushdie Fatwa,[142] have not been published in real time, not published in a legal database. The texts of what I call the 'missing volume of international legal materials', were thus not analysed as *legal* texts.[143] The void is filled by an unbalanced representation of religious law in contemporary publications, media and public discourse, with extreme positions gaining prominence. Violence ensures that the fundamentalist voices are heard – in academia, media and by leaders. Religious voices that categorically endorse and embrace all international law endeavours are heard too. Both extreme voices are disproportionately strong (relative to their constituency in religion),[144] and gain strength from this misrepresentation. The two extremes strengthen each other, by posing each other as illegitimate opposites. As a result, most academic research is dedicated to these extreme voices. A RILM database will give everyone access to all options within each religion, enabling and promoting discussion, thereby challenging the extremes and placing them within multiple contexts.

As opposed to relating only to the *results* of an extreme religious ruling, or relating to a phrase highlighted by the press, RILM will foster legal analysis of the full original texts in context of the full scope of options. This will enable

The rapporteurs participate in the online law reporting service "Oxford Reports on International law in Domestic Courts"'. The IDLC also enables various forms of access. See www.inasp.info/file/fe70e472c597268263f4fb9aa6ef6ca3/ildc.html.

141 www.vatican.va/holy_father/john_xxiii/encyclicals/documents/hf_j-xxiii_enc _11041963_pacem_en.html. The Encyclical outlines the Church's international law. This document is the foreign/global affairs law for more than a billion people around the world. Together with the Vatican II documents, they support some main international law concepts, institutes and ideas. Another important encyclical for international law is Pope Leo XIIIth, *Rerum Novarum* (1891), which has received more scholarly attention.

142 It included non-trivial influence of Islamic *law* on the international order, but the *legal* aspect of the 'religious – international' interface has been underrepresented. The full text is well worth reading. It was published by the Teheran radio, February 1989. See Anthony Chase, *Legal Guardians: Islamic Law, International Law, Human Rights Law, and the Salman Rushdie Affair*, 11 Am. U. Int'l L. and Pol'y 375 (1996).

143 Compare Shaybani, *The Islamic Law of Nations*, (Trans. and introduction M. Khadduri, Maryland 1966) with e.g., Westerbrook, *supra* note 12; G.M. Badr, *A Survey of Islamic International Law*, Religion and International law 95 (1999). Michael H.A. Reisman. *Islamic Fundamentalism and its Impact on International Law and Politics*, Idem 357; see also T.S. Twibell, *Implementation of the U. N. Convention on Contracts for the International Sale of Goods under the Shari'a (Islamic Law)*, 9 Int. Legal Persp. 25 (1997); M.A. Civic, *A Comparative Analysis of the Israeli and Arab Water Law Traditions and Insights for Modern Water Sharing Agreements*, 26 Denver J. of Int. L. and Pol. 26 (1998), 437 and Abdul An-Naim, *Human Rights in the Muslim World: Socio-Political Conditions and Scriptual Imperatives*, 3 Harv. Hum. Righ. J. 13 (1990) (appreciating the importance of the texts).

144 Progressive voices tend to have weak influence inside their respective religious communities. Fundamental extreme voices gain most of their power from the interaction with *outside* players, and are shaped by them.

to see additional aspects,[145] especially jurisprudential processes and community dynamics, and their interaction with international players.[146]

Publishing extreme positions with their argumentation serves as a 'sunshine method',[147] forcing the speaker and his followers to give account for their stand, even if not immediately. The sun also shines on the external sources of power of the extreme positions, the coalitions which support them, and who pays the costs of the positions taken. Given all the information, with multiple analyses offered, players are encouraged to ensure internalisation of costs, can offer incentives and sanctions, and follow their impact. Thus, the RILM can serve to empower the internal legal processes as well as empower individuals, leaders and communities vis-à-vis each other and vis-à-vis others. Going beyond mere tactical pragmatic sunshine, the RILM is a medium to richly engage religious culture and community.

The potential of RILM

Compiling and documenting religious law could enable to see religious legal processes happen in real time.[148] It will enable historical and comparative analyses as well as the use of further legal research. For example, we could ask if, how and when religious law incorporates prohibitions from the international criminal code like genocide, human trafficking and torture.[149]

Periodic publication of RILM would enable to measure the perceived impact and influence of international norms, institutions and organisations in wide populations.[150]

145 E.g. the choice of words and terms; the legal concepts and conceptualisation, the argumentation, the forum(s) of decision, the understanding of the reality and questions that preceded the ruling; the intended audience(s), the geographical and temporal extent of the ruling, what alternatives may have been considered and rejected, why the decision is formulated as it is, what precedents there are for such a ruling, what is the relation between law and politics in religious legal decisions, etc.

146 The Rushdie affair has been analysed and commented upon in various field of research, including law – as opposed to the Fatwa itself, as a legal text. Another recent example is the Fatwa forbidding nuclear weapons, published in the Iran daily (11 August 2005). See http://mathaba.net/0_index.shtml?x=302258. It was reported and analysed only as part of the Iranian statement to the IAEA. For a direct discussion of another (the Bin-laden) Fatwa see Mashood A. Baderin, International Law and Islamic Law 213–147 (2008).

147 Brown Weis & Jacobson, *supra* note 22.

148 We might see incorporation of international norms *de facto* without incorporation *de jure*, or the opposite (a ruling might accept CEDAW but empty it of any practical influence).

149 I discuss the lack of codification in the three monotheistic religions in an article to be published in the Jewish Law Association Studies 2015 (draft available from author), ch. 2.

150 When do institutions like the WTO, ILO, conventions like CEDAW and norms like the rights of children or handicapped persons appear in religious legal reasoning? In what capacity are they accepted and what normative status do they have? Careful reading of texts might also discover the incorporation of international norms within the internal religious language, without explicit references. Compare 2 J. of Hum. Righ. (2003, special issue: Religious Roots to Tolerance (Seligman, ed.)); see Summer B. Twiss, *Religion and Human Rights: A Comparative Perspective*, Explorations in Global Ethics: Comparative Religious Ethics and Interreligious Dialogue 163 (1998).

Religious law has strong tendency to reject foreign influence and transplantation of law, while at the same time, it has strong and established mechanisms for adaptation to realities. The choice between these options, as well as multiple others, is influenced by various factors, which will be revealed through the RILM database. The published variety might suggest options for other religious communities, as well as empower members of communities to promote different strategies.[151]

Finally, the RILM will present multiple religious perspectives on the relations between religions and international law,[152] and will directly enrich research regarding this and related topics (like church–state relationships and regional coping, e.g. in the EU).

Major concerns about the RILM project

I will outline some concerns regarding the proposed RILM,[153] which are inherent to efforts of empowerment:

1 Financing, organisation and infrastructure: the proposed project is expensive and as such would be prone to influence by financing institutions. In order to minimise this concern, the RILM could be part of an effort of an international institution (e.g. UN) or an academic setting. The basis should be a collaboration of a multinational, multi-religious team with technological resources and ongoing consultation and support. The initial stage should include contacting all existing projects on law and religion.
2 Abuse: (a) internal abuse – by users who have authorised access to the project. Distorting texts, biased reporting, censoring of self and others and other forms of abuse will have to be addressed. The best way of coping is

151 For the theory and dynamics of e.g. legal transplants, translation and dialogue see Alan Watson, Legal Tranplants: An Approach to Comparative Law (1993); David Nelken and Johaness Feest, Adapting Legal Cultures (2001); Langer, *supra* note 34; Anne-Marie Slaughter, *A Global Community of Courts*, 44 Harv. Int. L. J. 191 (2003).

152 For extrapolation from national relations see e.g. Lasia Bloss, *European Law of Religion – Organizational and Institutional Analysis of National Systems and Their Implications for the Future European Integration Process*, Jean Monnet Working Paper 13/03, New York Law School 2003. This attitude assumes (wrongly) that religions on local, state, regional and global levels should be treated and conceptualized in the same way. It also assumes that religion is one, stagnate, phenomenon. Witte and Vyver double volume dedicated one volume to each perspective, I: Religious Perspectives; II: Legal Perspectives (*supra* note 10). Note that 'religious' is posed in opposition to 'legal' – minimising the legal aspect of religious law. Patrick H. Glenn, Legal Traditions of the World (2004) includes religious systems.

153 At the current stage, this part of the proposal is incomplete for two reasons. Most concerns are dependent on the actual structure of the RILM, its creators and audiences. The initiating workgroup will probably consider a few options, each with its set of concerns. As well, for each set of concerns, it will be worthwhile to compare the utility of technological, institutional, legal solutions, as well as solutions based on motivation, incentives and commitment. The following is essentially an illustration.

disclosure. All special privileges will be possible only with identification and documentation. (b) External abuse – includes (virtual, real and even violent) intimidation of reporters or participants. Abuse of access (or other) rights; promotion of a restricted, biased portal.

3 Attacks: (a) on the database – the mere existence of the database might be conceived as harmful and come under attack. Backup and protection measures will be needed on an ongoing basis. Any attacks will be fully reported and all data about perpetrators disclosed as a public deterrence. (b) On the framework and portals – a more specific form of attack is to be anticipated towards certain aspects of the framework – disabling features (links, texts, etc) and portals. These are electronic ways of censoring access and will have to be dealt with.

The proposal calls to start creating several religious databases, while looking for a firm institutional and financial basis which can enable the development of the infrastructure. When such basis is found, a multi-religious, multinational, interdisciplinary team should be formed to plan the initial database, invite rapporteurs, etc.

Discussion: RILM as part of engaging and empowerment

RILM enables empowering religious law, while empowering religious players and communities vis-à-vis their religious law, their states and other players. The proposed database will challenge the prevailing limited religious discourse, encouraging development and refinements of arguments, choices and ability to account for their consequences. The public display of multiple scopes of legitimate religious options, and multiple debates about and around them, may confuse and reduce the power of unity and claim for truth in the short term, but will enhance powers of existing and newly emerging options and players in the long term. Interest of outside players into the religious legal texts may create reciprocity – interest of religious players in international texts, and other religions coping with similar issues. This process will empower those players in international, inter-religious and church–state arenas.

The RILM will emphasise the international and inter-religious aspects of each religion and of the religious phenomenon (or lack thereof). For example, the question of recognising other religious groups, non-religious groups and their (political, cultural, theological) claims is a major question in contemporary religious legal thought. The resolution of these and other internal legal questions in the various religions can have a major effect on international law. Religions are just starting to cope with the contemporary form of globalised, interdependent world, as well as with international law and institutions in their present form. The project will document – but also be part of – this process.[154]

154 Contemporary children are exposed, through the media, to the size of the world's population, its cultural diversity, the interdependence of states and to the flux of ideas, resources and people.

It is important to stress that not all the adherents of religious law actually read and study religious legal texts. There are various other ways in which laws, norms and tradition are conveyed, e.g. mimetic education and oral tradition. Religious law is a *living* legal system. It can and should be studied and engaged as such. The RILM will only portray part of these rich dynamics. The RILM may also over-emphasise the legal (as opposed to cultural) aspect of religions.

However, after accounting for these limitations the RILM will seek to provide an ongoing documentation of the laws *in action* in addition to the law in books;[155] and of religions as multi-faceted phenomena and not as a monolithic entity. Understanding the legal possibilities, the exact decisions and the political and social dynamics, broadens the possibilities for religious members, states and other parties.[156]

However, knowledge of laws is only a small part of empowerment, and is a very partial and limited form of engagement. Separate initiatives could use the preceding analysis of structures and incentives to enrich the empowering engagement of religions.

The resulting understanding of the world challenges two common religious worldviews. The first is that a single idea, regime or religion can conquer the world. The second is that a community can live isolated from the external world. Both are perceived as practically impossible and as humanly undesirable. The RILM project will endorse the new understanding of the world, and facilitate religious legal coping with these new conceptualisations of history, culture and humanity. Because of the structure of a small community of nations – ideas, products and people *can* gain (almost) universal attention or influence (but never permanently and totally conquer). See Immanuel Levinas, in the time of the nations 1–3 (1994).

155 See Karen Knop, Ralf Michaels and Annelise Riles, *International Law in Domestic Courts: A Conflict of Laws Approach,* 103 ASIL Proceedings (2009).

156 Religious players sometimes hide or downplay the significance of these religious texts, to hide these options and the resulting possible latitude.

8 Negotiating religious orthodoxy, state neutrality and religious freedom

The case of the Ahmadiyah controversy in post-Suharto Indonesia

Supriyanto Abdi

Introduction

Ahmadiyah first came to Indonesia in the early 1920s, and after a short-lived initial welcome, its non-conformist teachings have been opposed by the country's mainstream Muslim groups ever since. For most of the following eight decades, however, the controversy over Ahmadiyah did not break into open conflicts. During the same period, the Ahmadis have lived in peace in Indonesia. The fall of the authoritarian Suharto regime in 1998, however, has given way to a new and tragic development in the Ahmadiyah's history in Indonesia. In the post-Suharto era, and especially during the presidency of Susilo Bambang Yudhoyono (SBY), Ahmadiyah has been subject to more aggressive negative campaigning and its members have become the target of an unprecedented level of violence committed by their adversaries.

This chapter attempts to examine the Ahmadiyah controversy and situate it in the broader struggles over religion–state relations and against the background and conditions for the legal empowerment of religious minority groups in post-Suharto Indonesia. The chapter will begin with a brief theoretical account, followed by an overview of the main distinctive teachings of Ahmadiyah. It then traces the history of the Ahmadiyah controversy in Indonesia and its revival in the post-Suharto era, especially during the SBY presidency (2004–2014). Special attention will be paid to the significance and limits of liberal Muslim voices in this controversy, indicating the extent to which they help shape the current discourse of religion–state relations and religious freedom in this Muslim-majority democracy. The analysis will argue that the Ahmadiyah controversy, within which the relationship between religious orthodoxy, the state and religious freedom is contested, reflects the renewed struggles between different interpretations of Islam and competing constructions of national identities in post-Suharto Indonesia. It further argues that, apart from reflecting more contested Muslim politics, the controversy also suggests the remaining ambiguous nature of the Indonesian state and its constitutional-legal construction of religious freedom.

Brief theoretical framework

Discussions on religion–state relations in the Muslim world are often framed within cultural essentialist premises. Cultural essentialist accounts tend to focus on the fundamentally different approaches of Islam and Christianity towards secular and religious authority. Scholars subscribing to this approach generally assume that the latter is doctrinally and culturally more hospitable to secularism and secularization. Bernard Lewis, for example, argues that 'the distinction between church and state, so deeply rooted in Christendom, did not exist in Islam'.[1] He further argues that:

> The Islamic religion is concerned with life as a whole, exerting its jurisdiction, not in limited, but in global terms. In a society like this, the mere idea of a separation of the Church and the State is devoid of sense, in that the Church and the State, religious power and political power, do not exist as two distinct units able to be separated; they are one.[2]

The cultural essentialist approach towards Islam and Muslim societies, however, has been increasingly challenged. For most of its critics, the main problem with this approach is its perennial, unitary and totalizing premises of Islam.[3] Olivier Roy, for instance, challenges those who approach Islam as 'a discrete entity, a coherent and closed set of beliefs, values and anthropological patterns embodied in a common society, history and territory, which allows us to use the term as an explanatory concept for almost everything involving Muslims'.[4] Roy also disagrees with the ways in which culturalists overemphasize the role of Islam in contemporary societies, viewing culture as 'a fairly homogenous and closed set of values, downplaying a centuries-old history of civil wars and ideological conflicts'.[5]

Challenging this essentialist and unitary reading of Islam, some scholars offer an alternative reading which stresses the multivocality of its doctrine. Alfred Stepan, for example, challenges the assumption of the univocality of world religions, including Islam. In discussing their relationship to democracy, Stepan notes

1 Bernard Lewis, *The Political Language of Islam* (Chicago: University of Chicago Press, 1991), pp. 2–3. See also his 'Islam and Liberal Democracy: A Historical Overview', *Journal of Democracy*, 7:2 (1996) and his *Faith and Power: Religion and Politics in the Middle East* (Oxford: Oxford University Press, 2010).

2 Quoted in Mohamed-Cherif Ferjani, 'Islam and Politics: The Terms of the Debate', *History and Anthropology*, 16:1 (2009), p. 78.

3 Critiques of essentialist perspective can be found, among others, in Aziz Al-Azmeh, *Islams and Modernities* (London and New York: Verso, 1993); John L. Esposito and John A. Voll, *Islam and Democracy* (New York and Oxford: Oxford University Press, 1996); and Alfred Stepan, 'Religion, Democracy and the "Twin Tolerations"', *Journal of Democracy*, 11:4 (October 2000).

4 Olivier Roy, *Globalised Islam: The Search for a New Ummah* (London: Hurst, 2004), p. 9.

5 Ibid., pp. 11–15.

that 'doctrinally, the world's religious systems should not be assumed as univocally democratic or nondemocratic'.[6] Other scholars such as Talal Asad, John L. Esposito, Aziz Al-Azmeh and Ebrahim Moosa have also challenged the essentialist and monolithic view of Islam. Talal Asad argues that 'Islamic religious, legal, political ideologies do not have an essential significance which moulds the minds of believers in a predictable way. They are part of changing institutions, and discourses which can be, and often are, contested and reconstituted'.[7] John L. Esposito urges that people ask the question 'Whose Islam?' because Islam is always presented through the voices and representatives of Muslim groups and individuals.[8] Aziz Al-Azmeh and Ebrahim Moosa both note that there are many 'Islams' and many Muslims with differences in terms of their practices and understandings.[9]

Unlike cultural essentialism, the multivocality approach thus offers more nuanced discussions on religion–state relations in Muslim societies. It is not, however, without critiques. John Anderson argues that the multivocality argument 'tends to focus on "theological" debates or rely on interviews with religious leaders out of power and as such offer only a partial aid'.[10] According to Anderson, 'in the political "real" world, one has to deal with "actually existing" systems and ideological tendencies, not the interpretations of a handful of "liberally" inclined intellectuals'.[11] Anderson thus suggests that Protestantism, Catholicism, Orthodoxy, Islam, Judaism, Confucianism, etc. should be dealt with as they are to be found in the 'real world' rather than in the idealized form presented by many of their spokespersons. While acknowledging the possibility of major changes in religious doctrines and discourses, Anderson urges scholars 'to look less at what might be than at what in practice are the dominant themes or arguments within a religious tradition at any particular time and how these might impact upon the political order'.[12] For Anderson, whilst many Muslims may aspire to democracy or secularism and intellectuals may find supportive elements within the tradition, the actual dominant ideological trends may not necessarily have similar aspiration and interpretative position.[13] Anderson also notes that in many parts of the Muslim world '"liberal" intellectuals generally have limited influence, especially when they find themselves in competition with more radical groups'.[14]

6 Stepan, 'Religion, Democracy, and the "Twin Tolerations"', p. 44.

7 Talal Asad, 'Ideology, Class and the Origin of the Islamic State', *Economy and Society*, 9:4 (November 1980), p. 467.

8 See John L. Esposito, *Islam and Politics* (Syracuse: Syracuse University Press, 1998).

9 See Aziz Al-Azmeh, *Islams and Modernities* (London: Verso, 1993) and Ebrahim Moosa, 'The Debt and Burdens of Critical Islam', in Omid Safi (ed.), *Progressive Muslims: On Justice, Gender and Pluralism* (Oxford: Oneworld Publication, 2003), pp. 113–114.

10 John Anderson, 'Does God Matter, and if so Whose God?: Religion and Democratization', *Democratization*, 11:4 (2004), p. 207.

11 Ibid., p. 207.

12 Ibid., p. 207.

13 Ibid., p. 211.

14 Ibid., p. 211.

Some of Anderson's critiques have some merits, particularly in stressing that Muslim discourses and the actors who articulate them are historically situated. Here, Asad's notion of Islam as a 'discursive tradition' is particularly useful. According to Asad, rather than constituting a systemic homogeneity, the Islamic discursive tradition is characterized by debate, disagreement and contestations.[15] This is particularly true in relation to another important concept, 'orthodoxy', which is defined by Asad as 'not a mere body of opinion but a distinctive relationship—a relationship of power'.[16] According to Asad, 'wherever Muslims have the power to regulate, uphold, require, or adjust correct practices, and to condemn, exclude, undermine or replace incorrect ones, there is the domain of orthodoxy'.[17]

Therefore, in face of multiple and competing religious voices, attention should not merely directed to what religious texts literally suggest. More attention should be paid instead on the material bases and specific conditions that allow particular readings or interpretations of religious texts to become hegemonic and thus socially and politically more powerful. It also becomes a question of methodology, though many writers see this more as an issue of power. As succinctly argued by Asef Bayat:

> we need to examine the conditions that allow social forces to make a particular reading of the sacred texts hegemonic. And this is closely linked to groups' capacity to mobilize consensus around their 'truth' . . . The challenge is to give democratic interpretation material power, to infuse them with popular consciousness.[18]

Benefiting from this more historical and contextual approach towards Muslim discourses and politics, the following pages will discuss the Ahmadiya controversy in Indonesia as a case study to examine how Indonesian Muslims negotiate and grapple with the liberal discourse of state neutrality and religious freedom within the historical and political contraints they find themselves in.

Ahmadiyah and its distinctive teachings

Ahmadiyah was founded as an independent Islamic movement by Mirza Ghulam Ahmad in Punjab, India, in 1889. The Ahmadi, like Muslims generally, believe in the five pillars of Islam. As such they pronounce *shahadah* (the confession of faith), perform *salat* (prayer) five times daily, practise *sawm* (fasting, especially

15 Sean McLoughlin, 'Islam(s) in Context: Orientalism and the Anthropology of Muslim Societies and Cultures', *Journal of Beliefs & Values*, 28:3 (December 2007), pp. 273–296.

16 Talal Asad, 'The Idea of Anthropology of Islam', Occasional Paper Series, Center for Contemporary Arab Studies, Georgetown University, Washington, DC, pp. 15–16.

17 Ibid., pp. 15–16.

18 Asef Bayat, *Making Islam Democratic: Social Movements and the Post-Islamist Turn* (Stanford: Stanford University Press, 2007), p. 5.

during Ramadan), pay *zakat* (a percentage of their earnings to charity) and, in theory, perform *hajj*, pilgrimage to Mecca.[19] However, there are certain distinctive Ahmadiyah teachings that are not shared by, and set it apart in a significant way from, mainstream Islam. The most controversial of these revolve around the issue of prophethood, Jesus and jihad.

Concerning prophethood, mainstream Islam teaches the doctrine of the finality of prophethood (*khatamun nabiyin*) and the idea that the Prophet Muhammad is 'the seal', the greatest and the last of the prophets sent with a message by God. For the Ahmadis, however, the doctrine of *khatamun nabiyin* is to be understood as the greatest of all prophets and the last law-bearing prophet. The Ahmadis thus claim that there can still be lesser, non-legislative, or *zilli* (shadowy) prophets.[20] On this basis, they believe that their founder, Mirza Ghulam Ahmad, was one such non-legislative, *zilli* prophet. Furthermore, Ahmad is also considered as *ummati nabi* (a subordinate prophet), the imam mahdi and the 'promised messiah', prophesied by the Prophet Muhammad.[21]

The Ahmadiyah also diverges from mainstream Islam concerning the teachings on Jesus and jihad. According to the Ahmadi, instead of dying on the cross or being taken alive into heaven, Jesus escaped from the Romans, travelled to the East and finally settled and died in Kashmir.[22] On the concept of jihad, mainstream Muslims hold that Islam teaches a just war doctrine which supports the right to use force in self-defence or if the faith is threatened. The Ahmadis, however, 'strongly reject violence and terrorism in any form and for any reason'.[23] They further argue that *jihad-bil-qalam* (jihad of the pen) must take the place of *jihad bi-saif* (jihad of the sword) in the present age.[24] Mainly because of these distinctive teachings, the Ahmadi are rejected by mainstream Muslims as *kuffar* (unbelievers), *murtadd* (apostates) and *zindique* (heretics).[25]

In 1914, the movement split into two schools: the Ahmadiyah Muslim Community and, a much smaller wing, the Lahore Ahmadiyah Movement. The two streams differ in their interpretation of Ahmad's status. The Ahmadiyah Muslim Community insists on their belief that Mirza Ghulam Ahmad was a prophet but one who is subordinated to Muhammad. The Lahore Ahmadiyah Movement on the other hand sees its founder more strictly as a religious reformer,

19 K. Zirvi, *Welcome to Ahmadiyyat: The True Islam, Ahmadiyya Movement in Islam* (Silver Springs: Islamic Publications Ltd, 2002), p. 11.

20 Mahzarnama, *The Memorandum: submission by the Ahmadiyya Muslim Jamaat to the National Assembly of Pakistan regarding its basic tenets* (Tilford: Islam International Publications Ltd, 2002), p. 108 as quoted in S.R. Valentine, 'Prophecy after the Prophet, albeit Lesser Prophets? The Ahmadiyya Jama'at in Pakistan', *Contemporary Islam* (2014) 8:99–113.

21 Zirvi, *Welcome to Ahmadiyyat*, p. 285.

22 Ibid., p. 285.

23 M. Ali, *The Ahmadiyya Movement* (Lahore: Ahmadiyya Anjuman Isha'at Islam, 1984), p. 13.

24 K.S. Bakhsh, *The Debt Forgotten* (Lahore: Ahmadiyya Anjuman Isha'at Islam, 1993), p. 36.

25 See Valentine, 'Prophecy after the Prophet, albeit Lesser Prophets?', 8:99–113.

hence getting closer to the mainstream Islamic view that there can be no prophet after Muhammad.[26] Despite their differences, however, both have continued to engender heated controversy in many Muslim countries. In Pakistan, for example, after a fierce debate, the Ahmadis were in 1974 constitutionally declared as a non-Muslim religious minority, which means they are forbidden to refer to themselves as Muslims. In Saudi Arabia, the Ahmadis are classified as heathen (*kafir*), and hence prevented from entering the country for *hajj*. Ahmadiyah is also banned in several Southeast Asian countries such as Brunei and Malaysia. In Indonesia, the Ahmadiyah's status has been subject to a heated debate since its arrival in the mid-1920s.

The Ahmadiyah controversy in Indonesia

Ahmadiyah first came to Indonesia in 1925 when two preachers Maulana Ahmad and Mirza Wali Ahmad arrived in Yogyakarta. In the beginning, they were welcomed by the local Muhammadiyah branch and permitted to speak at the thirteenth National Congress of this modernist Islamic organization. Soon, however, Muhammadiyah and the traditionalist Nahdlatul Ulama (NU) declared Ahmadiyah to be 'deviant'.[27] In 1929, Muhammadiyah issued a *fatwa* declaring that people who do not accept this doctrine are '*kafir*' (unbelievers).[28] Similarly, NU's fifth National Congress in Pekalongan in 1930 proclaimed Ahmadiyah as being outside Islam.[29]

By the early 1970s, the controversial teachings of Ahmadiyah had become an international issue in the Muslim world. During its annual conference in Mecca, Saudi Arabia, on *Rabiul Awwal* 14-18, 1394 H (April 1974), *Rabita alam al Islami*, a world Islamic organization, issued a *fatwa* and a resolution against the Ahmadiyah. The *fatwa* declares that the Ahmadiyah is outside the pale of Islam and its followers are infidels and apostates. The issuance of the *fatwa* and resolution has strong connection with two factors: first, the movement in Pakistan that culminated with the 1974 Constitutional Amendment in which the government, under Zulfiqar Ali Bhutto, declared 'the Qadianis a separate community' or non-Muslim minority, and second, the rise of Saudi Arabia as a petro-dollar country and their intention the spread the Wahhabi ideology around the Muslim world.[30]

It is under the influence of this international propaganda that the Council of Indonesian Islamic Scholars (*Majelis Ulama Indonesia*/MUI) issued its first *fatwa* against Ahmadiyah in 1980. The *fatwa* of the MUI on the Ahmadiyah was entitled 'Ahmadiyah Qadiyan' which means that it is specifically directed to the Qadian

26 Bernhard Platzdasch, 'Religious Freedom in Indonesia: The Case of the Ahmadiyah', *ISEAS Working Paper: Politics & Security Series*, No. 2 (Singapore, 2011), p. 2.

27 Ibid., p. 2.

28 Ahmadi Najib Burhani, 'Treating Minorities with Fatwas: A Study of the Ahmadiyya Community in Indonesia', *Contemporary Islam* (2014), p. 291.

29 Platzdasch, 'Religious Freedom in Indonesia', p. 2.

30 Burhani, 'Treating Minorities', p. 292.

faction of the Ahmadiyah, and excluded the Lahore faction from it. This *fatwa* was issued during the second *Musyawarah Nasional* (National Congress) of this institution in Jakarta on 26 May – 1 June 1980 and consists of two points: first, the Ahmadiyah is a community outside the pale of Islam; it is a deviant and misleading community. Second, in dealing with the Ahmadiyah the MUI is expected to always communicate with the government.[31]

The Suharto regime, however, did not give any support for executing the *fatwa* in concrete and implementable policy. This was in line with the regime's main policy of restricting public discussion on the issue of SARA (*Suku, Agama, Ras, and Antar golongan*/ethnicity, religions, and inter-group relations). Open discussion on these matters was strictly prohibited and seen as potential sources of inter-group conflict and therefore it could harm national stability and security. As a result, the MUI's *fatwa* against Ahmadiyah had only little social and political resonance in the public realm and did not break into open conflicts.

The fall of the Suharto regime in 1998 has paved the way for new developments of the Ahmadiyah controversy. Radical and fundamentalist Islamic groups which were suppressed under the Suharto regime have now found a more fertile ground to express their voices, concerns and agendas. The anti-Ahmadiyah sentiment has been one of the main rallying points by which conservative and fundamentalist Islamic groups reorganize themselves and reassert their significance and influence in the more open public sphere of the post-Suharto era.

In 2000, Ahmadiyah caliph Mirza Thahir Ahmad visited Indonesia for the first time and met with President Abdurrahman Wahid. The visit fuelled suspicions among the Ahmadiyah's critics of a plan to make Indonesia a hub for Ahmadiyah activities. Some even claim that the Ahmadiyah headquarters in England aimed to make Ahmadiyah Indonesia the largest Ahmadiyah community in the Muslim world.[32] It is no surprise that this visit then sparked a more aggressive campaign against Ahmadiyah. Central to this reinvigorated campaign against Ahmadiyah has been the Institute for the Study and Teaching of Islam (*Lembaga Penelitian dan Pengkajian Islam*, LPPI), a Jakarta-based research institute with significant funding from Saudi Arabia. Led by Amin Djamaluddin, a member of Persatuan Islam (Persis) and Indonesian Islamic Propagation Council (*Dewan Dakwah Islamiyah Indonesia*/DDII), the institute is particularly dedicated to the struggle against 'deviant' sects. Other main groups in the campaign against Ahmadiyah include the Front of the Defenders of Islam (Front Pembela Islam/FPI), the Muslim Community Forum (*Forum Umat Islam*/FUI), DDII, the Islamic Scholars' Ulama (*Forum Umat Ulama Islam*/FUUI) and Hizbut Tahrir Indonesia (HTI).[33]

The year 2005 saw a significant development in the anti-Ahmadiyah campaign in the post-Suharto era when the MUI issued its second *fatwa* on this movement. Reaffirming its first *fatwa* in 1980, the second fatwa holds that 'Ahmadiyah stands

31 Ibid., p. 292.
32 Platzdasch, 'Religious Freedom in Indonesia', p. 7.
33 Ibid., p. 9.

outside Islam, deviant and misleading, and that Muslims who follow it have abandoned Islam [*murtad*]'. It further stated that 'the government has the responsibility to prohibit the spreading of the Ahmadiyah faith everywhere in Indonesia, to dissolve the organization and to close down all the places of its activities'.[34] Compared with the first *fatwa*, this *fatwa* is stronger in demanding that the government should disband this movement. It can be seen as a reflection of the MUI's strengthended confidence that it has higher authority on religious issues than the government and that the government has to listen to and obey their decisions.[35]

For conservative and radical Islamic groups, the MUI's fatwa is a welcome development for their campaign against Ahmadiyah. Strong criticism, however, was levelled against the MUI's *fatwa* by a number of liberal Muslim intellectuals and activists. Ulil Abshar Abdalla, one of the prominent figures of Liberal Islam Network (*Jaringan Islam Liberal*/JIL), was among those who strongly criticized the MUI's fatwa. Ulil was particularly concerned that the MUI, with its strong demand for the government action to ban Ahmadiyah, has blurred the line between fatwa and law. A fatwa, he argues, is the internal business of a particular religion, while the law is something that is universal and cuts across different religious practices and interpretations. Therefore, he argues, the MUI's fatwa on the deviancy of Ahmadiyah is an internal matter of Muslims and the state cannot be bound by it. He further argues:

> when the state is allowed to determine which interpretations are straight and those that are crooked, there is already a blurring between law and fatwa. The role of the state is to implement the law for all groups, sects; not a fatwa which is partisan. A state that becomes the tool of a particular sect to condemn another sect is a state of the middle-ages that has no right to be maintained. It appears that some groups within Islam are guiding the nation to this dangerous condition.[36]

The campaign against Ahmadiyah turned both more intense and more hostile following the MUI's second *fatwa*. At the same time, conservative Islamic groups intensified their lobbying efforts in parliament, with the Ministry of Religion, the Attorney General's office and other policy-makers.[37] One of the fruits of their campaign and lobbying efforts, in mid-February 2008, was that the parliamentary commission assigned to the Ahmadiyah question issued its own report, calling on the government to ban Ahmadiyah. The report also recommended the issuance of a presidential order to dissolve Ahmadiyah and to declare it as being barred permanently.[38]

34 Platzdasch, 'Religious Freedom in Indonesia', p. 9.

35 See Burhani, 'Treating Minorities', p. 294.

36 Ulil Abshar-Abadalla Hukum, 'Fatwa, dan Ahmadiyah', *Tempo,* 21 April 2008.

37 Platzdasch, 'Religious Freedom', p. 9.

38 Ibid., p. 11.

The Ahmadiyah controversy further escalated following a violent incident during a march at Jakarta's National Monument square to celebrate the birth of *Pancasila* on 1 June 2008. The march was organized by the National Alliance for Freedom of Religion and Belief (*Aliansi Kebangsaan untuk Kebebasan Beragama dan Berkeyakinan*/AKKBB). The coalition was formed by a number of human rights groups and activists and several prominent liberal Muslim intellectuals. The coalition planned the march to draw attention to religious tolerance issues by proclaiming that *Pancasila* was the ideological basis for religious freedom and tolerance and that the actions of Islamist conservatives were endangering that freedom. Ahmadiyah's opponents, however, saw the event as a show of support solely for Ahmadiyah. On the day of the march, an Islamist umbrella group calling itself the Defenders of Islam Command (*Laskar Komando Islam*) appeared at the square and assaulted the marchers, leaving several prominent Muslim social activists injured.[39]

In response to the increasingly violent controversy over the Ahmadiyah status, the government finally gave its official response. On 9 June 2008, the government issued its verdict on the Ahmadiyah question in the form of a Ministerial Joint Decree (*Surat Keputusan Bersama*/SKB) signed by the Minister of Religious Affairs, the Minister of Home Affairs and the Attorney General. The Decree was addressed to followers, members and/or board leaders of Ahmadiyah Indonesia. While it points out that 'the right to practice one's religion is a human right that must not be reduced in whichever situation' and that 'every man is free to adhere to his respective religion and worship in accordance with his religion and belief', it goes on with an important qualification. The qualification is based on the Law No.1/PNPS/1965 on the prohibition of blasphemy and/or defamation of religion ('the Blasphemy Law'). The first provision of the Blasphemy Law prohibited every person from deliberately expressing and promoting interpretations or activities of recognised religions in Indonesia which deviate from the central teachings of those religions. Clearly informed by this Law, the most important part of the decree then:

> warns and orders followers, members, and/or board members of Ahmadiyah Indonesia, for as long as they refer to themselves as Muslims [*mengaku beragama Islam*], to stop spreading interpretations and activities that deviate from the central teachings of Islam, that is, the spreading of the view which acknowledge that there is a prophet fully versed in all teachings after the Prophet Muhammad.[40]

Here, the government appears to say that Ahmadiyah members are liable of the blasphemy charges for 'spreading interpretations and activities that deviate from central teachings of Islam' by 'spreading of the view which acknowledges that

39 Ibid., p. 13.
40 Ibid., p. 14.

there is a prophet fully versed in all teachings after the Prophet Muhammad'.[41] On closer examination, the decree left the legal status of the Ahmadiyah unresolved. It banned Ahmadiyah from proselytization but not from internal activities, thus leaving its members in a legal limbo.[42]

Many liberal Muslim intellectuals and activists were highly critical of the SKB. Some argued that by ordering a stop to activities that went against central interpretations of Islam, the government had interfered in the personal lives of Indonesians. By deciding what a 'proper' definition of Islam is, the government, they held, had thus abandoned what was supposed to be a neutral stand on religion. Rumadi, a liberal Muslim activist of the Wahid Institute, for example, argues that religious interpretation is part of religious freedom and belief that cannot be criminalized. By issuing the SKB, he further argues, the government is trapped in taking sides in the matter of religious interpretation.[43] In a similar vein, Ulil argues that 'the Indonesian government is tasked with only one thing, i.e. to respect and guarantee the right of all its citizens to exercise their freedom to embrace any religion and faith of their choice'.[44] 'The state', he argued, 'has no stake whatsoever in delineating what is "straight" and what is "crooked" with respect to religious doctrinal debate within any community!'.[45]

The judicial review of the Blasphemy Law

In October 2009, the petition for the judicial review of the Blasphemy Law was officially filed to the Constitutional Court by the Religious Freedom Advocacy Team (*Tim Advokasi Kebebasan Beragama*). The Team was a coalition of a number of human rights lawyers representing seven human rights Non-Government Organizations (NGOs) and four individuals as the formal applicants of the petition. These seven NGOs consisted of Imparsial, the Indonesian Legal Aid Foundation (*Yayasan Lembaga Bantuan Hukum Indonesia*/YLBHI), the Association of Indonesian Legal Aid (*Perhimpunan Bantuan Hukum Indonesia*/PBHI), the Institute for Study and Community Advocacy (*Lembaga Studi dan Advokasi Masyarakat*/ElSAM), the Centre for Study of Human Rights and Democracy (DEMOS), the Desantara Foundation and the Setara Institute. The four individual applicants were widely known liberal and progressive Muslim figures: former President Abdurrahman Wahid, Siti Musdah Mulia, M. Dawam Rahardjo and Maman Imanul Haq. The four names have established themselves as widely respected figures and are well-known for their intellectual and political concerns on religious freedom and religious minorities.

41 Ibid., p. 14.

42 Ibid., p. 14.

43 Rumadi, 'SKB Stengah Hati', *Kompas*, 11 June 2008; available at http://cetak.kompas.com/read/xml/2008/06/11/01335564/skb.setengah.hati.

44 Ulil Abshar-Abdalla, *Ahmadiyah Controversy in Indonesia*, available at http://islamlib.com/en/article/ahmadiyahs-controversy-in-indonesia-vying-for-an-authority/ (accessed 23 July 2011).

45 Ibid.

The petition for the judicial review of the Law soon sparked a fierce public debate. A large number of Islamic groups appeared to be unhappy with and highly critical of the proposal to revoke the Law. Conservative and radical Islamic groups were among the loudest critics of the proposal, with some accusing it as a pretext for hidden agendas of atheists and liberals who promote 'unlimited freedom' (*kebebasan tanpa batas*).[46] While there was no representative of Ahmadiyah in the coalition, some have also closely associated this legal initiative with the Ahmadiyah case. Amidhan of the MUI, for example, suspected that 'the request for judicial review cannot be separated from the struggle of the applicants in the case of Ahmadiyah'.[47] The two largest Islamic organizations, the Nahdlatul Ulama (NU) and Muhammadiyah, were also among those who oppose the proposal, arguing that the Law is necessary for maintaining religious harmony and public order. Leaders of both organizations also claimed that the Law is primarily about the defamation of religion, which they saw as necessary to avoid horizontal conflicts, and not about religious freedom.[48] This position largely echoed and supported the similar position of the government as often represented by the comments by Minister of Religious Affairs, Suryadharma Ali and Minister of Justice and Human Rights, Patrialis Akbar.[49]

Liberal and progressive Muslims, on the other hand, were largely supportive of the judicial review of the Law. Three main problems were particularly associated with the Law by these liberal and progressive Muslims. The first main problem for them is that the Law allows too much room for state involvement and intervention in religious matters. This problematic aspect of the Law was identifed, for example, by Luthfi Assyaukanie, an important figure in the *Jaringan Islam Liberal* (JIL). In his speech he gave before the court entitled '*Negara Harus Melindungi Semua Agama dan Keakinan*' (The State has to protect all religions and beliefs), Assyaukanie argued that the Law is highly problematic because it allows the state to interfere with religious matters.[50] For Assyaukanie, 'belief and faith is an individual matter in which the state is not allowed to interfere'.[51] The same view was also put forward by Ulil Abshar-Abdalla. For Abdalla, the Law is problematic because it allows religious *fatwas* to be enforced by the state.

46 Margiono *et al.*, *'Bukan Jalan Tengah' Eksaminasi Publik atas Keputusan Mahkamah Konstitusi perihal Pengujian Undang-Undang Nomor 1 PNPS Tahun 1965 Tentang Penya lahgunaan dan/ atau Penodaan Agama* (*'Not the Middle Path' Public Examination on the Constiutional Court's Decision on the Judicial Review of the Law No.1/PNPS/1965 on Abuse of Religion and/or Blasphemy*) (Jakarta: The Indonesian Legal Resource Centre, 2010), p. 25.

47 Quoted in Melissa Crouch, 'Judicial Review and Religious Freedom: The Case of the Indonesian Ahmadis', *Sydney Law Review* (2012).

48 See 'Kebebasan Beragama: Hasyim: Jangan Berlogika Terbalik', *Republika*, 10 February 2010 (accessed 15 December 2011).

49 See Constitutional Court Decision No.140/PUU-VII/2009, p. 139

50 Luthfi Assyaukanie, 'Negara Harus Melindungi Semua Agama dan Keyakinan', available at his personal website www.assyauknie.com (accessed 10 April 2011).

51 Ibid.

This, for him, cannot be accepted since Indonesia is not a religious state, but a democratic state which must be neutral on religious matters.[52]

The second main problem of the Law is that it fails to provide an inclusive and equal guarantee for religious freedom by granting freedom only to certain religions and religious understandings and discriminating against others. For Assyaukanie, for example, the Law is discriminatory and as such it is clearly in conflict with the inclusive and equal guarantee for religious freedom provided by the Constitution. As he suggested, 'our constitution clearly protects all religions, without exception. There is no limitation on the number of religions or sects. Every religion and sect is protected to grow and develop'.[53] Jalaludin Rakhmat, another prominent liberal Muslim scholar, also found the Law problematic for its possibility of being manipulated by both the state and religious establishments to marginalize and suppress religious minorities.[54]

The third main problem of the Law is its tendency to blur the distinction between religious interpretations (*penafsiran agama*) and defamation of religion (*penodaan agama*). Most liberal and progressive Muslims argue for a clear distinction between the two. For them, religion is subject to multiple interpretations and there have been historically ongoing competing interpretations even on fundamental religious issues. Assyaukanie, for example, stressed that historically, multiple interpretations, including those initially or for political reasons considered 'heretical' or 'deviant', have been central to the growth and development of religious traditions.[55]

On 19 April 2010, after lengthy hearings and submissions from a large number of concerned parties, the Court decided to uphold the validity of the Blasphemy Law. In its decision, the Court endorsed a broad interpretation of the legitimate limitations on religious freedom. Two particular grounds, 'public order' and 'religious values', appear to be the main justifications of the Law by the Court. First, the Court agreed that in the interest of public order the state has the right to intervene in religious matters and restrict certain religious interpretations. Affirming the concerns expressed by many Islamic leaders and government officials, the Court argued that the revocation of the Law would lead to horizontal conflict and anarchy within the community.[56]

Second, the Court also justified the Law on the ground of 'religious values' as found in the Indonesian Constitution, but not in international human rights law. Stressing what it considers as distinctive historical close relations between state and religion in Indonesia, the Court considered the Law 'as a compromise between the state and religious leaders, allowing the state to restrict religious activities on the grounds of "public order" or "religious values", while also

52 Constitutional Court Decision No.140/PUU-VII/2009, p. 217.

53 Luthfi Assyaukanie, 'Negara'.

54 Margiono *et al.*, 'Bukan Jalan Tengah', p. 19.

55 Luthfi Assyaukanie, 'Negara'.

56 Melissa Crouch, 'Law and Religion in Indonesia: The Constitutional Court and the Blasphemy Law', *Asian Journal of Comparative Law* 7:1 (2012), p. 42.

delegating some power to religious leaders to act as gatekeepers to define the "correct" interpretation of their religion'.[57]

As far as the Ahmadiyah case is concerned, there are two major implications of this decision for Ahmadiyah. First, by upholding the validity of the Blasphemy Law, it justified the SKB that 'warns' Ahmadiyah to stop promoting their teachings, which are considered as 'deviating' from the core tenets of Islam. This is because the power to warn Ahmadiyah is derived from the Blasphemy Law. Second, it leaves open the possibility that followers of Ahmadiyah could potentially be prosecuted for insulting Islam under the widely defined Blasphemy Law in the future.[58]

The changing landscape of Muslim politics

While the controversy over Ahmadiyah has a long history in Indonesia, its revival in a more aggressive and violent way in the post-Suharto period cannot be detached from the changing landscape of Muslim politics. Since the late 1970s, Indonesia has seen the emergence of a liberal and progressive intellectual movement that transcends the 'traditionalist' and 'modernist' divide in Indonesian Islam. This new Islamic intellectual movement strongly claims that 'the modern ideals of equality, freedom, and democracy are not uniquely Western values, but modern necessities compatible with, and even required by, Muslim ideals'. More importantly, in the context of state–Islam relations, the movement's orientation is 'the establishment not of a monopoly-creating and diversity-denying "Islamic" state, but of a Muslim civil society dedicated to the Islamic values of justice, freedom, and civility in difference'. The movement's two most acclaimed leaders, Nurcholish Madjid and Abdurrahman Wahid, for example, argued that the case for an Islamic state 'rested on faulty exegesis and that the concept had wrongly been sacralised by successive generations of Muslim politicians'. Many have argued that the pluralist and democratic religious discourse developed by these two leaders and their contemporaries has been instrumental in the continuing support of *Pancasila* as the final foundation of Indonesian nationhood and non-sectarian and harmonious relations between various faiths.

The fall of the Suharto regime, however, has paved the way for major reconfiguration of Muslim politics and power relations between the state and different Islamic groups and orientations. As some scholars have noted, one of the significant transformations of Indonesian Islam following the fall of the Suharto regime has been the declining hegemony of liberal-progressive Muslim discourse in the face of the revival of long-suppressed conservative and fundamentalist Islamic discourses and movements.[59] The hegemonic position of

57 Ibid., p. 46.

58 Crouch, 'Judicial Review and Religious Freedom', p. 571.

59 See, for example, Martin van Bruinessen (ed.), *Contemporary Developments in Indonesian Islam: Explaining the 'Conservative Turn'* (Singapore: Institute of Southeast Asian Studies, 2013).

liberal-progressive Muslim discourse in the 1980s and 1990s, partly due to the strong endorsement of state, has now been put into question. The degree of institutional support that liberal and progressive Muslim discourse enjoyed during those periods no longer exists, whereas other Muslim discourses, including some that were suppressed under the Suharto regime, have gained greater prominence and official endorsement.[60]

Central to this changing landscape of Muslim politics has been a more assertive campaign for an 'orthodox' Islam as opposed to 'unorthodox', 'heretic' or 'deviant' interpretations or groups. The Majelis Ulama Indonesia (MUI) has been the major player in this struggle. The MUI was created in 1975 as part of Suharto's agenda to control Islam, and developed relatively moderate positions during Suharto's New Order. In the post-Suharto period, however, it has taken a more independent stance and transformed itself into a more conservative body.[61] Increasingly penetrated by Muslim leaders of conservative and puritan persuasion, the MUI leadership lent their support to orthodox and puritan understandings of the *shari'a* by taking a more aggressive stance against 'deviationist' currents in Indonesian Islam. The growing influence of conservative and puritan understanding in the MUI was most clearly observed in a number of fatwas that the MUI issued in 2005, two of which were particularly suggestive of its concerns with maintaining the 'pure' and 'established' Islam. One *fatwa*, as discussed before, declared the Ahmadiyah movement as 'deviant' sect, and the other stated liberalism, pluralism and secularism as antithetical to Islam. Some observers regard this development as the clearest expression of 'the conservative turn' in contemporary Indonesia.[62]

The increasing role of the MUI in 'the conservative turn' in post-Suharto Indonesian Islam was accompanied by its reconfigured relationship with the state. After its mostly conflictual relationship with President Abdurrahman Wahid and Megawati Sukarnoputri, it has increasingly gained more explicit endoresement from the SBY government in the following periods. During the decade of SBY's presidency (2004–2014), the MUI – which *nota bene* has no constitutional standing – has been treated almost as if it were a legislative body.[63] In opening the MUI's national congress in 2005, SBY made the following statement:

> We open our hearts and minds to receiving the thoughts, recommendations and fatwas from the MUI and *ulama* at any time, either directly to me or to the Minister of Religious Affairs or to other branches of government. We

60 Martin van Bruinessen, 'Postscript: The Survival of Liberal and Progressive Muslim Thought in Indonesia', in Martin van Bruinessen (ed.), *Contemporary Developments in Indonesian Islam: Explaining the 'Conservative Turn'* (Singapore: Institute of Southeast Asian Studies, 2013), p. 244.

61 M.C. Ricklefs, *Islamisation and Its Opponents in Java, c. 1930 to the Present* (Singapore: National University of Singapore Press, 2012), p. 284.

62 See John Olle, 'The Campaign Against "Heresy": State and Society in Negotiation in Indonesia', paper presented at the 16th Biennial Conference of the Asian Studies Association of Australia in Wollongong, 26–29 June 2006.

63 Ricklefs, *Islamisation and Its Opponents*, p. 286.

> want to place MUI in a central role in matters regarding the Islamic faith, so that it becomes clear what the difference is between areas that are the preserve of the state and areas where the government or state should heed the fatwas from the MUI and *ulama*.[64]

At the MUI meeting in November 2007, the president further states: 'In accordance with its regulations, the MUI issues *fatwas*. The president cannot issue a *fatwa*. But after a *fatwa* is issued, the tools of the state can do their duty.'[65] Hoping for further cooperation with the MUI, the president went even further, suggesting that 'we must all take strict measures against deviant beliefs'.[66] Whether or not SBY's statement was politically motivated, it has a significant implication on religion–state relations in contemporary Indonesia. With this statement, the state has positioned itself in a non-neutral position with regard to religious matters, allowing particular religious interpretations – in this case those sanctioned by the MUI – to dictate its policies in dealing with problems arising from differing religious interpretations in society.

Apart from his strong support for MUI's *fatwa*, SBY also included in his cabinet some ministers whose religious views are very hostile to religious minorities. Suryadharma Ali, the Minister of Religious Affairs, was particularly well-known for his strong anti-Ahmadiyah sentiment. Many human rights activists as well as liberal Muslim intellectuals were very disappointed with his public statements. Luthfi Assyaukanie, a leading fugure of *Jaringan Islam Liberal* (JIL), even suggests that he was the first minister in Indonesian history who is well known for his intolerant views and inhospitable attitudes towards minority groups.[67]

The ambiguous nature of the Indonesian state

The Ahmadiyah controversy, however, does not only reflect the more fragmented religious authority and Muslim politics in contemporary Indonesia. It also illustrates the remaining contentious nature of the Indonesian state. The basis of the independent Indonesia state was vigorously debated by the country's founding fathers in the *Badan Penyelidik Usaha Persiapan Kemerdekaan Indonesia* (BPUPKI), which was specifically inaugurated to draft the foundation of the Indonesian state. The body was largely dominated by two main competing ideological groups: the 'Islamic group' and the 'nationalist group'. The Islamic group argued for the establishment of Indonesia as an Islamic state on the ground that the majority of Indonesian are Muslims. The nationalist groups, on the other hand, were concerned that such a decision would eliminate the Christians and

64 Ibid., p. 286.

65 International Crisis Group, 'Indonesia: Implications of the Ahmadiyah Decree', Asia Briefing No. 78, Jakarta/Brussels: 7 July 2008, p. 9.

66 Ibid., p. 9.

67 Luthfi Assyaukanie, *Islam dalam Transisi Demokrasi di Indonesia*, available at www.islamlib.com/?site=1&aid=1827&cat=content&title=kolom.

other religious minorities. They thus argued in favour of a religiously neutral state in which religious and secular affairs would be kept separate.

On 1 June 1945, Sukarno, who later became the first president of Indonesia, introduced the first version of *Pancasila* (literally, five pillars) in an attempt to resolve the ideological deadlock. It comprised of:

1 Indonesian nationalism;
2 internationalism or humanitarianism;
3 deliberation or democracy;
4 social welfare;
5 belief in God.

The fifth principle of this first formulation of *Pancasila*, 'belief in God', exemplified Sukarno's effort to find an acceptable compromise by making Indonesia neither an Islamic state nor a secular state, but a state which would have a 'religious state philosophy so that the ideals of every religious denomination could be realised'.[68] Sukarno's concept of *Pancasila* was accepted as a compromise but its initial formulation was modified by leaders of both camps. In its final formulation, the principle of Belief in One God (*Ketuhanan Yang Maha Esa*) was put as the first principle, signifiying its ideological and political significance. It is this principle that has been instrumental in constructing the political identity of the Indonesian state as neither a secular nor religious state ever since. Mukti Ali, former Minister of Religious Affairs, formulated his famous sentences concerning the nature of the Indonesian state in the following way:

> Indonesia has chosen its own path. Indonesia is not a theocratic state, nor a secular state. The basis of our state, *Pancasila*, is right in stating that this state is based on Belief in One God, which shows that Indonesia is a multireligious state. But religion (Islam), in its official form, is not the basis of the state . . . it was not made a state religion. However, the government will formulate operational principles for development of religion, which is oriented towards all religious communities in Indonesia, in order to protect, assist, support and develop (*membina*) all religious activities.[69]

While many have agreed that *Pancasila* serves as the best ideological and political formula for multi-religious Indonesia, some have argued that the compromising nature of *Pancasila* has led to some ambiguities in the relationship between religion and state in this country. Kim, for example, argues that Article 29(2) of the

68 Anthony Johns, 'Indonesia: Islam and Cultural Pluralism', in John L. Esposito (ed.), *Islam in Asia: Religion, Politics and Society* (New York: Oxford University Press, 1987), p. 210.

69 Ali Munhanif, 'Prof. Dr. Mukti Ali: Modernisasi Politik-Keagamaan Orde Baru', in Azyumardi Azra dan Saiful Umam (ed.)., *Menteri-Menteri Agama RI* (Jakarta: INIS, PPIM, dan Puslitbang Depag RI, 1888), p. 299.

1945 Constitution ('The Indonesian state is based on Belief in One God') has three fundamental problems:

1 it is not clear in terms of religion–state relations;
2 it is not clear on the extent to which the state can interfere with the internal domain of religion; and
3 it does not guarantee whether someone can disseminate his religious understanding.[70]

This ambiguous nature of the Indonesian state and its relationship with religion has significant implications on how religious freedom is constitutionally and legally constructed. The normative framework for freedom of religion or belief in Indonesia is provided in the Indonesian Constitution of 1945 and has been strengthened during its amendments in the post-Suharto period. In 2001, in the second amendment to the Constitution, Article 28E was inserted as part of a new chapter on Human Rights. Parts of the Article read 'Each person is free to profess his or her religion, and to worship in accordance with his/her religion' and 'Each person has the freedom to possess convictions and beliefs, and to express his/her thoughts and attitudes'. Article 28I (1) reaffirms that the right to freedom of religion or belief is part of 'human right that cannot be reduced under any circumstance'.[71]

There are, however, certain limitation clauses made in some parts of the Constitution that highly qualify the normative guarantee for religious freedom in Indonesia.[72] The most significant limitation clause is set out in Article 28J(2) of the Constitution. The Article holds that:

> In carrying out his or her rights and freedoms, every citizen has responsibility to abide by restrictions set out by laws with the sole aim to guarantee the recognition and respect for the rights of others and to fulfil a just cause, taking into consideration morality, *religious values* [emphasis added], security, and public order in a democratic community.[73]

The limitation clause as set out in Article 28J(2) qualified Indonesia's normative commitment to international human rights discourse at least in two ways. First, this limitation clause seems to blur the distinction carefully made in international human rights discourse between the internal (*internal forum*) and external aspect (*external forum*) of the right to freedom of religion or belief. According to the international human rights discourse, limitations may only apply to the external aspect of the right, but only to the extent that such limitations are prescribed by

70 See Hyung-Jun Kim, 'The Changing Interpretation of Religious Freedom in Indonesia', *Journal of Southeast Asian Studies*, 29:2 (1998).
71 Article 28I (1), the Indonesian Constitution of 1945
72 Platzdasch, 'Freedom in Indonesia', p. 21
73 Article 28J(2).

law and are necessary to protect public safety, order, health or morals or the fundamental rights of others.[74] Second, the inclusion of 'religious values' as one of permissible grounds for restriction on freedom of religion or belief also departs significantly from the international human rights discourse. While international human rights discourse does allow restrictions on the external aspect of freedom of religion or belief, it does not recognize 'religious values' as one of the permissible grounds for these restrictions.[75] There has been in recent years a concerted effort among members of the Organisation of Islamic Conference (OIC) at various international forums on human rights to push for an international legal document on defamation of religion, which would allow certain restrictions of freedom of expression and freedom of religion on the basis of religion. This effort, however, has gained little support so far and the traditionally dominant understanding in international human rights discourse remains that religion is an acceptable ground for restrictions.[76]

Despite these ambuiguities, however, it seems that Mukti Ali's view on the nature of the Indonesian state has become the standard view in the Indonesian constitutional and political discourse in the last few decades. It is this view that highly influenced the reasoning of the Indonesian Constitutional Court in making its decision on the Blasphemy Law case. For the Constitutional Court's judges, Article 29(1) of the 1945 Constitution constitutes a unique characteristic of the principle of rule of law (*negara hukum*) in Indonesia, that is, 'a rule-based state which places the principle of Belief in One God as a main principle'. As explained by the Constitutional Court:

> The Constitution of the Republic of Indonesia does not permit free campaign for freedom not to have a religion, freedom to promote anti-religion as well as freedom to insult or denigrate religious teachings or scriptures that become the sources of religious teachings or defame the name of God. This is one of the elements that demarcates between the principle of rule of law in Indonesia and that of the West, so that in administration of the state, law making, and the judicial system, the basis of Lordship and religious teachings become the yardstick within which to demarcate good laws from bad ones, even to decide whether they are constitutional or inconstitutional.[77]

More importantly, the idea that Indonesia as a state based on belief in One God has an obligation to protect religion and the purity of its teachings has been firmly entrenched in the current constitutional-legal discourse. For example,

74 Ibid., p. 678

75 See Jeroen Temperman, 'Blasphemy, Defamation of Religion and Human Rights Law', *Netherlands Quarterly of Human Rights*, 26:4 (2008), pp. 525–526.

76 For a critical account on the so-called 'defamation of religion debate', see Malcolm Evans, 'Advancing Freedom of Religion or Belief: Agendas for Changes', *Oxford Journal of Law and Religion* (2011).

77 Constitutional Court's Decision, p. 275.

former Chief Justice of the Constitutional Court, Prof. Dr Moh. Mahfud MD, argues that in the context of the *Pancasila*-based state which recognizes the important position of religion:

> protection of religious freedom should be integrated with the protection of the purity (*kemurnian*) of religion. This means that freedom of religion is guaranteed, but religious deviation can not be justified. The responsibility of the State towards religion is not only limited to protect freedom of religion but also to provide service for religious communities and to protect religious teachings from any deviation.[78]

The problem with this view, however, is that it is not really clear what is meant by the 'purity of religious teachings' as it is subject to the ongoing struggles between competing religious interpretations whose boundaries are not clear and continuesly contested. Despite this continuing ambiguity, what the Court's decision makes clear is that this compromising nature of *Pancasila* – that Indonesia is not a theocratic, nor a secular state – in fact opens wide room for state intervention in religious matters.[79]

This does not mean, however, that the debates on religion–state relations and religious freedom have been sealed off and liberal discourse has been silenced. Alternative interpretations of *Pancasila* and its first principle are continuesly negotiated by various actors, including liberal and progressive Muslim intellectuals. One of the alternative discourses, for example, is offered by Yudi Latif, a young liberal Muslim intellectual. Latif argues that *Pancasila* must be understood proportionally; it is not a religion that tries to regulate the system of beliefs, rituals, norms and religious identities in the private realm and internal domain of each religious community.[80] Moreover, he further argues, the concern of *Pancasila* is more directed towards public morality; it does not have pretention to intervene with private morality or belief. As he writes:

> The principle of Belief in One God in *Pancasila* constitutes a conception of 'civil religion' which contains universal ethical values of religions but can be clearly differentiated from religion. Its pretention is to make ethico-religious values as the foundation for managing political and public life within the context of multi-religious and cultural society, without letting one particular religion (or one religious interpretation) dictate the state.[81]

78 Trisno Sutanto, 'Negara, Kekuasaan, dan Agama', in Zainal Abidin *et al.*, *Pluralisme Kewargaan: Arah Baru Politik Keragaman di Indonesia* (Bandung: Centre for Religious and Cross-Cultural Studies and Mizan, 2011), p. 124.

79 Ibid., p. 125.

80 Yudi Latif, *Negara Paripurna: Historisitas, Rasionalitas dan Aktualitas Pancasila* (Jakarta: Gramedia Pustaka Utama, 2011), p. 110.

81 Ibid., p. 110.

For Latif, the first principle of *Pancasila* is 'an attempt to search for a common ground within the spirit of togetherness in providing a strong ethical foundation for political life based on Godly morality'.[82] Within this framework of common ground, he further argues, Indonesia 'is not an extreme secular state which pretends to restrict religion within the private sphere because the first principle clearly requires religious values to be the basis of political and public life'.[83] At the same time, *Pancasila* also does not necessitate the establishment of a state religion which represents one particular aspiration of religious group which will lead to 'a religious tyranny that undermines the plurality of the nation and renders the followers of other religions as second-class citizens'.[84]

Concluding remarks

The chapter has attempted to discuss the recent Ahmadiyah controversy in Indonesia and put it in the larger context of the country's contentious politics of religion–state relations and religious freedom. The analysis has demonstrated that the Ahmadiyah controversy within which competing discourses of religion–state relations and religious freedom were waged has been influenced by the dynamics of Muslim politics that has been significantly reshaped in the post-Suharto era. It has showed that the liberal and pluralist understanding of religion–state relations and religious freedom, as advocated by some liberal Muslim intellectuals and activists, has been largely sidelined in the controversy. On the other hand, the state seems to be increasingly under considerable influence of conservative Islamic groups who promote highly restrictive and particularistic understanding of religion–state relations and religious freedom. The Constitutional Court's decision to uphold the Blasphemy Law further confirms the lack of support for a more liberal constitutional-legal discourse.

The analysis of the chapter further suggests, however, that the deeper underlying factor lies in the ambiguous nature of the Indonesian state. The government's response to the Ahmadiyah case and the Constitutional Court's decision on the judicial review of the Blasphemy Law seem to point at the ambiguity in religion–state relations remains. What now becomes clearer, however, is that the Constituonal Court's landmark decision on the Blasphemy Law case affirms that the compromised path of *Pancasila* – with its ambiguous proposition that 'Indonesia is not a theocratic nor secular state' – in fact paves the way for state intervention in religious matters. It is this inherent ambiguity that renders the liberal discourse of state neutrality and religious freedom highly contentious in contemporary Indonesia.

This does not mean, however, that more liberal dicourse of religion–state relations and religious freedom have been effectively marginalized in post-Suharto

82 Ibid., p. 110.
83 Ibid., p. 110.
84 Ibid., p. 110.

Indonesia. Liberal discourse remains and will continue to be among the main parts in the ongoing struggles and contestations over these issues. To conclude, it is safe to argue that the relationhsip between religion, and more specifically Islam, and the Indonesian state has been historically and politically contested and will continue to be a matter of contention and tension. This tension is unlikely to be settled with any finality. As Indonesia continues to wrestle with its competing 'secular' and 'religious' identities, the proper meaning of religious freedom and its limits will continue to be contested.

References

Al-Azmeh, Aziz. *Islams and Modernities* (London: Verso, 1993).

Ali, M. *The Ahmadiyya Movement* (Lahore: Ahmadiyya Anjuman Isha'at Islam, 1984).

Anderson, John. 'Does God Matter, and if so Whose God? Religion and Democratization', *Democratization*, 11:4 (2004).

Asad, Talal. 'Ideology, Class and the Origin of the Islamic State', *Economy and Society*, 9:4 (November 1980).

Bakhsh, K.S. *The Debt Forgotten* (Lahore: Ahmadiyya Anjuman Isha'at Islam, 1993).

Bayat, Asef. *Making Islam Democratic: Social Movements and the Post-Islamist Turn* (Stanford: Stanford University Press, 2007).

Bruinessen, Martin van (ed.). *Contemporary Developments in Indonesian Islam: Explaining the 'Conservative Turn'* (Singapore: Institute of Southeast Asian Studies, 2013).

Bruinessen, Martin van. 'Postscript: The Survival of Liberal and Progressive Muslim Thought in Indonesia' in Martin van Bruinessen (ed.), *Contemporary Developments in Indonesian Islam: Explaining the 'Conservative Turn'* (Singapore: Institute of Southeast Asian Studies, 2013).

Burhani, Ahmadi Najib. 'Treating Minorities with Fatwas: A Study of the Ahmadiyya Community in Indonesia', *Contemporary Islam* (2014).

Crouch, Melissa. 'Judicial Review and Religious Freedom: The Case of the Indonesian Ahmadis', *Sydney Law Review* (2012).

Esposito, John L. *Islam and Politics* (Syracuse: Syracuse University Press, 1998).

Ferjani, Mohamed-Cherif. 'Islam and Politics: The Terms of the Debate', *History and Anthropology*, 16:1 (2009).

International Crisis Group. 'Indonesia: Implications of the Ahmadiyah Decree', Asia Briefing No. 78, Jakarta/Brussels, 7 July 2008.

Johns, Anthony. 'Indonesia: Islam and Cultural Pluralism' in John L. Esposito (ed.), *Islam in Asia: Religion, Politics and Society* (New York: Oxford University Press, 1987).

Kim, Hyung-Jun. 'The Changing Interpretation of Religious Freedom in Indonesia', *Journal of Southeast Asian Studies*, 29:2 (1998).

Latif, Yudi. *Negara Paripurna: Historisitas, Rasionalitas dan Aktualitas Pancasila* (Jakarta: Gramedia Pustaka Utama, 2011).

Lewis, Bernard. *The Political Language of Islam* (Chicago: University of Chicago Press, 1991).

McLoughlin, Sean. 'Islam(s) in Context: Orientalism and the Anthropology of Muslim Societies and Cultures', *Journal of Beliefs & Values*, 28:3 (December 2007).

Mahzarnama. *The Memorandum: submission by the Ahmadiyya Muslim Jamaat to the National Assembly of Pakistan regarding its basic tenets* (Tilford: Islam International Publications Ltd, 2002).

Margiono, Muktiono, Rumedi, Sulistyowati Irianto *'Bukan Jalan Tengah' Eksaminasi Publik atas Keputusan Mahkamah Konstitusi perihal Pengujian Undang-Undang Nomor 1 PNPS Tahun 1965 Tentang Penyalahgunaan dan/atau Penodaan Agama* (Jakarta: The Indonesian Legal Resource Centre, 2010).

Moosa, Ebrahim. 'The Debt and Burdens of Critical Islam', in Omid Safi (ed.), *Progressive Muslims: On Justice, Gender and Pluralism* (Oxford: Oneworld Publication, 2003).

Munhanif, Ali. 'Prof. Dr. Mukti Ali: Modernisasi Politik-Keagamaan Orde Baru', in Azyumardi Azra dan Saiful Umam (ed.)., *Menteri-Menteri Agama RI* (Jakarta: INIS, PPIM, dan Puslitbang Depag RI, 1888).

Olle, John. 'The Campaign Against "Heresy": State and Society in Negotiation in Indonesia', paper presented at the 16th Biennial Conference of the Asian Studies Association of Australia in Wollongong, 26–29 June 2006.

Platzdasch, Bernhard. 'Religious Freedom in Indonesia: The Case of the Ahmadiyah', *ISEAS Working Paper: Politics & Security Series*, No. 2 (Singapore, 2011).

Ricklefs, M.C. *Islamisation and Its Opponents in Java, c. 1930 to the Present* (Singapore: National University of Singapore Press, 2012).

Roy, Olivier. *Globalised Islam: The Search for a New Ummah* (London: Hurst, 2004).

Stepan, Alfred. 'Religion, Democracy, and the "Twin Tolerations"', *Journal of Democracy*, 11:4 (October 2000).

Sutanto, Trisno. 'Negara, Kekuasaan, dan Agama', in Zainal Abidin Bagir and Endy Saputro, *Pluralisme Kewargaan: Arah Baru Politik Keragaman di Indonesi*a (Bandung: Centre for Religious and Cross-Cultural Studies and Mizan, 2011).

Temperman, Jeroen. 'Blasphemy, Defamation of Religion and Human Rights Law', *Netherlands Quarterly of Human Rights*, 26:4 (2008).

Valentine, S.R. 'Prophecy after the Prophet, albeit Lesser Prophets? The Ahmadiyya Jama'at in Pakistan', *Contemporary Islam* (2014).

Zirvi, K. *Welcome to Ahmadiyyat: The True Islam, Ahmadiyya Movement in Islam* (Silver Springs: Islamic Publications Ltd, 2002).

9 Must the infringement of women's rights within religions be tolerated?

A Swiss perspective

Adrian Loretan

Introduction

Religious beliefs are a cornerstone of many people's lives. However, it is a sad fact that infringement of women's rights is frequently tolerated or even encouraged by many religious communities.

In a world where the confluence of people and cultures presents itself as a plural environment with an 'understandable urge to return to old conventions, traditional cultures . . . and the familiar, seemingly secure, sense of one's identity',[1] questions are being constantly and increasingly asked on the universal character of human rights. The debate is clearly not new: on one side, cultural relativists argue that human rights vary according to the different cultural perspectives. They equip cultural relativity, thus, with a questionable prescriptive force. On the other hand, universalists claim the established universal character of human rights, as reflected in international law and most indicatively in the Universal Declaration of Human Rights. In Charles Norchi's words, the Universal Declaration 'represents a broader consensus on human dignity than does any single culture or tradition'.[2]

The essence of this universality implies that every human being is entitled to human rights without discrimination of any kind, including of gender and/or religion. While this principle of non-discrimination does not allow denial of rights on the basis of cultural distinction, it does not ipso facto exclude the overall flexibility of human rights so as to become tolerant to diverse cultures. This flexibility is available because human rights establish minimum standards and as importantly include and incorporate cultural rights. Culture in this context, refers to habits, beliefs, customs, activities, history, traditions and symbols of an identifiable social group[3] (e.g. the right to be maintained in a marriage). As a legal anthropological concept, it suggests that through the exercise of individual

1 Diana Ayton-Shenker, *The Challenge of Human Rights and Cultural Diversity*, UN Background Note, www.un.org/rights/dpi1627e.htm [accessed on 15.01.2015]

2 Ibid., at 2. See also the Preamble of the UDHR that declares the Declaration to be a 'common standard of achievement for all peoples and all nations'.

3 Justin Cox, 'The Limits of Toleration: Applying Rawls' Public Reason to Multicultural Rights', *Aporia*, Vol. 14, No. 1 (2004), 13–29 at 14.

autonomy, it places individuals, as right-holders, in a position of giving meaning to one's actions leading him/her towards a fulfilling human existence.[4]

The link, however, between individual autonomy and exercise of cultural rights is not established without difficulties: for instance, the Islamic tradition of female head-to-toe covering problematizes the extent to which cultural practices promote individual autonomy. Similarly, the right of the Muslim bride to be given property in marriage, as dowry, is another facet of cultural rights affecting individual autonomy, for both female and male believers.

Justin Cox maintains three ways in which culture (and the exercise of cultural rights) enhance this autonomy: first, the exercise of cultural rights for all groups in a given society provides a measure of comparison to reflect on one's own culture, second, the same exercise secures cultural goods and third, it allows for an exit option for those unable/unwilling to continue belonging to a group. The ramification of the granting and exercise of cultural (and religious) rights thus create an internal tension between pluralism per se and individual autonomy that is complex, context-dependent and often unchartered in the legal discipline.

In the context of a human rights frame of analysis, the centre of debate becomes the clash of human rights as 'assessed and regarded differently by individuals and groups'.[5] Apart from the fact, however, that human rights are constantly evolving to the point of becoming reflective, disagreement remains as to which actions can be legitimized within this framework. Parts of the difficulties surrounding this question are linked to our limited knowledge on the issue of the impact of globalization processes on the right to culture.[6] In that sense, the pursuit of cultural rights can certainly not be viewed as an end to itself, especially when it relied on the cultural legitimisation of oppression and violence of basic human rights.

If culture is conceptualized as a 'network of perspectives'[7] and we accept that cultural penetration, also in the form of religious norms and practices, affects increasingly social space, then the question on the position of human rights as transferrable and cross-cultural frames of actions of governments and individuals retains its relevance.[8] The essential question remains one of setting the limits of what is tolerable in the name of culture, which is certainly not a new issue, neither in the legal or other social science disciplines. Human rights, however, do not operate on a 'cultural tabula rasa'.[9] This point reinforces one's

4 Ibid., at 15. Ann Swidler approaches the concept as follows: 'Culture shapes action, not by providing ultimate ends, but by providing a repertoire or tool-kit of habits, skills and styles from which people construct strategies of action.' (Cf. Ann Swidler, 'Culture in Action: Symbols and Strategies', *American Sociological Review*, Vol. 51, No. 2 (1986), at 41.)

5 Dana Irina, 'A Culture of Human Rights and the Right to Culture', *Journal for Communication and Culture*, Vol. 1, No. 2 (Winter 2011), 30–48 at 38.

6 Ibid., at 41.

7 Ulf Hannerz, *Cultural Complexity: Studies in the Social Organization of Meaning* (1992), 266.

8 There are voices in anthropology that argue that human rights, by virtue of their universalization, can also be labelled as 'culture'. (Cf. Ann-Belinda S. Preis, 'Human Rights as Cultural Practice: An Anthropological Critique', *Human Rights Quarterly*, Vol. 18 (1996), 286–315 at 290.)

9 Ibid., at 306.

perception of culture as an ongoing debate, based on the flow of norms between countries and continents.[10]

As a result of such complexities, gender equality is a topic debated within the human rights community where universalism and cultural relativism often collide. The collision is due many times to the confusion in this discourse between values (such as justice, equity, humanity) and actual rights as entitlements, that give a special force to claims, vested in social practice.[11] The critique of cultural relativism, affecting also the gender dimension of the equality principle in religious communities, includes *inter alia* the essentialist and reductionist perception of 'right' as 'traditional', of the 'obligatory' as 'habitual', the assertion of the infallibility of culture, the assumed superiority of one's culture over others, the idealized representation of reality that culture is seen to reflect or the understanding of culture as static and homogenous.[12] To this matrix of considerations, human rights scholars have added the trajectory of class or social group that is helpful in certain contexts.[13]

In a radio broadcast[14] on the subject 'How universal are Human Rights?' Swiss international law expert, Walter Kälin, suggested that human rights be theologically established within different religions so that fundamental freedoms may find their proper place. This chapter explores this concept of whether the state should promote human rights within religious groups. First, the chapter explains how the human dignity of individuals is protected by law, then the chapter describes in detail how religious group rights might conflict with other individual human rights. Next, the chapter shows how collective rights create legal pluralism, which can be a threat to individual rights. It then explains how there are divergent opinions within religious groups as to the importance of protecting individual rights in religious frameworks.[15] Finally, several approaches for resolving this conflict are explored in society.

Human dignity and the rule of law

The legal existence of the individual[16] as such emerged towards the end of the Middle Ages, in the Reformation, in humanism and in late Spanish scholasticism. It broke out from the community ties established by the civic republics of the time. It was later the Enlightenment that connected individualism with universalism.

10 Ibid., at 306. This process of negotiating and adapting at times human rights does not happen with consideration of the influence of power and agency: various actors in each case act in the pursuit of specific ends.

11 Jack Donnelly, 'The Relative Universality of Human Rights', *Human Rights Quarterly*, Vol. 28, No. 2 (May 2007), 281–306 at 284.

12 Ibid., at 295–296.

13 See for example Paulin J. Hountondji, 'The Masters Voice: Remarks on the Problem of Human Rights in Africa', in Paul Ricaeur (ed.), *Philosophical Foundations of Human Rights: A World Survey*, 325 (1988).

14 Radio DRS 2, broadcast 'Kontext', Whit Monday, 24 May 2010.

15 Cf. Joachim Güntner, 'Mehr als nur ein Stückchen Haut. Das Verbot der religiös motivierten Beschneidung von Kindern durch Kölns Landgericht hat eine Debatte ausgelöst', *Neue Zürcher Zeitung*, 13 July 2012, at 41.

16 Cf. Neclek Kelek, *Über die Freiheit im Islam*, Vontobel Foundation Series, Zürich, 2010.

The human being was no longer defined by means of external attributes (role, gender, race, etc.). Value was equally accorded to each human being considered as an individual on the grounds of the dignity to which he or she was entitled.[17]

Human dignity, as a value, is prominently recognized in national international human rights law. Article 1 of the Universal Declaration of Human Rights reflects this recognition ('All human beings are born free and equal in dignity and rights'[18]). The recognition of human dignity as a universal value reflects precisely the understanding that each human being has inherent dignity that is the direct consequence of his/her nature and also the basis for his/her entitlement to a basic series of rights, awarded equally among humans.

Included in this construct is the notion of respect for the autonomy of each individual, in other words, his/her right to choose and control their life. In turn, this signifies that the protection of human dignity will involve two components: first, the respect for everyone's humanity and, second, the corresponding duty towards the creation of conditions for everyone's self-realization.[19] Whether we consider human dignity as Hannah Arendt's 'right to have rights' or as an overarching principle that aims to protect the necessary conditions to live life as a human being, it does not solve the instances where competing human rights claim precedence in a given socio-legal context.[20]

The dignity of each individual can only be considered effective in as far as it is universal. For this reason, human rights are not only a question of ethics, but also a question of human dignity and its implementation in legal norms. In the words of Gret Haller:

> If human dignity counts as a religious category, it is then particularised and loses its universal character. Such exactly happens when a religion, a nation, a cultural or an ethnic group claim to have understood human rights better than other religions, nations, cultural or ethnic groups, and when they go about forcing human rights, as they understand them, upon others.[21]

17 Cf. Kurt Seelmann, 'Recht auf Achtung und Schutz der Menschenwürde – leere Floskel oder Grundlage der Rechtsordnung?', in Adrian Loretan (ed.), *Religionsfreiheit im Kontext der Grundrechte*. Religionsrechtliche Studien vol. 2 (Zurich, 2011), 101–120.

18 The widespread character of the value has even reached the work of international organizations that have a primarily economic character (Cf. Article 2 of the Treaty of the EU that states: the EU 'is founded on the values of respect for human dignity, freedom, democracy, equality, the rule of law and respect for human rights').

19 Andrew Clapham, *Human Rights in the Private Sphere* (Oxford, 1993), at 148–149.

20 There is intense discussion on the various understandings of human dignity (liberal versus conservative, as a legal or as a moral concept, as a norm, a right or a principle of law, etc.). The approach to the concept determines also its use in concrete situations of clashes of rights. On this point, cf. Roger Brownsword, 'Human Dignity from a Legal Perspective', and Marcus Düwell, 'Human Dignity: Concepts, Discussions, Philosophical Perspectives', both in M. Düwell *et al.* (eds), *The Cambridge Handbook of Human Dignity: Interdisciplinary Perspectives* (Cambridge, 2014), at 1–22 and 23–49 respectively.

21 Gret Haller, *Politik der Götter. Europa und der neue Fundamentalismus* (Hamburg, 2005), 189, translated by Ch. Gallo.

However, if 'dignity is no longer ascribed to the individual but to a group of humans collectively, then human rights are threatened, since the universality of human dignity is lost. This is the case, for example . . . when dignity is ascribed not to the individual but to a religious group or only to those persons who belong to that group'.[22]

Affiliation to a particular group may therefore lead to inequality. Universal affiliation through the link of human dignity will lead inevitably to equality. Precisely for that reason, Gret Haller sees the constitutional state as the guarantor of rights and freedoms, that is, of human rights.[23] Internally, these rights can come into conflict with each other. Therefore a balance of legally protected interests becomes necessary, as shown in the following section. However, in striking a balance, should one set of rights prevail?

Two basic rights in conflict: religious freedom versus equality

In the context of the deliberations of the Federal Commission against Racism, a female Muslim participant disclosed a new perspective on the clash of rights between religious freedom and equality: she was of the view that gender equality in Switzerland was not guaranteed. The obvious response to her claim was to refer her to Article 8 BV of the Constitution of Switzerland on equal rights under the law.

She persisted in her statement on the grounds that religious freedom (Art 15 BV) is given precedence over the non-discrimination rule (Art 8 §2BV) and that it therefore very heavily restricted other basic rights. My subsequent advice to her was to abandon her religious community if she found it above all to be discriminatory. I myself was merely following the injunctions given by most of the commentaries on basic law. The Muslim participant replied that were she to abandon her religious and cultural community, it would seem to her as if she were removing all her clothes and trying to continue life naked.

The conversation made it clear to me that most commentaries on basic law do not equitably address the issue of the actual problem of discrimination within religious communities under the aspect of personal needs, since commentaries always start with the *de jure* possibility of withdrawal from the community, thereby overlooking the fact that for many a *de facto* retirement from a religious group is a complete impossibility, especially for the more vulnerable sections of believers, such as women.

Women, such as the Zurich-based political scientist Elham Manea, openly refer to violations of human rights even within their own religion.[24] Similar research applied the same line of argument to the Roman Catholic Church[25]and

22 Ibid., 65–66.

23 Cf. ibid., 70–72.

24 See, for example, Elham Manea, *Ich will nicht mehr schweigen: Der Islam, der Westen und die Menschenrechte* (Freiburg in Breisgau, 2009).

25 Stella Ahlers, *Equality of Women in Church and State: A Problematic Relationship of Conflict* (Münster, 2006).

this despite the fact that after 1945, equality of women has become a fixed component of universal European and national law. Various religious communities position themselves against the right to equality. Considering this, can the state on its own territory, in the name of religious freedom, allow communities to support equality-free zones? Will national and international courts of law share this stance? Furthermore, what will be the repercussions for the legal empowerment of individuals and groups directly affected by these significant limitations of rights?

Women who experience their religious community as discriminating against them must have the right to leave that community. However, they must also have the right to offer their own new interpretation to their religious tradition. Manea has opted for this latter.[26] The constitutional state provides women with a means of pressure to be able to modify religious concepts by guaranteeing the right of withdrawal. In the absence of such a right, religious communities become social prisons from which escape is impossible. This stands in contradiction to the secular concept of religious freedom.

The basic rights of collective religious freedom and of gender equality can thus get into an irresolvable tangle.[27] Resolution of such conflicts becomes almost impossible: for example, 'genital mutilation' cannot be euphemistically paraphrased as and levelled down to the equivalent of 'female circumcision'.[28] After all, genital mutilation is not a part of any religious dogma, but in places where women have few rights, as Manea[29] stresses, it tends to be tolerated. There must be a clear differentiation made here with the circumcision of boys of Muslim or Jewish descent.[30]

The right to exit, consent and the state's duty

Religion is being increasingly recognized as a legitimate (and legal) source for exemption from the principle of non-discrimination.[31] The interpretation of these

26 Cf. Manea (2009), 15–187.

27 Cf. Judith Wyttenbach, 'Kooperation von Staat und Religionsgemeinschaften in der Schweiz im Kontext der Grundrechte', in Adrian Loretan (ed.), *Religionsfreiheit im Kontext der Grundrechte* (Zürich, 2011), 377–413, 387–390.

28 Timothy Garton Ash, 'Der Islam in Europa', in Thierry Chervel and Anja Seeliger (eds), *Islam in Europa: Eine Internationale Debatte* (Frankfurt am Main, 2007), 30–54, 45.

29 See Manea (2009), 31–32.

30 Cf. Güntner (2012).

31 Indicatively, for the British case cf. Moira Dustin, 'Deference of Interrogation? Contrasting Models for Reconciling Religion, Gender and Equality', *Religion and Gender*, Vol. 2, No. 1, (2012), 9–35; for the US, cf. Gila Stopler, 'The Free Exercise of Discrimination: Religious Liberty, Civic Community and Women's Equality', *William and Mary Journal of Women and Law*, Vol. 10, Issue 3 (2004), 459, at 463, who goes as far as to claim that a right to 'free exercise of discrimination' has been created (ibid., at 470); at European Union level, see the European Employment Equality Directive 2000/78/EC, available at http://eur-lex.europa.eu/LexUriServ/LexUriServ.do?uri=CELEX:32000L0078:en:HTML, that permits Member States to maintain laws and practices that allow religious organizations to treat differently individuals on the basis of religion (e.g. when there is a genuine occupational requirement for employment purposes), without this treatment constituting discrimination.

exemptions suggests that religious identity takes precedence over general equality norms. The threat for the position and rights of women is obvious: religious protection could undermine the rights of more vulnerable (and marginalized) segments of religious communities. Martha Nussbaum nicely sets the background of the complex debate on the discrimination against women in religious contexts, when she acknowledges that women's ability to exercise their full capabilities is often hindered by 'traditional religious cultures'.[32] The 'reification of group identities' begs also the question as to whether claims based on religion are (and should be) considered different from any other equality claims so as to justify exemption.[33] Nussbaum continues by prioritising the rights (and the position) of women in religious contexts by granting them individual rights of exit as a guarantee and a safeguard against discrimination, within the religious communities to which they belong. Is this option realistic? When the religious community includes family, friends and other strong social ties, the option becomes less likely for women wishing to escape discriminating religious practices.[34] Discrimination then gradually leads to subordination.[35]

The right to exit a religious community that applies discriminatory practices is not a sufficient guarantee against the withdrawal of the state in requiring the same standards of equality to be applied within these groups. This option raises the question of voluntary membership: the centrality of religion and its hierarchical structure, coupled with the fact that individuals remain faithful to the denomination in which they were raised, suggest a strong social dynamic from the group towards the individual, alienating free choice of the latter.

Mary Becker takes a further step in this direction when she adds that children are not born with religious commitments, they are socialized in them by their families and social network.[36] This process is clearly not in line with a liberal definition of the individual as a free and autonomous entity. It also does not correspond to the reality of women's experiences in such communities.[37]

A second level of justification of discriminatory practices within religious communities against women relies on the concept of consent. This is also not clear: framing women's preferences against a background of limited opportunities with their (apparent) acceptance, does not satisfy an argument against the combat

32 Martha Nussbaum, *Women and Human Development: The Capabilities Approach* (Cambridge, 2000), at 188.

33 Term in brackets borrowed by Nancy Fraser, 'Rethinking Recognition', *New Left Review*, Vol. 3 (May/June 2000).

34 Dustin (2012), at 19; Stopler (2004), at 468.

35 According to Sunstein, 'The remedy of "exit" – the right of women to leave a religious order – is crucial but it will not be sufficient when girls have been taught in such a way as to be unable to scrutinize the practices with which they have grown up.' (Cass Sunstein, 'Should Sex Equality Apply to Religious Institutions?', in J. Cohen, M. Howard and M. Nussbaum (eds), *Is Multiculturalism Bad for Women? By Susan Moller Okin* (Princeton, 1999), at 88.)

36 Mary Becker, 'The Politics of Women's Wrongs', *University of Chicago Law Review* (1992), at 477.

37 Stopler (2004), at 516.

of discrimination.[38] At the same time, the role of the state that grants the exemption is merely contributing towards the perpetuation of women inequalities, far from its neutral protector of religious freedoms role. Madhavi Sunder resonates well this reality when she finds:

> Individuals in the modern world increasingly demand change within their religious communities in order to bring their faith in line with democratic norms and practices. Call this New Enlightenment: Today, individuals seek reason, equality and liberty not just in the public sphere, but also in the private spheres of religion, culture and family.[39]

The reconciliation or re-alignment between religious norms and international human rights principles is nevertheless not impossible: it presupposes the acceptance by legal decision-makers that religion is fluid, evolving and 'an ever-shifting, subjective construct'.[40] It also involves reflection on what is and what is not a fundamental requirement for each religion.[41] This latter process is of course connected inherently with the recognition of the diversity of religious views within each faith, otherwise religious 'orthodoxy' will inevitably claim religious authority for each rule and practice it abides to. This acceptance will ultimately empower women to bring religious norms in line with their needs and their rights. This process will be impossible without the active participation of the groups mostly affected and in need of a 'voice' when claiming their rights. The role of the state is limited to providing the frame for such empowerment, in the direction of Rawls' 'overlapping consensus'.

The Swiss dimension of the debate

Switzerland is not a religiously homogeneous country: it includes the major Christian confessions, Jewish communities, the Muslim communities, the free churches but also religious groups such as the Seventh Day Adventist Church, the Salvation Army, Jehovah's Witnesses and atheists as well.[42] The conflict between religious discriminatory practices and gender equality is not therefore new.

One of the recurring issues remains strict role stereotyping within the conservative faith communities which results in sex discrimination. Whether it concerns employment (e.g. appointment of priests) or education (e.g. dispensation from swimming classes), the question of the role of the state is posed. It is clear that all discriminatory practices do not carry the same weight: a distinction can be made between grave violations of human rights such as child marriage, forced marriage

38 Ibid., at 518.

39 Madhavi Sunder, 'Piercing the Veil', *Yale Law Journal*, Vol. 112 (2003), 1399–1472, at 1403.

40 Ibid., at 1424.

41 Dustin (2012), at 30.

42 Swiss Confederation, Federal Commission for Women's Issues (FCWI), Gender Equality and Cultural/Religious Practices – A position paper, June 2010, at 3.

or acts of violence (FGM, 'honour' killings) with moral customs (e.g. wearing of headscarves, chadors or wigs).[43] The latter constitute a case where the state is called to balance the individual's right with society's interests.

The constitutional role of the state, however, is broadly the same: to protect women from practices that are irreconcilable with the basic values of the Swiss constitution. On the ground, for instance, Swiss cantons tend to take a tolerant and pragmatic line with regard to religious clothing and symbols in education, which is more restricted for teachers that are bound to confessional neutrality. In the opposite direction, the position in Switzerland on class dispensations is harder in that the dispensations at issue are not considered conducive to integration efforts.[44] More ambiguous remains the role of the state as soon as religion becomes 'privatized' and enters the realm of one's private sphere, with the obvious exception applying to serious human rights violations mentioned previously.

Collective religious freedom leads to legal pluralism

Legal pluralism is a situation whereby several systems of regulation exist side by side. Whereto a strong collective religious freedom may lead to religious rules serving the function of law, even in states that have robust separation of church and state regimes. This can be seen in the following examples that Elham Manea recalls in her book cited above: a German female judge that dismissed an accelerated divorce case of a German female of Moroccan descent from her violent Moroccan husband, on the following grounds: the woman should be aware 'that her husband who grew up in a country influenced by Islamic tradition would exercise the right "to use corporal punishment" which his religion concedes. In other words, if her religion is Muslim then it is perfectly in order for her husband to beat her'.[45]

The second example refers to a similar view that was upheld by the legal authority of St. Gallen in Switzerland who refused an extension of a residence permit. The female applicant had, after brief matrimony, divorced her validly resident Muslim husband. She argued that she had been treated as a housemaid or a slave within the marriage. It was countered that the adverse effects she had suffered corresponded to the social norm in a marriage conducted on traditional Muslim principles.[46]

The Swiss Federal Supreme Court sanctioned her appeal. It returned the case to the administrative tribunal of St. Gallen for reappraisal. According to the Federal Supreme Court, it was necessary to clarify with greater precision whether the failure of the marriage was due to the aggrieved party being forced

43 Ibid., at 4–5.

44 The Swiss Federal Supreme Court has also ruled in this direction in 2008 (BGE 135/ 79). These decisions should be read in conjunction with Article 8 of the Swiss Federal Constitution that places the responsibility for promoting equality in education and training in the hands of the state.

45 Manea (2009), 19.

46 Cf. decision of the Swiss Bundesgericht 2C_821/2011 of 22.06.2012.

into the role of a 'slave', constantly against her will, under a patriarchal behavioural role which she refuted.[47]

Does collective religious freedom authorize a female member of a religious community to be beaten by her husband? Are there no universal legal values? Or does collective religious freedom open up areas of absence of equal footing? This effectively exempts some religious groups from adhering to human rights laws that the state has obliged itself to ensure. In the second example, above, the Swiss Federal Court did not accept the arguments of the St. Gallen legal authority. Therefore, the Court rejected any suggestion of parallel legal normativities precisely because they represented an attempt to reduce the right to equality that would lead to a result of a woman being forced to be a virtual slave.

By means of collective religious freedom, legal pluralism can and is systematically advocated. At the solemn opening in Emmenbrücke of the largest mosque in German-speaking Switzerland, in my capacity as a religious-constitutional lawyer, I was invited by an Imam to deliver a word of introduction. After the first meeting, representatives of Islam in Switzerland demanded that special religious courts be set up even in Switzerland in the name of collective religious freedom. What would this legal pluralism here signify?

By allowing religious groups to enforce their own rules that might conflict with state law, legal pluralism could allow religious communities, to a large degree, to supersede state law. This can lead to considerable injustice, for example in the law of inter-religious marriages and in the law of succession. Ultimately, it leads to the practical abolition of individual religious freedom, which is reduced to the practice of *forum internum*.[48]

How aspects of this internal community system of justice might be actually realized, even in liberal Switzerland, was the subject of a debate at the University of Zurich.[49] All of the women who opposed such discrimination at the debate, dissidents of Islam such as Ayaan Hirsi Ali, Taslima Nasrin, Irshad Manji, Necla Kelek or Seyran Ates, did so in the name of multiculturalism: 'Their passionate defence of self-determining lifestyle [of women], of the freedom of the individual as against a religious domesticated collective, demands . . . our support . . . or else, by whom should self-reflection and reform in Islam be activated other than by these courageous dissidents?'[50] This argument can also apply to other religious communities.

47 Ibid.

48 Cf. Marcel Stüssi, *Models of Religious Freedom: Switzerland, the United States and Syria by Analytical, Methodological and Eclectic Representation* (Münster, 2012), 337–380.

49 How aspects of this internal community system could be played out, even in liberal Switzerland, was the subject of a debate at the University of Zurich. (Religiös-kulturelle Varianz des Familien- und Erbrechts? Tagung für Juristinnen und Juristen, für Vertreterinnen und Vertreter von Behörden und Religionsgemeinschaften und für interessierte Privatpersonen, veranstaltet von: University of Zurich, Center for Islamic and Middle Eastern Legal Studies; Schweizer Institut für Rechtsvergleichung und Institut für Religionsrecht der Universität Freiburg, 21 May 2011).

50 Ulrike Ackermann, 'Lob der Dissidenz', in Thierry Chervel and Anja Seeliger (eds*), Islam in Europa. Eine internationale Debatte* (Frankfurt, 2007), 140–146, 145.

The approach of Elham Manea refutes all forms of cultural relativism that limit the human rights of Muslim women. For example, she mentions the legal request of the former Canadian Attorney General, Marion Boyd, to set up voluntary religious arbitration instances for Muslim women on the grounds of the Arbitration Act.[51] It took the outcry of the Canadian Council of Muslim Women to impede this. At a time 'when the supporters for women's rights in Arabic countries are starting campaigns to alter [religious] family laws . . . the Canadian government enacted of its own free will to endorse a religiously biased jurisdiction'.[52] In addition to the actions of the Canadian Council of Muslim Women, international protest forced the Canadian government to retract its proposal limiting human rights.

Pluralism in society

The philosophy of the Enlightenment developed concepts of tolerance and religious freedom in the face of 'civil strife provoked by beliefs' during the wars of religion.[53] It formulated concepts of a multi-religious society with the same civil rights for adherents to a minority religion.[54] The Jewish philosopher Mendelssohn abandoned the concept of 'Church and State'[55] or rather 'State and Religion'[56] by asking 'To whom should we consign the problems and concerns of eternal life? To the Church or to the State?'[57] Mendelssohn, the proponent of Enlightenment, rejected both and developed a third instance, seeing that both Church and state 'seldom tolerate each other in a different way to a third moral entity, the freedom of conscience, which knows how to draw several advantages from their disunity'.[58]

Among all the early colonies of the United States of America, it was Maryland alone that established no official church.[59] The proposers wished to declare Christianity as the 'established religion' of the state.[60] Christianity was thereby projected to become the state religion of the United States. At the beginning of

51 The wider debate concerned proposals for possible modifications of the Ontario Arbitration Act 1991 on alternative dispute resolution. In her report *Protecting Choice Promoting Inclusion*, released in December 2004, Marion Boyd, former attorney-general of Ontario, included the maintenance of the possibility for the Muslim community to use religious arbitrators and apply sharia law to solve disputes (section 32(1) of the Act). In September 2009, the Ontario government announced that it did not plan to follow Boyd's recommendations.

52 Manea (2009), 35.

53 Hermann Lübbe, *Politik der Aufklärung: Philosophische Ausätze* (München, 2001), 40.

54 Moses Mendelssohn, *Jerusalem oder über die religiöse Macht und Judentum* (Hamburg, 2005).

55 Ibid., 29.

56 Ibid., 33.

57 Ibid., 38.

58 Ibid., 33.

59 Cf. Patricia U. Bonomi, *Under the Cope of Heaven: Religion, Society, and Politics in Colonial America* (Oxford, 2003).

60 Cf. Stüssi (2012), 79–93.

US constitutional history, James Madison,[61] Thomas Jefferson[62] and the Berlin philosopher Moses Mendelssohn,[63] however, had opted not to recognize any state religion, but only the conscience of the individual – that is to say, religious freedom for all. With the first amendment of 1797[64] barring any form of state religion, a new epoch of religious constitutional law started in the United States. Religious freedom of the individual, as Mendelssohn had demanded, found its place in a constitution. It was in fact constitutional texts of the state that paved the way for religious tolerance – and not the ecumenical discussions among Christian denominations which begun faint-heartedly only in the twentieth century.

Since then, religious citizens in a liberal democracy have had to come to terms with the secular principles of a constitutional state, also including those basic principles which prescribe a separation of state and religion, or religious freedom as the case may be. Therefore, individuals must integrate these principles within the understandings of their faith.

In Western societies that arise from the basic idea of individual self-determination as widely as possible, the consequence of freedom leads to a multiplicity of religious opinions. From the point of view of the liberal state, according to John Rawls, only those religious communities merit the title 'equitable', which, from their own insight, reject any assertion of their religious truths by force, as well as any militant moral constraint exercised over their own members.[65] Without the stimulus of reflection, religious communities in modern societies unfold destructive capacities. The terminological difference between 'equitable' and 'non-equitable' pluralism must be applied to the question of withdrawal of membership. As far as the Swiss legal order, the *ordre public*, is concerned, legal adjudication and legislation which do not protect an individual's right to membership withdrawal, for example Muslim women, even within the framework of 'equitable pluralism', can no longer be accepted.[66]

If we stay with Rawls' terminology, we must also address the question of the cohesion of a Swiss multi-religious society, to which the response ran for centuries in terms of '*cuius regio, eius religio*'.[67]

61 Madison believed this approach was required in order to protect the church from the state. Cf. ibid., 88–96.

62 To Jefferson's mind, religious tolerance was best achieved by 'building a wall of separation between Church and State', ibid.

63 Samuel Feiner, *Moses Mendelssohn: Ein jüdischer Denker in der Zeit der Aufklärung* (Göttingen, 2009), 167.

64 'Congress shall make no law respecting an establishment of religion, nor prohibiting the free exercise thereof', Stüssi (2012), 92.

65 Cf. John Rawls, *Political Liberalism* (New York, 1998), 132–141.

66 Cf. Georg Kohler, 'Vernünftiger Pluralismus – Der liberale Staat als Hüter der Religionsfreiheit', in Bernhard Ehrenzeller, Peter Gomez, Constance Grewe, Andreas Kley, Markus Kotzur, Kerstin Odendahl, Benjamin Schindler and Daniel Thürer (eds), *Religionsfreiheit im Verfassungsstaat. Zweites Kolloquium der Peter Häberle-Stiftung an der Universität St. Gallen* (Zürich, 2011), 69–88 and Discussion on pp. 89–100.

67 Martin Heckel, 'Der Augsburger Religionsfriede', in Joachim Gaertner and Erika Godel (eds), *Religionsfreiheit und Frieden: Vom Augsburger Religionsfrieden zum europäischen Verfassungsvertrag* (Frankfurt, 2007), 13–33, 14.

> How can a stable and just society, consisting of free and equal citizens, permanently exist if the latter are drastically separated from each other by their 'equitable' religious, philosophical and moral teachings? . . . The question should be put more specifically as follows: how can those who advocate teachings based on religious authority, for instance, the Church or the Bible or the Koran, hold an equitable political conception destined to sustain a lawful democratic order as well?[68]

That Muslims, Protestants, Catholics, non-religious persons and religious fundamentalists all attempt living peacefully together in a pluralistic society is a challenge. Believers of different faiths and branches of atheism in a pluralistic society must adapt to the premises of the constitutional state founded on a morality which is secular.[69] In this, the creative transformation of basic rights in religious societies becomes an important theme for discussion.[70] In 1975, the World Council of Churches in Nairobi declared:

> Religious freedom is and remains a primary concern of the members of the WCC . . . This right cannot be separated from other basic rights of freedom of human beings. No religious community may claim religious freedom for itself without respecting and protecting the religious convictions and basic human rights of others.[71]

The basic rights of religious freedoms require that religious and ideological conflicts do not disrupt societies, which have in the meanwhile become pluralistic. These rights provide the religious communities within the constitutional state with an institutional framework for the solution of their own conflicts.

Conflict within the religious community and its theoretical interpretations

From the analysis so far, the following principal question arises: how can conflicts between a member and his or her religious community be solved? For as far as the constitutional state is concerned the propagation of heretical teaching[72] leads to no infringement of the law.

In part, religious communities form great worldwide organizations and are employers within large educational establishments. In addition, for believers, they

68 Rawls (1998), 35.

69 Cf. Jürgen Habermas, *Glauben und Wissen, Friedenspreis des Deutschen Buchhandels* (Frankfurt, 2001), 14.

70 Cf. Adrian Loretan, *Religionen im Kontext der Menschenrechte*. Religionsrechtliche Studien, Teil 1 (Zürich, 2010).

71 Hanfried Krüger and Walter Müller-Römheld (eds), *Bericht aus Nairobi 1975: Ergebnisse – Erlebnisse – Ereignisse* (Frankfurt, 1975), at 80.

72 A basic definition of heresy is adherence to a religious opinion contrary to church dogma.

represent an emotional and cultural homeland that cannot easily be abandoned without severing ties of family and friendship. Thus the question stands: how can conflicts between the individual and the religious community be solved within the community itself? What role does the state play? Does the collective freedom of religion, guaranteed by the state, partially override other basic rights of a constitution in the field of religion? Do human rights also apply to religious groups?[73] What is the relationship between collective religious freedom and the other basic rights of a constitution?[74] How does the state, for example, react to 'the many faces of Islam'[75] and to those representatives who repudiate a secular constitutional state?[76] What is the relationship between religious freedom and equality of treatment?

The communitarian approach

Communitarianism advocates the wish to justify collective rights as being independent from the rights of individual members of the group. The importance of the group for the individual allows basic rights of the members concerned to be curtailed. This results in 'a potential for suppression within the group',[77] as shown by the texts of Charles Taylor[78] and Michael Walzer. Walzer is prepared to tolerate internal suppression as long as the choice to be affiliated with the religious group remains free of constraint. In the case of encroachment, as for example in forms of discrimination based on gender, except in the case of women subjected to certain practices, he argues for letting tolerance prevail.[79] In this approach, the barring of women from offices in various churches, or the inequality between men and women in the understanding of marriage within certain religious communities, can be justified. In the private sphere, the full enforcement of effective equality between man and woman, according to Walzer, proves to be a problematic instrument leading to the disintegration of traditional and pre-modern cultures. State and social majorities therefore must forego the implementation of gender equality as far as members of a religious group are concerned, resulting in the limitation of basic rights.

It is recognized that, up to a certain point, intolerant attitudes are accepted, because cultural traditions and religious groups that subsist on such attitudes have an intrinsic and collective cultural value worthy of legal protection. Such an approach, according to Walter Kälin, is 'more equitable to the peace-promoting role of state

73 Cf. Loretan (2010).

74 Cf. Loretan (2011).

75 Manea (2009), 80–95.

76 Cf. Beat Stauffer, 'Kräftemessen oder Kollusion? Das undurchsichtige Verhältnis zwischen gemässigten und radikalen Islamisten in Tunesien', *Neue Zürcher Zeitung*, 20 July 2012, 41.

77 Jürgen Habermas, 'Kulturelle Gleichbehandlung – und die Grenzen des postmodernen Liberalismus', *Deutsche Zeitschrift für Philosophie* 51 (2003), 367–394, 388.

78 Cf. Charles Taylor, *Multikulturalismus und die Politik der Anerkennung* (Frankfurt a.M., 1993), 52.

79 Cf. Michael Walzer, *On Toleration* (New Haven/London, 1997), 62ff.

neutrality, since state intervention within the internal structures of closed groups and communities fosters conflict'.[80] This attitude, according to Kälin, is more realistic and more easily reconciled with the precepts of traditional basic law than with the liberal and feminist approaches that are portrayed below. In other words, it is completely acceptable in jurisprudence to overrule gender equality in order to favour religious freedom. Whoever demands true equality should apparently have no religious adherences: for he or she would either have to quit his or her religious community or face discrimination. For some jurists, to associate gender equality with religious freedom is either difficult or impossible.

The feminist approach

Women judge discriminating cultural and religious groups differently.[81] They assert that the reticence of the state towards group-internal discrimination denotes, in fact, partiality towards the discriminating party. Reticence on the part of the state and on the part of the society of the majority towards group-internal discrimination can result in the surrender of women to social pressures and intrinsic repression. The state may not remain neutral simply because traditional pre-modern privileges and discrimination cannot otherwise be put aside. The state must intervene in the private sphere if it genuinely aims to implement basic rights.[82] In that respect, it is worth questioning the role played by the courts of law with regard to the enforcement and implementation of the principle of equality. However, in relation to religious freedom, some jurists resist the fact that within religious communities, collective religious freedom should overrule other basic rights such as gender equality – or at least severely reduce such rights.[83]

The liberal approach

In the liberal interpretation the question on how to resolve the clash of rights between freedom of rights and equality is posed in different terms: which interest is to take preference, the protection of group autonomy or the protection of its members' freedom towards self-determination?

Will Kymlicka takes up the communitarian criticism of liberalism. He associates individual autonomy with the protection of cultural group identity. To

80 Walter Kälin, *Grundrechte im Kulturkonflikt. Freiheit und Gleichheit in der Einwanderungsgesellschaft* (Zürich, 2000), 47.

81 Cf. Denise Buser and Adrian Loretan (eds), *Gleichstellung der Geschlechter und die Kirchen. Ein Beitrag zur menschenrechtlichen und ökumenischen Diskussion* (Freiburg, 1999); Stella Ahlers, *Gleichstellung der Frau in Staat und Kirche. Ein problematisches Spannungsverhältnis* (Münster, 2005).

82 Cf. Susan Moller Onkin, *Justice, Gender and Family* (New York, 1989), 116f.

83 Cf. Felix Hafner and Denise Buser, 'Frauenordination via Gleichstellungsgesetz? Die Anwendbarkeit des Gleichstellungsgesetzes auf die Dienstverhältnisse in der römisch-katholischen Kirche', *Aktuelle juristische Praxis* 10 (1996), 1207–1214, 1207.

understand the teachings of one's own religion and culture (the study of texts) is a prerequisite for being able to take expedient decisions for leading our lives. Cultures are not valuable in themselves, but only because it is through cultural experience that human beings have access to different options. According to Kymlicka, cultures need to be protected in the interest of individual autonomy; and because of this, Kymlicka differentiates between justifiable and unjustifiable group rights. Armed with the former, a religious organization can defend its social environment against outside pressures. On the other hand, such group rights become problematic when attempts are made within a religious community, on the basis of these rights, to clamp down on discriminated members who have suggested changes to the established community way of life.

Group rights as derivative rights

Jürgen Habermas sees acknowledging rigid cultural group rights as a threat to democracy.[84] What seems above all to be dangerous for democracy is the acknowledgement of groups with strong fundamentalist tendencies. Group rights are only justifiable, in accordance with the liberal tradition, if they are understood to be derivative rights in the sense of a deflection from the cultural rights of individual group members. In pluralistic societies, religious groups can only transmit their heritage from one generation to the next if their members agree to. It is not through the state's granting of group rights that the survival of churches and religious communities can be guaranteed. The transmission of heritage should be envisaged in such a way that the members of a society protected by law also be convinced that the tradition is worth carrying on. It is possible that the question becomes whether the right to self-determination is the proper means for protecting diversity and non-culturization and transformation of a culture of human rights within religions frameworks. Is it also a question of a state-imposed, 'religious National Trust' for which the state, neutral in religious affairs, has no legal mandate? In other words, ought the state, neutral in religious affairs, protect religious communities from the demands of their members? In that case, one may, of course, question the limits of a state's neutrality vis-à-vis religion, in itself is an old and much debated issue, which is presented nevertheless under light if one takes account of the issue of the limits of culture and cultural rights. The intervention of the state would not be without complications in both administrative, constitutional as well as religious terms.

Conclusion

It seems at present that *either* religious freedom *or* gender equality are the alternatives in the minds of certain supporters of the communitarian idea and of certain courts of law. This, however, is a rather mono-dimensional representation of the

84 Cf. Jürgen Habermas, 'Kulturelle Gleichbehandlung – und die Grenzen des Postmodernen Liberalismus', *Deutsche Zeitschrift für Philosophie* 51 (2003), 3, 367–394, 390: 'Staat im Staate'.

question: it leaves out the (useful) discussion of the cultural settings in which the debate of universalism as opposed to relativism takes places. This is clearly not to suggest that the two fundamental rights are incompatible but rather that they have to be placed into context.

Those who wish to combine religious freedom *together with* gender equality have set themselves a very high goal to be attained. They have in front of them a challenging task to perform. One possibility is for the state to intervene in promoting human rights within religious groups. Another option would be to empower religious communities to address those issues internally to the groups concerned. This latter option is further away from the scope of strict legal regulation. It would enhance nevertheless the notion of human agency, within a more actor-oriented approach. The attractive point in it lies in its connection with actual practice of the religion.[85]

Human dignity, as a value, prominently recognized in national and international human rights law, provides a helpful starting point in this quest. As already mentioned, article 1 of the Universal Declaration of Human Rights reflects the recognition of one's agency in deciding their path of life.[86] In turn, this signifies that the protection of human dignity will involve two components: first, the respect for everyone's humanity and, second, the corresponding duty towards the creation of conditions for everyone's self-realization.[87] At the very least, however, it provides firmer ground for the serious consideration of the rights of more vulnerable segments of society, in particular women that refuse to choose between religious rights and equality.

85 Preis (1996), at 311.

86 The widespread character of the value has even reached the work of international organizations that have a primarily economic character (cf. Article 2 of the Treaty of the EU that states: the EU 'is founded on the values of respect for human dignity, freedom, democracy, equality, the rule of law and respect for human rights').

87 Andrew Clapham, *Human Rights in the Private Sphere* (Oxford, 1993), at 148–149.

10 Polygyny in Sub-Saharan Africa

A practice that empowers or disempowers women?

Lauren Fielder

Polygyny in Africa is an interesting area to study the dual empowering and disempowering effects of religion on women. Polygyny's historical context across several religions shows that the practice has an important role in providing social security, social cohesion and social benefits. This was the case in Sub-Saharan Africa, where polygyny has both religious and cultural roots. Religion and culture have become intertwined in African society, and have worked in conjunction to entrench the practice of polygyny across the continent. While the practice of polygyny continues to serve some of the original social functions that empowered women, however, polygyny in modern Africa also has the effect of disempowering women.

This chapter will discuss the historical evolution of polygyny in Africa, including its religious origins, then explore the living realities of women living in polygynous marriages to analyze whether polygyny currently empowers or disempowers women. Next, the chapter will briefly consider how polygyny is situated in the multi-layered legal framework in African law and explore the role constitutional courts have in the question of whether the practice of polygyny should continue lawfully in Africa. Finally, the chapter will conclude with observations that polygyny disempowers women in Africa and should be eliminated. This part will also discuss the role that religious groups may play in the process of legal change, toward the empowerment of African women.

Overview of polygyny in Africa

Polygamy is a form of marriage where there are more than two parties. There are two types—polygyny, where there is more than one wife; and polyandry, where there is more than one husband.[1] Polygyny is prevalent and polyandry is extremely rare.[2] The terms "polygamy" and "polygyny" are frequently used

1 Jonas "The practice of polygamy under the scheme of the Protocol to the African Charter on Human and Peoples' Rights on the Rights of Women in Africa: A critical appraisal" (2012) 4(5) *J of African Studies & Development* 142 at 142.

2 Ibid. See also Zeitzen *Polygamy: A Cross-Cultural Analysis* (Kindle ed. 2008) loc 252.

interchangeably, with "polygamy" being the more common, but less accurate term for a marriage between one man and more than one woman.[3] While some forms of relationships are similar to polygyny, such as affairs and concubinage, we can draw a distinction between these polygamous-like practices and polygyny, itself. Polygamy is a situation where all the parties intend to be a single matrimonial or family entity, whereby polygamous practices occur without the intent to be one family unit.[4]

Polygyny is an ancient practice found in many religious traditions, including Judaism, Islam, and Christianity.[5] It is currently practised in over 850 societies in the world, many in Africa.[6] It was common for kings in pre-colonial Africa to have many wives to show their high position.[7] Historically, polygyny was a sign of prosperity.[8] Now polygyny continues to be a common practice in Africa and spans the whole range of classes.[9] Some estimates place the percentage of polygamists across the continent at between 20 to 30 percent of men.[10] Its numbers are increasing in some parts of Africa rather than declining.[11] It is especially robust in African states with high Muslim populations.[12] For example, in Senegal, where 94 percent of the population is Muslim,[13] half of all women are in a polygamous relationship.[14] However, polygyny is no longer tied exclusively to religion, and is now part of African culture and customary law.[15]

3 Jonas (n 1) 142. See also Shepard et al. "Perpetuating polygamist tradition: An exploratory qualitative study of Senegalese women" (2010) 3(1) *J of Global Social Work Practice* 1 at 2, available at www.globalsocialwork.org/vol3no1/Shepard.html; Shepard, "The impact of polygamy on women's mental health: A systematic review" (2013) 22(1) *Epidemiol Psychiatr Sci.* 47, 47. (2013). While this chapter will use the term "polygyny," some quotes use the term "polygamy."

4 Law Reform Commission of Canada, "Bigamy" Working Paper No. 42 (Ottawa: Law Reform Commission of Canada, 1985). Polygyny offers a formal marriage. Zeitzen (n 2) loc 350.

5 Zeitzen (n 2) loc 350

6 Shepard et al. (n 3) 2. *See also* Zeitzen (n 2) loc 82. Africa is the region with the most polygyny. Zeitzen (n 2) loc 91.

7 Jonas (n 1) 143.

8 Ibid.

9 Zeitzen (n 2) loc 91.

10 Jonas (n 1) 143 (citing research by Welch & Glick, "The incidence of polygamy in contemporary Africa: A research note" (1981) 43(1) *J. of Marriage & the Family* 191, 192).

11 Zeitzen (n 2) 197.

12 Shepard et al. (n 3) at 3.

13 Ibid.

14 "Senegal – polygamy" in *Marriage and Family Encyclopedia*, available at http://family.jrank.org/pages/1482/Senegal-Polygamy.html. Togo is another heavily polygamous state, with over 50 percent of married women participating in polygyny. Cook "Polygyny: Did the Africans get it right?" (2007) *J of Black Studies* 1 at 6. In Tanzania, about 28 percent of married women are in polygynous marriages. Meekers & Franklin "Women's perceptions of polygyny among the Kaguru of Tanzania" (1995) 34(4) *Ethnology* 315 at 318.

15 Zeitzen (n 2) loc 153.

Polygyny in African religion and culture

Polygyny is a practice that is central to some religions and many African cultures/states. As seen above in the discussion of the prevalence of polygyny, this part of custom and the customary law that regulates it has a huge impact on African women. It is important to further explore how polygyny fits into this culture and take a close look at a number of indicators across disciplines to see what a woman's lived reality is under polygyny.

Why is polygyny such an integral part of many African cultures? First, polygyny has ties to religion. In the African context, Islam is especially important. As mentioned earlier, heavily Islamic areas have higher links to polygyny.[16] Islam's growth in Africa contributes to polygyny's staying power.[17] Of course, the connection between Islam and polygyny is not automatic, and different religious groups within Islam interpret the issue of polygyny differently.[18] Historically, polygyny among Muslims was permissive, rather than imperative, and served a protective function for women.[19] It was created in a spirit of compassion for widows and orphans and put parameters around the practice that was already in existence in seventh-century Saudi Arabia.[20] The Quranic text permits polygyny as follows:

> If ye fear that ye shall not
> Be able to deal justly
> With the orphans,
> Marry women of your choice,
> Two, or three, or four;
> But if ye fear that ye shall not
> Be able to deal justly (with them),
> Then only one, or (a captive)
> That your right hands possess.
> That will be more suitable,
> To prevent you
> From doing injustice.[21]

16 Islamic family law includes "marriage, divorce, polygyny, custody, guardianship, and inheritance." Amien "Overcoming the conflict between the right to freedom of religion and women's right to equality: A South African case study of Muslim marriages" (2006) 28 *Human Rights Q* 729 at 731.

17 Amien (n 16) 730. A Pew report on the future of the Muslim population showed that the Muslim population is projected to grow by nearly 60 percent from 2010 to 2030 in sub-Saharan Africa (from 242.5 million to 385.9 million). "The future of the global Muslim population: Projections for 2010–2013" 2011 *Pew Forum on Religion & Public Life*, available at www.pewforum.org/Global-Muslim-Population.aspx.

18 Pearl & Menski *Muslim Family Law* 3 ed (1998) 237, and Ssenyonjo "Women's rights to equality and non-discrimination: Discriminatory family legislation in Uganda and the role of Uganda's constitutional court" (2007) 21 *Int'l J.L. Pol'y & Fam.* 341 at 350.

19 Ssenyonjo (n 18) 350.

20 Ibid.

21 Pearl & Menski (n 18) 238. *See also* Ssenyonjo (n 18) 350.

Polygyny that meets this standard of justice is practically impossible.[22] In other places, such as Uganda, "justice" is interpreted more loosely, allowing men to practice polygyny more easily.[23]

Polygyny's entrenchment in African culture is not limited to Islamic groups. In Africa under colonization, some colonizers (and the Apartheid government in South Africa) refused to recognize non-monogamous marriages because they were seen as uncivilized.[24] This refusal created great hardships for women, who were in polygynous relationships that had no legal recognition, and ignored the cultural importance of polygyny to Africans.[25] Therefore, post-colonial Africans have embraced polygyny as part of African culture that was suppressed by oppressors.[26] To some, this makes the practice "automatically desirable."[27]

Another way to understand this connection is to look at the role of the family and the purpose of marriage in African culture. Africans value the collective good of the group (community, clan, family) in addition to, and sometimes higher than, the value of the individual.[28] Therefore, marriage serves many functions for the good of the group, such as good and peaceful group relations, and social security.[29] Polygyny may serve to consolidate families and stabilize society, ensuring the stability and continuation of the family and clan;[30] sometimes even the very survival of the group.[31] Polygyny also increases fertility in a family,[32] creating a stable or growing population size,[33] and allows a man to have a large family very quickly.[34]

For men who have unequal power in many African cultures, this increase in fertility equates to power and prestige, both real and perceived.[35] Large families

22 Ssenyonjo (n 18) 350 (stating that the Quran explains: "You will never be able to do perfect justice between wives even if it is your ardent desire." This is the interpretation taken by Tunisian Code of Personal Status (1956)); Pearl & Menski (n 18) 242.

23 Ssenyonjo (n 18) 351.

24 Amien (n 16) 733. Another approach was for governments to tax polygynous families. Armstrong et al. "Uncovering reality: Excavating women's rights in African family law" (1993) 7 *Int'l J. of L. & Fam.* 314 at 335.

25 Amien (n 16) 736.

26 Armstrong et al. (n 24) 333. See also Dlamini "The role of customary law in meeting social needs" (1991) *Acta Juridica* 71 at 75; and Cook (n 14)

27 Armstrong et al. (n 24) 333.

28 Fielder "African courts and African values: Harmonizing international human rights and customary law" in Topidi & Fielder (eds) *Transnational Legal Processes and Human Rights* (2013) 177 at 187.

29 Ibid.

30 Jonas (n 1) 143. In pre-colonial Africa, a king would marry women from as many families as possible to avoid conflicts. Ibid.

31 Cook (n 14) 4 (explaining that on the macro level, polygyny is an adaptive cultural practice).

32 Al-Krenawi & Graham "A comparison of family function, life and marital satisfaction, and mental health of women in polygamous and monogamous marriages" (2006) 52 *Int. J. Soc. Psychiatry* 5 at 6.

33 Cook (n 14) 6.

34 Jonas (n 1) 143. Studies show that polygamous men have more children on average than monogamously married men. Cook (n 14) 7. See also Gould et al "The mystery of monogamy" (2008) 98 *American Economic R* 333 at 333.

35 Gould et al. (n 34) 331.

can produce wealth in agriculturally based societies,[36] because women and children are inexpensive labour.[37] Historically, men were allocated land when they acquired a new wife, so in addition to having a wife as a worker, the man acquired the land necessary to support the larger family.[38] In addition to the actual wealth producing capacity of a polygamous family, polygyny itself is and/or becomes a sign of wealth,[39] so men with more than one wife are perceived to be more prosperous.

The social security function of polygyny provides benefits for families and women within those families. As a result, some women in Africa have a positive attitude toward polygyny.[40] Having co-wives can be cooperative in addition to being competitive.[41] In a society with heavy demands on women to care for the household and family, a shared workload may be welcome.[42] Women also may see the benefit of having the companionship that comes with polygyny, which can foster a sense of solidarity between women.[43] This is especially true where the husband/wife relationship is a difficult one. Where a wife is not happy with her husband, polygyny can be a way to share the misery with another person.[44] Where sexuality is viewed as a burden, an additional wife can be a relief.[45] Therefore, where a husband is not valued highly, polygyny may be an alternative to divorce.[46]

Because of the high priority African culture places on marriage and children, women in some parts of Africa face tremendous pressure to marry and bear children.[47] Polygyny gives most women this opportunity.[48] For many women in

36 Jonas (n 1) 143. This is magnified when women are competing for their husbands' favor. One way the women are forced to compete is through their economic production. Ibid. *See also* Maillu *Our Kind of Polygamy* (1988) 14.

37 Cook (n 14) 8. This works in urban areas, as well, providing a man who owns multiple shops free labor in more than one business. Armstrong et al. (n 24) 335.

38 Armstrong et al. (n 24) 333.

39 Cook (n 14) 8. However, a study of Nigerian students showed that "there is the feeling that monogamy is a more prestigious and socially approved form of union." Nevadomsky "Attitudes of Nigerian students toward marriage and family relationships" (1991) 21(2) *Int'l J. of Soc. of the Fam.* 201, 207. This perception of wealth comes from the way that polygyny worked in historically, where a man paid bridewealth for each of his wives, so he had to be prosperous to have more than one wife. Armstrong et al. (n 24) 334 (explaining that polygyny allowed men "ultimately to become an ancestor to a larger clan of people").

40 Shepard et al. (n 3) 3.

41 Koktvedgaard Zeitzen (n 2) loc 2694.

42 Al-Krenawi & Graham (n 32) 6.

43 Honig 'My Culture Made Me Do It' in (Okin ed., 1999) *Is Multiculturalism Bad for Women* 35, 38.

44 Meekers & Franklin (n 14) 321 ("Polygamy is considered a deprivation or a gain, depending on whether the husband is viewed positively or negatively").

45 While this would be traumatic for many women, again, it may be a positive occurrence for women in an unhappy union. Of course, this brings us back to the harsh reality that in many ways, society has much entrenched inequality, restricting women's ability to make choices about her life, for example, the choice to leave an unhappy marriage or refusing unwanted sexual acts with her husband.

46 Meekers & Franklin (n 14) 321.

47 Most women in Africa marry. Cook (n 14) 3. Further, women in traditional Africa are socialized to marry and have children. Maillu (n 36) 57.

48 Cook (n 14) 8.

Africa, their feeling of dignity is closely tied to their marital status,[49] and the closely related role of child bearer.[50] "[I]n some societies [polygyny may] be the only acceptable way for a women who is keen to have a child to fulfill that wish,"[51] and may explain why women feel that they would rather be a second or later wife than to stay unmarried.[52] The birth of a child is a great event in African cultures, an important assurance that a woman will be taken care of in her old age.[53]

In societies where women are powerless, the social security aspects of polygyny are important. Women are often vulnerable without a man.[54] The ability to join another marriage upon the death of her husband is essential. While polygyny always provides more opportunity for women to wed, one type of polygyny, levirate marriage, directly addresses this problem.[55] In some parts of Africa, it is customary for a widow to be married by one of her deceased's husband's family.[56] One African explains it this way:

> To leave the widow with her children out in the cold is seen as a great lack of love for the family . . . In America and western European countries, and it seems among the so-called modernization Africans, the death of a husband throws his wife out into the cold and insecurity . . . In traditional Africa, loneliness of widows and of children who have lost their father is virtually unknown.[57]

Therefore, in societies where women are unable to take care of themselves without a man, polygyny serves an important social function.

Polygyny and women's lived reality

Despite certain benefits of polygyny and its importance to African culture, polygyny also raises serious concerns for women and children.[58] First and most

49 Jonas (n 1) 143. Polygyny also traditionally conferred status on women when they married a rich man. Armstrong et al. (n 24) 334.

50 This is due in part to the high value Africans place on children. Cook (n 14) 3 (stating that in many African cultures, the attitude is the more children the better.).

51 Banda "Project on a mechanism to address laws that discriminate against women" Commissioned by: Office of the High Commissioner for Human Rights – Women's Rights and Gender Unit, (6 March 2008) 93, available at www.ohchr.org/Documents/Publications/laws_that_discriminate_against_women.pdf. Banda "Protocol to the African Charter on the Rights of Women in Africa" in Evans & Murray (eds) *The African Charter on Human and Peoples' Rights: The System in Practice, 1986–2006* 2 ed (2008) 441 at 450.

52 Banda (n 51) 92.

53 Maillu (n 36) 3.

54 Armstrong et al. (n 24) 334.

55 Jonas (n 1) 143; *see also* Zeitzen (n 2) loc 224.

56 Jonas (n 1) 143.

57 Maillu (n 36) 13.

58 Polygyny also hurts men, since it gives wealthier men the chance to monopolize women, making polygyny "unequal and class-based." Armstrong et al (n 16) 334. See also Henrich et al. "The puzzle of monogamous marriage" (2012) 367 *Phil. Trans. R. Soc. B* 657 at 661, explaining that polygyny leaves men without mates.

obviously, polygyny has an "inherent gender asymmetry," i.e. the relationship is unequal.[59] In fact, issues of power are central to polygyny.[60] Polygyny is also sexually unequal, because a man in a polygamous relationship has the opportunity to have sex much more than the women in the marriage, leading to sexual dissatisfaction by the women.[61] This sexual dissatisfaction can also be explained by the greater average age gap between wives after the first wife and the husband than in monogamous marriages.[62] The end result is that women usually experience negative outcomes in polygynous marriages.[63] Much research on polygyny shows that it is detrimental to women.[64] We can roughly group these harms into three categories: personal, economic, and health.

Personal

Despite some studies that show that polygyny may decrease divorce in some instances,[65] polygyny weakens the bonds of marriage,[66] possibly causing romantic love to fade away.[67] The relationship between husband and wife changes when a new wife is added.[68] Exclusivity in a marriage fortifies family relationships,[69] and adding a new wife is likely to take this away.[70] "The prospect of having to share their husband's sexual, material and emotional attention with other wives . . . deprives women of an exclusive connection to their husband."[71] This is especially problematic for the first wife/husband relationship.[72] Second wives

59 Zeitzen (n 2) loc 179.

60 Zeitzen (n 2) loc 2649.

61 Gage-Brandon "The polygyny–divorce relationship: A case study of Nigeria" (1992) 54(2) *J of Marriage & Family* 285 at 286.

62 Ibid. 286.

63 Sanni *La Polygamie au Bénin: Résistance au Changement ou Diversification des Formes de Conjugalité?* (2010) 5–6.

64 Zeitzen (n 2) loc 2646.

65 For example, when a woman faces infertility and her husband wants a child, he can add a new wife to the family instead of divorcing his first wife. Dlamini "The role of customary law in meeting social needs" (1991) *Acta Juridica* 71 at 77. Pearl and Menski give another example when they ask "[i]s it better to be a discarded and divorced elderly women, or a respected first wife in a polygamous household?" Pearl & Menski (n 18) 241.

66 Meekers & Franklin (n 14) 321–322.

67 Ibid. Romantic love is important to many African women; however, not all societies value romantic love in the same way. Kaganas & Murray "Women and the family: The question of polygyny in a new Africa" (1991) *Acta Juridica* 116 at 116. See also Shepard et al. (n 3) 5.

68 Meekers & Franklin (n 14) 321–322.

69 Cook & Kelly "Polygyny and Canada's obligations under international human rights law" Family, Children and Youth Section, Department of Justice Canada (September 2006) 10.

70 Cook & Kelly explain that this is especially negative where the new wife or wives reside in the same house as the first wife (ibid., 10–11).

71 Ibid., 11. But see Zeitzen (n 2) loc 2676, explaining that sharing a man's sexual attention may not be problematic for every woman.

72 Meekers & Franklin (n 14) 316; for more studies on polygyny and divorce. See also Ross *Women's Human Rights: The International and Comparative Law Casebook* (2008) 552; and Gage-Brandon (n 61) 286, citing Goody "Conjugal separation and divorce among the Gonja of

feel the addition of a wife as a betrayal, as well.[73] Consequently, statistics from studies on polygamous families show more problems in family functioning than in monogamous marriages,[74] and more problems in the marriage relationship.[75]

Jealousy is another problem that appears in polygamous relationships. While some wives cooperate and enjoy each other, polygyny often creates the feeling of competition between co-wives.[76] The situation arises especially where the husband shows favoritism to one wife. Depending on the culture, it could be the first wife, the youngest wife[77] or the wife in the most recent marriage.[78] Polygyny and the ensuing jealousy "can lead to violence, favoritism, competition, and sabotage" within the family.[79] There are numerous studies that highlight jealousy in polygyny.[80] In addition, senior and junior wives may have different experiences and conditions.[81] Jealousy is not restricted to the wives. Children also feel it. There is competition and jealousy among children of different wives that exceeds that of sibling rivalry experienced in monogamous families.[82] Children can become enemies, and experience significant levels of mental distress.[83] The co-wife cannot always show her displeasure to another co-wife and might instead act out these feelings on the children of the co-wife, by reprimanding them or by being aggressive to them.[84]

Women in polygamous marriages often suffer from a loss of dignity.[85] They describe this as feeling incomplete as a woman.[86] The addition of a new wife

northern Ghana" (1962) 2 *Man* 226. A study from Dakar shows polygyny to be a tremendous accelerator for divorce by a first wife when a second wife is added. Antoine & Nanitelamio "Peut-on echapper à la polygamie à Dakar?" (1995) 32 *La Chronique du CEPED* 1 at 17.

73 Gage-Brandon (n 61) 290.

74 Al-Krenawi & Graham (n 32) 10. See also Gould et al. (n 34) 334. Gould et al. also show that well-being decreases when women have to compete for resources. Gould et al. (n 34) 333.

75 Al-Krenawi & Graham (n 32) 10.

76 Cook and Kelly (n 69) 11. See also Ssenyonjo, 'Women's rights to equality and non-discrimination: Discriminatory family legislation in Uganda and the role of Uganda's Constitutional Court' (2007) 21 *Int'l J.L. Pol'y & Fam.* 341 at 351. Bao and Jankowiak explain that conflicts between co-wives are often a result of competition for resources. Bao & Jankowiak "Introduction: Privilege disguises torment" (2008) 47(3) *Ethnology* 137 at 138.

77 Meekers & Franklin (n 14) 321–322.

78 Cook & Kelly (n 69) 12.

79 Shepard et al. (n 3) 5, citing the example of a woman who forcibly removed the ear of a co-wife and another example of a woman who poured boiling water on a co-wife (5–6).

80 Zeitzen (n 2) loc 2739. See for example, Shepard et al. (n 3) 3, citing Ware "Polygyny: Women's views in a transitional society, Nigeria" (1975) 41(1) *J of Marriage & the Family* 185 at 190; and Fainzang & Journet *La Femme de Mon Mari – Anthropologie du Mariage Polygamique en Afrique et en France* (1988) 87, and 92–93.

81 Zeitzen (n 2) loc 2676.

82 Al-Krenawi "Women from polygamous and monogamous marriages in an out-patient psychiatric clinic" (2001) 38(2) *Transcultural Psychiatry* 187 at 195.

83 Shepard et al. (n 3) 5.

84 Fainzang & Journet (n 80) 113.

85 Meekers & Franklin (n 14) 322. Traditionally, a first wife might have acquired status when junior wives were added to the family, but now she might feel "neglected and ignored." Armstrong et al. (n 16) 335. See also Ssenyonjo (n 60) 355.

86 Meekers & Franklin (n 14) 322.

feels degrading,[87] and leads to a decreased perception of personal value.[88] It feels like an act of denigration of the husband to his wife.[89] A senior wife, especially, may feel that a new wife signifies her personal failure.[90] This leads to low self-esteem,[91] less life satisfaction,[92] loneliness,[93] and an extensive array of mental health ailments, as described below. This is especially acute where women do not have their own home, a problem that is growing rapidly with urbanization. Especially in cities, not every wife has her own room; sometimes all the co-wives have to share a room; when it is their turn, they can sleep in the room of their husband.[94] This can create even bigger conflicts between the co-wives, because they do not have their private living space.[95]

How women feel about polygyny can be seen from the very words they use to define it:

> In several societies, the potential for jealously or rivalry is reflected in the terminology used to refer to co-wives. For example, among the Luo (Kenya) a co-wife is called nyieka (my partner in jealousy), the Hausa (Nigeria) use the term kishiya (jealousy) . . . and the Yoruba (Nigeria) word for co-wife is orogun (rival or competitor) . . . Likewise, among the Bakgalagadi of Botswana the term for co-wives, bagadikano, means rivals, and the term for polygyny, lefufa, implies jealousy.[96]

There is a strong correlation between polygyny and gender-based violence,[97] which can come at the hand of the husband or co-wives.[98] A study showed polygyny to be a significant cause of domestic violence in Uganda.[99] Polygyny can also subject

87 Meekers & Franklin (n 14) 322.

88 Moosa et al. "A review of multispousal relationships: Psychosocial effects and therapy" (2006) 12(2) *South African J of Psychiatry* 12 at 12.

89 Mondain et al. "L'évolution de la polygamie en milieu rural sénégalais: Institution en crise ou en mutation?" (2004) 33(2) *Cahiers Québécois de Démographie* 273 at 287.

90 Al-Krenawi & Graham (n 32) 6. Contrast with the situation in traditional African culture, where the first wife was often held in high esteem.

91 Moosa et al. (n 88) 12. Self-esteem is a person's feeling of worth and "the condition in which an individual feels 'good enough'". Al-Krenawi (n 82) 194, quoting Rosenberg *Conceiving the Self* (1979).

92 Al-Krenawi & Graham (n 32) 10.

93 Ibid., 6, and Al-Krenawi (n 82) 196.

94 Fainzang & Journet (n 80) 100.

95 Ibid.

96 Meekers & Franklin (n 14) 316, citing Potash "Gender relations in sub-Saharan Africa" in Morgan (ed.) *Gender and Anthropology: Critical Reviews for Teaching and Research* (1989) 189 at 199; Ware (n 80) 190; and Solway "Affines and spouses, friends and lovers: The passing of polygyny in Botswana" (1990) 46 *J of Anthropological Research* 41 at 48.

97 Banda (n 51) 450; Henrich (n 58) 663. See also Gould et al. (n 34) 331; and Bove & Valeggia "Polygyny and women's health in sub-Saharan Africa" (2009) 68 *Social Science & Medicine* 21 at 22.

98 Al-Krenawi & Graham (n 32) 6; and Sanni (n 63) 5–6, reporting violence between co-wives.

99 Schnier & Hintmann "An analysis of polygyny in Ghana: The perpetuation of gender based inequality in Africa" (2001–2002) 2 *Geo. J. Gender & L.* 795 at 812, citing Law & Advocacy for

children to abuse at the hands of a jealous co-wife or even their own mother, if she is not coping well with polygyny and suffering psychologically.[100]

Polygyny further entrenches patriarchy, which hurts women. It strengthens gender stereotypes, and places women in the reproductive or service roles.[101] Men are seen as superior and women as inferior;[102] men see polygyny as a way to keep women in line. Even when a man is not polygamous, in a society where polygyny is allowed, a man can threaten to take an additional wife in an effort to control his existing wife.[103] This was acknowledged by the UN Special Rapporteur on Violence Against Women, in a 2002 report on cultural practices that were harmful to women.[104] Women in Senegal reported that they felt they could not do anything about additional marriages of their husbands, leading them to believe that polygyny subjugates women. The women in the study felt helpless and subject to men as the definitive decision-makers.[105] Another report found that "[o]verall, the participating women communicated that polygyny can contradict women's liberty and agency, leaving them to feel subjected and helpless."[106]

Economic

While polygyny can be economically advantageous to men, it is usually economically harmful to women. The UN Convention on the Elimination of Discrimination Against Women (CEDAW) committee's General Recommendation 21 from 1994 highlights these economic inequalities.[107] Economic power enhances a husband's dominance.[108] In addition, in a family economy there is only a finite amount of resources that must be divided between women and children.[109] These resources

Women-Uganda (LAW_U) *Research Findings on Domestic Violence in a Study Carried Out in the Districts of Ignaga, Kabale, Kampala and Kitgum* (completed Mar. 1, 2000) 11–12.

100 See, e.g., Henrich et al. (n 58) 658.

101 Cook & Kelly (n 69) 9.

102 Ibid.

103 Ibid., citing an immigrant from Mali: "One wife on her own is trouble. When there are several they are forced to be polite and well behaved. If they misbehave, you threaten that you'll take another wife." Ibid., quoting Okin *Is Multiculturalism Bad for Women?* (1999) 15. Bao and Jankowiak give an example from northern Pakistan: "tension between the couple often results in the husband marrying another woman to embarrass the first wife." Bao & Jankowiak (n 76) 140.

104 Cook & Kelly (n 69) 9, quoting UN Special Rapporteur on Violence Against Women "Cultural practices in the family that are violent towards women" UN ESCOR, 2002, 48th Sess., UN Doc. E/CN.4/2002/83 (2002) para 63.

105 Ibid. See also Bove & Valeggia (n 97) 21.

106 Shepard et al. (n 3) 5.

107 CEDAW General Recommendation 21 "Equality in marriage and family relations" (Thirteenth session, 1992) UN Doc. A/49/38, at 1 (1994).

108 Zeitzen (n 2) loc 2784, and the "*power* within a marriage" (emphasis in the original); Armstrong et al. (n 24) 336.

109 Meekers & Franklin (n 14) 316. See also, Armstrong et al. (n 24) 336.

must be stretched further in a larger family. In some cases, there are simply not enough resources to provide every child with the essential things they need, such as food, medical care, clothing, and school fees.[110] While polygyny may make a family more prosperous because there are more workers, this increased profitability does not make up for the economic hardship it places on women and children. Economic hardship is a recurrent problem in Africa, but polygyny exacerbates this situation, increasing what is known as "the feminization of poverty."[111] Men are often too poor to adequately support large families.[112] Even where a man has money to support a large family, "the money that could be used lavishly to maintain one family is often stretched to provide elementally for two families."[113] Not only is there a division, which makes the shares smaller, the shares themselves are often unequal, because a man may treat wives and children from different wives differently.[114] Women report that they are particularly upset about polygamy's inequality when it comes to reduced social and economic support for their children.[115] The end of a husband's life does not mean the end of inequality for the polygamous family. Laws of succession coupled with polygyny lead to further economic inequality.[116]

Health

The health implications of polygyny for women are overwhelming. These effects can be roughly grouped into two interrelated categories—mental and physical health.

Mental health

CEDAW's General Comment 21 recognizes that polygyny can have "serious emotional . . . consequences" for women and children.[117] As we have seen, family functioning is diminished within polygynous marriages.[118] This is not surprising, where women have to live with jealousies, insecurities, sexual dissatisfaction, decreased feelings of self-worth and dignity, and other negative emotions. The consequence is a higher than normal chance that women will

110 Zeitzen (n 2) loc 2739.

111 Cook & Kelly (n 69) 15. This is especially true where polygyny is associated with patriarchy. Ibid.

112 Meekers & Franklin (n 14) 318.

113 Shepard et al. (n 3) 5; see also Al-Krenawi & Graham (n 32) 6.

114 Meekers & Franklin (n 14) 320.

115 Ibid., 316 and 323. Women are especially upset when their husbands do not provide equally for sick children (323).

116 Under traditional African customary law, men gained land with the addition of wives, creating a system that was more balanced. This is now usually not the case. Armstrong et al. (n 24) 336 to 338.

117 CEDAW General Recommendation 21 (n 107) 564.

118 Shepard (n 3) 47; see also Henrich et al. (n 58) 665.

experience mental illness.[119] Multiple studies across borders and across disciplines have shown the extreme mental effects polygyny has on women.[120] These include somatization,[121] body aches,[122] headaches,[123] chest pains,[124] interpersonal sensitivity,[125] insomnia,[126] fatigue,[127] breathlessness,[128] nervousness,[129] bad thoughts,[130] stress,[131] anxiety,[132] depression,[133] obsession-compulsion,[134] hostility,[135] and phobia.[136] Women may also suffer higher psychopathology that accompanies infertility when they are in polygynous relationships, as they watch co-wives bear children; and depression around the birth of a child, since they feel sexually and emotionally abandoned.[137]

Physical health

Women's physical health is compromised by polygyny, as well. As stated earlier, there is a correlation between domestic violence and polygyny.[138] Domestic violence causes physical harm and even death.[139] Polygyny increases the age gap

119 See Moosa et al. (n 88) 12, and Al-Krenawi & Graham (n 32) 10. See also Bove & Valeggia (n 97) 25.

120 See, generally, Shepard (n 3), for a systematic review of research on the mental health of polygynous women. Shepard reports that women in polygynous relationships are three times more likely than women in monogamous relationships to have psychological distress, stating that "polygamy was a significant predictor of psychiatric distress," even psychosis (58).

121 Moosa et al. (n 88) 12; Al-Krenawi & Graham (n 32) 10; and Shepard (n 3) 58. Somatization is where a psychological problem manifests itself as a physical complaint. Kirmayer & Young "Culture and somatization: Clinical, epidemiological, and ethnographic perspectives" (1998) 60 *Psychosomatic Medicine* 420.

122 Al-Krenawi & Graham (n 32) 6.

123 Ibid.

124 Al-Krenawi (n 82) 196.

125 Moosa et al. (n 88) 12; and Al-Krenawi & Graham (n 32) 10.

126 Al-Krenawi & Graham (n 32) 6.

127 Ibid.

128 Ibid.

129 Ibid.

130 Al-Krenawi (n 82) 196; Shepard reports higher levels of paranoid ideation, as well. Shepard (n 3) 58.

131 Sanni (n 63) 5–6.

132 Moosa et al. (n 88) 12; and Shepard (n 3) 58.

133 Al-Krenawi & Graham (n 32) 10; Sanni (n 63) 5–6; and Shepard (n 3) 58.

134 Compare Al-Krenawi & Graham (n 32) 10.

135 Ibid.; and Shepard (n 3) 58.

136 Al-Krenawi & Graham (n 32) 10.

137 Bove & Valeggia (n 97) 25–26. Some African cultures mandate abstinence during the postpartum and breastfeeding periods, and watching her husband engage in a sexual relationship with a co-wife or wives can be difficult. Meekers & Franklin (n 14) 319.

138 See n 99.

139 Henrich et al. report higher levels of homicides within polygynous families and explains one possible reason is the decrease in relatedness within families. Henrich et al. (n 58) 665.

between spouses and drives down the age at which women get married.[140] This leads to higher fertility, and younger age of first birth, both factors which increase maternal mortality.[141] There are also studies linking polygyny to higher rates of sexually transmitted infections, including HIV/AIDS.[142] This connection was recognized by the CEDAW Committee General Recommendation 24, which states that multiple partners give a greater chance of disease.[143] HIV/AIDS is one of the most serious and devastating problems African women face. As a group, women account for over 50 percent of new infections as well as a rapidly increasing infection rate.[144] The correlation between polygyny and HIV/AIDS can be explained by several factors.[145] One study explained the correlation by decreased condom use, poor communication of the marriage partners, multiplication of sexual partners, and age and power differentials between spouses.[146] Polygyny decreases a woman's ability to make sexual decisions for herself.[147] In addition, husbands can bring the virus to their wives.[148] Wife-sharing polygyny (levirate) is another way polygyny can spread HIV.[149] When a husband has AIDS, he may pass it on to his wife and then die. When his wife remarries, her new spouse passes the virus on to *his* existing wife or wives.[150] In addition, sexual deprivation gives women the incentive and opportunity to engage in extramarital relations, which may bring HIV into a family.[151] Finally, children are exposed to the HIV infection in communities where polygamous wives breastfeed each other's children.[152] In countries like Swaziland with high rates of polygyny and a 40 percent HIV infection rate, this is a massive problem.[153] AIDS is a central part of the vicious cycle of poverty, disempowerment, vulnerability, suffering, and illness.

140 Henrich et al. (n 58) 663–664.

141 Henrich et al. (n 58) 663–665. See also Bove & Valeggia (n 97) 23, for more information on the link between polygyny and higher fertility rates.

142 Gage-Brandon (n 61) 286, citing Frank "Infertility in sub-Saharan Africa: Estimates and implications" (1983) 9 *Population & Development R* 137. See also Rwenge *Facteurs Contextuels de la Transmission Sexuelle du Sida en Afrique Subsaharienne: Une Synthèse* 223, available at www.codesria.org/IMG/pdf/12LRWENGE_.pdf, explaining that increased incidence of HIV/AIDS in polygamous families can be explained by the dual factors of a man being more likely to have extramarital sex if he is already sleeping with more than one woman, and of wives being more open to extramarital sex because of the increased age differential between spouses in polygamous families.

143 CEDAW General Recommendation No. 24: Article 12 of the Convention (Women and Health) 1999, A/54/38/Rev.1, chap. I, at para 18.

144 Zeitzen (n 2) loc 3790.

145 Ibid.

146 Bove & Valeggia (n 97) 21.

147 Zeitzen (n 2) loc 3790.

148 Ibid., loc 3796.

149 Ibid.

150 Ibid.

151 Ross (n 72) 552–553. See also Zeitzen (n 2) loc 3796.

152 Zeitzen (n 2) loc 3796.

153 ibid., loc 3809.

Polygyny and law

Now that we have seen the place of polygyny in African culture and the lived reality of women in this form of marriage, we must examine how polygyny is situated in the different layers of law present in Africa.

African customary law

At the local level, African customary law explicitly permits polygyny. Customary law may be defined as "a normative order observed by a population, having been formed by regular social behavior and the development of an accompanying sense of obligation."[154] It remains a highly relevant source of law in Africa, particularly in family law.[155] Customary law is not all the same. First, because Africa is a diverse continent, home to a multiplicity of cultures, it follows that there are wide variations in customary law.[156] "Customary law in Africa is not one unified system of law but rather varies by ethnic group; it can even vary in its implementation by community."[157]

Across African cultures, the specifics of customary marriage are different, but there are some similarities in the broader contours, one of which is that a man can marry more than one wife.[158] There is no limit to the number of wives under customary law a man can have, as there is under Islamic law, so a man can potentially marry any number of wives.[159] A customary marriage is "a marriage celebrated according to the rites of an African community and one of the parties to which is a member of that community."[160]

Domestic law

Domestic family law codes may also permit polygyny by acknowledging that form of union and providing some parameters for it. These parameters, such as formal

154 Gordon R. Woodman "A Survey of Customary Laws in Africa in Search of Lessons for the Future" in Fenrich et al. (eds) *The Future of African Customary Law* (2011) 9, 10. [C]ustomary law is based upon the customs of a community. Common attributes of customary legal systems are that they are seldom written down, they embody an organized set of rules regulating social relations, and they are agreed upon by members of the community. Although such law systems include sanctions for law infractions, resolution tends to be reconciliatory rather than punitive. A number of African states practiced customary law many centuries prior to colonial influences. Following colonization, such laws were written down and incorporated to varying extents into the legal systems imposed by their colonial powers.

155 Oba, 'The future of African customary law' in Fenrich et al. (eds) *The Future of African Customary Law* (2011) 58 at 79.

156 Kent "Custody, maintenance and succession: The internationalisation of women and children's rights under customary law in Africa" (2007) 28 *Mich. J. Int'l L.* 507, 514.

157 Kent (n 156) 514 (citing Kolajo, "Customary law" in *Nigeria Through the Cases* (2000) 1).

158 Twinomugisha "African customary law and women's human rights in Uganda" in Fenrich et al. (eds) *The Future of African Customary Law* (2011) 446 at 457. In many parts of Africa, people can marry under Islamic law, which is also polygynous.

159 Ssenyonjo (n 18) 349. Islamic law limits the number of wives to four. Pearl & Menski (n 18) 238.

160 Ssenyonjo (n 18) 349.

but ineffective registration requirements, permit polygyny impliedly by remaining silent about the issue. South Africa's Recognition of Customary Marriages Act 120 of 1998 (RCMA) is a good example of a statute permitting polygyny. The RCMA was created to formally recognize customary marriages.[161] Historically, the colonial and Apartheid governments of South Africa did not recognize customary marriages.[162] Polygynous marriages under this Act are explicitly recognized and are set in a framework of legal protections, including requiring both parties to consent to the form of the customary marriage, equalizing rights to divorce, creating a scheme of community property, and creating an element of judicial oversight, whereby a man must get the court's permission to marry additional wives.[163] Contrast South Africa's approach with Ghana's Marriage Ordinance Law, which requires marriages to be monogamous.[164]

Most constitutions in Africa are silent about polygyny. For example, the Constitution of the Republic of South Africa, 1996 does not explicitly address polygyny, although it is argued by some that the provisions on the right to equality indirectly forbid the practice,[165] especially in light of the central status of equality under the Constitution.[166] Rwanda's Constitution explicitly states in Article 26 that the only legally recognized form of marriage is monogamy:[167] "[o]nly civil monogamous marriage between a man and a woman is recognized."[168] Where a state's constitution is silent about the question of polygyny, a constitutional court may fill this gap with jurisprudence making polygyny unconstitutional. Benin's Constitutional Court has taken this approach in *Review of Constitutionality of Family Legislation*,[169] a constitutional challenge to Benin's Code of Individuals and Family, which permitted polygyny.[170] The Court found this provision of the family code to be unconstitutional, making polygynous marriage unconstitutional in Benin.[171] However, the Court made provisions for polygynous marriages contracted before the code, so that there would not be unjust transitory effects on women.[172]

161 Ibid.

162 Higgins & Fenrich "Customary law, gender equality, and the family: The limits of the choice paradigm" in Fenrich et al. (eds) *The Future of African Customary Law* (2011) 423 at 440.

163 Ibid.

164 Higgins & Fenrich (n 162) 432, citing Marriage Ordinance, Cap. 127 (1884) (Ghana). Numerous African states have made polygyny legally impermissible; for example Zaire, Nigeria, Côte d'Ivoire, Burundi, Somalia, Mauritius and Rwanda. See Schnier & Hintmann (n 99) 826.

165 Pierre de Vos "Is polygamy unconstitutional?" (4 January 2010), available at http://constitutionallyspeaking.co.za/is-polygamy-unconstitutional/. However, South Africa permits polygyny in customary marriages under the RCMA (Art. 2(3)).

166 Amien (n 16) 747.

167 Banda (n 51) 94.

168 Rwandan Constitution, art. 25.

169 Review of Constitutionality of Family Legislation (2004) *AHRLR* 127 (BeCC 2002).

170 Ibid at paras 1 & 4.

171 Ibid at para 10.

172 Ibid at para 19.

International law

Under international law, "there is a growing consensus that [polygyny] violates women's right to be free from all forms of discrimination."[173] While most treaties do not specifically ban polygyny, their treaty bodies make clear that polygyny violates women's right to equality.[174] Several treaty bodies in many instances have clearly stated that polygyny is inconsistent with equality, such as the Human Rights Committee (HRC) in General Comment 28,[175] and the CEDAW treaty body, which has been extremely active in urging states to eradicate polygyny in line with their Article 5(a) obligations.[176] CEDAW General Recommendation 21 on Marriage and Family Relations, which has been mentioned above, clearly admonishes states that polygyny is not compatible with equality.[177] State reports also make the point that polygyny is a clear women's rights violation.[178]

Regional law

The African regional system is less clear on polygyny than the treatment of polygyny under international law.[179] The African Charter contains no explicit prohibition against polygyny. However, Article 18(3) is a powerful equality provision. It requires that "[t]he State shall ensure the elimination of every discrimination against women and also ensure the protection of the rights of the woman and the child as stipulated in international declarations and conventions."[180] This equality provision, however, must be considered in light of the object and purpose of the treaty and its other features. "The drafting of the Banjul Charter was inspired by the traditions and values of African society, including African concepts of law and rights, prompted further by negative historical experiences."[181] It is important to keep in mind that one of the overriding features of the African Charter is that it is

173 Cook & Kelly (n 69) 3.

174 Ibid., 5, stating "[s]everal of these treaty bodies including CEDAW, the HRC, the CESCR, and the CRC have expressly stated in their concluding observations that polygyny violates the rights articulated within their respective treaties." See also Banda (n 51) 92.

175 General Comment No. 28: Equality of rights between men and women (article 3), UN HRCOR, 68th Sess., UN Doc. CCPR/C/21/Rev.1/Add.10 (2000) at para 24.

176 CEDAW Dec. 18, 1979, 1249 UNTS 13, Article 18, Art. 5*(a)*, available at http://www.un.org/womenwatch/daw/cedaw/text/econvention.htm.

177 CEDAW General Recommendation 21 (n 107) para 14.

178 See, for example, CEDAW *Concluding Comments of the Committee on the Elimination of Discrimination against Women: Kenya*, 10 August 2007, CEDAW/C/KEN/CO/6, at para. 22, and CEDAW *Report of the Committee on the Elimination of Discrimination against Women: Thirty-second Session (10–28 January 2005*), 18 March 2005, A/60/38 (Part I), at paras. 25–6. These are only two among many.

179 Banda (n 51) 91.

180 Organization of African Unity, African Charter on Human and Peoples' Rights ("Banjul Charter"), 27 June 1981, CAB/LEG/67/3 rev. 5, 21 I.L.M. 58 (1982).

181 Naldi "The African Union and the regional human rights system" in Evans & Murray *The African Charter on Human and Peoples' Rights: The System in Practice, 1986–2006* 2 ed (2008) 20 at 25.

less focused on individuals and more centered on "peoples" as rights bearers.[182] Combining the benefits of polygyny we have seen for groups,[183] with the Charter's focus on promoting African Culture,[184] it is no surprise that the Charter does not contain an explicit ban on polygyny.

The African Women's Protocol[185] is the only African treaty to specifically address the issue of polygyny.[186] Article 6(c) states that "monogamy is encouraged as the preferred form of marriage and that the rights of women in marriage and family, including in polygamous marital relationships are promoted and protected."[187] This confusing and contradictory provision is deeply unsatisfying for many women's rights groups and was born of a compromise.[188] Early drafts of the conventions wholly disavowed polygyny,[189] but pro-polygyny groups argued heavily against an outright prohibition.[190] The resulting provision makes it unclear whether polygyny is prohibited or accepted.[191] The convention's goal is to promote equality,[192] yet its lack of clarity on the polygyny issue may violate the object and purpose of the treaty, which is to "eradicate gender based discrimination and promote equality between the sexes."[193] It also appears to be inconsistent with other treaties that many African states have obligated themselves to, such as the ICCPR and CEDAW.[194]

The courts' role in the polygyny question

In places where the constitution does not specifically prohibit polygyny, it is clearly the role of the courts to figure out how to implement the international law obligations within the legal framework of the specific state law. This requires careful balancing of women's rights and the right to culture, which is difficult because as we have seen earlier, African culture and customary law frequently include polygyny.

The question, then, is whether polygyny is inconsistent with international and regional law. As we have seen, state allowance of polygyny does not seem to

182 Viljoen "An introduction to the Protocol to the African Charter on Human and Peoples' Rights on the Rights of Women in Africa" (2009) 16 *Was. & Lee J.C.R. & Soc. Just.* 11 at 20.

183 See pp. 223–226.

184 Banjul Charter (n 180).

185 African Union, Protocol to the African Charter on Human and People's Rights on the Rights of Women in Africa ("Women's Protocol"), 11 July 2003.

186 Gaffney-Rhys "Polygamy: A human right or human rights' violation?" (2011) 2 *Women in Society* 1 at 2.

187 "The African Union has thus acknowledged that women in plural marriages require protection, but it did not go so far as to outlaw polygyny."Ibid. (n 186) 2.

188 Jonas (n 1) 144.

189 Viljoen (n 182) 22.

190 Banda (n 51) 92.

191 Jonas (n 1) 144.

192 Woman's Protocol (n 185) Article 8(f).

193 Jonas (n 1) 144, citing Banda *Women, Law and Human Rights* (2005) 117.

194 Ssenyonjo (n 18) 354.

be entirely inconsistent with regional law, while it is clearly inconsistent with international law. Therefore, the courts must consider this issue, as "it is not only desirable but possible for States to outlaw a practice that so clearly constitutes de jure discrimination against women."[195]

One of the considerations courts should take into account when handling this balancing is whether polygyny can be a valid choice for women. Some women do experience polygyny as a choice. In some states, there is a trend in favor of polygyny. For example, in Senegal, educated and professional women are entering into polygynous marriages.[196] The assumption is that when these women enter polygynous marriages, it is by choice. One writer explains: "when women contract polygamous marriages, they do so in exercise of their right to free choice, that is choosing for themselves the form of marriage to enter, whether it being [*sic*] monogamous or polygamous."[197] Why would a woman choose polygyny? Or stated another way, what would make polygyny an attractive choice for a woman? As discussed above, some women see polygyny as advantageous for them. For example, in the African context, women perceive marriage as central to their dignity,[198] and the only socially sanctioned way to have children, which itself seems to be an imperative in African society.[199] Further, choosing polygyny may be a choice that is in harmony with a woman's religious or cultural beliefs.

There is great value in a woman having greater choice in all areas of her life. It would seem that taking away a woman's right to choose polygyny is taking away her autonomy. Therefore, are laws prohibiting polygyny a step backwards for women's empowerment? Is jurisprudential curtailment part of a larger alarming trend of rights contraction instead of expansion? Should each individual woman not have the right to choose what form her marriage takes?[200] Along the same thread, there seems to be a simple solution to the equality/polygyny conundrum: allow polygamy in both its forms, polygyny and polyandry. The result would be that any person, male or female, would have the right to have more than one spouse.

Yet, law cannot be isolated from the society of which it is part. The reality is that in Africa, society is still extremely patriarchal,[201] and polygyny further entrenches this state of affairs. Unequal bargaining power and illiteracy make women vulnerable.[202] There are myriad reasons for polygyny entrenching

195 Banda (n 51) 94.

196 Shepard et al. (n 3) 6; but see discussion at pp. 000–000; and Meekers & Franklin (n 14) 315–316, explaining that educated women choose polygyny less.

197 Jonas (n 1) 143.

198 Ibid.

199 See Section 2, above.

200 Advocates of polygyny in the United States have argued that the right to privacy, which began with the right to birth control and now includes rights of gays and lesbians, should be extended to protect persons who choose polygamous marriage. See Zeitzen (n 2) loc 3642.

201 See pp. 000–000.

202 Banda (n 51) 93.

patriarchy, many of which operate to create a vicious cycle, keeping women illiterate, undereducated, disempowered, and in poverty.[203] In addition, "modern polygyny differs from polygyny under the ideal customary law,"[204] which had protections for women built in.[205] Therefore, with all these societal structures in place, giving women the power to choose polygyny is in the best case giving women very little, and in the most likely situation, fueling their subjugation. Even if a women could marry more than one man, under a patriarchal society, that could result in suffering even greater oppression, because of what it means to be a "wife" in African societies, where men dominate.[206] Put another away, men and women, due to society's norms, view even gender-neutral laws in very different ways.[207] This means that women's "lived realities" are very different to men's, even when laws are neutral.[208] Women's circumstances may force them into polygyny even when it seems there is a choice.[209] For example, less access to land and lower wages for women motivate some women to enter into a polygynous marriage.[210] Even when women may have a choice, they are socialized to believe that they do not. Girls are socialized to believe that polygyny is hard to avoid.[211] This societal pressure may be so strong that those women with co-wives articulate satisfaction with polygyny when in fact they are not satisfied.[212]

Courts must respond to these cases in a way that is sensitive and respectful to traditional cultures and religions, and find a legal response that carefully balances the rights of women (and children) to achieve gender equality with the right to religion and culture. They must realize that, while polygyny may be good for some individual women, women's rights as a whole are incompatible with the practice.[213] Indeed, equality in general suffers where polygyny is allowed; likewise, studies have shown polygyny decreases where equality is greater, including men's equality.[214] Most importantly, women must have a greater say in the shaping of norms of customary law by being a part of this process by entering into a

203 Meekers & Franklin (n 14) 316. Henrich et al. report that polygyny suppresses women's freedom, and leads to loss of household decision-making power ((n 58) 663).

204 Armstrong et al (n 24) 336.

205 Armstrong et al. explain that where polygyny once offered security for older women, it is now "often the justification for abandoning older women, particularly those beyond child-bearing age" (ibid., 338).

206 Kaganas & Murray (n 67) 127–128.

207 Tsanga & Stewart *Women and Law: Innovative Regional Approaches to Teaching, Research and Analysis* (2011) xii.

208 Ibid.

209 Bao & Jankowiak (n 76) 138.

210 Armstrong et al. (n 24) 336.

211 Meekers & Franklin (n 14) 320.

212 Meekers & Franklin (n 14) 321.

213 Armstrong et al. (n 24) 338, explain that polygyny in the modern context causes women to be used "as symbols of wealth and status, and is employed as an excuse for male sexual promiscuity which may harm women both emotionally and physically."

214 Kanazawa & Still 'Why monogamy?' (1999–2000) 78 *Soc. F.* 25, 30. See also Gould et al. (n 34) 335.

dialogue with each other and the courts. They must participate because women are affected so deeply by this practice.[215] This requires educating women on their rights and taking steps to increase women's participation in all levels of society, including government. A consideration of whether it is more appropriate to make immediate changes or whether the judiciary should shape rights more slowly to gradually eliminate the practice must be explored. These limitations should be viewed as a "starting point towards the ultimate goal of eliminating polygyny."[216] Finally, all efforts to eradicate polygyny must be accompanied by legislation that protects women and children in *de facto* and *de jure* polygamous relations, so as not to ignore the real situations that women find themselves in.[217]

Conclusion

Polygyny has been a central feature of customary marriage in Africa. It has served a beneficial purpose, and, as a religious practice and a part of African culture, should not be lightly discarded. Yet, the inherent inequality present in polygyny and the enormous negative consequences for women and society necessitate legal change that empowers women. It is inevitable that courts will increasingly grapple with this tension between an established cultural practice and women's rights, under many layers of law from international to regional to constitutional.

Despite religion's role in perpetuating polygyny, a practice with features that disempower women, the church has an important role in empowering African women. One effect of this empowerment is for women to be able to have a role in ending harmful practices such as polygyny. This can happen in three ways: socialization, education, and facilitation of women's groups.

The church is an agent of socialization in Africa.[218] Therefore, it can be used as a tool for social change that empowers women rather than disempowers them. Women should be socialized to believe that they have value equal to men. For example, some Islamic scholars believe that God endows all people with human rights without distinction.[219] This comes from the "Qur'anic idea that all human beings are unconditionally equal in dignity through God's act of creation."[220]

Churches in Africa provide an important role in the education of women, both formally and informally.[221] Formally, churches are an important provider

215 Al-Krenawi (n 82) 197. Polygyny is "a social practice that has deep and long-lasting negative implications for women and their children."

216 Ssenyonjo (n 18) 356.

217 It is important to note that polygyny will not be eradicated by law prohibiting the practice and women in polygynous relationships must be protected. Kaganas & Murray (n 67) 125.

218 Anaeme "Reducing gender discrimination and violence against women through library and information services" (2012) *Library Philosophy and Practice* 844, available at www.webpages.uidaho.edu/~mbolin/anaeme.htm.

219 Sachedina *Islam & The Challenge of Human Rights* (2009) 113.

220 Ibid.

221 The church has a long and controversial history educating African children. For example, in 1942, 97 percent of Nigerians in schools were in parochial schools. Ghana in 1950 had the same

of primary and secondary education in Africa. Informally, churches can be involved in improving adult literacy and creating job skills classes for women. Further, churches can educate women that they are rights bearers.[222] A bishop from Malawi describes the churches' efforts to provide literacy classes for adult women, skills training workshops for women, primary and secondary schools for girls, and offer family health and family planning clinics.[223]

Churches can also facilitate women organizing themselves into groups. Women comprise the majority of active church-goers in many African churches.[224] Therefore, the church is a natural place for women to come together to form groups to empower themselves. African people understand their church is a center in the struggle for social change.[225] For example, the church in South Africa played an active role in opposing Apartheid.[226] The church, therefore, is a natural site for a multi-faceted approach to the empowerment of women, which could have the result in African women having the tools they need to end harmful practices like polygyny.

percentage. The state subsequently became more involved in education as concerns rose about the mission purpose of parochial education. Berman "African responses to Christian mission education" (1974) 17(3) *African Studies Review* 527, 527.

222 Acheampong "Human rights and the African renaissance" (2000) 5(1) *Afr. J. Pol. Sci.* 105, 113, 118.

223 Ibid.

224 Kasomo "The role of women in the church in Africa" (2010) 2(6) *International Journal of Sociology and Anthropology* 126, 130.

225 Bvumbwe "Understanding the contextual challenges facing pastoral leadership in African church leadership today" (2002), available at http://synodresourcecenter.org/evang/global_missions/companion_synods/malawi/0008/church_society.html.

226 Ibid.

11 Tolerance of liberal values in Romania

Anti-abortion strategies – between religious belief and civil society mobilisation

Bogdan Mihai Radu and Cosmina Paul[*]

Introduction

The ways in which people form attitudes towards such issues as abortion are to be understood in the context of forming more or less consistent value systems. Especially in a recent democracy such as Romania, forming such a system is a cumbersome process, since all liberal values are adopted for the first time, and the way people integrate them in their broader view of the world may result in many inconsistencies. Moreover, value formation is very much influenced by critical debates existant in mass media and the public sphere in general, some of them benefitting from significant support from stakeholders involved. In the case of abortion, we argue that a change of paradigm from humanitarianism to sustainable development, adopted by civil society, and, in this case, by religious non-governmental organisations, resulted in simultaneous discourses advocating both tolerance for minorities and alternative lifestyles and promotion of family values. Hence, Romanian people's attitudes towards liberal values relating to private life and mores can end up characterised by antagonism, such as the one between accepting homosexuality but rejecting abortion and divorce. In the following, we first discuss the role of religion in the post-modern world, especially emphasising the religious revival in East Central Europe and the importance of the church in influencing choice of core values. Second, we explore the delicate relationship between religion and democracy, in order to show that the commonly held belief that most democracies are secular states may be erroneous, and that in fact religion can be a source of value formation – without necessarily having to be so. Third, we analyse quantitative and qualitative data in order to show how people form attachments to different liberal values in Romania, and showcase increasingly conservative attitudes towards abortion in a context of growing liberal orientations.

* This work was supported by a grant of the Romanian National Authority for Scientific Research and Innovation, CNCS – UEFISCDI, project number PN-II-RU-TE-2014-4-0032.

Secularisation and its critics

After acute irreversible secularisation was proclaimed in the late 1970s, a decade of religious revival followed, and a whole range of hypotheses on inevitable secularisation were disconfirmed.[1] According to Casanova, religious revival is not a surprising phenomenon, since secularisation – conceptualised as the diminishing role of religion in the post-industrial world – is limited only to some parts of Western Europe.[2] Nonetheless, this did not stop international democratising agents from attributing secularisation a normative feature, constructing it as a pre-condition for successful democratisation.[3]

The pre-eminence of Western discourse on religion is spelled out in Talal Asad's collection of essays gathered in the volume *Genealogies of Religion*.[4] The author offers a perspective on the 'West' and its religious alterity, in the language of culture, religion and power. His focus is on the anthropological method that originated in Western Europe and therefore contains 'the grain' of cultural imperialism. It is modernity that initiated anthropological studies, as both, a path towards understanding 'the others' and of defining itself: 'The West defines itself in opposition to all non-Western cultures, by its modern historicity.'[5]

Modernity, usually preceded and partially caused by economic growth, offers resources for research, and impregnates the study of foreign culture with the stigmata of non-modernity. Rationalisation of religion and the separation between state and church in medieval Western Europe led to the contemporary end point at which the West has a specific understanding of religion, power and culture. In this view, religion acquires an optional status.

Asad argues against capitalist-imperialist tendencies identifiable in these anthropological studies. While people are 'locable' and thus tied to a certain context, modernity gives the upper-hand to the West that seems more efficient in 'localising' other cultures. The author asserts the impossibility of universally defining religion, because 'the definition is itself the historical product of discursive processes'.[6]

Attempts to understand outer worlds are biased by considering the Western modern context as the reference point. Power and rationality, separation of state and church are assumptions undermining any effort to understanding the 'others'.

Nevertheless, not all authors agree on the imminence and necessity of secularisation. According to Casanova, there are three different understandings of secularisation in the literature: secularisation as a result of differentiation of society, secularisation as religious decline and, finally, secularisation brought about by the privatisation of religion. Secularisation through differentiation is

1 Berger (2001).
2 Casanova (1994).
3 Burgess (1997).
4 Asad (1993).
5 Asad (1993, p. 18).
6 Asad (1993, p. 29).

theoretically rooted in the rivalry between reason and faith, between science and the divine. Noting that the distinction between the religious and the secular spheres only makes sense if perceived from one or the other members of the dichotomy, the secular paradigm becomes a true and worrisome rival of religion when it starts undergoing the modern processes of differentiation, most importantly in the context of the rise of nation states and markets. Four factors are important in the process of differentiation – the Protestant Reformation, the formation of modern states, the rise of capitalism, and the early modern scientific revolutions. These processes slowly start taking away from the realm of church its monopoly over society and eroding its legitimacy. After all, religion and church did have a tight grip on all sectors of human activity, ranging from strictly individual and mystical acts, to societal and political control.[7]

Secularisation through religious decline has an almost mythical aura by predicting the disappearance of religion at the end of a period of religious decline. Even at first glance, this theory is not verified, and an obvious counterexample is the sustained vitality of religion in the non-Christian world. Moreover, within the Christian world, it is solely in Western Europe that religious beliefs and levels of participation declined, while in the United States, religious beliefs and levels of church attendance remained constant. Therefore, what needs to be explained is not the high levels of popularity that religion enjoys all over the world, but rather the low levels of religiosity in Western Europe. Casanova argues that the relationship between church and state took dramatically different forms in Western Europe and America respectively:

> What America never had was an absolutist state and its ecclesiastical counterpart, a caesaro-papist state church . . . It was the caesaro-papist embrace of throne and altar under absolutism that perhaps more than anything else determined the decline of church religion in Europe.[8]

The privatisation of religion thesis claims that as modernity advances, so does differentiation among institutional roles and religion becomes a strictly personal, individual and intimate matter. Modern societies do not need to legitimise themselves through the church and so religious experience loses most of its social functions and that is because modern secular governments limit their intervention in church matters to the regulation of religious competition, and the interaction between church and state.

> Modern societies do not need to be organized as 'churches,' in the Durkheimian sense, that is, as moral communities unified by a commonly shared system of practices and beliefs. Individuals are on their own in their private efforts to patch together the fragments into a subjectively meaningful whole.[9]

7 Foucault (1984).
8 Casanova (1994, p. 29).
9 Casanova (1994, p. 37).

The author also warns against a common confusion, namely the collapsing into one category of examples of liberal democratic societies that have privatised religion and normative assertions of privatisation. This distinction is particularly important for democratising societies, which often times are led to believe (by international democratising coalitions) that a clear separation between church and state is mandatory in order to democratise successfully.

Secularisation understood as differentiation remains 'the valid core' of the theory, in the sense that 'differentiation and emancipation of the secular spheres from religious institutions and norms remains a general modern structural trend'.[10] The consequence of this trend, especially in relationship to such institutions as the state and the economy (but also institutions of the society, such as science, education or the arts) is the forced isolation of religion within its own sphere. Correlatively, 'established churches are incompatible with modern differentiated states and that the fusion of the religious and the political community is incompatible with the modern principle of citizenship'.[11]

The thesis of the decline of religious beliefs and practices does not find empirical support in Casanova's study. Moreover, privatisation of religion is not a structural trend, because religions in the modern world 'do not need to endanger either modern individual freedoms, or modern differentiated structures'.[12] Privatisation of religion has both internal and external sources. The internal sources are linked to the rationalisation of religion, and the preference for more individual and reflexive forms of religious experience. Externally, privatisation is encouraged, if not forced, by the trend of differentiation 'which tend(s) to constrain religion into a differentiated, circumscribed, marginalized, and largely "invisible" religious sphere'.[13] More intriguing, Casanova believes that privatisation of religion is also mandated ideologically 'by liberal categories of thought which permeates not only political ideologies and constitutional theories but the entire structure of modern Western thought'.[14]

Therefore, Casanova sees no privatising structural trend, although the process itself is encouraged internally, externally and ideologically. Nonetheless, he argues that privatisation is not the necessary consequence of differentiation. Concluding that the decline and privatisation of religion are not necessary corollaries of secularisation through differentiation, Casanova coins the concept of religious de-privatisation. By arguing against privatising religion, he implicitly lends support to democratising countries that are either religious, or choose not to create a clear separation between church and state.

The de-privatisation of religion proceeds in four steps. First, originating in Durkheim's idea of religion as social integration, and Weber's idea of religion as salvation, the author shows that religion cannot be limited to either of the two:

10 Casanova (1994, p. 212).
11 Casanova (1994, p. 213).
12 Casanova (1994, p. 215).
13 Casanova (1994, p. 215).
14 Casanova (1994, p. 215).

> Religion always transcends any privatistic, autistic reality, serving to integrate the individual into an inter-subjective, public, and communal 'world'. Simultaneously, however, religion always transcends any particular community cult, serving to free the individual from any particular 'world' and to integrate that same individual into a trans-social, cosmic reality.[15]

Second, while liberals insist that religion must be confined to its own separate and isolated sphere, civic republicans value public religion's contribution to the common good and civic virtue, and see public religion as coextensive with the political or societal community. Third, mostly grounded in Habermasian thought, the experience of transition to democracy creates a possibility through which public religion can enter the space of civil society, without threatening the inner core of liberal vales, or long-standing requirements of modern differentiation. Fourth, building on feminist theory and Seyla Benhabib's theory of the proceduralist discursive model of the public sphere, Casanova sees public religion's individual and societal benefits as follows:

> The de-privatization of religion has a double signification here in that it simultaneously introduces publicity, that is, inter-subjective norms into the private sphere (analogous to the feminist dictum 'the personal is political'), and morality into the public sphere of state and economy (the principle of the 'common good' as a normative criterion).[16]

For all these reasons, de-privatisation of religion is possible, without menacing the inner core of democracy. Allowing churches back in the public space may also carry advantages for the democratic system per se.

Romania as a virtually homogenous Orthodox and religious country defies the imminent secularisation thesis, and, to some extent challenges even the relationship between secularisation, modernisation and differentiation. If anything, throughout the last 25 years, the Romanian Orthodox Church became more involved in all spheres of social and political life, and yet Romania is more or less a consolidated democracy. This is why we now turn to exploring the relationships between religion and democracy.

Religion and democracy in a global context

In the last 20 years religion became more prominent on the political stage. From the religious revival in Central and Eastern Europe after the collapse of communism, to the bloodshed in former Yugoslavia, to the fear of Muslim terrorism, the role of religion in today's democratic societies is one of the most debated issues.

15 Casanova (1994, p. 216).
16 Casanova (1994, p. 217).

Religion and democracy are in a relationship characterised by ambiguities: 'In the "West" . . . the Christian tradition struggled with a political vision that placed sovereignty in the hands of the people and increasingly treated its institutions as just one amongst a plurality of competing interests.'[17] While experiences with democracy in the 'East' and 'South' have been less consistent and shorter lived than in the 'West', 'a few Islamic commentators stressed the inherent democratic qualities of their tradition, sometimes said to pre-date the European and North-American development of formal democracy'.[18]

The debate on the compatibility between religion and democracy is a multi-faceted issue. Its most controversial facet is the so-called 'natural' symbiosis between Western Christianity and liberal democracy. Starting off with Max Weber's *Protestant Ethics and the Spirit of Capitalism* the marriage between Protestantism and capitalism was gradually extended to include liberal democracy and Catholicism, into what became a deterministic argument – the values embedded within Western Christianity create fertile soil for the flourishing of democracy. Although the Catholic Church was a force of conservatism for centuries, the *Vatican II Council* and the *Aggiornamento* signalled its formal recognition of religious freedom and pluralism, and its commitment to change. The reform within the Catholic Church was intended to make the church respond better to the spiritual needs of modern-day society – hence including the values of liberal democracy.

Liberal democracy is grounded in the principles of the Enlightenment and of Christian religion. Nonetheless, Western Christianity itself is very different nowadays than even one century ago. It is through a process of adjustment to new political contexts and ideas that Western Christianity now welcomes democracy. There are a few defining features of Western Christianity, both Catholic and Protestant that specify the role of religion in consolidated democracies. First, state and church are separate entities, with the latter belonging to the civil society. Second, in consolidated democracies, religion is increasingly privatised. Religion became more a matter of individual introspection, rather than a mobilising *mot de force*. Third, most consolidated democracies constitutionally guarantee freedom of religion, and, implicitly, religious pluralism.

Nonetheless, we argue that the private, separate and pluralistic religion is a result of adjusting religious dogma and structure to the structures of liberal capitalist democracy. Protestantism fits more 'naturally' into the category of private, competitive and separate religion because of the multiple streams of Protestantism, their historical coexistence and separate functioning from that of the state. Catholicism had difficulties accommodating these three features, mostly because of its worldwide coverage under one leader and its strict hierarchical structure. However, the so-called Aggiornamento signified the Catholic Church's readiness to change and accommodate progress and liberalism.

17 (Anderson, 2006, p. 1)
18 (Anderson, 2006, p. 1)

Eastern Orthodoxy is traditionally in close relationship with the state, especially through autocephaly – a sign of national identity and unity, and, therefore, it does not come close to democratic Christianity. Islam has the hardest time adapting because of its collective aspect, the omnipresence of religion in every day life, and a conflation of the religious and secular spheres.

Analysing the ways in which religion in itself transformed the political, cultural and social context in which it historically evolved is crucial. Through the acceptance of the dynamic and historical character of the relationship between church and state, and also of the status of religion in society, one amends the discourse on the compatibility between religion and democracy. Religions are or can be flexible, as the example of the Catholic Church showed.

It is more useful to understand under which conditions religion and church can be promoters of democratic values – initiating the inquiry from the perspective of embedded religion and church. Moreover, religions are also multi-vocal, with competing discourses within each denomination,[19] though not so conflicting when Christian alliances form out of different other Christian denominations.

Public religions and protection of values

Public religion can mobilise resources in defence of traditional values, against the increasing penetration of states and markets. Church mobilisation against abortion is such an example. While it is always possible to see a blunt regress into the fundamentalism of pre-modern religion, the fact that churches can be mobilising agents, is essentially democratic. Churches can 'push' issues into the public sphere, make them salient, and thus force societies to contemplate their own understanding of good and bad, their own normative standards. A second type of de-privatisation is seen when public religions enter the public sphere to oppose and criticise states and markets. Either opposing militarism, or the 'economical individualist' paradigm prevalent today, churches constantly remind people of a common good. With the advent of globalisation, Casanova notes that transnational churches are also in a privileged position to promote a universal common good that transcends borders. Third, de-privatisation of religion can be directly related to critiques of liberal versions of the common good as the mere sum of its parts, portraying churches as the moral conscience of societies. Through the church, morality becomes an essentially inter-subjective concept – a public concern. Public religions, through their interventions, are 'immanent critiques of particular forms of institutionalization of modernity from a modern normative perspective'.[20] Of course not all religions are fit for this task of resetting normative standards, but as long as a particular civil religion has internalised the Enlightenment criticism, it seems that it will serve as true opponent to the differentiated spheres of our societies, forcing them to

19 Stepan (2000).
20 Casanova (1994, p. 231).

specify and change their claims over good and bad. Public religions can revitalise modern public sphere. It is true that some religions are not playing this role, and especially non-Western religions will use their difference to construct themselves against the Western model. If Weber was right about Protestantism containing the grain of capitalism, then one must admit that other religions themselves can contain such seed for major social change.

Marc Juergensmeyer brings a significant contribution to the normative analysis of the relationship between state and church.[21] He notes that there is a conceptual and societal closeness between secular nationalism and religion. He cites Muslim thinkers that affirm the religious nature of Western secular nationalism. Some of them go so far as to analyse secular nationalism as a disguise of Christianity: 'to these Muslims, Buddhists, Hindus and Sikhs it is perfectly obvious: the West's secular nationalism competes in every way with religion as they know it'.[22] Indeed Western civilisation overlaps with what is known as Christendom. The author calls both religions and nationalism 'ideologies of order', because of them belonging to the same genus:

> Both religious and secular nationalistic frameworks of thought are ideologies of order in the following ways: they both conceive of the world around them as a coherent, manageable system; they both suggest that there are levels of meaning beneath the day-to-day world that explain things unseen; they both provide identity for and evoke loyalty form secular communities; and they both provide the authority that gives social and political order a reason for being. In doing so they define how an individual should properly act in the world, and they relate persons to the social whole.[23]

The author observes a resurrection of religions that compete with states in telling what is good or wrong, or even, sometimes, questioning who has the monopoly of violence. Religion can provide a basis for the construction of societal fabric, just as adequately as states and their official nationalisms can: 'religion is ready to demonstrate that, like secular nationalism, it can provide a faith in the unitary nature of a society that will authenticate both political rebellion and political rule'.[24] While in the 'West' the rise of the nation state led to the rise of secular nationalism that incorporates religion, in the countries undergoing either state formation or regime transition, there is rivalry between secular nationalism and religion. This tension is not unheard of in the 'West', but countries in the 'South' or the 'East' did not have sufficient time at their disposal to peacefully blend 'the religious' into 'the secular'.[25] In most of these cases, the nation state is a recent accomplishment, most transition democracies having acquired this status when

21 Juergensmeyer (1995).
22 Juergensmeyer (1995, p. 380).
23 Juergensmeyer (1995, pp. 380–381).
24 Juergensmeyer (1995, p. 381).
25 Juergensmeyer (1995, p. 384).

colonial ties were broken, and independence was acquired. The tensions between the religious and the secular sphere are more pronounced in situations where religion had a historically important political role:

> Given religious histories that were part of national heritages, religious institutions that were sometimes the nations' most effective systems of communication, and religious leaders who were often more devoted, efficient, and intelligent than government officials, religion could not be ignored. The attempts to accommodate it, however, have not always been successful.[26]

Juergensmeyer provides a nuanced analysis of the problematic compatibility between religion and political regime. He offers examples of different non-Western countries, in which religion and politics end up in 'happy marriages': 'Buddhism in the case of Sri Lanka, for example – has a strong affinity with socialism . . . the constitution of the Islamic Republic of Iran, for instance, guarantees the right of private property.'[27] Of course, there is much disagreement over how much of a role religion should play in every day political life, since 'the political role of religion is primarily in formulating national identity and purpose'.[28] Similarly, Filali-Ansary compares democracy or, at least Western democracy with 'a religious faith or "mystical ideal"'.[29] By the same token by which political attitudes are not immutable, religious attitudes can also change. Nevertheless, a change in religious attitudes should not be expected along the lines of how Reformation occurred in Europe since 'the Reformation is a singular event in history, linked to a particular environment and to specific conditions. It cannot, as some observers suggest nowadays, be "replicated" in the context of another religion and under twentieth century conditions'.[30] This message should get across to proponents of secularisation and religious pluralistic markets in Central and Eastern Europe, since it is this lack of contextuality of reforms that makes some transitions tedious, and some democratic consolidations hard to attain. Religious attitudes can and do undertake change, within a more universalistic framework derived from modernisation and through a process that

> leads the majority of the population to give religious dogmas symbolic truth-values, and to consider religious narratives contingent, historical manifestations or expressions of the sacred that are amenable to rational understanding and scientific scrutiny. Religious dogmas and narratives no longer define, in a monolithic way, people's ideas about the world and society, nor do they determine the views that believers are supposed to be guided by in their social and political interactions. This 'disenchantment' may discard the meanings of sacred

26 Juergensmeyer (1995, p. 384).
27 Juergensmeyer (1995, p. 388).
28 Juergensmeyer (1995, p. 388).
29 Filali-Ansary (2001, p. 44).
30 Filali-Ansary (2001, p. 47).

> words and rituals, but it maintains and reinforces the overall ethical and moral teachings . . . Faith becomes a matter of individual choice and commitment, not an obligation imposed upon all members of the community.[31]

Liberal values and world order in the new millennium

Inglehart and Norris take on the Huntingtonian thesis with a catchy title: the true clash of civilisation.[32] They analyse a large cross-national data set and conclude that procedural democracy is something that even citizens in Muslim countries strive for. It is the embracing of liberal values that proves to be more problematic:

> Samuel Huntington was only half right. The cultural fault line that divides the West and the Muslim world is not about democracy but gender. According to a new survey, Muslims and their Western counterparts want democracy, yet they are worlds apart when it comes to attitudes toward divorce, abortion, gender equality and gay rights – which may not bode well for democracy's future in the Middle East.[33]

Starting from the empirical findings which show that liberal values divide the new world order more than the appetite for democracy, and that non-Western societies draw more from the religious traditions rather than taking in democratic values without scrutiny, we aim at understanding in a longitudinal perspective the attitudes towards abortion in Romania after 1990 to the present, the country which rates the highest in Europe, and in the world top. Therefore we look at the liberal values in the framework proposed by Ronald Inglehard, who makes the difference between post-materialist and materialist values.

> Postmaterialists have been shaped by security during their formative years and are far more permissive than Materialists in their attitudes toward abortion, divorce, extramarital affairs, prostitution, and euthanasia. Materialists, conversely, tend to adhere to the traditional societal norms that have favored child-bearing, but only within traditional two-parent family, and that heavily stigmatized sexual activity outside that setting.[34]

Though we expect a slight percentage of the population increase in manifesting post-materialist values, we are concerned here with understanding why some materialist values are increasing, some stay steady and some decrease. Moreover, we are also interested in exploring how religious beliefs and participation, practically religious identification, influence political values, and whether that influence is an effect of an overarching value system or the result of exposure to church message.

31 Filali-Ansary (2001, p. 47).
32 Norris and Inglehart (2004).
33 Inglehart and Norris (2003, p. 62).
34 Inglehart (2004).

Democratisation in Romania

Understanding democratisation in Romania and in East Central Europe for that matter is usually channelled through modernisation. Modernisation theses start the discussion at the country level, and trickle down to individual level. Lipset's 1959 article on the determinants of maintaining democratic government is strongly correlated with his modernisation theory. As economic development takes place, levels of education increase, and the social stratification of the society changes, making space for the middle class – the main promoter of democracy:

> First, economic development is closely associated with increases in education which in turn promotes political attitudes conducive to democracy (e.g. interpersonal trust and tolerance of opposition). Second, economic development alters the pyramid-shaped social stratification system, in which the majority of the population is lower class and poor, to a diamond shape, in which the majority of the population is middle class and relatively well-off.[35]

According to Lipset, the middle class, the main driver of democratisation, has to become more educated because of their occupational status, and, through this process, they develop pro-democratic attitudes. These attitudes spread into the larger society because of the increasing size of the middle class, 'the middle class emerges as the main pro-democratic force in Lipset's analysis, and this class gains in size with socio economic development'.[36] Alternatively, Rueschemeyer *et al.* see the advent of democracy as a direct function of the growing urban working class. In their view, it is neither political culture nor education that affects the diffusion of democracy, but the fact that the working class accumulates more power, and, it is only logical for the working class to engage in democratic opening dialogue.[37]

Complementarily, Muller argues that neither of the two theses stated above are necessary to explain democratic development and survival; he adds the critical importance of income inequality in predicting the survival of a democratic system.[38] However, Bollen and Jackman oppose Muller's newly found effect of inequality, and assert that a better specification of the model would leave inequality out of the equation. They find that one of the strongest predictors of democratic survival is the presence of a previous democratic system.[39]

Most scholars of Central and Eastern European democratisation, however, find support for the modernisation theory. Age, gender, education, place of residence and size of the community have been mentioned in several studies as independent variables affecting people's attitudes towards democratic opening and towards the

35 Muller (1995a, p. 967).
36 Rueschemeyer *et al.* (1992, p. 14).
37 Rueschemeyer *et al.* (1992).
38 Muller (1995a, 1995b).
39 Bollen and Jackman (1995).

market economy system.[40] The effect is consistent with the modernisation theory that Lipset formulated more than five decades ago. More educated individuals are more supportive of democracy and the market by virtue of their higher social status that, in turn, makes them understand its net qualities. Similarly, older people (although not the oldest generations) and males also support democracy more, because of their occupational status that brings them more to the forefront of democratisation, and allows them to play a more important part. Finally, the place of residence and the size of the community affects one's attitudes because larger urban settings are also more cosmopolitan, and more exposed to the diffusion of foreign ideas. Overall, socio-economic status and demographic indicators such as gender and place of residence work through a process of empowerment, that results in people with higher status playing more important roles in the polity; at the very minimum, empowerment provides them with skills and abilities improving their subjective feelings of political efficacy.

Peffley and Rohrschneider make an interesting argument claiming that the fact that Central and Eastern Europe is democratising does not mean that tolerance of other liberal values is also widespread.[41] They note that the literature on democratisation and political tolerance rarely intersect. According to the authors, there is overwhelming evidence that democracy is at its widest coverage ever and enjoys incredibly widespread support.[42] They document the spread of support for democracy across the globe,[43] and identify two causes for this unexpected avalanche of countries manifesting high levels of support for democratic polities, even outside of the Western hemisphere. The first cause is the diffusion of democratic norms through mass media, personal contacts, and rising levels of education.[44] This argument is a quintessential version of both modernisation and democratic contagion theses. The second cause is the changing value structure of citizens, in the sense of more personal autonomy and post-material values, that occurs in non-Western contexts too.[45] They complement these optimistic perspectives with the bleaker prospects of levels of tolerance not increasing correlatively with the spread of democratic regimes. Moreover, there is evidence that intolerant people hold stronger, more powerful, beliefs and attitudes than more tolerant people.[46] They observe that in consolidated democracies, especially in the United States, tolerance is harder to learn than abstract democracy. Among predictors for tolerance, the first is the longevity of a democratic system – the longer a country's experience with democracy, with the rough and tumble of politics and increased quality of governance, the more tolerant its people are.

40 Fleron, Jr. and Ahl (1998), Kullberg and Zimmerman (1999).
41 Peffley and Rohrschneider (2003).
42 Norris (1999), Klingemann (1998).
43 Mishler and Rose (2002).
44 Weil (1989, 1993), Inglehart (1997).
45 Inglehart (1997).
46 Sullivan *et al.* (1982), Gibson and Duch (in Russia) (1993), Rohrschneider (in East Germany) (1996).

In Romania, democratisation brought about a series of principles, among which religious freedom and pluralism rank high, that are in tension with the historically constructed relationship between church and state. Privileging the Romanian Orthodox Church through the legal mechanisms of public policy and public financing embodying the principle of proportionality is also a way in which the state shows its support for Orthodox identity. In other words, the state constructs the Orthodox Church and its adherents as the main and most important actor in the religious space, one that should both benefit from financial support and be shielded from the potentially harmful influences of other denominations. The religious market in Romania is quasi-monopolistic, and the Romanian state supports the dominating position of the Orthodox Church. The privileging of the Orthodox Church becomes part and parcel of the process of constructing identity. Indeed, one of the most popular definitions of Romanian identity equals Romanian-ness with Orthodoxy. How is that then plural?

The relationship between church and state and its regulation in Romania is under opposite pressures. On the one hand, the Orthodox Church gathers up almost 85 percent of the population, and asks for a privileged status according to its strong representation within the society. On the other hand, democratisation and European integration entails the adoption of pluralism and in fact of multiculturalism. Consequently, public policy as a tool for creating deservingness also becomes subject to different pressures, and striking a balance between the equal representation of interests required by pluralistic democracy and privileging historically significant sources of stability can be difficult.

Churches contribute to democratisation in several ways: they respect the rules of the game, they avoid demagogical or populist discourse, and they are tolerant. Churches, thus, are part of civil society, but with limits usually imposed by the state. In Hungary, for example, the Catholic Church is vocal against new-Protestant religious groups, and enjoys quasi-immunity from the state, not having to transform into a transparent, democratic institution. The relationship between church and state therefore influences a church's behaviour in new democratic societies.

The cultural base of a church represents those segments of the participants' cultural terrain that the church appeals to, those common unifying traits of the population that offer the legitimising base for the church's actions. The cultural strategy indicates what part of community life the organisation will draw upon. These two factors lead to the formation of an internal political culture, made up of shared assumptions, perceptions and symbols that facilitate the understanding of the surrounding world. The political culture affects the projection of social power and the ability to shape the public realm.

Wood details the challenges that churches face in their formation and preservation of internal political culture.[47] Wood's approach is designed for the pluralist religious space existing in the United States. His announced goal was to determine the effectiveness of church participation in the representation of minorities. So part of his analysis will not apply to cases of dominant religion or even state religion.

47 Wood (1999).

The overall framework, though, is useful. Cultural base and cultural strategy carry meaning when applied outside the North American context.

Abortion in Romania: context, meanings and relationship with religion

Abortion shall not to be understood as the epitome of modernisation, but of the social values at a given time. Indeed, technology does not enter the life of citizens as it advances, but through public policies which advance values. That was why the Soviet Union was the first country in the world to give women the right to abortion at the beginning of the twentieth century as a consequence of women's emancipation and the right to decide the matters of their own body. But it did not take too much time for the empire to go back to the patriarchal order and to put the abortion decision in the hands of the state, as a mother's health, future children, population health and reproductive rights became matters of national interest as soon as the Soviets stabilised their political power. If at first Soviet women were envied for their equal rights, especially the rights over their own body and for access to education, in the 1980s they were silently enslaved in a patriarchal order more than ever. The West took a different approach, as prevention had been their chosen path. Prevention was the way to emancipate women and abortion remained a sensitive issue, never taken for granted. Even if movements for women's emancipation kept defending the right to make decisions regarding their own body, there have always been other voices seeking to have the right of a child to be born recognised. During the 1980s, though in an extreme way, abortion has been seen to epitomise women's rights: pro-choice became prevalent over pro-life as a consequence of gender equality and human rights. Change on the international agendas took place in the 1990s and, nowadays, worldwide abortion is not anymore promoted as a right in itself or a matter of gender equality.

Here, the debate on abortion epitomises the idea that public policies are just the expression of the values system at that time, which are consistently shaped by religion in traditional settings. That is not to say that there is a religious consensus as it depends on the way one sees life's inception in order to define murder and accountability. In an unreligious setting, morality of abortion is recognised even if the foetus is seen as a person or an infant (implying a more protective attitude), as there is an imposition on people not just to give life but also to protect it so as to assume responsibility towards it.[48] Different religions have different viewpoints concerning abortion. Islam believes that the soul enters the foetus after four months, Buddhism offers compassion rather than condemnation, Judaism has neither a pro-choice, nor a pro-life, stand. But Christianity puts forth a greater variety of opinions. Catholics can support a pro-choice stand on abortion, essentially being in disagreement with the pope.[49]

48 Kamm (1992), Kaczor (2011).
49 Abortion (2011).

With respect to the Romanian Orthodox Church (ROC), the Holy Spirit enters the foetus at its very conception. The ROC perceives comprehensive sex education as a way to manipulate people in order to sell contraceptives, as it teaches that only after 14 days, after the cell is implanted in the womb, does life appear. The ROC sees contraceptives being as murderous as abortion and fights against the ideology of sexual rights and family depreciation. It also stands against comprehensive sexual education as it encourages the teenagers to start their sexual life earlier.[50]

According to Silent Voices, Romania has the highest abortion rate in the world, following Vietnam (Mercy's Action Mission). Abortion, however, is legal only up to the 14th week of pregnancy. The burden of Decree 770 issued in 1966, when abortion was criminalised, ended with a very liberal abortion law in 1990. It has been also a symbolical liberation since tens of thousands of women died during Ceausescu's procreation policy, which outlawed abortion and allowed no contraceptive to become available to the population. Like in the Soviet Union, abortion was used in Romania as a means of contraception and it seems that it continues to be used for the same purpose. Ever since, the law has been challenged by religious civil society. On 24 July 2013, an open letter was addressed to the Health Minister, Eugen Nicolaescu, by 22 religious non-governmental organisations to ask for a public debate on the abortion law. The letter impeaches the national institutions and, especially, the national medical care system, for the ways in which abortion and sexual education are institutionalised. A decrease, however, in the number of abortions can be noted according to the data on abortions in a given age group: in 1990, the number of abortions per 1,000 women was 177.6; in 2000 the rate was 44.3 and in 2008 the rate was 23.5 (meaning that out of the 127,410 women who had abortions, 13,883 were between 15 and 19 years old, 27,010 were between 20 and 24 years old, 28,952 were between 25 and 29 years old, and 28,796 were between 30 and 34 years old).[51]

The liberalisation of abortion was paired with poor comprehensive sex education. It took years for the population to become informed, although the number remains high. We should also look at the case of Romania through the lens of the new humanitarian agenda and in the specific context of societal development.

Predictors of favourable attitudes towards abortion[52]

The European Values Survey (EVS) includes Romania in its three last waves, and so data is available for 1993, 1999 and 2008. We believe that the three waves are telling

50 Todea Gross (2008).

51 www.johnstonsarchive.net/policy/abortion/ab-romania.html.

52 Dependent variables are measures on a 10-point scale, with 1 meaning never justifying, and 10 meaning full agreement; religious variables are multiple categories ordinal variables, and low values means more religious/more prayer/more frequent church attendance, while high values means less; socio-economic indicators are measured from low to high, low means young, uneducated, smaller income, small town or rural residence, and high means older, more educated, higher income and living in big cities; postmaterialism is a 4-point scale variable, with 1 meaning materialist and 4 post-materialist.

for the different periods of political and overall social, economic and cultural change that marked Romania in the last 25 years. The first wave captures attitude towards such change very early on, only a few years after the breakdown of the communist regime. The second wave captures the societal landscape in the middle of democratic transition, while the third wave offers a snapshot of Romanian society one year after EU integration, and in a moment when its democratisation was at its peak.

In Table 11.1, we look at different measures of religious identification and involvement in Romania, throughout the years of democratic transition and consolidation. As already mentioned elsewhere, Romania is one of the most religious countries in East Central Europe (perhaps only comparable to Poland), at least judging by the number of people declaring a religious affiliation – there are virtually no atheists. Moreover, the country is almost homogenous from the perspective of religious denomination, with almost 90 per cent of the people belonging to the Orthodox faith. We present below religious variables tackling both religiosity (the believing aspect – subjective religiosity and prayer) and religious participation (the belonging aspect – church attendance).

It is apparent that throughout the 15 years captured in the three waves of the EVS, Romanians became more and more religious, in both believing and belonging terms. If at the beginning of transition only less than 20 per cent went to church once a week or more often, in 2008 the percentage went up to 30 per cent and more than 80 per cent of the respondents pray on a weekly matter. This result is interesting especially in comparison to the situation in other countries in the area where people flocked to church in the early 1990s, especially given the forced secularisation during the communist regime, but by the late 1990s religious identification and involvement decreased dramatically. For example, the Czech Republic is one of the most non-religious countries in the whole of the EU.

Tolerance towards homosexuality is decreasing and the religious social discourse accordingly shows that homosexuality is understood and treated as a disease, which may be cured. Indeed, video materials claim the non-discrimination of homosexuals when preventing them from marriage, explaining why treating people who are different as different does not constitute discrimination in the first place. Many materials, informational and testimonials instruct on the possibility of curing the disease or spiritual handicap of homosexuality and promote marriage while defending the value of family, again in terms of equality in rights, but recognising different rights for men and women, the latter being protected as mothers. Families and mothers receive increased attention through various counselling schemes. The consolidation of the discourse of Religious Non-Governmental Organisations (RNGOs) and their upbringing along with the increased church attendances, explain the raising of intolerance towards abortion and divorce. All the RNGOs find themselves categorically against euthanasia, but the percent expressed in the polls shows quite a steady and biased attitude, as just about half of the population declare that they would never justify it. We should be cautious with these findings as confusion was raised by the large national campaigns for euthanasia for dogs in the last decade, when scandals became highly broadcasted and attitudes divided. Adding also that euthanasia is not a common word and

Table 11.1 Longitudinal view on religious attitudes and practices in Romania (based on EVS longitudinal data, N>1000 for each survey)

Survey wave	*Religious belonging*	*Denomination (Orthodox)*	*Subjective religiosity*	*Prayer outside of religious service (often, weekly or more)*	*Church attendance (1/week or more)*	*Church attendance (1/month)*	*Church attendance (special days/religious holidays)*
EVS 1993	94.1%	93.4%	74.5%	40%	18.7%	12%	23.2%
EVS 1999	97.6%	87.7%	84.8%	75.9%	24.9%	21.6%	30.7%
EVS 2008	98%	88.8%	82.9%	80.7%	30.3%	19.6%	36.2%

not a daily concern that may explain the splitting into two groups. In the case of attitudes towards suicide, the numbers stay high, a clear influence of the church prohibition and conservatism.

In Table 11.2, we analyse longitudinally changes in attitudes towards homosexuality, prostitution, abortion, divorce, euthanasia, suicide and adultery. We chose these variables in order to circumscribe a concept of internalisation of some liberal values associated with modern democracies. It is interesting to analyse both how Romanians' attitudes towards these items changed over time, but also how these items group themselves in order to create the profile of a 'liberal' citizen (if we were to replicate the Western typology). Nevertheless, we do not believe that these items necessarily form a particular overarching factor, but rather that they all reflect changes in society from the perspective of alternative lifestyles and the liberalisation of private life, also because they have something to do with morality, and hence religion/church.

Table 11.2 shows that tolerance of homosexuality and prostitution increased throughout time, thus confirming the pattern of post-communist societies liberalising. Attitudes towards euthanasia, suicide and adultery are fairly constant, and the high level of intolerance towards adultery is somewhat disconcerting. Finally, the most important result in Table 11.2 is the clear increase in intolerance towards abortion, and the more moderate one in tolerance of divorce. It appears that as Romania democratised, the society adopted more conservative views towards abortion and divorce (family life and pro-life approaches), while it accepted other morals challenging transformation, such as homosexuality and increasing prostitution. The finding is all the more interesting given that at the onset of democratic transition Romania had one of the highest rates of abortion in the world, probably also as a consequence of abortion being decriminalised after decades of communist policies of birth control and promotion.

In Table 11.3, we ran linear regression models on all dependent variables and aimed to assess the effect of religious variables on them. We also included socio-economic indicators as control variables, a score of post-materialism, and we differentiated between Orthodox and other believers, because we wondered whether the Romanian Orthodox Church may be a cause of pro-choice socialisation. From the socio-economic indicators, age and residence are the most important predictors, and they grant validity to our models. Younger and urban people are more tolerant regarding all our dependent variables, with education sometimes also contributing to this. Interestingly, prayer, as a measure of religiosity, is positively

Table 11.2 Longitudinal view exploring the percentages saying that they would 'never justify . . . ' (based on EVS longitudinal data, N>1000 for each survey)

Survey wave	*Homosexuality*	*Prostitution*	*Abortion*	*Divorce*	*Euthanasia*	*Suicide*	*Adultery*
EVS 1993	86.4%	78.2%	22.7%	22.5%	48.7%	75.5%	60.9%
EVS 1999	79.8%	73.6%	39.9%	32.6%	56%	87.3%	71.5%
EVS 2008	68.6%	71.6%	42.2%	28.1%	50.1%	80.8%	66.6%

Table 11.3 Regression analysis (based on EVS three-wave integrated survey, N = 2640)

Independent variables	*Homosexuality*	*Prostitution*	*Abortion*	*Divorce*	*Euthanasia*	*Suicide*	*Adultery*
Religious person	0.044	0.061	0.031	0.032	0.103	0.071	0.043
	(1.188)	(1.670)*	(0.861)	(0.903)	(2.667)**	(1.871)*	(1.157)
Church attendance	−0.022	0.032	0.097	0.071	−0.037	0.004	0.030
	(−0.631)	(0.913)	(2.873)**	(2.141)**	(−0.990)	(.110)	(0.841)
Prayer	0.103	0.094	0.112	0.088	0.076	0.088	0.102
	(2.574)**	(2.375)**	(2.924)**	(2.332)**	(1.832)*	(2.125)**	(2.555)**
Post-materialism	0.084	0.075	0.000	0.049	0.006	0.079	0.087
	(2.483)**	(2.227)**	(0.010)	(1.519)	(0.175)	(2.245)**	(2.550)**
Age	−0.147	−0.072	−0.067	−0.094	−0.198	−0.060	−0.171
	(−4.227)**	(−2.079)**	(−1.995)**	(−2.815)**	(−5.418)**	(−1.646)	(−4.848)**
Education	0.062	0.119	0.122	0.059	0.021	0.008	0.028
	(1.460)	(2.811)**	(2.953)**	(1.429)	(0.477)	(0.182)	(0.640)
Income	−0.005	0.059	0.037	0.042	0.057	−0.057	0.006
	(−0.121)	(1.504)	(.948)	(1.105)	(1.372)	(−1.357)	(0.148)
Urban/rural	0.190	0.099	0.215	0.271	0.171	0.018	0.044
	(5.286)**	(2.764)**	(6.158)**	(7.891)**	(4.492)**	(0.492)	(1.198)
Orthodox	−0.034	−0.063	0.053	−0.004	0.013	−0.048	0.000
	(−1.054)	(−1.957)*	(1.706)*	(−0.132)	(.381)	(−1.421)	(0.012)
Rsq	0.139	0.133	0.180	0.186	0.135	0.040	0.093

and significantly correlated with intolerance towards all eight dependent variables, even when controlling for all other variables. While this result speaks volumes about traditional people being intolerant to all our dependent variables and also more religious, it does not say anything about the effect of the church. However, the effect of religious participation is significantly associated with intolerance only to abortion and divorce, which are also the strongest models we ran. An interpretation of this result may be that it is within the church that pro-life and pro-family (stricto sensu) attitudes are formed, since the church attendance indicator is significant even when controlling for socio-economic indicators and other religious variables. This finding may be corroborated by the lack of significance of the post-materialist variables for attitudes towards divorce, abortion and euthanasia, while being significant in all other models.

Abortion and the local, national and global civil society

Abortion is taken here as a case in point: it represents the ending point for a broader discussion about new humanitarianism and religious civil society in the post-communist countries. It reflects as well the culmination of the debates over life, over conception and contraception, over abstinence and sexual education, purity in marriage and sexual diseases; the matter of abortion also reverberates on concerns about population health and falling birthrates in relation to sustainable development. Abortion is linked both to poverty and a person's level of education. The church's takeover of both social assistance and abstinence-only education has not proven to decrease the number of abortions in spite of the vast number of women who are overtly self-declared Christians.[53] That proves that materialist values might be conflicting, as abortion is perceived much as a self-defence action. Romania finds itself at the crossroads in this respect.

A turnaround in the discussion occurred once the framework of talking about human rights and the envisaged role of the state changed. The agenda of strengthening state institutions and exporting state structures failed and a new agenda on sustainable development and civil society was shaped. Towards this agenda, which goes to the grassroots level of society, the church was rediscovered. How can we understand the puzzling church involvement in the most progressive of fields, such as education and development? After a long time of fighting off concurrent ideologies, churches began to get involved in development projects and poverty alleviation, legitimising themselves as the light to lead obscure science development, to impregnate with morality the new scientific, medical and technological discoveries, such as stem cell treatment, contraceptives, and environmental protection. The position of secularists is clear: they want the church out of public policies. Interestingly enough, the church is open to debate, has opened its own charity resources to everyone, and piously adopted a more ecumenical stand. So ecumenical indeed, that it was in the year 2000 when the Christian churches

53 Mcfarlane (2007).

became deeply involved in relieving third world debt. It is thought to be one of the largest transnational mass movements. 'Please, wish me a merry Christmas', seemed to be the telling message of many third world countries, Christianised during colonisation, now resonating with the struggle against capitalism. Out of this situation, the church seems to triumph again.

One very recent book on collective action coordinated by Francisco, disenchants revolutions, protests, social movements and dissidents.[54] All in all, it draws upon the entrepreneurial character of collective action, which has been a great achievement for the theory since 1965. The ROC was the first group in Romania to understand the importance of civil society, which remains up to date on the most developed concepts in the social sciences: it includes networking, social capital and assessment. Nevertheless, the ROC takes advantage of its privileged position by being able to mobilise volunteers, reach more donors, both religious and secular, and motivate people by faith. The organisation is widely considered legitimate and '(b)ecause of its unique place in Romanian society, the Church can play a pivotal role in spreading knowledge about HIV/AIDS and can provide the moral leadership necessary for a more effective response to this growing problem'. To roughly portray the religious context of Romania since 1989, we note that the number of self-appointed transnational and national religious NGOs and church organisations has been increasing in Romania; Romanians overtly declared themselves religious (90 per cent),[55] and that volunteer work for religious organisations, including the church, has one of the highest rates of participation (4 per cent for people aged between 18 and 29 and this increases with age up to 9 per cent).[56]

RNGOs from all denominations come together in an alliance against abortion. They are voicing the values of Orthodox, Catholic and Evangelical churches and cover all geographical areas.[57]

When liberal values are discussed, the secular NGOs appear rather as a countermovement to the religious ones. Secular NGOs form networks and mobilise based on commonly identified values. That has been the case of the pro-choice movement in Romania, which actually reacted to the pro-life movement's demonstrations every March, starting in 2011. The debate covered the issues of religious education and

54 Francisco (2010).

55 IRES (2011).

56 Study of Volunteering in the European Union, Country Report Romania (2011).

57 Hence, the Orthodox Church is represented by the Federation of Pro-Vita Orthodox Organizations from Romania (Federatia Organizatiilor Ortodoxe Pro-Vita din România) through 12 associations and foundations, the Pro-Vita Association Media, Bucharest (Asociatia Provita Media, Bucuresti), Foundation Pro Vita Medica, Timisoara (Fundatia Pro Vita Medica, Timisoara), Association Provita 'Sf. Brâncoveanu' (Asociatia Provita 'Sf. Brâncoveanu'), Association Pro-Vita for the Born and the Unborn, Galati (Asociatia 'Pro-Vita pentru nascuti si nenascuti', Filiala Galati), Association Pro-Vita for the Born and the Unborn, Filiala Calarasi, Foundation 'Solidarity and Hope' (Fundatia 'Solidaritate si Speranta'), the Alliance of Families (Alianta Familiilor), M.A.M.A Miriam Organization Hunedoara (Organizatia MAMA, Hunedoara), Iochebed Foundation (Fundatia Iochebad, Brasov). The Catholic Church is voiced by Caritas Association (Asociatia Caritas Bucuresti) and by the Association The Gift of Life (Asociatia darul vietii, Timisoara).

the impact of ROC as the main provider of social assistance in Romania. According to Lichbach's theory, secular NGOs mobilise people based on the pre-existing organisation and community values.[58] There is neither a hierarchy, nor selective incentives. Secular values are perceived as community values because only a small minority in Romania is secular. It is the overwhelming entrepreneurship of religious organisations that creates the movement. Among the secularists we merely find people who are rejected by the church or excluded from redemption, people who suffer from addictions, like drugs and alcohol, and the homosexual community.[59]

Much of the legitimacy of humanitarianism has been constructed on the right of intervention but international NGOs opted against it more than two decades ago. Instead, they committed themselves to long-term sustainable development by empowering communities and protecting families. Therefore, the concept of development received a vision, which consistently resonates traditional values. 'The anti-state approach and basis of "sustainable approaches" is hostile to short-term relief. Developmentalists argue that relief creates dependency and reduces the capacity of local communities, while long-term developmental support builds capacity.'[60] Here, strengthening civil society became the centre of the humanitarian agenda. In traditional and modernising societies, religious institutions are seen both as traditional and civic and they are now taking up the cause of sustainable development. Due to their long-standing establishment, they present themselves as legitimised actors to be the voice for civil society.

In 1994, the UN Conference on Population and Development took place and the conference was taken as an impetus for the church to enter through the front door in the international debate on reproductive health taking place in international courts, rooms and foyers. After all, the secular debates were born around the church and they continue to be motivated by the church. Population control has been the primary concern of missionary churches ever since. At the moment, international society's concerns with regard to overpopulation are overtaken by the discourse on development. If the state had been seen as the primary agent of furthering development, civil society now receives extra attention as the main force for promoting grassroots democracy, community based services and everything else that may be connected to sustainable development. Governments and private donors give civil society the power to promote peace, democracy and human rights. The issue of reproductive rights received attention and debate due to its intimate connection with abortion rights or family planning. In sum, no right to abortion has been sustained by either the European Union or by the United States, two entities which

58 Lichbach (1995).

59 Asociaţia Integration, Asociaţia Samusocial din România, ALIAT – Alianţa pentru Lupta Împotriva Alcoolismului şi Toxicomaniilor, Fundaţia Parada, Centrul de Relaţii Internaţionale, Mişcarea Verzilor, Asociaţia Solidaritatea pentru Libertate de Conştiinţă, Asociaţia Umanistă din România, Asociaţia Sens Pozitiv, Asociația Secular-Umanistă din România, Fundaţia Estuar, Liga Pro Europa, Grupul pentru Acţiune Socială, ECPI-Centrul Euroregional pentru Iniţiative Publice, PSI România, Asociaţia ACCEPT, A.S.C.H.F-R filiala Argeş.

60 Chandler (2001, p. 7).

could tackle the subject based on their legislation and their global leverage. The term 'reproductive health' was defined by the United Nations in 1994 at the Cairo International Conference on Population and Development: 'All Member States of the Union endorsed the Programme of Action adopted at Cairo. The Union has never adopted an alternative definition of "reproductive health" to that given in the Programme of Action, which makes no reference to abortion.' Reproductive health has no direct link to women's rights except those shaped by human rights. Women become, again, mothers.

As religious organisations were facilitated to enter debate and voice their concerns as factors to bring about social change, international and national political agendas changed their focus from individual rights issues such as gender equality, women rights or human dignity into social issues, such as development and education.

Since the RNGOs are present in international fora, communities and families are empowered at the expense of individual rights, gender equality is discussed in terms of the differences between women and men and protecting women as mothers. Social justice is promoted through compassion and philanthropy, as it has always been in the Christian Church tradition. Therefore, the concerns over families, unborn children or euthanasia became visible, which were overlooked by the Western civil rights movements as ethical concerns. Indeed, matters of life, which were seen as rather philosophical, have come to be listed as values (i.e. the right to life was not listed in the human rights agenda). That is why the debate over life, more than any other debate, comes to the fore. Abortion, homicide, suicide, death penalty, euthanasia and assisted suicide are all brought into attention. Indeed, recent history has witnessed the increase of RNGO involvement in global issues of civil rights and social justice concerns. Women's rights and gender equality are topics of high priority on the agenda of collective action enterprises in Romania, as are family and child protection. As women are often seen as promoters of peace and education, the cement for sustainable development, many initiatives end up emancipating women by providing work outside the households. How progressive are the values promoted by an appointed progressive civil society?

Church ties to US international aid

In 1992, International Orthodox Christian Charities (IOCC), the official humanitarian aid agency of the Standing Conference of Canonical Orthodox Bishops in the Americas (SCOBA), launched major programmes with the Romanian Orthodox Church to strengthen their capacity to deliver social services.[61] Their

61 Building on ten years of collaboration with the Romanian Orthodox Church, IOCC began two programmes valued at US$3.4 million to further develop the organisational capacity of the Romanian Orthodox Church at a central level and in three dioceses and to empower a national network of faith-based non-governmental organisations to gradually become a strategic partner in improving social inclusion and services at local, regional and national levels (IOCC, 2010).

objectives include fighting AIDS, family violence, coping with the abortion trauma and so on.[62]

In 1996, the US government started instructing American students to abstain from sexual activity. Along with the right to abortion, contraception is denigrated. It has now been more than a decade since abstinence-only education began to receive funds, the amount of which continues to be increased in spite of the rising voices debating on the one hand the ineffectiveness of the whole educational enterprise and, on the other hand, the prevalent religious discourse over the scientific. As it was not considered to be enough for abstinence to be taught in American schools, two-thirds of the President's Emergency Plan for AIDS Relief is directed for abstinence-until-marriage programmes towards the top 15 countries of AIDS concern worldwide. Again, contraceptives and condoms are excluded from the programme's budget and attention.[63]

> . . . the Personal Responsibility and Work Opportunities Reconciliation Act of 1996 into law, it contained language that included the deliberate encouragement of states to support state cooperation with community and faith based charities in serving needy families . . . The goal of the charitable choice provisions: to encourage states to involve community and faith based organizations as providers of services under the new welfare reform bill while protecting the religious character of the participating religious organizations and the religious freedoms of the beneficiaries.[64]

Since the beginning of 2000s, the ROC started organizing its efforts. A myriad of Christian enterprises soon realised that by networking they could strengthen their capacity to act. Therefore they organised their work on social assistance in accordance with the guiding principles of sustainable development. They published a manual of management and assessment, which has also been a guide to other collective action enterprises.[65] By being constituted as NGOs, they were able to actively work towards change and applied to receive European funds for strengthening civil society.

The debates become relevant for our analysis from two perspectives: they give broader understanding as to how the discourse on abortion is undertaken by the Christian church and Christian NGOs and they make the picture of changing liberal values more clear.

Conclusion

We aimed at comparing the findings resulting from the quantitative data with those provided by the self-presentations of these RNGOs on the Internet in

62 IOCC (2010).
63 Ito *et al.* (2006), Hess (2010).
64 AIDSAction (July 2003).
65 Vasiliada (2011).

order to see if the data is consistent. RNGOs promote child-bearing, marriage only of opposite-sex, sexual abstinence before marriage, express views against divorce by offering consultancy for married couples, and disagree with concubinage and sexual perversities. They also affirm values of non-discrimination and equality by offering to cure homosexuality, and promoting education in the Christian values and ethics but against sexual education, and take social actions to fight poverty for a more just society. The educational video material presented by the RNGOs on their web page is produced in USA and Ireland and document abortion as a criminal act (i.e. 'The Silent Scream' by Bernard Nathanson), and teach why the values of marriage may not be translated to couples of the same sex.[66]

Looking at the discourse promoted by the RNGOs we notice that compassion is the key value, which inspires the promoted attitudes. Divergent from the laic sense of empathy, in the religious tradition, compassion is directed towards disabilities or weaknesses being social, physical or spiritual. Therefore they work for orphans, people with disabilities, and the disadvantaged. Henceforth, their mission is spiritual but somewhat intrinsically social and medical.

The present analysis aimed at providing a comprehensive understanding of the new framework of the discussion on abortion and sought to illuminate the religious aspects that came to play a formative role. We addressed the debate on abortion waged by myriad collective action enterprises motivated by religion, in Romania. The topic is relevant for two reasons: on the one hand, as Romania is strengthening international ties, religious enterprises flourish as a result of the impetus of civil society; on the other hand, the debate on abortion epitomises the religious, rather than the secular, origin of values in the pursuit of social change.[67] Even though they formulated their creeds differently for centuries and even developed their own way of evangelising, they now found themselves united by the same concerns, by ecumenism and by civil empowerment created by the increasing investment in civil society in the last two decades. Therefore, Catholic charities, Eastern Orthodox philanthropy and Protestant dioceses achieve their goals via the public mission of NGOs. What role do religious NGOs play in the overall debates of civil society? Does the debate on abortion law, which is furthered by religious NGOs and church organisations, result in the advancement, stagnation or regression of women's rights? How present are they in the overall debate? How much does the understanding of women's rights change, as a consequence of the changing agenda of humanitarian interventions? Do Christian activists endorse women's rights? How are missionaries transformed into entrepreneurial dissidents or likewise how are entrepreneurial dissidents mobilised in religious NGOs within traditionally appointed secular realms? Setting the scene of debate on liberal values and especially on abortion, all the above questions are necessarily important in order to obtain a clearer picture. They reflect a real need

66 I.e. 'For the sake of our children', www.alianta-familiilor.ro/.
67 Berger (2003).

to reconsider and review the alignment of the rights of women with the internal norms and values of the church in Romania and elsewhere.

References

Abortion, Global Viewpoints (2011). Greenhaven Press, Ed. Noah Berlatsky.

AIDS Action, Policy Brief (July 2003). Faith-Based Response to HIV/AIDS.

Anderson, J. (2006). Introduction: Religion, Democracy and Democratization. In

Anderson, J. (ed.). *Religion, Democracy and Democratization*. New York: Routledge, 1–2.

Asad, T. (1993). *Genealogies of Religion: Discipline and Reasons of Power in Christianity and Islam*. Baltimore: Johns Hopkins University Press.

Berger, Julia (2003). Religious Non-Governmental Organizations: An Exploratory Analysis, September 2003, Harvard University.

Berger, P.L. (2001). Reflections on the Sociology of Religion Today. *Sociology of Religion*, 62(4), 443–454.

Bollen, K.A. and Jackman, R.W. (1995). Income Inequality and Democratization Revisited: Comment on Muller. *American Sociological Review*, 60(6), 983–989.

Burgess, A. (1997). *Divided Europe: The New Domination of the East*. London: Pluto Press.

Casanova, J. (1994). *Public Religions in the Modern World*. Chicago: Chicago University Press.

Chandler, David (2001). The Road to Military Humanitarianism: How the Human Rights NGO's Shaped A New Humanitarian Agenda. *Human Rights Quarterly*, 23(3), August.

Filali-Ansary, A. (2001). Muslims and Democracy. In Diamond, L. and Plattner, M.F. (eds). *The Global Divergence of Democracies*. Baltimore: Johns Hopkins University Press, 37–51.

Fleron, F.J. Jr. and Ahl, R. (1998). Does the Public Matter? What We Have Learned from 'Third Wave' Transitions and Public Opinion Surveys. In Eckstein, H. *et al.* (eds). *Can Democracy Take Root in Post-Soviet Russia*? Lanham: Rowman & Littlefield.

Foucault, Michel (1984). *The Care of the Self*, vol. 3. New York: Random House.

Francisco, R.A. (2010). *Collective Action Theory and Empirical Evidence*. Dordrecht: Springer.

Gibson, J.L. and Duch, R. (1993). Political Intolerance in The USSR: The Distribution and Etiology of Mass Opinion. *Comparative Political Studies*, 26, 286–329.

Hess, Amie (2010). Hold the Sex, Please: The Discursive Politics between National and Local Abstinence Education Providers. *Sex Education*, 10(3), 251–266.

Inglehart, R. (1997). *Modernization and Postmodernization: Cultural, Economic, and Political Change in 43 Societies*. Princeton: Princeton University Press.

International Orthodox Christian Charities (IOCC) (2010). Annual Report.

Ito, Kristin E., Gizlice, Ziya, Owen-O'Dowd, Judy Foust, Evelyn, Leone, P.A. and Miller, W.C. (2006). Parent Opinion of Sexuality Education in a State with Mandated Abstinence Education: Does Policy Match Parental Preference? *Journal of Adolescent Health*, 39(5), 634–641.

Juergensmeyer, M. (1995). The New Religious State. *Comparative Politics*, 27(4), 379–391.

Kaczor, Christophor (2011). *The Ethics of Abortion*. New York and London: Routledge.

Kamm, F.M. (1992). *Creation and Abortion: A Study in Moral and Legal Philosophy*. New York and Oxford: Oxford University Press.

Klingemann, H.-D. (1998). Mapping Political Support in the 1990s: A Global Analysis. Wissenschaftszentrum Berlin fur Sozialforschng gGmbh (WZB), FS III 98–202.

Kullberg, J.S. and Zimmermann, W. (1999). Liberal Elites, Socialist Masses, and Problems of Russian Democracy. *World Politics*, 51(3), 323–358.

Lichbach, Mark Irving (1995). *The Rebel's Dilemma*. Ann Arbor: University of Michigan Press.

Mcfarlane, A. (2002). Abortion Methods in England. www.alanmacfarlane/com/savage/A-ABORT.PDF, last accessed: 2015.

Mishler, W. and Rose, R. (2002). Comparing Regime Support in Non-Democratic and Democratic Countries. *Democratization*, 9(2), 1–20.

Muller, E. (1995a). Economic Determinants of Democracy. *American Sociological Review*, 60(6), 966–982.

Muller, E. (1995b). Income Inequality and Democratization: Reply to Bollen and Jackman. *American Sociological Review*, 60(6), 990–996.

Norris, P. (ed.). (1999). *Critical Citizens: Global Support for Democratic Government*. New York: Oxford University Press.

Norris, P. and Inglehart, R. (2004). *Sacred and Secular: Religion and Politics Worldwide*. New York: Cambridge University Press.

Peffley, M. and Rohrschneider, R. (2003). Democratization and Political Tolerance in Seventeen Countries: A Multi-Level Model of Democratic Learning. *Political Research Quarterly*, 56(3), 243–257.

Rohrschneider, R. (1996). Institutional Learning Versus Value Diffusion: The Evolution of Democratic Values Among Parliamentarians in Eastern and Western Germany. *The Journal of Politics*, 58(2), 422–446.

Rueschemeyer, D., Stephens, E.H. and Stephens, J.D. (1992). *Capitalist Development and Democracy*. Chicago: University of Chicago Press.

Stepan, A.C. (2000). Religion, Democracy and the 'Twin Tolerations'. *Journal of Democracy*, 11(4), 37–57.

Sullivan, J.L., Pierson, J. and Marcus, G.E. (1982). *Political Tolerance and American Democracy*. Chicago: University of Chicago Press.

Todea Gross, Christa (2008). Avortul – *Curs 1 pentru elevi*.

Weil, F.D. (1989). The Sources and Structure of Legitimation in Western Democracies: A Consolidated Model Tested with Time-Series Data in Six Countries since World War II. *American Sociological Review*, 54, 682–706.

Weil, F.D. (1993). The Development of Democratic Attitudes in Eastern and Western Germany in a Comparative Perspective. *Research on Democracy and Society*, 1, 195–225.

Wood, R.L. (1999). Religious Culture and Political Action. *Sociological Theory*, 17(3), 307–332.

Web sources

Alianta Familiilor din Romania, www.alianta-familiilor.ro/, last accessed: 14 January 2014.

'Asociatia pro vita pentru nascuti si nenascuti', www.provitabucuresti.ro/, last accessed: 14 March 2013.

Asociatia Caritas Bucuresti, www.caritasbucuresti.org/new3/index.php/ro/, last accessed: 14 March 2013.

Asociatia Darul Vietii, Timisoara, www.darulvietii.ro/, last accessed: 14 March 2013.

Asociatia M.A.M.I., Hunedoara, http://hunedoaraevanghelica.wordpress.com/tag/asociatia-mama-miriam-hunedoara/, last accessed: 14 March 2013.

Fundatia Iochebed, Brasov, http://brasovulevanghelic.ro/organizatii/fundatia-iochebed/, last accessed: 14 March 2013.

Fundatia Solidaritatea si Speranta, www.fundatia.mmb.ro/index.php, last accessed: 14 March 2013.

'Strigatul Mut' ('The Silent Scream'), www.strigatulmut.ro/, last accessed: 14 January 2015.

12 Public education and religious rights

A comparative analysis

Kyriaki Topidi

> The fact that some members of some minority religious movements choose to order aspects of their lives in accordance with different priorities makes them objects of suspicion because, among other things, their non-conventional ways of living imply that something is wrong with the machinery of 'normalization'.[1]

Introduction

One of the persisting queries related to the interplay between law and culture(s) relates to the question to which extent all cultural practices (including religious ones) should be defended and therefore tolerated. Deriving from this more general question are sourced also the questions as to whether the denial of the recognition of a particular ethnic practice constitutes a denial of human rights as well as whether the non-recognition of a practice can be automatic because it constitutes a violation of human rights.

Law and anthropology adopt different positions on these points, while the dominant legal doctrine largely continues to base its discourse on the human rights paradigm and its universal character.[2] Anthropology has claimed a 'more nuanced recognition that tolerance of difference was one of several important ethical considerations'.[3] But what exactly counts as 'culture' in a given context?

1 J.E. Beckford, 'The Continuum between "Cults" and "Normal" Religion', in P. Coté (ed.), *Chercheurs de Dieux dans l'espace public: Frontier Religions in Public Space*, Ottawa, University of Ottawa Press, at 14.

2 See indicatively Jack Donnelly, 'Cultural Relativism and Universal Human Rights', *Human Rights Quarterly*, 6:4, Nov. 1984, 400–419; M. Mutua, 'Change in the Human Rights Universe', *Harvard Human Rights Journal*, 20, 3–5; Cyra Akila Choudhury, 'Beyond Culture: Human Rights Universalisms versus Religious and Cultural Relativism in the Activism for Gender Justice', *Berkley Journal of Gender Law and Justice*, 2015 [available at http://papers.ssrn.com/sol3/papers.cfm?abstract_id=2520581] .

3 Sally Engle Merry, 'Human Rights Law and the Demonization of Culture (And Anthropology Along the Way)', *Polar: Political and Anthropology Review*, 26:1, 2003, 55–77, at 57. One clear demonstration of the inconsistency across disciplines is shown by Merry (2003) in the context of the CEDAW general recommendations. She points out pertinently that the CEDAW Committee views culture as a 'barrier to progress'. The critique of culture adopts an 'imperial understanding'

As importantly, to what extent are given expressions of culture worthy of legal protection? International human rights still rely on a conception of culture as '*kultur*', the German romantic concept that 'responds to the need for a nation to define itself, to constitute its boundaries, and to ask how it is different from other groups'.[4] It does not take account necessarily of circumstances of co-existence of more than one culture, i.e. conditions of multiculturalism, let alone *de facto* or *de jure* legal pluralism.

Legal pluralism represents a concept and an analytical tool that introduces this discussion and explains at least some parts of the debate surrounding the legal fragmentation that classrooms around the world are increasingly reflecting.[5] Predictably, a structure that reflects genuine legal pluralism is perceived as a risky strategy leading to the disintegration of classrooms and by extension to that of societies.

Relying on Kymlicka's and Shachar's work,[6] legal protection today has a dual aim: first, to protect individual members and groups from external protections, but also, second, from internal ones too imposed on the most vulnerable members (e.g. children and women typically) in the name of cultural integrity and tradition.[7] Public education is a particularly appropriate policy area and legal field to cultivate this dual protection but with a parallel quest for those values that are common to the different legal systems in action in a given space.

These broad questions are repeatedly addressed to legal practitioners and legal systems in infinite combinations. One way to start answering them is to accept that culture is by no means a 'bounded and static'[8] concept. This is in fact a common anthropological view of culture, but one that the discipline of law still has difficulties to embrace, because it tends to privilege and presuppose a certain degree of legal certainty. If culture, however, is a dynamic and hybridised factor, then not every practice/belief is defendable. The question becomes where are the limits of tolerance of diversity. An-Na'im' s work attempts in his numerous contributions to this debate to point at the possibility of integration of local cultural understandings into human rights, reconciling the two views.[9] The wider concern, however,

of the context (other works label this as 'orientalist') and these arguments ultimately influence and shape contemporary human rights law (ibid., at 62).

4 Merry (2003) at 20.

5 For more on this point in the area of Family Law, cf. Andrea Büchler, *Islamic Family Law in Europe? Legal Pluralism and its Limits in European Family Law*, Farnham, Ashgate, 2011.

6 See indicatively Will Kymlicka, 'The Governance of Religious Diversity: The Old and the New', in Bramadat and Koenig (eds), *International Migration and the Governance of Religious Diversity,* McGill Queens University Press, 2009, 323–334; Ayelet Shachar, *Multicultural Jurisdictions: Cultural Differences and Women's Rights*, Cambridge University Press, 2001.

7 Büchler at 20.

8 Ibid. at 7.

9 With respect to Islam, An-Na'im suggests the use of liberal interpretations of Islamic law to make it amenable to human rights and argues that a reformation of Islamic law through a modern interpretation of the Shari'a would be better for the advancement of human rights in Muslim states than a secular approach. [Cf. Abdullahi An-Na'im, ed. by Mashood A. Baderin, *Islam and Human Rights: Selected Essays of Abdullahi An-Na'im,* Farnham, Ashgate, 2010.]

stands both scientifically and socially: our consciousness, understanding of and respect for cultural diversity needs to exclude instances of strong cultural relativism in order to avoid to have to tolerate the intolerable.[10]

Another systemic shortcoming in the discussion of the role of culture (with-)in law pertains to the over-emphasising of cultural factors and beliefs to the exclusion of socio-political and economic considerations. This is particularly relevant for women and their rights in minority cultures (e.g. headscarf issue in Europe). As Tariq Modood has already noted, however, 'the road to social integration and race equality politics has to go through ethnicity, not against it'.[11] In other terms, it has become more and more difficult (if not untenable) to dissociate expressions of culture, belief and/or identity from social integration in multicultural settings.

From the stricter legal perspective, one of the main obstacles in taking into systematic consideration cultural difference in legal claims lies in the uncertainty that it would create for the users of each legal system, as already mentioned.[12] In the UK context, as of the mid-1980s, the following balancing act was proposed:

> We would . . . regard a democratic pluralist society as seeking to achieve a balance between, on the one hand, the maintenance and active support of the essential elements of cultures and lifestyles of all the ethnic groups within it, and, on the other, the acceptance by all groups of a set of shared values distinctive of the society as a whole.[13]

The two sides of the balancing equation operate as limitations to each other but this does not signify that tensions are absent. This complex balancing act begins with and in schools.

Against this complex background, the purpose of this study is to account for the debate of the exercise of religious rights in public schools, but on a legal comparative basis. The comparison will operate on three levels: first, it will consider the main legal concepts (*secularism* v. *post-secularism*) in setting the scene for the consideration of their implications and effects. The second level will effectively look at the protection of legal diversity in Europe and two other case studies, Canada and South Africa. In parallel to this second level of comparison, the third level of comparative inquiry will observe and question the ways that non-discrimination, prevalent in European countries, as opposed to reasonable accommodation used in Canada and

10 William Twining, *Human Rights Southern Voices*, Cambridge, Cambridge University Press, 2009, at 218.

11 Tariq Modood, 'Alabama Britain', *Guardian*, 22 May 1989.

12 See for example the critique of the commercial case of *Ting Sing Ning* v. *Ting Chek Swee* (2008) 1 SLR 197, decided in Singapore, where the Court of Appeal was faced with the question on whether there has been wrongdoer control control of a company. The Asian origin of respondents played a determinant role in the Court's decision. For more see Nurmatha Murthi, 'Does Culture Have a Role to Play in a Legal System?', *Singapore Law Review*, 30.01.2013, Blog Archive.

13 Swann Committee Report, *Education for All*, at p. 6, as quoted in Sebastian Poulter, 'Cultural Pluralism and its Limits: A Legal Perspective', at p. 4.

South Africa, answer the calls in response to the increasing religious diversity in public schools. The following part of the chapter will then reflect on these realities against a multicultural and post-multicultural policy frame. Ultimately, the chapter will conclude with remarks asking if and how students in these schools can become empowered agents and subjects of the law when it comes to their religiously diverse identities. The entire analysis is conditioned *ab initio* by the assumption that it is impossible to ignore the state of plurality that modern law and society has nowadays acquired.

A legally plural environment: the background

A contemporary reading of the relationship between the legal aspects of interaction of religion and education requires a legal pluralist lens. What people and right-claimers consider as law, when exercising their rights, gains increasingly importance. Equally important is the superimposition of norms and their hierarchy, whether we are referring to official and/or unofficial law.[14]

This is particularly so if one accepts that legal pluralism is 'the key concept in a post-modern view of law'.[15] This statement comes with many questions attached to it, such as what is really law (definitional problems), whether and how law reflects cultural practice (culturalist dimension) and what is ultimately law's role (functionalist dimension) in the award of religious rights in public schools. None of these issues, however, are the direct concern of this analysis, although they affect the ways law is ultimately practised.

The present analysis, however, unambiguously operates within Santos' third phase of the debate on legal pluralism: that of 'post-modern legal plurality where the concept of the global challenges the concept of the nation-state'.[16] Religious diversity in public school classrooms is most often the result of twentieth-century migratory movements, especially and particularly in Europe, and as such fits squarely in the global dimension of the phenomenon.

For the purposes of this study, globalisation is and remains the relevant background and the way legal provisions respond to religious rights claims clearly reflects this background. Santos' observations on 'post-modern legal plurality' suggest two strong features/movements: the first is the communication between the various legal

14 The basic types of legal pluralism are STRONG, referring to 'legal systems in which the sovereign commands or validates or recognizes different bodies of law for different groups in the population' and WEAK, in cases where the central state retains 'the ultimate power to acknowledge or refuse the existence of such different bodies of law'. [John Griffiths, 'What is Legal Pluralism?', *Journal of Legal Pluralism and Unofficial Law*, 24, 1986, 1–56, cf. also Baudouin Dupret, 'Legal Pluralism, Plurality of Laws and Legal Practices: Theories, Critiques and Praxiological Re-specification', *European Journal of Legal Studies*, 1, 2007, available at www.ejls.eu/1/14UK.pdf.]

15 Santos, B. de Sousa, 'Law: A Map of Misreading. Toward a Postmodern Conception of Law', *Journal of Law and Society*, 14, 1987, 279 at 297.

16 B. de Sousa Santos, *Towards a New Common Sense: Law, Science and Politics in the Paradigmatic Transition*, London, Routledge, 1995, at 117.

orders (which he labels as *legal porosity*) and the second relies on 'a cultural political strategy aimed at revealing the full range of social regulation'.[17] Both paradigms are relevant and in full operation as the following discussion reveals.

In fact, reflecting on the clash of rights in public schools, often involving the freedom of belief opposed to that of education, or to the 'rights of others' (translated also as the *public interest*), hides a second reading of the same clash: that of a religious practice/custom perceived as law by its claimer as opposed to the 'official' practice and content of certain rights. In that sense, we are openly facing a situation of plurality of laws, plainly revolving around 'what people conventionally refer to as law'.[18]

Dominant global legal conceptual tools and concepts

The model of arrangement between religion and the state has direct influence on the position and treatment of religious identity in public schools. There is a very rich debate taking place in academic literature of many disciplines of the social sciences, including law, on the role of religion in constitutional settings of contemporary societies.[19]

The principle of state neutrality is often invoked as a standard that guarantees a certain degree of religious diversity in the public sphere. At the level of European jurisprudence, the understanding of the concept signifies that the state cannot favour or disfavour religions and must, in all cases, act as an impartial arbiter and benevolent co-ordinator of faiths within its territory,[20] in other words, secularism understood as equidistance. The limits to the state's duties are nevertheless placed

17 Ibid., at 115.

18 Tamanaha's definition of law is resonating here ('what law is , is determined by the people in the social arena through their own common usages, not in advance by the social scientist or theorist', B.Z. Tamanaha, 'A Non-Essentialist Version of Legal Pluralism', *Journal of Law and Society*, 27, 2000, 296–321 at 314).

19 See indicatively J. Temperman, 'The Neutral State: Optional or Necessary? A Triangular Analysis of State-Religion Relationships, Democratisation and Human Rights Compliance', I *Religion and Human Rights*, 269, 2006; J. Temperman, 'State Neutrality in Public School Education: An Analysis of the Interplay Between the Neutrality Principle, the Right to Adequate Education, Children's Right to Freedom of Religion or Belief, Parental Liberties, and the Position of Teachers', *Human Rights Quarterly*, 32:4, 2010, 865; R. Uitz, 'Aiming for State Neutrality in Matters of Religion: The Hungarian Record', *U. Det. Mercy L. Rev.*, 83, 2005–2006, 761; E. Brems, 'Above Children's Heads, The Headscarf Controversy in European Schools from the Perspective of Children's Rights', *Int'l J. Child. Rts*, 14, 2006, 119; S. Langlaude, 'Indoctrination, Secularism, Religious Liberty, and the ECHR', *Int'l & Comp. L.Q.*, 55, 2006, 929; Karl-Heinz Ladeur and Ino Augsberg, 'The Myth of the Neutral State: The Relationship between State and Religion in the Face of New Challenges', *German Law Journal*, 8:2, 2007, 143; B. Chélini-Pont, 'Religion in the Public Sphere: Challenges and Opportunities', *BYU L. Rev.*, 3, 2005, 611; M.W. McConnell, '"God is Dead and We Have Killed Him!" Freedom of Religion in the Post-Modern Age', *BYU L. Rev.*, 1, 1993, 163.

20 Indicative ECtHR case-law on this matter includes: *Serif* v. *Greece,* 14.12.1999; *Hasan and Chaush* v. *Bulgaria,* 26.10.2000; *Metropolitan Church of Bessarabia* v. *Moldova,* 13.12.2000; *Svyato-Mykhaylivska Parafiya* v. *Ukraine,* 14.06.2007.

in cases where religious moral doctrines appear to conflict with the law, values or the legal system as a whole.[21]

Neutrality, however, is far from a uniform concept and includes numerous nuances as to how relations between the state and religion could be organised. Ultimately, the 'model' applied in each case remains, at its base, a political choice infused by the historical and cultural traditions of a given state.

The purpose of this contribution is not to reproduce the arguments and findings of earlier studies. Its focus, instead, is more on how these 'paradigms' are reflected in public schools and on what types of rights they lead to for students, teachers and parents. The two extremes, theocracy and thoroughly militant, perhaps even anti-religious secularism, assign unambiguous positions to religion: in the first case, there is a fusion between law and religion where religion becomes law. In the second case, there is 'no government support for religion and no government interference in the religious practices of both the majority and minority religions in a state',[22] and every expression of religious identity including claims for exemptions, tends to be banned from the public sphere.

Questions and controversies arise more often in the context of intermediate models, which tend to reflect more pragmatic responses to the needs of a given society, often too the fruit of historical circumstances.[23] This linear representation of the state–religion relationship suffers, however, from one significant drawback: it assumes that religiosity (and the exercise of religious rights) and secularity are opposite and incompatible poles.[24]

Secularism: conceptual mapping

Modern secularism, in the sense of separation of law and religion, represents a complex picture, whereby commitment to religion does not necessarily go hand in hand with constitutional and practical support of believers to their respective faiths. It is essential to determine for the purposes of this analysis how the concept of secularism is understood: there are, indeed, many definitions of the term: from *political secularism*, that brings together religion and law through policy, to *radical secularism* that is characterised by a strict separation of law and religion, passing through a *moderate* type of secularism that aims at relative separation between law and religion.[25]

Morini, in her work, proposes two essential forms of secularism:[26] a *pluralist* one, which identifies religion as a purely private matter but one that deserves

21 See for example *Refah Partisi and Others* v. *Turkey*, 31.07.2001 (Chamber), 13.02.2003 (Grand Chamber).

22 Fox (2006) at 538.

23 Daryn Jensen, 'Classifying Church-State Arrangements: Beyond Religious versus Secular',in N. Hosen and R. Mohr (eds), *Law and Religion in Public Life: The Contemporary Debate*, London, Routledge, 2011, 15–33. The examples of the United States, France or the UK are indicative.

24 Ibid. at 16.

25 Werner Menski, *Fuzzy Law and the Boundaries of Secularism*, PER/PECJ 2010(13) at 30–31.

26 Claudia Morini, 'Secularism and Freedom of Religion: The Approach of the European Court of Human Rights', *Israel Law Review*, 43, 2010, 611–630 at 618.

a position in the public space (essentially through manifestation). This implies that the state must abstain from taking a position on core aspects of each faith and at the same time it must guarantee the principle of non-discrimination on groups on the basis of religion. The second type of secularism, of a *fundamentalist* kind, suggests that religious beliefs have no place in the public domain. The risk inherent in this second type is that secularism is likely to prevail over religious pluralism[27] and is then perceived as politically contested and therefore unacceptable.

This and other broad categorisations, however, are far from self-sufficient in guiding us within an environment of intense and multi-layered plurality. Vertovec's *super-diversity* highlights the inadequacy of the current legal frameworks to address the boundaries of secularism.[28] Accepting that legal pluralism is a fact,[29] which is one of the main assumptions of this analysis, the challenge of religious diversity in public school education appears as a testing ground about the ways that 'law as culture is accepted but culture as law creates irritations'.[30] Precisely because of the plurality of law, it becomes increasingly difficult to separate formal law from values.[31] This implies that secularism becomes a concept that is constantly 'adjustable' to a given society's needs. In other words, a culture-specific legal order.

In a way, thus, it is not sufficient to assess the relationship between state and faith(s) solely in the light of formal constitutional commitments. At the same time, the notion of state neutrality vis-à-vis religion is becoming more and more contested: there is indeed no perfectly neutral state in the sense that culture (including religion) and political/constitutional values are already part of society and guide the legal and political system in drawing the line between the public–private, the individual and the collective, the morally acceptable and the prohibited.[32]

Post-secularism and public education: a shift?

If we accept, as Taylor claims, that contemporary democratic societies ought to be organised around a strong 'philosophy of civility', secularism almost automatically contains more than Rajeev Bhargava's 'principled distance' of the state from religion in the context discussed above.[33] It becomes a notion with at least three components: human rights, equality and democracy.[34]

27 See for example *Sahin* v. *Turkey*, Appl.N. 44774/98 (2005).

28 Steven Vertovec, 'Super-Diversity and its Implications', *Ethnic and Racial Studies*, 30:6, 2007, 1024–1054.

29 There is abundant literature that makes this point: see indicatively Griffiths (1986).

30 Menski (2010) at 35 and also R. Cotterrell, 'Law in Culture', *Ratio Juris*, 17:1, 2004, 1–14.

31 Menski (2010) at 45.

32 For a similar point, see Jensen (2011) at 19.

33 Charles Taylor, 'Why We Need A Radical Redefinition of Secularism', in Butler *et al.*, *The Power of Religion in the Public Sphere*, New York, Columbia University Press, 2011 34–59 at 47.

34 Ibid.

This understanding of secularism, labelled as post-secularism by others,[35] also implies the end of the phase of the strife against one religion dominating all others in a given space. To state only two of the numerous understandings of *post-secular,* one can claim that it reflects the struggle to come to terms with ideas and formats that were once called religious or it can also be used to describe religious features and continuity that are used in non-Western or non-Christian contexts.[36] Both definitions, however, resonate Habermas' more recent work that observes the continued and often enhanced existence of religious communities.[37] The current phase of the phenomenon is more concerned with the way(s) to balance religious rights with equality. The shift in the 'content' of secularism has nevertheless not completely eradicated the view that some hold of religion as a social threat.

An alternative vision of the relationship between state and religion, which embodies in a fuller way the notion of conflict in the exercise of religious rights is the one that draws a broad distinction between constitutional systems that leave room for only one system of values (i.e. religion), such as Saudi Arabia or Iran (*monism*), and those that accept that there cannot be only one set of beliefs or systems of faith to which members of society and the political community are expected to adhere, as in India (*pluralism*).[38] In the latter case, the state disposes of two options: it either supports the activities and expressions of rights of all religious communities or it does not support any of them. Concretely, for example, the application of secularist pluralism could signify either the financial support of all schools, independently of the faith that they belong to or the support of none of them.

The complexity of the pluralist option should not be, nevertheless, ignored. What happens in cases of parallel sub-community normative systems that 'compete' with the 'official' one in regulating a given set of circumstances? Again more concretely, how does one address a claim from a female student to be exempted from compulsory swimming lessons that are part of the official public school curriculum for religious grounds? These and other similar circumstances do not always make it easy to define with clarity the respective domains of authority of the different normative systems that seem to be potentially concurrently applicable.

The dilemma for the law and the state presents itself therefore as one where on the one hand the state cannot ignore the sensibilities of religious groups

35 See for example Hazel Bryan, 'Reconstructing the Teacher as a Post Secular Pedagogue: A Consideration of the New Teachers' Standards', *Journal of Beliefs and Values: Studies in Religion and Education*, 33:2, 2012, 217–228, at 222. In her view, post-secularism describes 'the state where individuals determine the extent to which they take part in religious activity' (at 222) not whether they are religious in the first place, but rather in what ways are they religious.

36 M.S. Roberts, 'Poetry in a Secular Age', *Poetry Review*, 98:69–75, 2008.

37 J. Habermas, 'Religion in the Public Sphere', *European Journal of Philosophy*, 14:1, 2006, 1–25.

38 Ibid. at 21. For the Canadian conception of state neutrality see Justice Deschamps' definition of the ideal of 'neutrality' in *S.L.* v. *Commission sclaire des Chênes*, 2012 SCC 7(2012) 1 S.C.R. 235, understood as follows: 'following a realistic and non-absolutist approach, state neutrality is assured when the state neither favors nor hinders any particular religious belief, when it shows respect for all postures towards religion, including that of having no religious beliefs whatsoever, while taking into account the competing constitutional rights of the individuals affected' (para.32).

(often minorities), if it wishes to remain committed to pluralism but at the same time, it has to fully embrace using the legal means it deems appropriate, certain values that it recognises as essential.

To that effect there are two prevalent conclusions that can be drawn from the start: first, there is widespread acknowledgement of the different possibilities in reflecting the presence of religion in the public space and, second, it is broadly accepted that religion matters.[39]

In direct opposition to Peter Berger's prediction in 1968, that in the twenty-first century, religion will only concern a small minority of individuals,[40] the debate is now framed, not anymore around the issue of finding a single general universal recipe on religion and secularity, but instead on the study of the multitude of complex and multi-layered understandings of secularity and religion.[41]

The implications in the area of education of post-secularism present us with two basic options: one option would place emphasis on preparing students for a 'global' citizenship that embraces and pushes the student to understand the world's multiple modernities.[42] The other option would revert to human rights education based on human rights universals.[43]

The real issue between these two options for our purposes is to what extent religion and the exercise of religious rights should be treated as a 'dangerous cultural force' for education, insofar as it is deemed to threaten human rights.[44] HRE scholarship is not unanimous on this point, however coming from a different angle, that of *de facto* legal pluralism in contemporary multicultural societies, the content of education cannot be easily separated from that of the identity of pupils. Issues of rights exercise arise precisely because of legal pluralism and societal diversity with a heavy influence from religious traditions. The vicious circle of rights, religious origin/values and education in the words of Bowie, moves then as follows: 'if the voices of religious traditions are silenced or portrayed in negative terms, then a climate of fear about difference is created'.[45] This leads ultimately to the denial of basic human rights.

Where would the balance lie then between religion as a source of rights' violations and religion as positive moral motivation? Habermas now suggests that

39 Bob Bowie, 'Human Rights Education and the Post-Secular Turn', *Journal of Beliefs and Values: Studies in Religion and Education*, 33:2, 2012, 195–205, at 195.

40 Peter Berger, 'A Bleak Outlook is Seen for Religion', *New York Times*, 25 February 1968, at 3.

41 Bowie (2012) at 196. Bowie refers to this latter aspect as multiple modernities.

42 Bowie (2012) at 199. Habermas's work reflects this when he states: '[s]ecular citizens in Europe must learn to live, the sooner the better, in a post-secular society and in so doing they will be following the example of religious citizens, who are have already come to terms with the ethical expectation of democratic citizenship'. [Jürgen Habermas, 'Religion in the Public Sphere', *European Journal of Philosophy*, 14:1, 2006, 1–25 at 1.]

43 The UN defines HRE as 'training, dissemination and information efforts aimed at the building of a universal culture of HR through the imparting of knowledge and skills and the moulding of attitudes' (UNESCO, *All Human Beings: A Manual for HRE*, Paris, 1998, at 3).

44 Bowie (2012) at 200.

45 Ibid. at 201. See also U. Baxi, *The Future of Human Rights*, Oxford, Oxford University Press, 2003, at 24–25.

'both religious and secular mentalities must be open to a complementary learning process if we are to balance shared citizenship and cultural difference'.[46] In other words, he proposes a critical and somewhat guarded acceptance of diversity. Any assumption that in order to be a constituent part of the national identity of a given state, prior identities should be relinquished, is inherently incompatible with the multicultural dimension of any post-modern state.[47]

Religious pluralism in European law

European law, far from being uniform, has adopted a clear preference for a cautious approach regarding the role of religion in the public sphere, including in education. Largely a cultural process, the position of religion and religious rights is reflected in national constitutional systems but also at the supra-national level, essentially through the findings of the European Court of Human Rights (ECtHR). The following part will first consider the contribution of the ECtHR in the debate surrounding the exercise of religious rights in public schools, with emphasis on cases involving religious symbols, which are the most common. Then, it will reflect on the debate as to whether it matters whether a religious claim is grounded in a Christian context (majority religion) or in a non-Christian context (minority religion) in a given constitutional setting.

The role of the European Court of Human Rights in adjudicating claims on religious rights' exercise in public schools

It has been often recalled that 'the US way to be secular – or modern – is to be religious – while the European way of being religious is to be secular'.[48] In this light, the Council of Europe's European Court of Human Rights has defined freedom of religion as follows:

> (f)reedom of thought, conscience and religion is one of the foundations of a democratic society within the meaning of the Convention. It is, in its religious dimension, one of the most vital elements that go to make-up the identity of believers and their conception of life, but it is a precious asset for atheists, agnostics, skeptics and the unconcerned. The pluralism indissociable from a democratic society, which has been dearly won over the centuries, depends on it.[49]

The right in itself is of course not absolute: the state may step in to protect the rights of others or other constitutionally protected liberties.

46 Habermas (2006) at 1.
47 Kymlicka (2012) at 18.
48 Sullivan (2009) at 1183.
49 *Kokkinakis* v. *Greece*, at para.31 (1994).

Against a rich variety of arguments and proposed solutions from domestic courts, the ECtHR has insisted on a tactic of 'decisional minimalism'[50] when it comes to religious human rights claims. This is because the Court has found that '(i)t is not possible to discern throughout Europe a uniform conception of the significance of religion in society . . . even within a single country such conceptions may vary'.[51] In practice, the Strasbourg court has built its decisions on pragmatic arguments and has cautiously avoided complex legal theorising in order to minimise political damage and severe judicial errors.[52] It also utilises the techniques of the *margin of appreciation* or the concepts of *reasonableness* and *proportionality* to shift attention from *stricto sensu* legal reasoning towards the prevalent values in a given national context.[53] Particularly regarding legal pluralism, the ECtHR's stance remains that parallel religiously inspired legal systems are incompatible with secularism and equality.[54] This latter point is to some extent incompatible with the Court's position that there is no uniformity in the significance of religion within society in European states, and hence special features and aspects of the role of religion in some states are deliberately ignored.

The recent and widely criticised Grand Chamber judgment, in the case of *Lautsi* v. *Italy,* highlights pertinently the difficulties of adjudicating religiously related claims in the realm of education. The common question of whether the presence of a crucifix in a public school classroom violated one's freedom of conscience and right to have his/her children receive an education in conformity with his/her philosophical beliefs, led to confusion as to what exactly is the duty of the state: an 'a-religious' order that serves pluralism by relegating religious rights completely to the absolutism of the individual sphere or rather the stage to present and support spiritual and moral values that are the common heritage of a state.

On the other hand, the ECtHR when considering the question as to whether mandatory Turkish religious education courses were compatible with the right to education as guaranteed by the ECHR,[55] did not hesitate to find a violation in the applicant's right to education[56] in conformity with her religious belief when it ruled that the absence of instruction on the elements of the applicant's and her

50 The term is borrowed from Cass Sunstein, *One Case At a Time: Judicial Minimalism on the Supreme Court*, Cambridge, MA: Harvard University Press, 2001.

51 *Otto Preminger Institute* v. *Austria*, 295 –A ECtHR (ser.A) at 14 (1994).

52 See for example the relatively recent *Lautsi* v. *Italy* (Grand Chamber) decision. Appl. N. 30814/06) (2011).

53 See *Sahin* v. *Turkey* and *Efstratiou* v. *Greece* (Appl. N. 24095/94) and *Valsamis* v. *Greece* (Appl. N. 21787/98).

54 Cf. *Refah Partisi and Others* v. *Turkey*, Appl. No. 41349/98, 41342/98, 41344798, Judgment of 13.02.2003 at 127, 128.

55 *Zengin* v. *Turkey* (Appl. N. 1448/04) (2007).

56 Article 2 of the First Additional Protocol stipulates that: 'No person shall be denied the right to education. In the exercise of any functions which it assumes in relation to education and to teaching, the State shall respect the right of parents to ensure such education and teaching in conformity with their own religious and philosophical convictions.'

father's faith (in this case Alevism), was not compensated for due to the lack of objectivity and pluralism in the contents of the school subject on 'Religious Culture and Ethics'.

In sum, the Court's approach at times embraces a 'fundamentalist' degree of secularism by imposing on individuals a secularist behaviour in the public domain, particularly affecting the manifestation of religious beliefs through symbols (e.g. in clothing).[57] Without renouncing the human rights ideals reflected in the Convention and in particular the principle of freedom of religion, the Court avoids general rules and consequently fails to create consistent interpretation of the content of the right. It also places barriers to the circulation and efficient transfer of norms between the various jurisdictions by placing a wall of legal obscurity vis-à-vis the interpretation of religious rights and their compatibility with the broader human rights culture that courts have been developing in the European continent.

Comparing this approach to other, non-European jurisdictions that have been faced with questions relating to the exercise of religious freedom at school, they have shifted their focus from objective to subjective criteria. They have focused on the sincerity of the belief that a student claims, which then leads to discussions of the possible justification of the interference with the right,[58] just as is the case before the ECtHR.

Taking each situation separately and avoiding negative qualifications, as is often the case for Muslim headscarf cases both in schools and elsewhere, the narrower approach to religious rights cases allows for the concretisation of competing interests in the spirit of diversity and tolerance.[59] The doctrine of reasonable accommodation appears essential in non-European settings but is still largely missing from the European one.

In the European space, it is however difficult to deny that the Strasbourg court contributes in significant ways through positive as well as negative findings in cases concerning religious beliefs and education in conditioning the ways that religion is perceived, interpreted and adjusted in the individual jurisdictions of its

57 Ingvill Thorson Plesner, 'The ECtHR between Fundamentalist and Liberal Secularism', 1–3, www.strasbourgconsortium.org/commentaries.php.

58 See indicatively the cases of *Pillay* v. *MEC for education, KwaZulu Natal and Others*, CCT 51/06 (South Africa) or *Multani* v. *Commission Scolaire Marguerite –Bourgeoys* (Supreme Court of Canada, 2 March 2006) as discussed in Hans-Martien Th. D. ten Napel and Florian H.K. Theissen, 'The ECtHR on Religious Symbols in Public Institutions –A Comparative Perspective: Maximum Protection of the Freedom of Religion through Judicial Minimalism?', in Silvio Ferrari and Rinaldo Cristofari (eds), *Law and Religion in the 21st Century: Relations between States and Religious Communities,* Ashgate, 2010, 317–320. These cases may be contrasted for example with the ECtHR case of *Karaduman* v. *Turkey* (1993), which concerned the refusal to a university graduate of a certificate asserting her qualifications because she would not submit a photograph without a headscarf, as required. The ECtHR held that 'Article 9 of the Convention does not always guarantee the right to behave in the public sphere in a way which is dictated by such a belief' (para.108).

59 Ibid., 319–210.

member states, especially with reference to immigrant groups. Elizabeth Shakman Hurd argues a step further by claiming that this is the beginning of a new form of horizontal religious governance.[60] It is indeed true that a state's authority to draw a line and designate the space where religious rights can be exercised is no longer exclusive: courts, constitutions and transnational bodies contribute to the exchange of norms and concepts creating webs of understandings that are becoming decreasingly easy to study in isolation. The *transnational embedding* of religious norms and rights has already been identified as a crucial characteristic of the various modes of religious belonging, particularly for migrants,[61] yet it is still too early to depict, let alone predict, the ways that the transnational element affects the practices of religious governance in Europe.

Religious symbols in education

The field area with the largest attraction of both social as well as legal instances of contention remains that of religious symbols.[62] The legal study of religious symbols in education presupposes the identification of at least three main axes of inquiry: first, the use of such symbols on the individual as opposed to the institutional level. The permission of the personal use of religious symbols entails a different legal account and balancing act from a similar generalised display of such symbols in public institutions, schools in particular.[63] Second, solutions adopted vis-à-vis the presence of religious symbols in schools also vary between the national level and the supra-national one (e.g. at the Council of Europe level).[64] Finally, a background parameter and dimension to the debate to be accounted for is the one where one needs to distinguish between public policies and the way that courts apply the relevant legal provisions affecting religious diversity in the public education systems.[65] A review of case law in those circumstances usually reveals self-restraint on behalf of both national and supra-national judges that are not constitutionally required to reflect on the appropriate characteristics of a certain policy, but instead to control its compatibility with the general constitutional principles applicable in each case.[66]

The conceptualisation of religious pluralism in public education has been also dominated in recent case law by the overarching concern of social cohesion. This concern is interpreted most often through the limitation that freedom

60 Elizabeth Shakman Hurd, 'Emergent Patterns in Global Religious Governance', ReligioWest Conference Paper, EUI, November 2011.

61 Bramadat and Koenig (2009) at 314.

62 Cf. W. Menski and R. Scarciglia (eds), *Islamic Symbols in European Courts*, CEDAM-Kluwer, 2014.

63 Javier Martinez-Torron, 'Institutional Religious Symbols, State Neutrality and Protection of Minorities in Europe', *L&W Journal*, 12/2013, at 23.

64 Ibid.

65 Ibid. at 24.

66 Ibid.

of religion can be subjected to when protecting 'public order' and/or 'the rights and freedoms of others'.[67]

To be clear, Article 2 of Protocol I ECHR does not confer any right to go to any particular school. It refers to one's right to obtain education from the system as a whole.[68] So, unless a given school system imposes a general ban on religious symbols, it is difficult to argue that there is an interference with a student's right to education. Even in the case of a general ban, however, it is legally required that the ban is justified as 'necessary' to protect a legitimate aim, in line with Articles 18(3) ICCPR and 9(2) ECHR. This rule is applicable for instance to both female students as well as teachers wishing to wear the Islamic veil, who deserve to see their claims considered on a case-by-case basis, with increasing consideration also of the social, economic and cultural conditions in which these women operate, 'so as to create favourable conditions in which autonomous and meaningful choices can be made'.[69]

In the European context where there is no single, uniform response to the position of religion in the public sphere, national interpretations of the right to religious freedom within public education share a common defensive attitude, as already mentioned, towards religious diversity precisely by invoking the social cohesion limitation.

For example, the German method highlighted in the case law of the Länder jurisdictions allows preferential treatment of Christian symbols in education and sanctions Muslim ones – in particular the headscarf – on the basis of the argument that 'a Muslim teacher could not credibly convey to her pupils the Christian values and traditions anchored in the Länder constitutions and the respective school laws'.[70] The above stands, despite findings of the German Federal Constitutional Court that the headscarf as an individual choice is covered by a teacher's fundamental right to freedom of religion, even within a public school.[71]

Similarly, the French approach, using a very different starting point, that of laïcité, together with its republican tradition, effectively denies the possibility of the exercise of religious rights in the public sphere.[72] But is laïcité really neutral? This becomes an important question when addressing religious pluralism in public schools. It is based and relies on the public–private sphere distinction in the expression of religious belief, which is after all a European Christian conceptualisation of faith.[73]

67 Daniel Augustein, 'Religious Pluralism and National Constitutional Traditions in Europe', in C. Ungureanu and L. Zucca (eds), *Law, State and Religion in the New Europe,* Cambridge University Press, 2011.

68 Manisuli Ssenyonjo, 'The Islamic Veil and Freedom of Religion, the Rights to Education and Work: A Survey of Recent International and National Cases', *Chinese Journal of International Law*, 6:3, 2007, 653–710, at 710.

69 Sahin Judgment at para.69.

70 See Augenstein (2011) and Verwaltungsgerichthof Baden-Württemberg, 14 March 2007 S 516/07 as well as Bayerischer Verwaltungsgerichthof, 15 January 2007, Vf. 14-VII-05.

71 BVerfG, 2 BvR 1436/02 of 3 June 2003 (Kopftuch Ludin).

72 See footnote 92 for more details.

73 Augenstein (2011).

At the supra-national level, faced with widespread resistance to the presence and display of non-majoritarian religious symbols in educational institutions, the ECtHR has proved unwilling to qualify the notion of 'social cohesion' as a limitation to religious pluralism. Instead, in a series of widely discussed cases,[74] it grants an unnecessarily wide margin of appreciation to member states in deciding these matters.[75]

The margin of appreciation becomes problematic in its domestic application when, for instance, once contrasts *Dahlab* with *Lautsi*. *Lautsi I* (Chamber Judgment) conveyed the message, albeit implicitly, that in public schools the absence of all religious symbols is a guarantee of freedom of belief and flows from the principle of state neutrality. *Dahlab* and *Lautsi I* appear compatible so far, at least with regard to outcomes. They remain, of course, open to critique insofar as both cases suggest the elimination of 'visibility' of de facto religious pluralism in European classrooms. One can also question whether and how this is a normatively 'acceptable' form of neutrality, as it reinforces the assumption of religion as being conflictive.[76]

Lautsi II[77] highlights the incoherence with *Dahlab* best as it delegates the decision about the presence of religious symbols to the state, in accordance with the latter's margin of appreciation. Ms Dahlab was not allowed to wear her headscarf in school by virtue of the principle of neutrality applicable at the Canton of Geneva but public schools in Italy could choose to append crucifixes in the classroom. The same right is invoked but ultimately cultural and socio-political factors and understandings of the concept have shaped the right's legal content in different ways.

Sticking to a rights-based discourse, one also needs to be aware of the increasingly pluralist legal environment that these jurisdictions operate in. As Werner Menski explains, the quest for 'good law' that he finds to be inherently plural, is also 'a matter of common sense and . . . equity, demanding cautious avoidance of jumping to hasty conclusions about what is "intolerable" and what is not'.[78]

The Muslim factor

As the comparison between *Lautsi II* and *Dahlab* seems to imply, the lack of sympathy for Muslims in Europe is symptomatic of the assumption that religious people are not worthy of protection, due to European historical experiences with

74 *Dahlab* v. *Switzerland*, 42393/98 (2001), *Sahin* v. *Turkey*, 44774/98 (2005), *Dogru* v. *France*, 27058/05 (2008), *Kervanci* v. *France*, 31645704 (2008).

75 The majority of Sahin nevertheless notes that the 'State's role as the neutral and impartial organizer of the exercise of various religions' should not be interpreted as being that of removing 'the cause of tension by eliminating pluralism' but instead ensuring that 'competing groups tolerate each other' (cf. Sahin, at para. 107).

76 For a similar point see Martinez-Torron (2014) at 35.

77 See footnote 50.

78 Werner Menski, Legal Pluralism as a Global Irritant of Critical Relevance: MM v POP, at p.8.

secularism. This societal 'suspicion' and legal restraint towards non-majoritarian religion(s) appears more clearly in the context of Muslim immigrant communities in Europe.

It is based on the growing 'Islamisation' of certain Muslim communities constructed as a response to modernisation by some authors.[79] The often-cited example of the headscarf is but one illustration of this issue. From a religious perspective, the requirements of the headscarf are interpreted differently by different Muslim religious schools. For some Muslims, it does not even constitute a religious obligation at all to cover their heads.

Overall, the debate of the headscarf as a symbol is quite widespread nowadays.[80] A purely legal analysis of the wearing of the headscarf carries however some inherent limitations: it ignores the socio-economic parameters for the (non-) exercise of religious rights. Placing this debate in the material scope of education would remedy to some extent this gap.

In the words of Niraj Nathawani, '[a]n Islamic headscarf could mean: loyalty to tradition, belief in chastity of women, symbol of religious identity, respect for wishes of parents and families, signal of not being sexually available, expression of cultural identity, refusal to westernize'.[81]

From the angle of the right to education, firmly recognised in human rights treaties worldwide,[82] states are obliged to eliminate racial discrimination in education.[83] Additionally, they are also under the obligation to respect the right of parents to have their children educated in conformity with parents' religious and philosophical content and to a lesser extent the wishes of the student herself.[84]

As Ssenyongo notes, two types of legal questions emerge as a result of the ban on the headscarf: first, the extent to which the ban interferes with the right to education of the female student that wishes to wear it and, second, the question as to whether there is a violation of the parents' right to have their children educated according to their convictions.[85]

79 Gellner's 'Muslim Society' is one such work.

80 For two opposing discourses see for example K. Bennoune, 'Secularism and Human Rights: A Contextual Analysis of Headscarves, Religious Expression and Women's Equality Under International Law', *Columbia J Transnational L*, 45, 2007, 367–426 and Ssenyonjo (2007).

81 Niraj Nathwani, 'Islamic Headscarves and Human Rights: A Critical Analysis of the Relevant Case Law of the European Court of Human Rights', *Netherlands QHR*, 25:2, 2007, 221–254, at 244 citing Ludin (at para.52).

82 Article 14 ECHR, together with Article 2 of Protocol I; Article 2 and 17(1) of the African Charter on Human and Peoples' Rights (ACHPR), OAU Doc. CAB/LEG/67/3 rev.5, 21 ILM 58 (1982), into force 21 October 1986; Article 11 of the African Charter on the Rights of the Child OAU Doc. CAB/LEG/24.9/49 (1990), into force 29 November 1999.

83 International Convention on the Elimination of All Forms of Racial Discrimination (CERD) UN GA Res. 2106 (XX) of 21 December 1965, into force 4 January 1969.

84 Article 13(3) ICESCR; Article 18(4) ICCPR; Article 2, Protocol I ECHR, Article 13(4) of Protocol of San Salvador; Article 11(4) of African Charter on the Rights and Welfare of the Child. The UN Convention on the Rights of the Child stipulates that in cases of conflict between rights of parents and the child in matters of the right to education, the parents' wishes take precedence (Art.5 UNCRC).

85 Ssenyonjo (2007) at 660.

Against this multiplicity and interpretative complexity, the role of law is to reflect the 'majority's' vision of justice as embodied in a series of rights. Hostility of the law, however, towards religion is a dangerous strategy insofar as it pushes even the more moderately religious persons to assume the incompatibility between one's religious beliefs with the normative requirements of a democratic society.[86]

Alternative legal approaches to the protection of religious difference: *reasonable accommodation* v. (*indirect*) *discrimination*

The protection of religious freedom is not addressed worldwide using the same tools. While in Europe, religious rights stem from a non-discrimination perspective, prohibiting a different treatment on the basis of religion, other legal traditions approach the same process from the perspective of reasonable accommodation. Very often, these latter traditions place this tool in the context of multiculturalism policies.

The origins of the notion of reasonable accommodation concerning religious diversity are to be found in the United States[87] and Canada and are the direct result of immigration. The duty of reasonable accommodation was at first recognised in the area of religious non-discrimination.[88] While in the US context, the concept has not penetrated the area of religious diversity in education, due to the Establishment Clause, the situation is strikingly different in Canada. The Canadian legal context recognises as generally applicable the duties of reasonable accommodation to all those socially vulnerable as a result of their belonging to a disadvantaged group (ethnic, religious or other).[89] Reasonable accommodation has been considered an 'instrument for negotiating cultural and religious plurality'.[90] It was introduced by courts in the context of the interpretation of the Canadian Human Rights Act and confirmed by the Supreme Court in *Ontario Human Rights Commission (O'Malley)* v. *Simpson – Sears Limited* in 1985.[91]

86 Joseph Catens, 'Free Speech and Democratic Norms in the Danish Cartoons Controversy', *International Migration*, 44:5, 2006, 33–42, at 40.

87 The Civil Rights Act of 1964, after amendement in 1972, has included the employer's duty to accommodate his/her employees' religious practices, unless they cause undue hardship to him/her (Civil Rights Act 1964, Title VII, Chapter 21, para. 701(j)).

88 Emanuelle Bribosia, Julie Ringelheim and Isabelle Rorive, *Reasonable Accommodation for Religious Minorities: A Promising Concept European Antidiscrimination Law?*, 2010, http://ssrn.com/abstract=1781182 at 139.

89 For more cf. Kristin Henrard, 'Duties of Reasonable Accommodation in Relation to Religion and the European Court of Human Rights: A Closer Look At the Prohibition of Discrimination, the Freedom of Religion and Related Duties of State Neutrality', *Erasmus Law Review*, 5:1 2012, in particular footnote 9 and pp. 64–65. The interpretation has been extended to cover the equality clause in the Canadian Charter of Rights and Freedoms, including for religious purposes.

90 Ibid. at 144.

91 2 S.C.R. 536.

The content of the principle entails a

> duty for the author of a provision, practice or policy, which *de facto* penalizes an individual on the basis of any prohibited ground of discrimination. It involves the use of all reasonable means to take into account as far as possible the specific needs of that individual . . . and to protect him/her from the discrimination effects of such provisions.[92]

The principle covers also education.

The idea and stimulus behind the concept is to allow participation and access to society and the public space to all on as equal terms as possible. In the case of the United States, the concept is limited under conditions where it causes *undue hardship* or/and *disproportionate burden* to the state. The threshold in Canada, however, is much higher than in the United States.[93] Canadian case law has treated *reasonable accommodation* as extending to individual and specific exemptions from general rules, adding the obligation of institutions to consider the situation of affected groups when establishing those standards.[94] In a sense, and given the general coverage of the concept, reasonable accommodation appears to form an integral part and component of the right to equality.

The alternative approach to anti-discrimination relying on the notion of reasonable accommodation, used in other national contexts such as Canada and South Africa, has been dismissed on six occasions by the ECtHR in 2009. All cases were education-related in the French context and concerned the exclusion of Muslim or Sikh students from high schools for wearing religious symbols, contrary to the stipulation of the 2004 Act prohibiting the wearing of ostentatious religious signs in public schools.[95] The Strasbourg Court's main argument rested on the state's legitimate objective of protecting the rights of others and public order more broadly. It was based also on the assessment that the prohibition contained in the Act does not violate Article 9 ECHR on the freedom of religion nor does it contain any elements of discrimination. As such, it is difficult to invoke a duty of reasonable accommodation of public schools towards pupils invoking their (minoritarian) religious rights.[96]

92 Bribosia *et al.* (2010) at 145. For the limits of this duty cf. *Alberta* v. *Hutterian Brethren of Wilson Colony*, 2009 SCC 37 [2009] 2 S.C.R. 567, where a pressing and substantial goal, a minimal impairment to the right and proportionality between the limitation and its effects are enough to justify the violation (at para.71).

93 US Supreme Court case *Trans World Airlines* v. *Hardison*, 432 U.S. 63 (1977) confirmed the need for a de minimis duty to make reasonable accommodation.

94 Henrard (2012) at 66.

95 *Loi n. 2004-228 du 15 mars 2004 encadrant en application du principle de laicité, le port de signes ou de tenues manifestnat une appartenance religieuse dans les écoles, collèges et lycées publics*, J.O. n.65, 17.03.04, p. 5190. The cases at issue were: *Aktas* v. *France* [2009] no. 43563/08; *Ghazal* v. *France* [2009] no.29134/08; *Bayrak* v. *France* [2009] no. 14308/08; *Gamaleddyn* v. *France* [2009] no. 18527/08; *Jasvir Singh* v. *France* [2009] no. 25463/08; *Ranjit Singh* v. *France* [2009] no. 27561/08.

96 For a similar conclusion, cf. Bribosia *et al.* (2010) at 156.

The classic non-discrimination approach with emphasis and impetus from a passive conception of secularism to the issue could support instead the understanding of accommodation through the prohibition of indirect discrimination. Henrard argues that accommodation measures can indeed be treated as a tool of prevention and/or remedy in cases of indirect discrimination.[97] This approach, while sustainable at the European level, in particular through the jurisprudence of the ECtHR,[98] has not been consistent and has not been extended to education in the European context. In order to be successfully invoked, it requires the absence of an undue or disproportionate burden on the duty bearer in the Canadian and the United States as well as the European contexts, as already mentioned.

It is not clear to what extent the concept of indirect discrimination – available in European jurisprudential contexts – can create a mechanical duty to accommodate religious (or other) differences. Indirect discrimination, as a concept, relies on group disadvantage so an individual's claim of a right to difference may not sit easily with it.[99] In addition, the prohibition of indirect discrimination does not necessarily include a duty to accommodate.[100] Under conditions, the obligation not to indirectly discriminate can provide the grounds for a duty to accommodate, especially in situations where the disputed measure can lead to disadvantage of a group of people that are affected due to their religion (or other characteristics).

Secularism, education and religious rights: dilemmas in contemporary culturally diverse societies from two case studies

Normative plurality, citizenship and religious identity protection in Canada

In terms of formal recognition of legal pluralism, Canada has been divided. In Quebec, options relying on faith-based normative systems have not become available, not even in the area of family law. In Ontario, the Arbitration Act[101] provided one possibility for individuals to hire third parties (also on religious criteria) to privately decide on conflicts. Debate in 2004–2005, led, however, the government in Ontario to announce legislation that eliminated all faith-based arbitration.[102]

97 Henrard (2012) at 67. See also indicatively the ECtHR case *Thlimmenos* v. *Greece* (2000) Appl.N. 34369/97 where the Court found that 'the right not to be discriminated against in the enjoyment of the rights guaranteed under the Convention is also violated when states without objective and reasonable justification fail to treat differently persons whose situations are significantly different'.

98 Another relevant case would be *Jakobski* v. *Poland* (2010), Appl. N. 18429/06 where the Court found a duty to accommodate the dietary needs of members of particular faiths in prisons.

99 For a similar point see Lisa Waddington, 'Reasonable Accommodation: Time to Extend the Duty to Accommodate Beyond Disability?', *NTM/N JCM-Bull.* 36 [2011], Nr. 2 at 194.

100 Ibid.

101 Arbitration Act, S.O. 1991, C.17.

102 For a feminist perspective on this process, cf. Sherene H. Razack, 'The "Sharia Law Debate" in Ontario: The Modernity/Premodernity Distinction in Legal Efforts to Protect Women from Culture', *Feminist Legal Studies*, 15, 2007, 3–32, at 5 onwards.

One of the recurring issues that came out of public debate and academic research on the topic leads us to question the extent to which we are or ought to be looking for arrangements in the public sphere that promote the idea that citizens (also as right-holders) need to be 'first and foremost' loyal to the state.[103] There is an underlying argument proposed by Talal Asad that advances the idea that secularism precisely operates on this basis, aiming to secure its own power first, vis-à-vis citizens.[104] It, therefore, excludes religious 'presence' in the public sphere, including the 'official' legal system, targeting the creation of 'normative' citizens, that have little or (ideally) no group-based loyalties.

Transposed and implemented in public education, where traditionally states 'shape' and participate in the formation of future citizens, the argument shows that secularism has been elevated to a preferred strategy of management in multicultural societies. This strategy, however, tends to oversimplify religious identity: for instance it finds in some contexts, such as the wearing of religious symbols, the exercise of religious rights to be incompatible with the practice of citizenship. It ultimately ignores the transnational loyalties of individuals as subjects of law.

If one accepts, as Razack argues, that citizens are those who leave aside group-based identities, those who choose to remain within the borders of group-based identities, should be treated then as 'non-citizens',[105] in a context of secularism, starting off from their period spent in public school systems. After all, the argument continues, 'multiculturalism has been instrumental in breeding terrorists by steeping them in their own culture and alienating them from . . . society'.[106]

The debate around the Arbitration Act in Ontario highlights the concern surrounding 'civilized' Canadians at risk of 'unassimilable immigrants'.[107] This point resonates well the observation made that dominant groups are thought to have values, while subordinate/minority groups have culture[108] (*modernity* v. *pre-modernity*).

At the other end of the spectrum, the policy background in pushing for reasonable accommodation in education was supported through the use of two core arguments, at least in Quebec: first, reasonable accommodation in public schools 'prepares all students to exercise their citizenship and integrate into civic culture' and, second, it is 'a tool to foster active participation by both the students and the parents in the schools'.[109] Translated into legal terms, this approach points to a consideration of the

103 Ibid. at 7.

104 Talal Asad, *Formations of the Secular, Christianity, Islam, Modernity*, Stanford University Press, 2003; Talal Asad, www.islamamerica.org/articles.cfm/article_id/94.

105 Razack (2007) at 23.

106 A. Sivanandan, 'Race, Terror and Civil Society', *Race & Class*, 47:3, 2006, 1–8, at 3.

107 Razack (2007) at 25.

108 Abdullahi An'Naim has written extensively on this point from a human rights and gender perspective.

109 M. McAndrew, 'The Muslim Community and Education in Quebec: Controversies and Mutual Adaptation', *Journal of International Migration and Integration*, 11, 2010, 41–58. An interesting parallel to this point is provided in the US context by Justice Brennan that in *Abington Township* v. *Schempp* described the American vision of public schools as places for 'the training of American citizens in an atmosphere free of parochial, divisive or separatist influences of

rights of students and parents within a timidly expressed post-multiculturalist context, quite in the opposite direction of secularism understood as the non-religious.

Reasonable accommodation and the nature of religious rights in Canada

Section 1 of the Canadian Charter of Rights and Freedoms explains that religious rights are not absolute: 'The . . . Charter . . . guarantees the rights and freedoms set out in it subject only to such reasonable limits prescribed by law as can be demonstrably justified in a free and democratic society'.[110]

In early post-Charter case law, the Canadian Supreme Court conceptualised religion as a group expression of rights, in mostly collective terms.[111] While religion, in those cases, was considered as the expression of individual beliefs, it was strongly connected with the community. *Syndicat Northcrest* v. *Anselem,* concerning a private dispute on the erection of *succahs* on balconies, despite the violation of condominium laws where defendants were lodged, demonstrated a more individualistic approach to religious rights.[112] The majority of the Court found that the impairment caused by reasonable accommodation of the owners' claim was minimal and accepted it. At the same time, the case introduced the need for an assessment of one's sincerity of belief in order to establish whether one's practices and beliefs would be covered by freedom of religion.

In the Canadian legal context, the collective nature of religion as a right has been connected to the cultural dimension and embedding of faith systems. The exercise of religious beliefs acquires thus elements of an 'exercise in agency',[113] guiding groups in their life in community, well beyond and outside the conception of religion as 'divine revelation'.[114] The lived experience of law, in a legal context of constitutionally declared multiculturalism, such as the one in Canada, suggests a propensity towards accommodation of religious legal claims also in the area of education. In fact, the duty to accommodate also takes the form of a request for an exemption from rules of general application.[115]

The *Alberta* v. *Hutterian Brethren of Wilson County* case[116] re-focused the debate on the nature of religious rights towards a much stricter individualistic

any sort – an atmosphere in which children may assimilate a heritage common to all American groups and religions'. [374 U.S. 2013, 242 (1963) (Brennan, J. concurring)].

110 Canadian Charter of Rights and Freedoms, Part I of the Constitution Act, 1982, s.1.

111 See for example *R.* v. *Big M. Drug Mart* (1985) or *R.* v. *Edwards Boooks and Art Ltd.* (1986).

112 2004 SCC 47, 2 SCR 551. See in particular para.39 of Justice Iacobucci's opinion as quoted in Louise Tardiff, 'Religious Freedom in Canada: Whither the Community?', *Regulating Religion e-journal,* December 2012, available at www.religionanddiversity.ca, at p. 6.

113 Ibid. at 8.

114 Ibid.

115 See for example the cases of *Lafontaine* and *Anselem* [see below footnote 117].

116 The Canadian Supreme Court held in this case that the Province of Alberta's requirement of a photograph on drivers' licences was reasonably limiting the freedom of religion of Hutterites who objected to it for religious reasons.

approach. The general understanding, however, that religious freedom has been designed to protect religious minorities, coupled with the multicultural heritage in section 27 of the Charter, imply an interpretation of the right to religious freedom through the lens of reasonable accommodation, reinforced by the state's encouragement for tolerance and debate of religious values in the public sphere, despite diverging opinions within the Canadian Supreme Court on perceptions of neutrality and secular democracy.[117]

Reasonable accommodation, in recent case law, remains at the core of a number of cases.[118] The background of the cases at issue includes the political uneasiness within Quebec over such claims.[119] The main issue which was common to all those claims that reached the Canadian Supreme Court was connected to the politics of collective identity and entailed a different understanding of secularism and the duty of the state in Quebec as opposed to that of the rest of the country.[120]

In the area of public education more narrowly, in *Chamberlain* v. *Surrey School District No.36 (2002)*, the question as to whether it was constitutionally acceptable to prohibit the use of books portraying families with same-sex parents as contrary to British Columbia's School Act requirement that public schooling be conducted on 'strictly secular' principles, was considered by the Supreme Court.

Chief Justice McLachlin found that the Act's 'insistence on secularism' does not signify that religious concerns should be accounted for in decisions of School Boards. To the contrary, they have to be merely considered. She added:

> the Act's requirement of strict secularism means that the Board must conduct its deliberations on all matters, including the approval of supplementary resources, in a manner that respects the views of all members of the school community. It cannot prefer the religious views of some people in its district to the views of other segments of the community.

By insisting on tolerance and non-sectarianism, the Court did not explain which decision should be reached in the given case but instead outlined how that decision should be taken: by respecting the multiplicity of religious views in the community.

117 According to Choudhry, these divisions are happening along ethno-linguistic lines between judges from Quebec and the rest of the judicial body of the Court. For more on this point, see Sujit Choudhry, 'Rights Adjudication in a Plurinational State: The Supreme Court of Canada, Freedom of Religion, and the Politics of Reasonable Accommodation', *Osgoode Hall Law Journal*, 50:3, Spring 2013, 575–608 at 580 et seq.

118 See *Anselem* (see above footnote 109); *Congrégation des témoins de Jehovah de St. Jerôme Lafontaine* v. *Lafontaine Village*, 2004, SCC 48, 2 SCR 650; *Multani* v. *Commission Scolaire Marguerite- Bourgeoys*, 2006, SCC6, 1 SCR 256; *Bruker* v. *Markovitz*, 2007, SCC 54, 3 SCR 607; *SL* v. *Commission Scolaire des Chênes*, 2012, SCC 7, 1 SCR 235.

119 Choudhry (2013) at 586.

120 Ibid. at 586. The current form of nationalism in Quebec is concerned with secular nation building, without any presence of religion in the public sphere, as it was previously about linguistic nation-building.

In *SL,* the Canadian Supreme Court had to apply reasonable accommodation in a case concerning the teaching of religion in public schools. Since 1995, public education is organised on the basis of language. Pre-1995 mandatory instruction on religion and morals is presently replaced by an Ethics and Religious Culture Program, providing education about different religious and ethics.

The claim in this case was issued by Roman Catholic parents that challenged the programme on the basis of their right to have their children educated according to their religious values. The Court unanimously dismissed the claim as being too abstract (i.e. implementation of the act at stake had not yet occurred at the time of the complaint).

On a more macroscopic level, and despite the considerable margin allowed in Canadian case law about which religious practices are considered 'reasonable', the fundamental question remains whether a claimant wishing to exercise his/her religious rights should submit a claim based on the principle of equality or on the right to religious freedom,[121] essentially in cases where there is a conflict between the rule at stake and a religious command. The ambiguity at this point lies with cases concerning a religious obligation that is contested within the faith community itself. The current jurisprudential response within numerous legal systems is one relying on the subjective conception of the freedom of religion, avoiding the court's interpretation of religious dogmas.

The Canadian context, however, of this debate is quite different: Canada, according to recent research, is one of the few (if not the only) Western countries 'where strength of national identity is positively correlated with support for immigration'.[122] In other words, immigrant minorities will identify with their new national identity in conditions where this identity is recognised and respected. The role given to the content of education in that respect remains crucial: cultural and linguistic diversity in the Canadian public school curriculum have contributed to the process of acculturation.

In furtherance of these aims, section 15(1) of the Charter of Rights and Freedoms stipulates: 'Every individual is equal before and under the law and has the right to the equal protection and equal benefit of the law without discrimination'. In early case law of the Supreme Court, it was found that 'the accommodation of differences . . . is the essence of true equality'.[123] The intention to achieve substantive equality, even to the extent that it would require different treatment, was further recognised in *Law* v. *Canada (Minister of Employment and Immigration)*.[124]

Section 27 of the Canadian Charter of Rights and Freedoms further states that 'the Charter shall be interpreted in a manner consistent with the preservation and enhancement of the multicultural heritage of Canadians'. Accordingly, multiculturalism has been also reflected in the school curriculum, with variations

121 Bribosia *et al.* (2010) at 149.

122 Kymlicka (2012) at 12. See also Richard Johnston, Keith Banting, Will Kymlicka and Stuart Soroka, 'National Identity and Support for the Welfare State', *Canadian Journal of Political Science*, 43:2, 2010, 349–377.

123 *Andrews* v. *Law Society of British Columbia* [1989] 1 S.C.R. 143 at para.169.

124 [1999] 1 S.C.R. 497.

encountered in Canada's provinces.[125] In 2005, the Supreme Court of Canada addressed the question of religious dress/symbols at schools. It found that a Quebec student of Sikh origin should be permitted to wear a kirpan at school under the condition that the kirpan be worn in a stitched sheath underneath his clothing.[126]

Overall, the broader strategic perspective of multiculturalism policies since the mid-1990s targets, however, inclusion and institutional change, instead of specific ethno-specific policies.[127]

Legal pluralism in South Africa and religious diversity in public education

The South African legal system contains numerous dimensions of legal pluralism. Historical context and socio-legal composition of the South African society have led to the expansion of non-state law with important repercussions. *Deep legal pluralism*[128] is therefore a reality of the 'lived law' in South Africa.

The specificity of the South African case is highlighted from a systemic point of view in the crucial role that the Constitutional Court has played in affording protection to religious or cultural groups.[129] The principle of equality is nevertheless well covered in the South African Constitution,[130] as reflected through the exercise of cultural and religious rights. This recognition is not without risks: in *MEC for Education, Kwazulu – Natal* v. *Pillay*,[131] involving the prohibition imposed on a Hindu pupil by her school to wear a nose stud, the Court placed the balancing of individual as opposed to collective rights involved in the context of dignity as an 'entitlement to respect for the unique set of ends that the individual pursues'.[132] The toleration of religious and cultural diversity, characterised as 'one

125 The Council of Ministers of Canada (2008, 52–53) have recognized in that respect that 'integrating immigrant children into the existing education systems of the provinces and territories involves establishing policies embodying the principles of diversity, equity and multicultural education as part of the daily classroom and school environment, as well as adapting the curriculum and providing teacher support that addresses students' real needs, especially for language learning' [Cf. *Multiculturalism Policies in Contemporary Democracies – Canada*, www.queensu.ca/mcp/immigrant/evidence/Canada.html.]

126 Ibid. at point 4.

127 Ibid. at point 6.

128 As explained in Christa Rautenbach's 'Deep Legal Pluralism in South Africa: Judicial Accommodation of Non-State Law', 2010, http://ssrn.com/abstract=1783574 at 145. According to Rautenbach's analysis, *deep legal pluralism* represents the 'factual situation which reflects the realities of a society in which various legal systems are observed, some officially and others unofficially' and is contrasted to *narrow legal pluralism*, which reflects the co-existence of officially recognised state laws. Section 15(3) of the South African Constitution recognises the possibility of legal pluralism in the context of family law.

129 For more on this point cf. Rautenbach (2010).

130 S.9(1), s.10, s.15(1), s.30. Cf. Rautenbach (2010) at 150–151.

131 2008(1) SA 474 (CC).

132 Ibid. at para.65.

of the primary treasures of . . . [the] nation',[133] leads to an understanding of equality as 'equal concern and equal respect',[134] with the limit being placed to practices that constitute human rights violations.

Du Plessis[135] explains well the dynamic of the exercise and assertion of religiously related entitlements in education. For these entitlements, case law

> has increasingly been interrogating, with transformative rigour, 'mainstream' preferences and prejudices regarding the organization of societal life, inspired by the desire to proceed beyond . . . all that used to contribute to and sustain marginalization of the Other.

The recognition of express provisions catering for difference marks the explicit new approach in South Africa that is based on social equality, with the understanding that accommodating normative plurality and religious difference should not come at the expense of the protection of individual human rights. In that respect, South African courts have demonstrated particular sensitivity towards claims emanating from parties in proceedings issued from vulnerable groups (e.g. women).[136]

The significance of the religious dimension of South African pupils in public education has been showcased in recent case law[137] and policy-making.[138] Section 15(1) of South African Constitution stipulates that all people have the right to 'freedom of conscience, religion, thought, belief and opinion'. Additionally, the South African Constitution recognises in its equality provision under s.9 that 'The state may not unfairly discriminate directly or indirectly against anyone on one or more grounds, including . . . religion, conscience, belief, culture'. In other words, the South African fundamental right to freedom of religion comprises both a free exercise element as well as an equal treatment element.

Evidently, the South African Schools Act 1996, in its preamble, supports the constitutional provision further by acknowledging that: 'whereas this country requires a new national system for schools which will . . . provide and advance our diverse cultures . . . and uphold the rights of all learners [and] parents'.[139] At a closer look, religiously related dress codes in public schools and their prohibition have brought back to the surface the issue of learners' constitutional rights to freedom of religion and equality.

133 Ibid. at para.92.

134 Ibid. at para.103.

135 As quoted in Rautenbach (2010) at 167.

136 Ibid. at 164.

137 See indicatively *Antonie* v. *Governing Body, Settlers High School* 2002 4 SA 738 (C); *Pillay* v. *MEC for Education, KwaZulu-Natal* 2006 6 SA 363 (High Court); *MEC for Education, KwaZulu – Natal* v. *Pillay* 2007 1 SA 474 (Const. Court).

138 Cf. Guidelines for the Consideration of Governing Bodies in Adopting a Code of Conduct for Learners GG 18900 of 1998-05-15 as quoted in Elda de Waal and Nelda Cambron-McCabe, 'Learners' Religious – Cultural Rights: A Delicate Balancing Act', *De Jure*, 2013, 93–113 at 94.

139 Act. No.84 of 1996.

The South African response to these clashes of rights differs significantly from other national or supra-national responses. The policy context of the disputes includes a set of *Guidelines on School Uniforms* issued by the Ministry of Education, with emphasis placed on support for public schools in establishing dress codes that do not infringe the pupils' constitutional rights.[140]

Constitutionally, however, the right at issue can be subject to limitations by virtue of section 36(1) of the South African Constitution, stating that fundamental rights may be limited 'to the extent that the limitation is reasonable and justifiable in . . . democratic society based on human dignity, equality and freedom'.[141] Constitutional practice surprisingly tends to widen the scope of the right,[142] quite in the opposite direction of the ECtHR's approach.

On the point of equality, the Court in *Pillay* justified its finding of unfair discrimination of the student on the ground, inter alia, that the standard identified in the Code of Conduct of the school imposed 'middle-of-the-road and historically privileged types of ornamentation . . . at the expense of alternative and previously barred types'.[143] The disposition of the rule was therefore not found to be neutral insofar as it imposed on students the 'tyranny of the mainstream'. The link between equality and religious rights passes through human dignity according to the Court, which represents an essential element of equality. As such, the Court does not hesitate to invalidate laws that force individuals to choose between their religious beliefs and abiding to the law.[144] In other words, the protection of voluntary religious practices serves as evidence of constitutional commitment to diversity.

Central to the evaluation of (unfair) discrimination of the case was also the implementation of the requirement of reasonable accommodation, which occupies a central position in the application of the principle of equality in South Africa. In *Pillay*'s case, the Court found that fairness required reasonable accommodation, particularly so in the light of the religious practice's 'significance . . . to the person concerned'.[145] The last point is well connected to the Court's stance that only

140 The relevant sub-sections dispose:
'29(1) A school . . . dress code should take into account religious and cultural diversity . . . [and] . . . accommodate learners whose religious beliefs are compromised by a uniform requirement
(2) If wearing . . . attire . . . is part of the religious practice of learner . . . schools should not, in terms of the South African Constitution, prohibit the wearing of such items.
(3) A uniform policy may . . . prohibit items that undermine the integrity of the uniform . . . such as a T-shirt that bears a vulgar message.'

141 Limitations are assessed with regards to the nature of the right at stake, how important the purpose of the limitation is; the nature and extent of the limitation; the relationship between limitation and purpose and whether less restrictive means would be available. [Cf. De Waal and Cambron-McCabe (2013) at 99].

142 Ibid.

143 Pillay judgment at para.50.

144 De Waal and Cambron-McCabe (2013) at 105.

145 Pillay judgment at para.91.

sincerely held religious beliefs are worthy of constitutional protection, without signifying nevertheless that all practices can and should be protected.

The appropriate balance between freedom of religion and the state's duty to dispense education is a perilous exercise of constitutional equilibrium. Ultimately, the South African Constitutional Court is aiming well when it observes that '[w]hat may be most difficult when school leaders attempt to make accommodations is to move out of the comfort of their own culture and recognize that a practice that seems different, exotic or even bizzare can be included and honoured without damaging the educational environment',[146] only to remind a bit further that 'our Constitution does not tolerate diversity as a necessary evil, but affirms it as one of the primary treasures of our nation'.[147] Only under this light, can the exercise of religious rights at school lead to legal empowerment.

From non-discrimination to post-multiculturalism: a reflective path

The contrast between religious diversity management approaches in the European continent and countries such as Canada or South Africa inevitably brings to the fore the discussion of the 'cost-benefit' analysis of the legal tools used in each case vis-à-vis the exercise of religious freedom. In all cases, legal pluralism is a reality that affects the general legal landscape in more than one ways. Religious diversity is also an uncontested reality in most contemporary societies and as such constitutes the relevant comparator for the examples mentioned in this discussion.

The aim of this part of the discussion is to elevate the observation of religious rights protection in public education to a more general level, that of policies with distinct (and concrete) legal repercussions.

Multiculturalism: a frame

Multiculturalism represents a particular approach to managing cultural diversity. It tends to focus on the strategies for the advancement of marginalised/disadvantaged groups.[148] It is casually defined as 'the existence of diverse cultures, values and traditions within the same society'.[149] In Europe's case, it has come to signify most often 'the management of Muslims'.[150] Structurally, multiculturalism as an approach places emphasis on difference over equality and includes rights

146 Pillay CC para.92.

147 Ibid.

148 Andrew Heywood, *Multiculturalism , Identity and Diversity*, available at http://andrewheywood.cp.uk/resources/MulticulturalismidentityDiversity.doc at 1 [accessed on 10.02.2015]

149 Ibid. See also Minstère de l'Education, du Loisir et du Sport (MELS) 2008, La prise en compte de la diversité culturelle et religiouese en milieu scolaire: De la théorie à la pratique – Module de formation à i'intention des gestionnaires préparé par M. Mc Andrew.

150 Bryan S. Turner, 'Managing Religions: State Responses to Religious Diversity', *Cont. Islam*, 1, 2007, 123–137, at 129.

to public recognition and respect, minority rights as well as qualified rights to self-determination.[151] It is characterised by the central premise that unity can be achieved within diversity through the legitimisation of the recognition of cultural differences.[152] In legal terms, it represents a combination of anti-discrimination law together with legislative accommodation of ethno-cultural practices. Attempts to study its implication for religious/ethnic groups focus on citizenship, constitutional protection and education.[153]

As an ideology, multiculturalism has received a multiplicity of definitions but in most cases was 'invented' as a response and an attempt to accommodate non-white immigration.[154] Whether of the *conservative*, *liberal* or *pluralist* type,[155] multiculturalism responds to a real need for the management of cultural and religious diversity. It calls for and embodies, from the legal perspective, the right to difference in the form of the recognition of the specific needs of *inter alia* religious minorities and attaches to that some form of 'entitlement' to occupy public space in order to express their identity. This public presence[156] and expression could then lead to the legal empowerment of those exercising it, with the qualification mentioned above, however, that the exercise of religious freedom is not an absolute right.[157]

Yet, one of the persistent and underlying critiques to this approach is nicely reflected in J.S. Mills' concept of 'despotism of custom' which describes the

151 Ibid. at 3.

152 There are various types of multiculturalism. Cf. Andrew Heywood discussing the liberal, the pluralist and the cosmopolitan type.

153 See Kymlicka (2012) at 7, referring to the Multiculturalism Policy Index (www.queensu.ca/mcp) that measures the evolution of multiculturalism according to the following policy criteria: constitutional, legislative, or parliamentary affirmation of multiculturalism at all levels of governance; adoption of multiculturalism in school curricula; the inclusion of ethnic representation/sensitivity in the mandate of public media or media licensing; allowing dual citizenship; the funding of bilingual education or mother-tongue instruction; affirmative action for disadvantaged immigrant groups.

154 Leonie Sanderock, 'Rethinking Multiculturalism for the 21st Century', Vancouver Centre of Excellence Working Paper Series, No 03-14, 2003 at 21.

155 For more on these definition, cf. ibid. at 21–22.

156 The concept of 'public presence' and 'public space' are heavily contested in the various jurisdictions. The same applies to the notions of 'public order' with respect to the limitations to freedom of religion, in particular related to religious symbols. See in this respect indicatively the recent decision of the Belgian Constitutional Court n.145/2012 of 6 December 2012 on a motion for annulment of the Law of 1st June 2011 on the prohibition of the wearing of all dress hiding substantially or totally the face (Loi du 1er Juin 2011 visant à interdire le port de tout vêtement cachant totalement ou de manière principale le visage). One of the arguments invoked concerned the discussion on the link between criminality and the burqua and at the same time the extent to which the burqa was conducive to the goal of 'vivre ensemble dans une société émancipantruce et protectrice des droits de tous et chacun' (point A.5.3). Interestingly, in this case the Court put forward three guiding principles in assessing the 'accessibility' of public space in terms of religious freedom expressed through symbols: public security, gender equality and a 'certain conception of living together' in society (B.17, 23 & 21). Ultimately, the contested measure was found justified and necessary in a democratic society.

157 ECtHR, *Leyla Sahin* v. *Turkey*, Grand Chamber, 10 November 2005 at paras. 66 and 105.

commonly observed culture pressure towards vulnerable groups to comply with cultural rules often against their individual rights and personal autonomy.

Multiculturalism, thus, differs from the classic non-discrimination approach in at least two ways: first, while non-discrimination is a legal and social construct above all, anchored on the principle of equality, multiculturalism carries a more pronounced cultural 'flavour' that relies on values and perceptions of 'otherness'.[158] Second, emphasis within multiculturalism is placed on the notion of difference, not on that of equality, as already mentioned.[159] As a direct consequence of this shift of weight, multicultural rights hint more at the group dimension of a community as this becomes evident through expression of cultural identity.

A critique

'We cannot claim to be a truly multicultural society if the various communities within it live . . . a series of parallel lives which do not touch at any point.'[160] The de- and re-territorialisation of cultures in 'global cities' has led to the formation of complex identities based increasingly on transnational elements.[161] These new identities have revealed a 'very liquid sense of identity and belonging',[162] which has been translated in a difficult balance in order to reconcile different lifestyles.

The recognition of multiculturalism, however, does not take place in a vacuum: it evolves within a certain constitutional setting, rooted in given political and legal traditions. This setting requires openness to new differences while remaining connected to the 'roots of contemporary democratic society'.[163]

The concept of multiculturalism emerged as a response to this need but one that was too cautious to avoid meaningful multicultural encounter when implemented.[164] Schools did not escape this trend.

A very different assessment of the notion of limitation of religious rights in the public space in connection with multiculturalism can be found in the Canadian context. Concerned with the question of religious symbols (such as the *niqab*), worn in Court while testifying,[165] the Supreme Court of Canada adopted a distinct methodological approach: first, it inquired whether the requirement to remove the symbol interfered with one's religious freedom. The standard used here is rarely used in European jurisdictions and relies on the sincerity of one's religious belief, not to be confused with one's strength of belief. The second

158 Ibid. at 3.

159 Ibid.

160 Home Office, *Building Cohesive Communities: A Report of the Ministerial Group on Public Order and Community Cohesion*, London, Home Office/Her Majesty's Government, 2001, at 13.

161 For more on this point cf. Sanderock (2003) at 10–11.

162 Ibid. at 12.

163 R.v. NS, 2012, Supreme Court of Canada, 20.12.2012, Case N.33989, SCC 72 at para. 72.

164 Ash Amin's *Ethnicity and the Multicultural City: Living With Diversity* (2002) makes a parallel point of failure of cultural interchange due to the non-use of public space as a forum of multicultural engagement (pp. 11–12).

165 Ibid.

issue, not strictly relevant for the purposes of this study, looked at the question of the extent to which the wearing of a niqab while testifying created a risk to trial fairness. The majority of the Court decided that this depended on the type of evidence that the witness must provide. Third, the salient question of whether there is room for accommodation of both rights exists. Again, this examination is strikingly different from the European context. The standard applicable places emphasis on whether there are reasonably available alternative methods 'reconciling' the two sides. The final question related to the overall effects assessment of allowing the witness to wear the symbol, in the sense of measuring the salutary effects of allowing her to wear it against the detrimental ones arising from the same behaviour, in cases where there is no reasonably available alternative. In essence, this represents a proportionality inquiry. The nexus between multiculturalism and reasonable accommodation appears very relevant.

In most Western-style democracies, however, it would be fair to say that multiculturalism has been developed against a liberal ideological context, with clear emphasis on access to rights for individuals rather than groups.[166] In many cases, this has resulted in policies that enforce, rather than mitigate, assimilation to the majority cultural background, eliminating or isolating cultural and religious repertoires that appear to be 'outside of the mainstream'.[167] In short, power relations including in schools, retain their hierarchical nature, leading to the assimilation of minority and immigrant students and at the same time indirectly disempowering them in the socio-legal sphere.

At the other end of the policy spectrum on religious diversity in schools, critical theoretical positions, such as those applicable in France, identify schools as public spaces that should remain clear of cultural and religious dynamics. Learning, however, that is dispensed while being unconnected to the students' cultural baggage produces similar results to policies that place emphasis on individuals, ignoring their collective belonging(s).[168]

166 See for example the study by June Beynon, Linda Larocque, Roumiana Ilieva and Diane Dagenais on 'A Sociocultural and Critical Analysis of Educational Policies and Programs for Minority Youth in British Columbia', in C. James (ed.), *Possibilities and Limitations: Multicultural Policies and Programs in Canada*, Halifax, Fernwood Publishing, 2005. The authors take issue with minority language policies in Canada emphasising how federal and provincial policies are using liberal pluralist conceptions of policy design in public schools.

167 Ibid. for similar findings.

168 In the opinion of the Human Rights Committee in *Singh* v. *France*, Comm.No. 1852/2008, CCCPR/C/106/D/1852/2008, the wearing of the Sikh turban (keski) at school was challenged by the applicant as not being a 'conspicuous' symbol of faith otherwise prohibited at school under Act No.2004-228 of 15.03.2004. The context of the Act is precisely on the consideration of the school as a public space clear from religion. The effect of the law as applied in Singh's case resulted in the removal of the student from the class and his subsequent permanent expulsion from his learning environment. The findings of the Committee, while acknowledging the need for a public policy of strict secularism in order to protect the rights and freedoms of others (para.8.6), stated clearly that the simple wearing of a turban was not convincingly shown to pose such as threat to rights and freedoms and incurred an injustifyingly and disproportionately strict penalty 'solely because of (the student's) inclusion in a broad category of persons defined by their religious conduct' (para.8.7).

Indicatively and on this point, the Canada Multiculturalism Act (1988) in order to address this concern, states that it is policy of the government to 'preserve and enhance the use of languages other than English and French' and adds that all federal institutions should 'make use, as appropriate, of the language skills and cultural understanding of individuals of all origins'.[169]

As a direct consequence of multiculturalism in the area of education, one can also consider the establishment of 'faith schools', often publicly financed. This is the case in the UK, where faith-based multiculturalism becomes 'government policy, based on communitarian theories, and claims by minorities increasingly defining themselves in religious terms'.[170] This direction in policy-making is not without its dangers.[171] The tension, in particular, between the beliefs and practices contained in the programme of these schools, with core liberal principles reflecting a post-multiculturalist take on the issue, points at the common critique on classic multiculturalism that fosters cultural relativism.[172] In case law, this shift has been reflected in the judiciary's scrutiny of such schools and their practices as incompatible with liberal principles,[173] in particular gender equality.

At the same time, the rise of multiculturalism has signalled the expansion of the interpretation of the notion of anti-discrimination on the basis of religion and equality to 'issues of recognition, voice, participation and promoti[on] of diversity'[174] as central axes. The dimension of legislation as conducive to addressing socio-economic disadvantages, at the root of inequalities, is less developed.

Current developments have added that the limits of religious rights in public education and elsewhere, are placed at the point where the minorities affected have to prefer complying with Western liberal values over their individual cultural and religious norms and beliefs. In other words, the balancing act is now phrased as the legal conflict between freedom of religion and freedom from discrimination.

A provocative reading of multiculturalism could frame the concept as 'a more sophisticated version of racism',[175] 'a racism with a distance',[176] in that it places new immigrants into groups based on cultural (and religious) difference. Beyond the recurring argument that multiculturalism is above all beneficial to international trade, it is difficult to negate that it has been instrumental in

169 Beynon *et al.* (2005).

170 Ralph Grillo, 'British and Others: From "Race" to "Faith"', in S. Vertovec and S. Wessendorf (eds), *The Multiculturalism Backlash: European Discourses, Policies and Practices,* Routledge, 2010, at 57–58.

171 See for example the 2004 TV report *Dispatches – Faith Schools Undercover: No Clapping in Class,* www.channel4.com/programmes/dispatches/episode-guide.

172 Christopher McCrudden, 'Multiculturalism, Freedom of Religion, Equality and the British Constitution: The JFS Case Considered', *Oxford Legal Research Paper Series,* No.72/2010, at 6.

173 In the UK context, see for example *R* v. *Governors of Denbigh High School,* [2007] IAC 100 at 65 or *R (on the application of X)* v. *Headteachers and Governors of Y School* [2007] HRLR 20.

174 McCrudden (2010) at 7.

175 David Ley, 'Post-Multiculturalism?', Research on Immigration and Integration in the Metropolis Working Paper Series, No.05-18, September 2005, Vancouver Centre of Excellence, at p. 4.

176 Ibid. at 4.

placing 'the ethnic card as a sign of a worldly cosmopolitanism',[177] albeit one largely exploited by elites.[178]

Designated as a distinctive Canadian value and labelled as a 'source of national identity and unity' for Canada[179] or as 'what unites us and makes us all British' in the UK,[180] multiculturalism has been criticised on a variety of grounds including its limited perspective on persisting issues of economic and political inequality, its 'blindness' to cultural/religious practices or norms that cannot be legally tolerated (e.g. forced marriages) or its conception of groups as sealed and static.[181] Kymlicka disputes the critique of multiculturalism by arguing that it is after all concerned with policies that are about access of immigrant groups to political and economic opportunities, with emphasis on the human rights paradigm.[182]

Post-multiculturalism: a credible option?

The concept of post-multiculturalism remains puzzling: it is still unclear whether it represents a continuation of multiculturalism or instead a retreat from it.[183] For a number of scholars, it reflects above all a format for 'the recognition of diversity and the maintenance of collective national identities'.[184] In essence, post-multiculturalism combines elements of national identity and values with the official recognition of cultural diversity as a reaction to the 'failures' of multiculturalism.

More concretely, post-multiculturalism seeks to escape a more inclusive national identity. These models aim at political participation and economic opportunities, human rights and freedoms over the respect for cultural traditions, as well as cultural mixing.[185]

Beyond the typology of what constitutes and what sets apart multiculturalism and post-multiculturalism, there is more and more academic analysis that emphasises the civic integration of immigrants following respect for basic values and the rule of law, as well as a basic knowledge of the host society's language and history.[186] What scholarship does not clarify is whether multiculturalism suffers from unsuccessful implementation but remains in principle

177 Ley (2005) at 4.

178 In this respect see the work of Katharyne Mitchell, *Crossing the Neoliberal Line: Pacific Rim Migration and the Metropolis*, Philadelphia, Temple University Press, 2004, for a study of the Canadian context.

179 Cf. D. Li, 'The Multiculturalism Debate', in P. Li (ed.), *Race and Ethnic Relations in Canada*, Don Mills, Ontario, Oxford University Press, 2003, 148–177.

180 Bhikhu Parekh, 'Multiculturalism is a Civilised Dialogue', *Guardian*, 21 January 2005.

181 Will Kymlicka, *Multiculturalism: Success, Failure and the Future*, MPI Europe, 2012, at 4–5.

182 Ibid. at 8–9.

183 Dorotha A. Gorzdecka, Selen A. Ercan and Magdalena Kmak, 'From Multiculturalism to Post-Multiculturalism: Trends and Paradoxes', *Journal of Sociology*, 2014, 50–64, at 52.

184 See indicatively, S. Vertovec, 'Towards Post-Multiculturalism? Changing Communities, Conditions and Culturalism in Europe', *International Social Science Journal*, 61:199, 2010, 83–95 at 83.

185 Kymlicka (2012) at 5.

186 To which Kymlicka (2012) at 16 adds employment and the necessity of anti-discrimination laws.

'normatively desirable' or whether it reflects a flawed conceptualisation of the modus operandi of diverse societies.[187]

From the legal perspective, the essence of the debate remains centred on what Roger Cotterrell described as being the uncertainty as to 'how law should reflect, express or even control an aspect of culture'.[188] To the extent that culture leads to divisions, even to the point of 'separating' the group from the larger national societal context to which it belongs, the role of law, particularly in educational contexts, is to propose tools that are conducive to cross-cultural communication. This goal can be achieved more easily through the increase of opportunities for pupils to exercise their religious rights, not with the aim to constrain others but rather in an effort to achieve the respect for others as individuals and as members of specific groups. Critical race theory can be of assistance in this case, insofar as it makes the point that legal rights can be empowering for marginalised populations, breaking the vicious circle of subordination and vulnerability.[189]

What becomes an essential inquiry for religious diversity in public education is the extent to which post-multiculturalism will signify a retreat in the interpretation and application of the relevant European norms on religious rights. *Dahlab* v. *Switzerland, Sahin* v. *Turkey*, *Köse* v. *Turkey* and *Dogru* v. *France* privileged the preservation of the national system over the religious rights of the applicants.[190] Inversely, *Lautsi* v. *Italy*, *S.H.* v. *Austria* and *A. B. and C.* v. *Ireland* privileged the constitutional traditions and religious beliefs of majorities in the respective countries. Legal empowerment of individuals exercising their freedom of religion becomes therefore more difficult to conceive, especially if the claimants belong to a religious minority. The state's compelling interests prevail seemingly in all of these instances. Put differently, the constitutive elements of post-multiculturalism, namely national values and cultural diversity, have to reach an equilibrium susceptible of enlarging agency of right claimers but barring those claims, which are totally in dissonance with these pre-designated values.

Conclusions: empowering students as agents and subjects of law

The right to education functions primarily as a gateway right in the sense that it empowers both socially and legally individuals to combat gendered and other

187 Kymlicka (2012) at 20 seems to argue in the direction of combining civic integration with multicultural accommodation. Ultimately, the question requires a lot of contextualisation and could be at the end of the day a matter of perception and trajectory. The results of this policy, on the other hand, are harder to contest.

188 Roger Cotterrell, 'Law and Culture – Inside and Beyond the Nation State', *Retfaerd Argbang 31*, 2008, Nr. 4/123, 23–36, at 24.

189 John Mikhail, 'Dilemmas of Cultural Legality: A Comment on Roger Cotterrell's "The Struggle for Law" and a Criticism of the House of Lords' Opinions in Begum', *Int'l J.L in Context*, 4, 2009, 385–393, at 388.

190 Gozdecka *et al.* (2014) at 57–58.

stereotypes.[191] Religious identity can be similarly empowering: there is strength involved in tolerance, in recognising other people's identity in non-hostile terms.[192] Furthermore, international human rights law does not guarantee freedom from religion so facing religious difference is inevitable and legal.

The social movements surrounding the debate on religious diversity in education cannot be strictly detached from the realm of law. Perceptions on women, domesticity, access to the labour market, not to mention ethnicity, exclusion and housing are not unrelated to religion, dignity, or national values as expressed and practised throughout public education.[193] The complexity that results from the characteristics of contemporary migration in Europe directly impacts on patterns of cultural and social diversity practices, particularly and emphatically on education.[194]

To respond to the need of states wishing to address the development of religious revivalism, post-multiculturalism resonates a classic liberal solution, which is at the same time distancing itself gradually from making religion a private matter and separating church and state.[195] Instead, contemporary liberalism, reflecting Rawls' 'The Laws of People' (1999), focuses on the rule of law, reasonableness and the protection of individual rights.[196] His vision of 'overlapping consensus' is not far from Habermas' vision of post-secular citizens. A liberal society, thus, is/should be based on an overlapping consensus of beliefs but predictably leaves no room or options for fundamentalism.

While the right to education can and does ultimately in certain cases conflict with the right to religious freedom,[197] secularisation in public schools is not sufficient to eliminate educational disparities. Rights-based education appears a more empowering option: if one accepts that education remains a useful tool to promote equality and eliminate prejudice, it would be self-contradictory to 'erase' all traces of religious identity provided that religion does not become an obstacle to equality.

191 Elizabeth Chamblee, 'Rhetoric or Rights? When Culture and Religion Bar Girls' Right to Education', *Va. J. Int'l L.*, 44, 2003–2004, 1043–, at 1077.

192 Amartya Sen, *Culture and Identity*, in Women Living Under Muslim Laws Dossier 23/24, at 27, 31 (Int'l Solidarity Network of Women Living Under Muslim Laws, Harsh Kapoor (ed.), 2001).

193 Turner (2007) at 130.

194 The United Nations Food and Population Agency has explicitly recognised that the need to improve basic levels of education is 'an important prerequisite to sustainable development and a . . . factor in the development of well-being through its links with demographic as well as economic and social factors' [UNESCO, Thematic Studies: Girls' Education, 14 (2001)].

195 Turner (2007) at 126.

196 Ibid. Rawls' 'reasonableness' is defined as the duty of citizens to be 'prepared to offer one another fair terms of cooperation of political justice', often at the cost of their own interests.

197 Reference is made here to instances where religious fundamentalism restricts the right to education (for example genderwise) or significantly attempts to affect the content of subject matters of education in secular states.

13 Conclusion

The normative dialogue between religion and law as a cultural endeavour – a plea for complexity and context•

Kyriaki Topidi

Religion is powerful. Its power takes sometimes a discrete, even silent form. Other times, it becomes loud, controversial and highly threatening. As the contributions in this volume have amply demonstrated, what determines the form of power that religion takes depends on the context.

An essential question when looking at the relationship between law and religion in contemporary, multicultural societies concerns the degree to which these two elements overlap and/or collide. Accepting the plurality of law inevitably begs the question of whether religion 'counts' as a form of normative ordering and if so, what are the implications that stem out of this inclusion.

Different voices in this collection of studies answer in the positive to the first question but further to that challenge at many levels the assumption that legal rules are a straightforward process, with little (if any) value-assessment. Instead, and to repeat what Werner Menski has pointed out explicitly in his latest work, 'today, we . . . recognize that any form of law-making – and decision-making in the name of law- has almost inevitable normative dimensions. Nothing is value-neutral'.[1]

The recurring question that many authors ask here is the following: what are the patterns and conditions for the mobilization of religion towards an expansion of one's legal rights? This perspective challenges the assumption that religion as a normative structure can only limit one's strategic choices. Instead, we explore how it can also change access and exercise of rights arising from individual and collective actions in response to new situations and opportunities.

The sum of the chapters in this book confirms the importance of context in defining and studying the impact of religion on legal empowerment. At the same time, the variation in the nature and importance of legal empowerment across contexts challenges the consistency and comparability of our assessments. This is,

• Expression borrowed from Will Kymlicka, 'The Governance of Religious Diversity: The Old and the New', in P. Bramadat and M. Konig (eds), *International Migration and the Governance of Religious Diversity*, McGill – Queen's University Press, 2009, pp. 323–334 at 332.

1 Werner Menski, 'Legal Simulation: Law as a Navigation Tool for Decision-Making', *Report for Japan Coast Guard Academy*, 59(2.1), 2014, 1–22 at 4.

however, inevitable and to a large extent desired in order to expose as many facets of the phenomenon as possible.

In more general terms, there is a clear link established in social sciences between good governance and legal empowerment. The previous chapters of this book contributed to this group of literature and showed how and why legal empowerment may be conducive to people acting as fully-fledged legal subjects with regard to the rights stemming from their freedom of belief. At the same time, all studies position themselves in the stream of academic literature that questions the thesis that holds that as societies become more modern, they also become less religious. We have proposed to look beyond the rule of law orthodoxy in its consideration of the freedom of religion as a human right and place this discussion in a more plurality-sensitive context.[2] We intended, instead, to shed more light on the informal and/or customary mechanisms that explain the limited impact of law on individuals and groups, especially in non-Western societies. The focus of the studies has been, therefore, to discuss precisely how religion and the exercise of religious rights may or may not empower individuals and social groups or various descriptions and improve access to human rights in general.

A significant number of studies in this book argue to different extents that providing more public space to religion due to its empowering features is necessary though not self-sufficient: if we are to challenge assumptions about the incompatibility of modernity with non-Western cultural and religious traditions, the space for the exercise of religious rights must be maintained and conditioned. Religions have a critical role to play in this respect not only with regard to the content of the rights that concern them, but also in relation to the format surrounding their exercise. Under certain conditions, they can play a unique role in making bottom-up legal empowerment practically possible with the assistance of civil society agents with strong value-based structures. The shared moral values of religious traditions also provide additional compelling arguments for the reasons why legal empowerment is a necessary and attainable.

Our starting point has been that there is surprisingly little attention in the legal discipline given to what law and public institutions applying the formal law, do (or fail to do) for people that are not fully able to exercise their religious rights or that are victims of discrimination based on their faith. These groups also tend to be statistically the weakest economically and furthermore, as a result of their poverty and exclusion, they stand largely outside the scope of protection and opportunities of a functioning rule of law.[3]

Accordingly, in this book, empowerment is treated and analysed as a process. Contributions try to stress the importance of agency in exploring how legal

2 We are inspired here by S. Golub, *Beyond Rule of Law Orthodoxy: The Legal Empowerment Alternative*, Carnegie Endowment for International Peace, Working Paper 41 (2003).

3 Olav Kjoven, 'Not Just Another Commission: How Legal Empowerment Could Energize the Fight Against Poverty', in M.E. Brother and J.A. Solberg (eds), *Legal Empowerment: A Way Out of Poverty*, Oslo: Norwegian Ministry of Foreign Affairs, 2007, pp. 17–29, at 17.

empowerment emerges from the 'bottom-up' and 'top down'. Ultimately, and in concrete settings, we show how religion and the exercise of religious rights may contribute towards the removing of various types of 'un-freedoms' that constrain individual choice. We did not aim to propose a universal approach to religion as legal empowerment, but instead a highly contextualized analysis within various and diversified sets of socio-legal circumstances.

Work on legal empowerment in general has been previously driven by empirical experimentation.[4] Pursuing this methodological avenue, this volume relied on individual contributions sourced from different geographical and legal backgrounds in order to illustrate the variety of experiences and lessons learned among the religions and legal systems studied. The chapters tested and enquired into (new) versions of modernity as they are expressed through cultural performances, symbols, and practices. Our main underlying theme, hopefully successfully, challenged *in concreto* the linear representation of modern and secular identities as designed to replace the more obsolete and dangerous religious, 'pre-modern' systems. We maintained, instead, that multiple modernities are better suited `to help humanity close the book on a long chapter of human misery',[5] a need that is felt today more acutely than ever.

The book also indirectly aimed to discuss the capacity of groups and communities to voice their values. By formulating these shared values and beliefs, such groups contribute towards their legal empowerment and also create space for others, even if that may not be the primary intention. The interface between religious minorities with state and local authorities is a recurring theme in the chapters of the entire volume, with emphasis on the ways in which governments and justice institutions understand and approach the claims of these communities.

The analysis has therefore focused on four axes: first, the issue of how the lack of aspects of legal identity (in this case religious affiliation) becomes a barrier to democratic participation; second, the question of embracing bottom-up solutions and claims in order to institute reform processes that reflect better the needs of specific groups; third, issues of organization that enhance the externalization of religious rights claims; and fourth, social policy strategies for improving legal awareness and understanding of the parameters of interfaith dialogue and religious rights.[6] The sum of these areas provides a more accurate picture on how certain practices hinder legal empowerment, how they can be changed or enhanced so as to increase governance *functionality*, understood here as the exercise of religious rights for all, subject to their usual limitations, with the legal system being responsive and their rights retaining their value/meaning to those claiming them.

4 Ana Palacio, 'Legal Empowerment of the Poor: An Action Agenda for the World Bank', http://rru.worldbank.org/legal *empowerment*_of_poor.pdf.

5 Hector Avalos, *Fighting Words: The Origins of Religious Violence*, Amherst: Prometheus Books, 2005, at 378.

6 The issues of legal identity, voice (as participation), organization and information are developed in Kjorven (2007) at 21.

With knowledge of the fact that there exists little agreement on an exact definition, we approached *legal empowerment* as the enhancement of the individual or the group to 'intellectually, financially and physically access the law and legal services'.[7] Towards this goal, users choose the system with which they feel most at ease to make their claims, accepting that what we label as 'systems' are in themselves fluid entities.

Often and in addition to the formal judicial authorities, parallel legal orders operate. These orders usually draw authority from religious beliefs, *inter alia.* These 'customary' justice systems evolve as society changes. Chapters in this volume also aimed to explore whether a new concept of religion that does not stand in the way of development, using law broadly understood, can be constructed, and under what conditions. The capacity and ability of individuals to organize as groups with religious character as a means to achieve real legal empowerment has also been discussed to some extent insofar as these groups may 'provide an arena for formulating shared values and preferences and instruments in pursuing them, even in the face of powerful opposition'.[8]

Similarly to other disciplinary contexts, we all seem to struggle in our individual discussions of religion as a potential empowering legal tool with the implications of legal pluralism. This struggle brings to the surface the processes of competition between the different forms of law. Whether we are concerned with Canon Law confronting Human Rights Law, Family Law confronting Religious Law or Constitutional Law as affected by religiously tainted power struggles, the competition is intense, unavoidable and occasionally fierce.[9]

The discussion obviously departs from the observation that many different non-state communities assert jurisdiction over a variety of issues, regardless of the lack of formal status of these communities. The consequence of these competing claims of jurisdiction is the phenomenon of multiple regimes occupying the same social field.[10] Religion has been traditionally and historically associated with these competing normative claims, even prior to the current resurgence of diasporic religious claims that are the result of immigration.[11]

In general, legal pluralist normative movements operate in two directions: vertically, already since the 1970s, legal pluralists have argued that the hierarchy in a social space dominated by many legal systems is not clear and a given.[12]

7 Ewa Wojkowska and Johanna Cunningham, 'Justice Reform's New Frontier: Engaging with Customary Systems to Legally Empower the Poor', *Legal Empowerment Working Papers No.7*, IDLO, 2010, at 3.

8 P. Evans, 'Collective Capabilities, Culture and Amartya Sen's Development as Freedom', *Studies in Comparative International Development*, 37(2), 2002, at 54.

9 Menski (2014) highlights this element of competition stressing the contribution of the growing significance of international law and human rights to this process (ibid., at 2).

10 Paul Schiff Berman, *Global Legal Pluralism: A Jurisprudence of Law Beyond Borders*, Cambridge: Cambridge University Press, 2012.

11 For example, in Europe, canon law overlapped with state legal systems.

12 Sally Falk Moore, 'Law and Social Change: The Semi-Autonomous Social Field as an Appropriate Subject of Study', *Law & Soc'y Rev.*, 7, 1973, 719.

Horizontally, the interaction between legal systems is *bidirectional*,[13] with one influencing the other. This horizontal dimension largely also explains why legal pluralism is not restricted to colonial societies but has become part and parcel of most industrialized societies, by virtue, as mentioned, of migratory movements.

A perception of the reality of legal pluralism allows us to concentrate on the issues of the patterns of people's actions on the basis of religious affiliations and how the expression of difference in religious beliefs is (or not) legally protected. Particularly the notion of 'personal law', which is often religious in character and is also exercised regardless of territorial location seriously challenges the state *qua* territory-centric conception of modern law.[14] It also demonstrates the link between territorial jurisdiction and citizenship.

The way jurisdiction through membership to a community constructs coherent communities of course is no longer the limited prerogative of the state: religion nowadays, through what Berman labels the 'language of law', brings together groups of individuals in order to assert its normative power.[15]

The dynamic nature and treatment of law allows arguments for and against religion as a legal empowerment tool to unfold in this book in a manner that empirically demonstrates these conflicts as they arise. By the same token, we are also reminded of the limits of the 'tolerable' in each case. It is therefore difficult, if not impossible, to extract from these contributions globally relevant criteria and standards on what is law or on what is tolerable. For the latter point, the majority of authors identify the protection of human rights as a legally (but also morally) valid limitation to what should be considered as 'acceptable' from the religious perspective. What authors also seem to accept, without always spelling it out fully, is that 'good law is . . . situation-specific'.[16]

Mario Ricca described the circumstances, which the studies of this book address, as situations where 'the normative encyclopaedias might collide and eventually conflate by themselves in a kind of magical convergence'.[17] He was, of course, not considering the findings of this volume but was referring to the common (nowadays) scenario whereby individuals while using normative standards, in order to make relations possible with others, are forced to adapt those standards in order to communicate.

The question for Ricca, as well as for many others, remains how to handle situations where individuals have to comply with laws imposing contradictory behaviours. Ricca suggests that these individuals ultimately opt out of all the alternatives surrounding them.[18] Analyses in this book, such as that of Federica Sona or Pietro Longo, demonstrate that often the individuals navigate the legal

13 Schiff Berman (2012) at 47.

14 Ibid., at 165.

15 Ibid., at 214.

16 Menski (2014) at 17, quoting Chiba.

17 Mario Ricca, 'Intercultural Law, Interdisciplinary Outlines: Lawyering and Anthropological Expertise in Migration Cases Before the Courts', *Rete*, 2014, at 1.

18 Ibid., at 3.

system in a way to achieve their stated aims. Other contributions, such as that of Dennis Xulu and Kalindi Kokal, show how formal law is replaced with other forms of normative orderings. In neither case, however, can one find a complete abandonment of all sets of rules.

Is then the dialogue between law and religion a cultural process and project? Multiculturalism has been steadily advocating the legitimacy of each and every culture and relying on the reciprocal recognition between cultures and their ensuing normative orderings. Its implications in terms of legal systems mainly require from states and their legal orders to award autonomy and protection of cultural communities to organize their activities based on their own values, in an attempt to escape scenarios of contradictory normative requirements.

A very standard limitation to this 'autonomy' is the requirement to respect human rights. The notion, philosophy and content of human rights limit the possibility of an intercultural normative experience, under the pretext of universality, while pushing a mono-dimensional track of an 'hierarchically ordered legal production'.[19] At the same time, however, human rights represent the safest path towards the protection of autonomy and difference. In other words, they safeguard individuals against the 'intolerable'. This is precisely why the human rights discourse is often subjected to culturally friendly interpretative exercises in an attempt to service the various cultural patterns, including religious ones, that have different needs from the so-called Western legal tradition.[20] Some contributions raise, therefore, the important issue of religious belonging and entitlement to fundamental rights protection. They touch on the controversial clash between equality and religious membership. The often debated issue of the clash between the normative dominance of liberal values, taking the form of fundamental rights, with religious values as norms is projected to the question of whether and how religious rights exercise may lead to access to a more expansive protection of one's human rights.

All contributions touching on this issue express caution and reservations about the possibility to empower believers in contexts of inequality sourced from traditional understandings of religion. Tradition, obligation and community appear to present, at times, irreconcilable poles of religious normative activity with human dignity, even after the consideration of the right to exit options.

As legal scholars, we are trained to argue, explain and justify with reference to pre-set legal categories, although at times legal representation asks for the exploitation of semantic ambiguities within those categories. But what if behaviours perceived as religious duties are sourced from another combination of values? The chapters of Waheeda Amien, Lauren Fielder and Adrian Loretan in this book problematize the difficulty to classify or re-classify under state law practices that are normatively religiously tainted.

Ultimately, the aim of studies on legal pluralism, if they are to retain resonance on how law is operating on the ground, needs to stick to the observation of the

19 Ibid., at 5.
20 Reference to An'Naim.

living law in order to witness and map the idiosyncratic ways in which the configurations of 'laws' operate in each set of circumstances studied. These accounts need, however, to reflect also the ways that power and agency trigger the law in action.

In our accounts of the interaction between law and religion, we should not neglect the dimension of the phenomenon that is linked to social class and in some cases, social deprivation. It is not rare to observe that socially discriminated groups revert to religion as a mode to resist and protest against what they perceive as the 'hegemonic legal ideology'.[21] The trend stands irrespectively of where one stands on the question of whether courts and the law can bring about social change, particularly for vulnerable groups.

In multicultural contexts, James Tully has proposed a method to address these conflicts. He made the case for 'intercultural dialogue in which the culturally diverse citizens of contemporary societies negotiate agreements on their forms of association over time in accordance with the three conventions of mutual recognition, consent and cultural continuity'.[22] The strategy is useful insofar as it presupposes a (constitutional) pluralist framework, which as the various analyses in the book demonstrate in concrete areas of social activity, is present and necessary. Similarly, all authors argue to various lengths for the need for law to be plural in the ways it attempts to regulate religious diversity. More originally, some of the same authors propose ideas and arguments as to how legal orders cannot be any more meaningfully distinguished or separated from the agents that created them, such as the chapter authored by Amos Israel-Vleeschhouwer.[23] In other, simpler terms, they engage with the issue of agency. The consideration of agency in legally plural contexts emerges as a fresh perspective that could allow us to reflect not only on the content of plural legal orders but also on their potential to operate as platforms for legal empowerment, which is the central question that we have been considering.

At the end of the day, the legal implications of religious pluralism can only be accounted for in coherent terms if we look at the processes of law-making, the content of the norms at stake and their application. The word of caution included in many parts of the present volume reminds us that not all differences ought to be legally protected. Essentially, what is already clear is that the rule of law and its interpreters can only survive if they have their limitations.[24]

21 Gad Barzilai, 'Introduction', in G. Barzilai (ed.), *Law and Religion*, Ashgate, 2007, pp. xi–xxv, at p. xxiv.

22 James Tully, *Strange Multiplicity: Constitutionalism in an Age of Diversity*, Cambridge: Cambridge University Press, 1995, as quoted in Meena K. Bhamra, *The Challenges of Justice in Diverse Societies: Constitutionalism and Pluralism*, Farnham: Ashgate, 2011, at 30.

23 This point in confirmed in Gavin W. Anderson, *Constitutional Rights After Globalization*, Hart Publishing, Oxford, 2005, at p. 39, as one of the main challenges faced by legal pluralism to be widely accepted as a dominant legal theory view.

24 Lisbet Christoffersen, 'Is Shari'a Law, Religion or a Combination? European Legal Discourses', in Jorgen S. Nielsen and Lisbet Christoffersen (eds), *Shari'a As Discourse: Legal Traditions and the Encounter with Europe*, Ashgate, pp. 57–75, at 75.

Retrospectively, society and religion and their patterns of interaction continue to represent undoubtedly a challenging area for the discipline of law to tackle. As Veit Bader has pointed out, in order to provide a relevant analysis of the workings in these two areas, studies 'have to analyze all mechanisms of action coordination – markets, networks, associations, communities, and private and public hierarchies'.[25] Bader's preference for 'associative democracy' based on moderate universalism reflects theoretically the findings of some of the authors of the present volume that stress the conflicts between equally important principles and basic rights.

Bader's understanding of a moderate universalist morality relies on the guarantee of basic needs and rights such as the right to life, liberty, physical integrity, due process and protection against violence. He lays out the possibility to complement this 'basic' form with liberal democratic morality that includes civil and political rights or a more pluralist one that covers socio-economic and cultural rights. Yet, Bader places the limit of what is tolerable and the corresponding need for accommodation at a low level: he argues '[i]n hard cases in which the practices of illiberal and non-democratic religions . . . conflict with the minimally interpreted standards of liberal democratic morality . . . I argue for maximum accommodation if they do not vie for public money'.[26]

In the light of these considerations, the next step in this reflective process initiated in this book would require the empirical testing through comparison of practices, conflict patterns, their effects and the broader policies from a normative perspective in order to assess the characteristics of conflict resolution strategies between values and rights in contemporary multicultural societies.

Towards that goal, this volume has addressed, albeit indirectly, a number of themes that are cross-cutting, independently of geographical or religious context, and that attract increasingly scholarly (but also social) attention despite them being discussed widely during the last decades. Echoing Bader's analysis on the advantages of associative democracy, these themes are the right to dissent and exit from religious organizations in meaningful terms, the discussion and reform from within religious organizations and the recognition of religions as a means to provide more efficient state supervision and a more comprehensive protection of the interests of the basic needs of the most vulnerable religious minorities.[27] Ultimately, one of the effects of these processes interacting leads to the empowerment of religious majorities and minorities.[28]

In parallel, and in more methodological terms, the accounts of this volume rely, for the most, on the 'national' experience of one given state. While in other

25 Veit Bader, 'The Governance of Religious Diversity: Theory, Research, Practice', in P. Bramadat and M. Konig (eds), *International Migration and the Governance of Religious Diversity*, McGill – Queen's University Press, 2009, pp. 43–74 at 44.

26 Ibid., at 61.

27 Ibid., at 62. Bader, for the last point, refers to the idea of *differentiated morality* as one of the characteristics of associative democracy.

28 Ibid., at 63.

academic contexts this exercise would have deserved the label of 'methodological nationalism',[29] in this project these accounts demonstrate the way(s) in which the proliferation of new rights that compete benevolently with the established 'universal' human rights discourse may create new forms of religious identity and legal empowerment.

Another window of inquiry that the present volume opens concerns the contribution of religion towards the development of social capital in religiously diverse societies. As these lines were being written, the debate resurfaced in a very violent manner by way of the 13 November 2015 terrorist attacks in Paris. While it may be a difficult moment to claim, as Putnam does, that religious groups are able to produce bonding social capital within each group but also and more controversially bridging social capital between different religious groups in society,[30] the perspectives presented in this book suggest that to be an undisputed reality. The typology and characteristics of social capital produced, however, need to be further explored.

It is hardly new or surprising to suggest that we belong to a world of multiple overlapping normative communities. What is much more contested is how non-state cultural/religious communities dispose, manage and sometimes impose normative force. Increasingly some of the non-state communities in question attempt (and often succeed) to introduce their religious beliefs as part of these overlapping normativities. As we are moving away from ideology, as an organizing force in our societies and states, culture steps in to create a new platform to understand global polarities.[31]

The debate has therefore shifted towards the ways to introduce 'order' in the disorder created by this legal hybridity.[32] The essence of the normative conflict centres around how much the (majoritarian) normative community can impose on another (minoritarian) normative community and what can be deferred. In that context, legal pluralism scholarship has focused on and accepted a broad definition of the understanding of law that extends the concept beyond the content of normative action issued by a sovereign power.[33]

29 Term borrowed by Matthias Koenig, 'How Nation-States Respond to Religious Diversity', in Paul Bramadat and Matthias Koenig, *International Migration and the Governance of Religious Diversity*, Montreal: McGill – Queen's University Press, 2009, pp. 293–322.

30 Reference from Paul Weller, 'Religious and Governance in the United Kingdom: Religious Diversity, Established Religion, and Emergent Alternatives', in P. Bramadat and M. Koenig (eds), *International Migration and the Governance of Religious Diversity*, McGill – Queen's University Press, 2009, pp. 161–190 at 183.

31 Austin Sarat and Jonathan Simon, 'Beyond Legal Realism? Cultural Analysis, Cultural Studies, and the Situation of Legal Scholarship', *Yale Journal of Law and the Humanities*, 13(1), 2001, 3–30, at 4.

32 See Schiff Berman (2012), in particular his proposal on cosmopolitan legal pluralism as a 'recognition of multiple refracted differences where people acknowledge the link with the "other" without demanding assimilation or ostracism' (ibid., at p. 12).

33 The list of scholarship is long. See indicatively Boaventura Santos de Sousa, *Toward a New Legal Common Sense: Law, Globalization and Emancipation*, Cambridge: Cambridge University Press,

Even if we accept that the issue of the definition of law is less urgent another essential question remains: what if the liberal state chose to take into account certain cultural differences, instead of applying a consistent rights-based approach to all religious and cultural claims? What if we tried to look on the other side of the mirror of culture? This is already happening in certain areas such as gender discrimination in employment within religious associations. This so-called *multiculturalism of fear*[34] is above all a policy consideration that is very difficult to defend from the viewpoint of law and human rights. It perpetuates inequality and gently shifts the debate away from more salient areas of minority discrimination reflected in socio-economic inequalities between immigrant groups and the rest of the population. Imposing, thus, the liberal minimum inevitably appears as the least problematic scenario. As much as individuals should not be forced by secular rules to abandon their religious identity, they should not be forced either by religious authorities to accept discriminatory practices. Here lies the strength of post-multiculturalism and the rights-based discourse: provide a safety net to coercion.[35]

Post-multiculturalism is not resistant to the idea that a religious *qua* cultural analysis of law may enhance traditional ideas of culture,[36] provided that core values of co-existence are not affected. To the contrary, this process is more than likely to advance new conceptions of law. In an era of legal pluralism, it is one option that policy-makers, legal practitioners and religious community leaders should not ignore. In the meantime, and as Adam Gopnik wittingly observed, 'every age has a term to explain things that resist explanation. The Elizabethans had Fate; the Victorians had History; we have Culture'.[37]

References

Avalos, Hector, *Fighting Words: The Origins of Religious Violence*, Amherst: Prometheus Books, 2005.

Augustein, Daniel, 'Religious Pluralism and National Constitutional Traditions in Europe', in C. Ungureanu and L. Zucca (eds), *Law, State and Religion in the New Europe*, Cambridge University Press, 2011, pp. 261–280.

Bader, Veit, 'The Governance of Religious Diversity: Theory, Research, Practice', in P. Bramadat and M. Konig (eds), *International Migration and the Governance of Religious Diversity*, McGill – Queen's University Press, 2009, pp. 43–74.

2002; John Griffiths, 'What is Legal Pluralism?', *J. Legal Pluralism and Unofficial Law*, 24, 1986, 1, Sally Engle Merry, 'Legal Pluralism', *Law & Soc'y Rev.*, 22, 1988; Brian Z. Tamanaha, 'A Non-Essentialist Version of Legal Pluralism', *J. Law & Soc'y*, 27, 2000, 296; Moore (1973).

34 The term belongs to Jacob Levy, *The Multiculturalism of Fear*, Oxford University Press, 2000.

35 There is a great degree of complexity in determining what is considered as coercive and what the product of choice. This is a particularly difficult question to answer especially for vulnerable groups such as women and children, the latter being the focus of this study. Answers need therefore to be highly contextualized and also take account of the important informal power of religion. On these issues, see Anne Phillips, 'Religion: Ally, Threat or just Religion?', UNRISD, 2009.

36 Sarat and Simon (2001) at 13.

37 Quote borrowed from ibid., at 22.

Barzilai, Gad, 'Introduction', in G. Barzilai (ed.), *Law and Religion*, Ashgate, 2007, pp. xi–xxv.

Bennoune, K., 'Secularism and Human Rights: A Contextual Analysis of Headscarves, Religious Expression and Women's Equality Under International Law', *Columbia J Transnational L*, 45, 2007, 367–426.

Beynon, June, Larocque, Linda, Ilieva, Roumiana and Dagenais, Diane, 'A Sociocultural and Critical Analysis of Educational Policies and Programs for Minority Youth in British Columbia', in C. James (ed.), *Possibilities and Limitations: Multicultural Policies and Programs in Canada*, Halifax: Fernwood Publishing, 2005, pp. 108–129.

Catens, Joseph, 'Free Speech and Democratic Norms in the Danish Cartoons Controversy', *International Migration*, 44(5), 2006, 33–42.

Christoffersen, Lisbet, 'Is Shari'a Law, Religion or a Combination? European Legal Discourses', in Jorgen S. Nielsen and Lisbet Christoffersen (eds), *Shari'a As Discourse: Legal Traditions and the Encounter with Europe*, Ashgate, pp. 57–75

Clover, M. Robert, 'The Uses of Jurisdictional Redundancy: Interest, Ideology and Innovation', *William & Mary L. Rev.*, 22, 1981, 639.

Cotterrell, Roger, 'Law and Culture – Inside and Beyond the Nation State', *Retfaerd Argbang 31*, 2008, Nr. 4/123, 23–36.

Evans, Peter, 'Collective Capabilities, Culture and Amartya Sen's Development of Freedom', *Studies in Comparative International Development*, 37(2), 2002, pp. 54–60.

Golub, S., *Beyond Rule of Law Orthodoxy: The Legal Empowerment Alternative*, Carnegie Endowment for International Peace, Working Paper 41 (2003).

Gorzdecka, A. Dorotha, Ercan, A. Selen and Kmak, Magdalena, 'From Multiculturalism to Post-Multiculturalism: Trends and Paradoxes', *Journal of Sociology*, 2014, 50–64.

Griffiths, John, 'What is Legal Pluralism?', *J. Legal Pluralism and Unofficial Law*, 24, 1986, 1.

Griffiths, John, 'The Idea of Sociology of Law and its Relation to Law and to Sociology', *Current Legal Issues*, 8, 2005.

Grillo, Ralph, 'British and Others: From "Race" to "Faith"', in S. Vertovec and S. Wessendorf (eds), *The Multiculturalism Backlash: European Discourses, Policies and Practices*, Routledge, 2010, pp. 50–71.

Habashi, Janette, 'Intersections of Education and Freedom of Religion Rights in the UNCRC and in Practice', in Beth Blue Swadener, Laura Lundy, Janette Habashi and Natasha Blanchet-Cohen (eds), *Children's Rights and Education: International Perspectives*, Peter Lang, 2013, pp. 236–246.

Joppke, Christian, 'The Retreat of Multiculturalism in the Liberal State: Theory and Policy', *The British Journal of Sociology*, 55(2), 2004, 237–257.

Kislowicz, Howard, 'Sacred Laws in Earthly Courts: Legal Pluralism in Canadian Freedom Litigation', *Queen's L.J.*, 39(1), 175–222.

Kjoven, Olav, 'Not Just Another Commission: How Legal Empowerment Could Energize the Fight Against Poverty', in M.E. Brother and J.A. Solberg (eds), *Legal Empowerment: A Way Out of Poverty*, Oslo: Norwegian Ministry of Foreign Affairs, 2007, pp. 17–29.

Kymlicka, Will, 'The Governance of Religious Diversity: The Old and the New', in P. Bramadat and M. Konig (eds), *International Migration and the Governance of Religious Diversity*, McGill – Queen's University Press, 2009, pp. 323–334.

Kymlicka, Will, *Multiculturalism: Success, Failure and the Future*, MPI Europe, 2012.

Ley, David, 'Post-Multiculturalism?', Research on Immigration and Integration in the Metropolis Working Paper Series, No.05-18, September 2005, Vancouver Centre of Excellence

Li, Peter, 'The Multiculturalism Debate', in P. Li (ed.), *Race and Ethnic Relations in Canada*, Don Mills, Ontario: Oxford University Press, 2003, pp. 148–177.
McCrudden, Christopher, 'Multiculturalism, Freedom of Religion, Equality and the British Constitution: The JFS Case Considered', *Oxford Legal Research Paper Series* No.72/2010
Martinez-Torron, Javier, 'Institutional Religious Symbols, State Neutrality and Protection of Minorities in Europe', *L&W Journal*, 12, 2013.
Menski, Werner, 'Legal Simulation: Law as a Navigation Tool for Decision-Making', *Report for Japan Coast Guard Academy*, 59(2.1), 2014, 1–22.
Merry Engle, Sally, 'Legal Pluralism', *Law & Soc'y Rev.*, 22, 1988.
Merry Engle, Sally, 'Anthropology and International Law', *Annu. Rev. Anthropol.*, 35, 2006, 99–116.
Michaels, Ralph, 'Global Legal Pluralism', Duke Law School Public Law and Legal Theory Research Paper No. 259, 2009, available at http://ssrn.com/abstract=1430395.
Mikhail, John, 'Dilemmas of Cultural Legality: A Comment on Roger Cotterrell's "The Struggle for Law" and a Criticism of the House of Lords' Opinions in Begum', *Int'l J.L in Context*, 4, 2009, 385–393.
Mitchell, Katharyne, *Crossing the Neoliberal Line: Pacific Rim Migration and the Metropolis*, Philadelphia: Temple University Press, 2004.
Moore, Sally Falk, 'Law and Social Change: The Semi-Autonomous Social Field as an Appropriate Subject of Study', *Law & Soc'y Rev.*, 7, 1973, 719.
Palacio, Ana, 'Legal Empowerment of the Poor: An Action Agenda for the World Bank', http://rru.worldbank.org/legal *empowerment*_of_poor.pdf.
Parekh, Bhikhu, 'Multiculturalism is a Civilised Dialogue', *Guardian,* 21 January 2005.
Phillips, Anne, 'Religion: Ally, Threat or just Religion?', UNRISD, 2009.
Reed, Jodie, 'Religion Renewed? The Right Path for English Schools', *Public Policy Research*, December 2005–February 2006.
Ricca, Mario, 'Intercultural Law, Interdisciplinary Outlines: Lawyering and Anthropological Expertise in Migration Cases Before the Courts', *Rete*, 2014.
Santos de Sousa, Boaventura, *Toward a New Legal Common Sense: Law, Globalization and Emancipation*, Cambridge: Cambridge University Press, 2002.
Sarat, Austin and Simon, Jonathan, 'Beyond Legal Realism? Cultural Analysis, Cultural Studies, and the Situation of Legal Scholarship', *Yale Journal of Law and the Humanities*, 13(1), 2001, 3–30.
Schiff Berman, Paul, *Global Legal Pluralism: A Jurisprudence of Law Beyond Borders*, Cambridge Univesity Press, 2012.
Ssenyonjo, Manisuli, 'The Islamic Veil and Freedom of Religion, the Rights to Education and Work: A Survey of Recent International and National Cases', *Chinese Journal of International Law*, 6(3), 2007, 653–710.
Tamanaha, Z. Brian, 'A Non-Essentialist Version of Legal Pluralism', *J. Law & Soc'y*, 27, 2000, 296.
Tamanaha, Z. Brian, 'Understanding Legal Pluralism: Past to Present, Local to Global', *St John's University Legal Studies Research Paper Series*, Paper 07-0080, May 2008.
Vertovec, Steven, 'Towards Post-Multiculturalism? Changing Communities, Conditions and Culturalism in Europe', *International Social Science Journal*, 61(199), 2010, 83–95.
Weisbrod, Carol, *Emblems of Pluralism: Cultural Differences and the State*, Princeton: Princeton University Press, 2001.

Weller, Paul, 'Religious and Governance in the United Kingdom: Religious Diversity, Established Religion, and Emergent Alternatives', in P. Bramadat and M. Koenig (eds), *International Migration and the Governance of Religious Diversity*, McGill – Queen's University Press, 2009, pp. 161–190.

Wojkowska, Ewa and Cunningham, Johanna, 'Justice Reform's New Frontier: Engaging with Customary Systems to Legally Empower the Poor', *Legal Empowerment Working Papers No.7*, IDLO, 2010.

Index

For Product Safety Concerns and Information please contact our EU representative GPSR@taylorandfrancis.com Taylor & Francis Verlag GmbH, Kaufingerstraße 24, 80331 München, Germany